AF594300

Data Structures Using Modula–2

Data Structures Using Modula-2

Richard F. Sincovec

Richard S. Wiener

University of Colorado
at Colorado Springs

John Wiley & Sons

New York Chichester Brisbane Toronto Singapore

Cover design: Anna Lieber
Text design: Nancy Field
Editorial supervision: Martha Cooley
Copyediting: Brenda Griffing
Production: Philip McCaffrey

Library of Congress Cataloging in Publication Data:

Sincovec, Richard.
Data structures using Modula—2.

1. Modula-2 (Computer program language) 2. Data structures (Computer science) I. Wiener, Richard, 1941– . II. Title.

QA76.73.M63S56 1985 005.7′3 85-26337
ISBN 0-471-81489-X

Printed in the United States of America

10 9 8 7 6 5 4 3 2 1

To our children

Mary and James

Erik and Marc

Preface

This book is designed for a two-semester undergraduate sequence on data structures using the Modula-2 language. It is assumed that a student has taken an introductory computer science course and has been introduced to the Pascal programming language (or Modula-2). The book is also aimed at practicing computer science professionals.

The major emphasis throughout the book is on abstract data types and their implementations. The concepts related to a data abstraction are presented first; then one or more implementations are analyzed.

The Modula-2 language was chosen as a vehicle to illustrate the implementation of abstract data types because of its power in enforcing data hiding, its readability, its simplicity, and its growing importance. Modula-2 allows a programmer to separate the definition of a data abstraction from its implementation. This makes it natural for the abstract data types to be presented separately from their respective implementations.

We believe that in the past, a major weakness in introducing the subject of data structures has been a tendency to confuse concepts with their implementation. Quite often, we have observed students thinking of a stack or linked list or tree in terms of a particular implementation rather than as an abstraction. This hampers their ability to wisely utilize abstract data types in the design and implementation of a software system. We hope to rectify the problem in this book by clearly separating concepts from data structure implementations.

One of the unique and important features of the book is the use of generic element types for all the major data structures (stacks, queues, lists, and trees). Modula-2's separate compilation facility allows us to encapsulate the base type of a given data structure in an elements module. By removing the dependence of a data structure on a particular base type, the student can focus on the essential features of the algorithms and not be distracted or confused by the presence of a particular base type. Furthermore, reusable generic data structure software components have much greater utility than data structure components for a particular base type.

We have found from our experience in using the notes for this book that a first course can comfortably cover the first eight chapters, allowing some time to review the differences between Pascal and Modula-2, and to review pointer variables and recursion.

A second course may be presented from the remaining chapters of the book, which include advanced topics in data structures, some appearing in a textbook for the first time (e.g., the detailed treatment of probabilistic hashing and virtual hashing). The chapter on B trees includes more implementation detail than normally is provided in introductory texts.

We thank Carol Beasley, former computer science editor and currently publisher at Wiley for helping to launch this project. We are most grateful to Gene Davenport, senior computer science editor at Wiley, for his support during the latter stages of the project. We thank Brenda Griffing for her outstanding work in copyediting the manuscript.

We are most appreciative of Logitech Inc. (805 Veterans Blvd., Redwood City, CA 94063) for developing a high-quality Modula-2 programming environment, which we used in developing and testing most of the programs in this book.

We are deeply grateful to all the students, too numerous to mention by name, who helped with the class testing of the manuscript.

We would like to thank Steve Mahone for coauthoring the high-quality text and program editor we used for writing some of the text and programs in this book.

Finally we would like to express our gratitude and love to our families (Deanna and Jim; Sheila, Erik, and Marc) for being so supportive during this project.

Richard F. Sincovec

Richard S. Wiener

Contents

Table of Listings

Table of Figures

List of Tables

1

Data Abstraction, Data Structures, and Modula-2

What role do data types and data structures play in problem solving and software development? What is an abstract data type? What is a generic data type? What is the difference between a data type and a data structure? What important features are contained in the Modula-2 language that support the development of abstract data types? We will discuss these issues in this chapter and set the stage for the presentation of data structures using Modula-2.

1.1 Modula-2, Abstraction, and Problem Solving in Software Development

The essence of problem solving is abstraction. Abstraction may be described as identifying essential concepts while ignoring inessential details. In software development, a problem solver may typically model a system in terms of a set of objects, operations, and processes. Such a model represents an abstraction of a system.

A software designer and programmer must translate a model involving objects, operations, and processes into a reliable software system. Abstraction is used to help us partition a complex problem into smaller, more manageable subsystems or modules. Each of the resulting subsystems or modules may be further partitioned into still smaller components. At the software design level the interrelationships among the objects, operations, and processes that define a system must be clarified. This methodology has been called structured problem solving.

Most programming languages provide constructs and facilities that support problem abstraction. For example, program variables defined in terms of predefined and programmer-defined types are used to represent objects in the problem domain that are an abstraction for memory locations in the computer domain. Decision and loop statements provide the software developer control abstraction. Procedures and functions provide the software developer functional abstractions.

Languages such as Pascal allow a software developer to represent a rich variety of objects with complex information structures. The array, record, and set structures in Pascal may be used in combination with each other and in combination with pointer variables to create a data structure model for almost any real-world object. For this reason Pascal and Pascal-like languages have enjoyed tremendous popularity. Many data structure books written in the past few years have featured Pascal. Unfortunately, Pascal fails to provide a programmer and software designer (problem solver) with certain tools that are important for problem solving and problem abstraction. We will carefully examine some of Pascal's shortcomings in these areas in section 1.4.

In 1980 Dr. Niklaus Wirth, the developer of Pascal, introduced Modula-2, a high-level programming language that grew out of Pascal. The features of Modula-2 that are most different from Pascal were introduced to support the development of reliable and cost-effective, large, sophisticated, software systems and low-level system programs.

Modula-2 provides several new constructs that significantly enhance problem abstraction at the highest and lowest levels. High-level abstractions allow problem solving to be performed more independently from a machine, whereas low-level abstractions allow a programmer to access entities closer to a machine.

At the highest level of abstraction, Modula-2 introduces library modules, namely definition and implementation modules, as separate compilation units. These modules are the syntactic entities that allow a programmer to express the data, functional, and process abstractions that are so important in modern software design.

Modules provide a software designer and implementer the basis for partitioning a software system into physical and logical units, each with a well-defined interface. Modules also allow a programmer to carefully control the visibility of declared entities and to ensure their inaccessibility, when appropriate, by hiding them from regions within a software system.

At the lowest level of abstraction, Modula-2 introduces the byte and word types, address arithmetic, bit masking, and other constructs that enable a programmer to manipulate bits and bytes within a computer.

As programming languages make available more powerful facilities for abstraction and effective problem solving, a greater burden is placed on the software designer and programmer to use the facilities wisely. For example, the module construct in Modula-2 allows a programmer to partition a software system into logically homogeneous units. The challenge to the designer and programmer is to find a logically sound partitioning of a complex system into smaller subsystems (modules). Once the module partitioning has been completed, the programmer must define for each library module a clear and precise interface that allows the module to be reused and to be useful to a large community of other programmers.

Although we have been discussing Modula-2, problem solving, and software development in general terms, we must remind the reader that this book will focus on a narrow but extremely important aspect of problem solving in software development, namely, the design and implementation of data structures. You may wish to consult books such as Wirth (1983), Wiener and Sincovec (1984), or Ford and Wiener (1985) for detailed information on Modula-2 and software engineering.

Let us informally illustrate the process of abstraction in problem solving by introducing an important problem in computer science, a discrete-event simulation.

Suppose we wish to write a discrete-event simulation program of toll booth transactions at the entrance to a lightly traveled bridge. The problem domain is described as follows. Cars arrive at random time instants at a specified average rate and form a line at a single toll booth at the entrance to a bridge. As each car reaches the toll booth, the attendant collects the toll fee from the motorist.

We assume that the sequence of service intervals (time intervals the toll booth attendant spends with each motorist) are independent and identically distributed. That is, although we assume no information about a particular motorist, we assume that the service intervals for all motorists come from the same service time distribution. We assume that the service time distribution is independent of the line length and the time of day. We wish to estimate the average line length, the average time spent by a motorist in line before service, and the fraction of idle time spent by the toll booth attendant.

We may abstract from the problem statement the following abstract data types (we will formally define abstract data types in section 1.2):

1. Service time (toll booth operator).
2. Queue (of cars or customers).
3. Customer arrival time (car arrival time).
4. Clock time.

We may abstract from the problem statement the following operations on the data types:

1. Generate next arrival time (operation on customer arrival time).
2. Generate next service time (operation on service time).
3. Add car to waiting line (operation on queue).
4. Remove car from waiting line (operation on queue).
5. Increment clock time (operation on clock time).

TABLE 1.1 Abstract Data Types for Toll Booth Simulation

Service time
Generate next service time
Queue
Initialize queue to empty
Insert element in queue
Remove element from queue
Determine whether queue is empty
Customer arrival time
Generate next arrival time
Clock time
Initialize clock time
Increment clock time

In addition, we will need the following operations:

6. Initialize the simulation clock (operation on clock time).

7. Initialize the queue to empty (operation on queue).

8. Test the queue to see whether it is empty (operation on queue).

Table 1.1 lists each of the four abstract data types with its associated operations.

We may visualize two processes operating in parallel: one that involves the toll booth attendant collecting the toll and a second that involves cars arriving at the toll booth. These processes are independent of each other, provided there is at least one car in the waiting line to serve; otherwise, the toll service process is suspended until the next car arrives at the bridge.

The problem abstraction (model) centers around a very important data structure, the queue. We must begin the simulation by setting the queue to empty. As cars arrive at the toll booth, they are inserted into the queue. As motorists complete the payment of their toll, their cars are removed from the queue. Implied in the queue structure is the first in/first out relation. We present a detailed discussion of the queue data structure in Chapter 2.

In more advanced queuing applications we may have a multiserver process with several waiting lines. Service time may depend on the time of day (accounting for fatigue) or the length of the lines (accounting for the personality of the human server); customers may shift from one line to another based on their estimate of their expected wait time, or customers may leave the line without using the bridge after a certain wait time interval has elapsed.

For each set of assumptions about the operation of the system, the problem-solving process requires us to represent each object (such as servers and customers) and each operation (such as determining the next arrival time). Abstract data types may be used to represent each class of object and functional abstractions (procedures and functions) to represent each operation.

You will note that at this stage of the problem-solving process we have not been concerned with the implementation details of the abstract data types or procedures and functions that represent each operation. Although these details are most important in the production of the final software product, the initial problem-solving process is best performed without concern about such low-level matters. Concept development must precede establishment of implementation details. Unfortunately, inexperienced or untrained software developers tend to worry about too many details too soon.

1.2 Abstract Data Types and Data Structures

Some of the discussion of data abstraction presented in this section is taken, with permission, from *Modula-2: A Software Development Approach* (Ford and Wiener 1985).

In the preceding section we informally distinguished problem-solving concepts (abstractions) from implementation details. In this section we establish a more formal basis for the separation between concepts and their implementation.

One may formally define an abstract data type as a pair $\langle V, O \rangle$, where:

V is a set of values
O is a set of operations defined on those values.

Most modern programming languages provide a variety of predefined data types. Examples include integer data types, cardinal data types, real data types, character data types, and boolean data types. Although the sets of values for these types, particularly the numeric types, may vary from one computer implementation to another, the operations are invariant. For example, on real types the operations of addition, subtraction, multiplication, division, negation, less than, greater than, and equal are the same. These operations are functional abstractions associated with the data type REAL. Strongly typed languages like Pascal, Ada, and Modula-2 enforce the requirement that only the operations defined for a particular data type may be performed on values of that data type.

Most programmers are content, if not delighted, that in many programming applications they can manipulate numbers (integers, cardinals, and reals) and characters without concern about the internal representation of these entities and without knowledge of the hardware operations used to support the data manipulations. The Modula-2 data types REAL, CHAR, BOOLEAN, INTEGER, and CARDINAL, each supported by a set of operations, are abstract data types even though they are predefined in the language.

The essential feature of an abstract data type is the separation between its concept and implementation. The term "data hiding" (or "information hiding") is used to describe this ability. The programmer or user of the data abstraction is given a precise description of the set of values and the set of operations that define the abstract data type, but the implementation of the type is inaccessible—that is, hidden.

The implementation of an abstract data type is called a data structure. For many years, software developers considered it important to identify data structures and algorithms early in the software design process. More recently, with the advent of programming languages such as Modula-2 and Ada, it has become desirable to defer decisions about the choice of data structures and algorithms until later in the design process.

Data hiding (the use of abstract data types) offers a programmer the ability to guarantee the integrity of the values of an abstract data type. The programmer cannot manipulate the internal representation of a data type because this representation is invisible and inaccessible. Consistency of usage is guaranteed because only the operations defined for the abstract data type may be performed by users of the type. This consistency of usage is very important in designing and implementing large, multiprogrammer software projects. Many common errors may be avoided because of the enforcement of consistency of usage.

The separation of the definition of an abstract data type from its implementation allows the programmer the option of changing the implementation without any fall-out effects on the rest of the software system. Only the interface to the abstract data type, its definition, determines its relationship to the rest of the software system.

As an example, suppose the predefined abstract data type INTEGER were implemented differently because of an upgrade in a compiler. The source code in a typical program that performs integer arithmetic would not have to be modified as a result of changing the implementation of INTEGER. The concept of INTEGER (i.e., the operations that may be performed on objects of type INTEGER) would remain unchanged.

Data abstraction provides a mechanism to group logically related software components together. This leads to cleaner software design, easier testing, and simplified maintenance.

The concept of data abstraction may be used to design software implemented in any high-level language. Modula-2 allows us to implement abstract data types so that a compiler can enforce data hiding. This enforcement of data hiding provides the Modula-2 programmer a strong incentive to design a software system using data abstraction.

We will illustrate data abstraction and data hiding with a short example. In section 1.3 we present a longer illustration.

We define the abstract data type complexnumber by the following operations:

define. Allocate the space for an object of type complexnumber. Space must be allocated before any operations may be performed on objects of type complexnumber.

assign1. Create a complex number with given real part and given imaginary part.
assign2. Create a complex number with given modulus and given angle.
real. Access the real part of an object of type complexnumber.
imaginary. Access the imaginary part of an object of type complexnumber.
modulus. Access the modulus of an object of type complexnumber.
angle. Access the angle of an object of type complexnumber.
add. Return the sum of two objects of type complexnumber.
subtract. Return the difference of two objects of type complexnumber.
multiply. Return the product of two objects of type complexnumber.
divide. Return the ratio of two objects of type complexnumber.

The 11 operations informally stated above define the concept of a complex number data type and form the basis for providing a precise interface to the complexnumber data abstraction.

Listing 1.1 shows a Modula-2 definition module that encapsulates the interface to the abstract data type.

Listing 1.1 Interface to Complex Number Abstract Data Type

```
DEFINITION MODULE complex;

  EXPORT QUALIFIED
    (* type *) complexnumber,
    (* proc *) define, assign1, assign2, real, imaginary,
               modulus, angle, add, subtract, multiply,
               divide;

  TYPE complexnumber;


  PROCEDURE define
            ( VAR c                 : complexnumber (* out *) );


  PROCEDURE assign1
            (      real, imag    : REAL        (* in   *) ) :
                   complexnumber;


  PROCEDURE assign2
            (      mod, angle    : REAL        (* in   *) ) :
                   complexnumber;
```

```
  PROCEDURE real
            (     c              : complexnumber (* in  *) ) :
                  REAL;


  PROCEDURE imaginary
            (     c              : complexnumber (* in  *) ) :
                  REAL;


  PROCEDURE modulus
            (     c              : complexnumber (* in  *) ) :
                  REAL;


  PROCEDURE angle
            (     c              : complexnumber (* in  *) ) :
                  REAL;


  PROCEDURE add
            (     c1, c2         : complexnumber (* in  *) ) :
                  complexnumber;


  PROCEDURE subtract
            (     c1, c2         : complexnumber (* in  *) ) :
                  complexnumber;


  PROCEDURE multiply
            (     c1, c2         : complexnumber (* in  *) ) :
                  complexnumber;


  PROCEDURE divide
            (     c1, c2         : complexnumber (* in  *) ) :
                  complexnumber;


END complex.
```

The definition module given in Listing 1.1 provides the software designer and programmer a precise interface to the data abstraction complexnumber. This logical collection of software components (we are using the word "component'' to mean procedure) is a physical unit as well. The definition module is compiled as a separate block of code that stands independent of other units.

The 11 procedures given in DEFINITION MODULE complex provide a functional socket, and any programmer who needs to manipulate complex numbers may plug into it.

Many programming applications require the use of complex numbers, and module complex is an example of a reusable software module. Once the implementation details for type complex have been perfected, this package of software components may be used over and over again with confidence.

A short Modula-2 main program that uses some of the software components defined in Listing 1.1 is presented in Listing 1.2.

Listing 1.2 Test Program for Complex Number Abstract Data Type

```
MODULE complextest;

  FROM InOut IMPORT
    (* proc *) WriteLn, WriteString;

  FROM RealInOut IMPORT
    (* proc *) WriteReal;

  FROM complex IMPORT
    (* type *) complexnumber,
    (* proc *) assign1, real, imaginary, add, multiply,
               define;

VAR
    c1, c2, c3 : complexnumber;

BEGIN
  define( c1 );
  define( c2 );
  define( c3 );
  c1 := assign1( 12.3, 6.5 );
  c2 := assign1( -2.4, 0.0 );
  c3 := add( c1, c2 );
  WriteLn; WriteLn;
  WriteString( " The real part of the sum = " );
  WriteReal( real( c3 ), 30 );
  WriteLn; WriteLn;
  WriteString( " The imaginary part of the sum = " );
  WriteReal( imaginary( c3 ), 30 );
  c3 := multiply( c1, c2 );
  WriteLn; WriteLn;
  WriteString( " The real part of the product = " );
  WriteReal( real( c3 ), 30 );
```

```
  WriteLn; WriteLn;
  WriteString( " The imaginary part of the product = " );
  WriteReal( imaginary( c3 ), 30 );
END complextest.
```

We contrast the Modula-2 program presented in Listing 1.2 with a typical Pascal implementation (Listing 1.3).

Listing 1.3 Pascal Program for Complex Numbers

```
program complex;

  type complexnumber = RECORD
                         rl   : real;
                         im   : real;
                       end(* record *);

var
   c1, c2, c3 : complexnumber;

begin
  c1.rl := 12.3;
  c1.im := 6.5;
  c2.rl := -2.4;
  c2.im := 0.0;
  c3.rl := c1.rl + c2.rl;
  writeln( 'The real part of the sum = ', c3.rl );
  c3.im := c1.im + c2.im;
  writeln( 'The imaginary part of the sum = ', c3.im );
  c3.rl := c1.rl * c2.rl - c1.im * c2.im;
  writeln( 'The real part of the product = ', c3.rl );
  c3.im := c1.im * c2.rl + c1.rl * c2.im;
  writeln( 'The imaginary part of the product = ', c3.im );
end.
```

The most striking difference between the Modula-2 program in Listing 1.2 and the Pascal program in Listing 1.3 is the presence in the Pascal program of the complex number data structure and its absence from the Modula-2 program. The Modula-2 declaration

```
TYPE complex;
```

is an example of an opaque type. The data structure (implementation) is given in the implementation module (not shown here). Modula-2's opaque types provide the basis for data hiding.

If the data structure for implementing a complex number were changed in implementation module complex, not a single line of code in the main program (Listing 1.2) would have to be changed. Indeed, the program would not even have to be recompiled but just relinked to the new implementation code.

This is not the case for the Pascal program (Listing 1.3). A change in the data structure for complexnumber would require the entire program to be rewritten. Although the penalty in this small example is tiny, program maintenance is greatly simplified when abstract data types are used in the software design.

We must point out that a better version of the Pascal program could be written. The adding and multiplying of complex numbers should be done by procedure, not in-line, as in Listing 1.3. A disciplined Pascal programmer can utilize data abstraction and enjoy its benefits. Unfortunately, most Pascal compilers cannot enforce the data-hiding feature so critical to data abstraction.

Thus far, we have focused on abstract data types and their advantages. What about data structures?

A data structure is an implementation of a data type that contains component parts such as the fields of a record or the index locations of an array. More formally, a data structure can be represented as:

1. A set of data components, some of which may be other data structures.

2. A set of rules governing the relationships of the elements to each other.

Data structures are created by a programmer using the predefined constructors array, record, set, and pointer in combination with other predefined data types such as REAL, CHAR, CARDINAL, INTEGER, and BOOLEAN and other programmer-defined data structures. Dynamic data structures implemented using pointer variables are powerful and commonplace. We review the use of pointer variables in Chapter 2.

In Modula-2 the implementation of an opaque type occurs in an implementation module (each definition module has an associated implementation module as a separate compilation unit). For example, we list three possible data structures for the opaque type complexnumber given in Listing 1.1.

1.
```
TYPE complexnumber = POINTER TO
                        RECORD
                          real : REAL;
                          imag : REAL;
                        END;
```

```
2. TYPE complexnumber = POINTER TO
                          RECORD
                            modulus : REAL;
                            angle   : REAL;
                          END;

3. TYPE complexnumber = POINTER TO
                          ARRAY [ 1..2 ] OF REAL;
```

The first implementation, similar to the one given in the Pascal program (Listing 1.3), is a rectangular coordinate implementation. The second implementation is a polar coordinate implementation. The third implementation could be either rectangular or polar, depending on the interpretation of each array component.

The algorithms for performing the 11 operations on a complex number depend heavily on the choice of data structure. For example, the procedure (algorithm) for multiplying two complex numbers is greatly simplified if the polar representation is chosen. We leave this as an exercise.

Since the choice of algorithm so closely follows the choice of data structure, the latter choice is most critical. A well-chosen data structure can lead to program efficiency. Considerations such as the speed of a processor and the memory available influence the choice of data structure.

One of the main objectives of this book is to introduce useful and efficient data structures and associated algorithms in the context of practical applications. Only by knowing the available alternatives can a software designer and programmer choose wisely.

Common structures such as stacks, queues, and trees contain elements such as integers, or characters (called the base type). They may contain more complex elements, data structures in their own right, such as arrays or records. If the operations on a data structure are written so that they are independent of the base type (element type), the data structure is said to be generic.

Most of the data structures in this book are presented as generic structures, which are quite important in software engineering because they may be used in many diverse applications. It often occurs that a stack of numbers (real or integer) and a stack of characters are required in the same programming application. (Stacks are discussed in Chapter 2.) If such an application were written in Pascal, with its strong type checking, two separate stack types would have to be defined: one having integers as its base type and one having characters as its base type. Using a generic implementation of a stack, only a single stack abstraction is required.

1.3 An Important Abstract Data Type: The String

Like most high-level programming languages, Pascal and Modula-2 provide facilities for manipulating character arrays or strings. In Modula-2, a string of say 20 characters may be declared as follows:

```
TYPE string20 = ARRAY [ 0..19 ] OF CHAR;
```

Such a programmer-defined string, like Pascal's strings, is static. That is, the memory allocation (20 bytes in this case) occurs when a variable of type string20 is declared at compile time. If one attempts to pack more than 20 characters into a data structure of type string20, an index range error occurs. This constraint may be very serious when concatenating two strings together or when inserting a substring into an existing string. In both cases, an out-of-range error may occur.

This section introduces a more powerful and generally useful dynamic string abstraction, one that allows string variables to grow and shrink dynamically to any size. Space for such dynamic strings is allocated at run time, on demand. Listing 1.4 presents the interface to our string package.

Listing 1.4 Interface to Dynamic String Abstract Data Type

```
DEFINITION MODULE dynamicstring;
(* This module defines a dynamic string abstract data
   type.                                                     *)

  EXPORT QUALIFIED
    (* type *)  string,
    (* proc *)  define, createnull, copy, concatenate,
                search, delete, insert, extract, length,
                equal, lessthan, readstring, writestring,
                convertarray, convertliteral;

  TYPE string;

  PROCEDURE define
           ( VAR str        : string         (* out    *) );
  (* This procedure must be used before any other procedures
     on str.                                                 *)


  PROCEDURE createnull
           ( VAR str        : string         (* in/out *) );
  (* A defined string, str, is set to blank.                 *)


  PROCEDURE copy
           (     str1       : string         (* in     *);
             VAR str2       : string         (* in/out *) );
  (* Defined string, str1, is copied into defined string
     str2.                                                   *)
```

```
PROCEDURE concatenate
        (     str1        : string          (* in     *);
              str2        : string          (* in     *);
          VAR result      : string          (* in/out *) );
(* Defined string str2 is concatenated to defined string
   str1 to produce defined string result.               *)


PROCEDURE search
        (     str         : string          (* in     *);
              pattern     : string          (* in     *);
              start       : CARDINAL        (* in     *);
          VAR location    : CARDINAL        (* out    *) );
(* The location of defined string pattern is output if
   pattern is present in defined string str.  If pattern
   is not present, the location zero is returned.       *)


PROCEDURE delete
        ( VAR str         : string          (* in/out *);
              start       : CARDINAL        (* in     *);
              count       : CARDINAL        (* in     *) );
(* For defined string str, count characters are deleted
   starting at start.  If count is too large, nothing
   is deleted.                                          *)


PROCEDURE insert
        ( VAR str         : string          (* in/out *);
              substr      : string          (* in     *);
              start       : CARDINAL        (* in     *) );
(* For defined string str, the defined substring substr is
   inserted into str beginning at position start.       *)


PROCEDURE extract
        (     str         : string          (* in     *);
              start       : CARDINAL        (* in     *);
              count       : CARDINAL        (* in     *);
          VAR substr      : string          (* in/out *) );
(* For defined string str, count characters beginning at
   start are deposited into defined string substr.      *)


PROCEDURE length
     (     str         : string          (* in     *) ) :
           CARDINAL;
(* The size of defined string str is returned.          *)
```

```
  PROCEDURE equal
           (     str1        : string          (* in     *);
                 str2        : string          (* in     *) ) :
                 BOOLEAN;
  (* If defined strings str1 and str2 are equal, true is
     returned otherwise false is returned.                 *)


  PROCEDURE lessthan
           (     str1        : string          (* in     *);
                 str2        : string          (* in     *) ) :
                 BOOLEAN;
  (* If defined str1 is alphabetically smaller than defined
     string str2, true is returned otherwise false.        *)


  PROCEDURE readstring
           ( VAR str          : string          (* in/out *) );
  (* Defined string str is assigned a value from keyboard
     using 'RETURN' as a terminator.                       *)


  PROCEDURE writestring
           ( str          : string          (* in     *) );
  (* Defined string str is written to terminal.            *)


  PROCEDURE convertarray
           (     chars        : ARRAY OF CHAR (* in     *);
                 count        : CARDINAL      (* in     *);
             VAR str          : string        (* in/out *) );
  (* An ordinary static "string", chars, of size count, is
     converted to a defined dynamic string str.            *)


  PROCEDURE convertliteral
           (     chars        : ARRAY OF CHAR (* in     *);
             VAR str          : string        (* in/out *) );
  (* A literal, chars, is converted to a defined dynamic
     string str.                                           *)

END dynamicstring.
```

The 16 procedures that define the data abstraction string are given in Listing 1.4; comments under each procedure stub indicate the procedure's purpose. Since the definition module dynamicstring represents the interface to the data abstraction, it is very important that a potential user (programmer) know how to connect the client program to the module dynamicstring. We recommend that the programmer include a small user's guide, embedded in the definition module as a set of comments.

The first procedure, define, establishes a memory reference for a string. It must be executed before any other string procedure.

Procedure createnull renders an existing string empty by dynamically deallocating memory for an existing string and leaving the string in a state comparable to having just been defined.

Procedure copy allows one defined string to be copied to another defined string. The memory previously allocated to the target string is deallocated before allocating new space to the target and copying to the target.

Procedure concatenate combines two strings, end to end. The memory previously allocated to the target string is deallocated before new memory space is allocated to the target and the resultant concatenated string is formed.

In procedure search, the location of the string pattern is output if the pattern is present in the input string, str. If the pattern is not present, the location 0 is returned.

In procedure delete, count characters are deleted starting at position start. If the parameter count is greater than the string size minus the start position, nothing is deleted.

In procedure insert, the substring substr is inserted into str beginning at position start. Since str is a dynamic string, there is no constraint on the size of the substring that is inserted into str.

In procedure extract, count characters beginning at start are extracted from str and output in substr. The memory previously allocated to the output substr is deallocated before new memory to contain the result is allocated.

In procedure length, the size, in number of characters, is returned.

Procedures equal and lessthan allow an alphabetical comparison to be performed between two strings.

Procedure readstring supports input from a keyboard into a dynamic string. The "RETURN" key acts as a string terminator. Procedure writestring supports output to a terminal.

In procedure convertarray, an ordinary static string with count characters is converted to a dynamic string str. Memory previously allocated to the target str is deallocated before new memory sufficient to contain the resultant is allocated. This procedure is useful in retrofitting dynamic strings into a program that previously used static strings.

In the final procedure, convertliteral, a literal, chars, is converted to a dynamic string str.

Are there any other operations you would like to have in the string package? If so, you must add a procedure declaration to the existing definition module and add the procedure name to the export list of the module.

The interface to the abstract data type string, defined in Listing 1.4, like the interface to the abstract data type complexnumber, defined in Listing 1.1, is a promise or contract between the author of the module and potential users. Because such a module is destined to be used by many programmers in many application areas, it is particularly important that the implementation of each procedure be efficient, and thoroughly tested. We present an implementation of the dynamic string module in Appendix A.

We deal with many important abstract data types and data structure in this book. For each new data type, we present its interface, discuss its application in important areas of computer science, and offer one or more implementations (data structures). We coupled our presentation to the Modula-2 language to permit us to separate the presentations of concepts and implementation details. Both are clearly important.

1.4 Important Differences Between Pascal and Modula-2

Modula-2, developed by Dr. Wirth, the creator of Pascal, was introduced in 1980 to overcome some of Pascal's deficiencies and to add features not present in the earlier languages. In this section we outline the major and important differences between Pascal and Modula-2. Some computer scientists have suggested that Modula-2 should be called Pascal-2. Dr. Wirth contends that Modula-2 is sufficiently different from Pascal to warrant the new name.

Modula-2 is a much more powerful language than Pascal but retains Pascal's simplicity, elegance, and readability. It is too early to say, but there is much speculation that Modula-2 will supplant Pascal, emerging as one of the most important and widely used programming languages.

At the time of this writing there are relatively few reference books and texts on Modula-2. The books by Wirth (1983) and Ford and Wiener (1985) contain precise descriptions of the language and its applications in software development. The book by Wiener and Sincovec (1984) on software engineering with Modula-2 and Ada assumes a prior knowledge of Modula-2 but provides extensive case studies illustrating the use of Modula-2 in a modern software engineering context. In Appendix, B, as a convenience to the reader, we reproduce the Modula-2 syntax diagrams from *Modula-2, A Software Development Approach* (Ford and Wiener, 1985).

Perhaps the most serious shortcoming of Pascal is the lack of facility for separating the specification of a data abstraction from its implementation. Subprograms in Pascal are bound to a particular data representation.

Various dialects of Pascal, such as UCSD Pascal, provide the separate compilation unit, called UNIT, as a half-way measure in the right direction. Unfortunately, the Pascal UNIT facility (interface portion) does not allow a physical separation between specification and implementation, which are tied together in the same compilation unit.

Because the interface section and the implementation section of a Pascal compilation unit are required to be in the same physical unit, the data structure for any Pascal data type must be completely specified in the interface portion except when only one variable of such a data type is to be allowed. In such a case the data structure can be hidden in the implementation portion of the compilation unit. This restriction is rather severe. For example, only one complex number variable, only one stack variable, only one string variable, only one list variable, could exist in a program at a given time. This is unrealistic in most cases.

In the Modula-2 dynamic string abstraction presented in section 1.3, each procedure contains a parameter of type string. This permits many string variables to coexist in a program. Each individual string variable may be manipulated independent of the others. The data structure for the type string is not specified in the interface unit (definition module) because of Modula-2's opaque type facility and the separation between specification and implementation.

To allow each Pascal procedure in the interface portion of a string compilation unit to contain a parameters of type string, the data structure for a string must be completely specified before the first parameter reference to type string is given. Thus the essential feature of data hiding is lost in Pascal, even with the limited facility of separate compilation available in some dialects of Pascal. Standard Pascal does not support any form of separate compilation.

Associated with the issue of separate compilation is the issue of version control. Modula-2 provides a powerful version control system that makes it impossible for a programmer to change the interface in a definition module without recompiling and perhaps making suitable changes to all client modules that import one or more components from the modified definition module. Many sources of subtle errors in large software systems have been traced to poor version control. In most Pascal systems with the UNIT facility, version control systems are limited or nonexistent.

Another severe limitation of Pascal is the absence of low-level access to the processor. There are times when manipulating the bits and bytes of the machine leads to programming efficiency. Perhaps the tremendous popularity of the programming language C is due to its support of bit manipulation. Modula-2 offers the programmer a low-level capability comparable to that of C.

Pascal does not provide variables other than global variables that remain active for the duration of program execution. Good software engineering practice suggests limiting the use of global variables because of thier universal visibility and accessibility. It is therefore very desirable to have another facility for controlling the lifetime of a variable. Modula-2 provides such a vehicle using its internal module construct. Important variables can be kept alive for the full duration of program execution without being universally visible and accessible. An extensive discussion and illustration of this may be found in Chapter 11 of Ford and Wiener (1985).

Standard Pascal provides no facilities for the process abstraction. Some dialects of Pascal provide the binary semaphore to control process communication. Modula-2 provides some powerful low-level facilities for supporting the process abstraction.

Many small deficiencies found in Pascal have been cleaned up in Modula-2. These include the following:

1. The declaration order for data objects is relaxed in Modula-2. It is thus possible to declare an object closer to its point of application.
2. Case statements in Modula-2 allow an ELSE branch, providing an escape route in the event that none of the case constants are satisfied by the case selector variable.
3. Subranges can be used in case constant lists, eliminating the need to list all case constant values individually.
4. Short-circuiting of boolean operators is prescribed in the Modula-2 language. Thus boolean expression are less ambiguous and more economy of code is possible.
5. Generic procedures may be written in Modula-2 because strong type checking may be suppressed using the ADDRESS type, the WORD type, and the open array of WORD parameter type.
6. Pointer arithmetic may be performed in Modula-2, allowing much closer control of dynamic memory management.
7. The syntax of Modula-2 has been simplified. For example, the need for the Pascal BEGIN statements on most block constructs has been eliminated.

We in no way wish to diminish the significance and importance of Pascal as a programming language. Pascal remains one of the most important programming languages ever created. Clearly, Modula-2 represents an important evolution of Pascal. It is our hope that the investment you make in learning to read and write in Modula-2 will be worthwhile. You will begin to accrue dividends from this investment when Modula-2 and its associated methodologies are applied to the problem-solving process.

1.5 A Few Words About Programming Style

The format conventions chosen by a programmer affect the readability and maintainability of the finished software product. We encourage you to adopt a consistent and sensible programming style. We have attempted to establish such a style in the program listings throughout this book. You may wish to note the use of binding mode comments for every procedure parameter.

Exercises

1.1 Write the Modula-2 procedures that implement the 11 complex number operations given in Listing 1.1. Assume that a rectangular representation is used for a complex number.

1.2 Write the Modula-2 procedures that implement the 11 complex number operations given in Listing 1.1. Assume that a polar representation is used for a complex number.

1.3 Write the Modula-2 procedures that implement the 11 complex number operations given in Listing 1.1. Assume that the array implementation (rectangular interpretation) is used.

1.4 Write a Modula-2 main driver program that uses each of the procedures given in Listing 1.4.

1.5 Describe and define five data abstractions. For each one, indicate the allowable set of values and the operations defined for each data type. Define Modula-2 definition modules for your abstractions by providing the formal interfaces to the defined operations.

1.6 Are there any additional procedures you would like to see in the dynamic string module presented in Listing 1.4? If so, add the appropriate procedure stubs to the definition module.

2

The Stack and Queue Abstractions and Some Implementations

2.1 The Stack and Queue as Abstract Data Types

Two data types common in computer science are the stack and the queue. In this chapter, we define the stack and queue as abstract data types (ADTs) along with their associated operations. We specify the interface to the operations independent of the implementation details. Finally, we present several implementations of the stack and queue. Each implementation is characterized by the use of a different data structure.

Definition of a Stack

A stack is an ordered collection of items in which the insertion of a new item or the removal of an existing item can be made only at one end, called the top of the stack. A stack is often referred to as a last in/first out (or LIFO) list.

The plates that are piled at the beginning of a cafeteria line represent a stack. Often the plates are in a spring-loaded cylindrical chamber so that it is possible only to remove the top plate from the stack or to insert a plate onto the top of the stack: the other plates in the stack are not accessible or visible. If there are no plates, then the stack is empty and we cannot remove a plate from the stack. Conceptually, the spring-loaded chamber can hold an arbitrarily

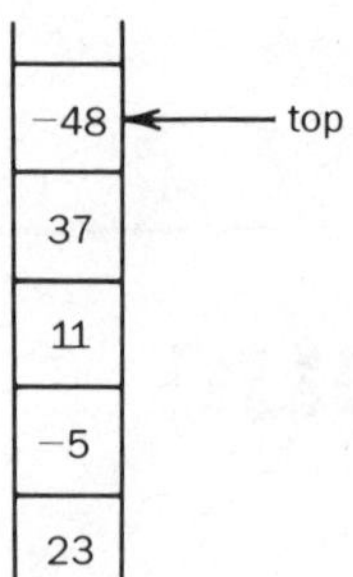

Figure 2.1 A Stack of Five Integers

large number of plates. Since we can see the top plate on the stack, we may merely examine it without removing it. If the plate is dirty or broken, for example, we may decide not to remove it.

The preceding description makes reference to four operations on stacks. The removal of the top item from a stack is commonly referred to as "popping" the stack or more simply as "pop." Inserting an item onto the top of the stack is equivalent to "pushing" an item onto the stack, so the corresponding operation is referred to as the "push" operation. If the stack contains no items, the "empty" operation returns a value of true; otherwise "empty" returns a value of false. The fourth operation is "topofstack," which returns the top item on the stack, permitting us to examine it without removing it from the stack.

Figure 2.1 shows a stack of five integers. That it happens to be drawn with the top toward the top of the page is irrelevant. It would be the same stack lying on its left side or right side, or even turned upside down.

A stack is conceptually a dynamic structure. It is continually changing depending on the insertion (push) and removal (pop) operations that are performed on the stack. Each push and pop operation changes the top of the stack. Figure 2.2 shows the dynamic changes in the integer stack as the following operations are performed: push 11 onto the stack, pop the stack, pop the stack,

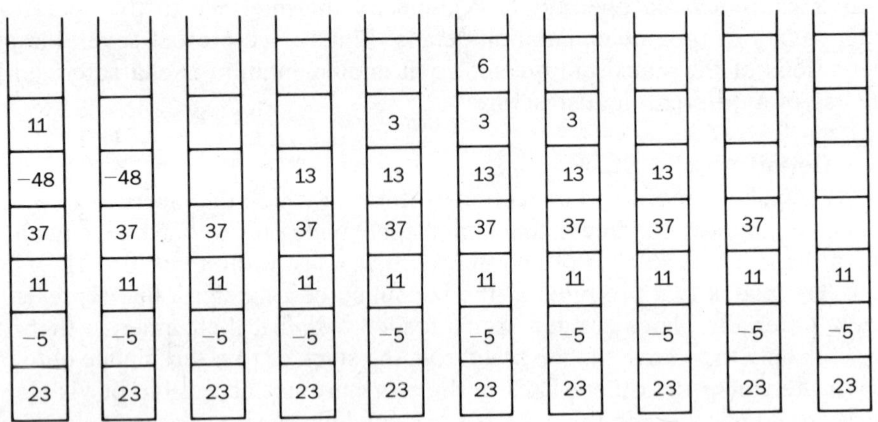

Figure 2.2 The Dynamic Behavior of a Stack

push 13 onto the stack, push 3 onto the stack, push 6 onto the stack, pop the stack, pop the stack, pop the stack and, finally, pop the stack.

A stack is not a single data type but a type constructor meaning that different stack types may be defined for different item types. To make our interface to the stack ADT more general, we will not choose a specific item type. Rather, we assume that some other module will provide that information. We accomplish this by importing the "elementtype" for the items in the stack from a module named elements. For example, to create a stack of integers we define

```
DEFINITION MODULE elements;
  EXPORT QUALIFIED elementtype;
  TYPE elementtype = INTEGER; (* Base type for the stack. *)
END elements.
```

A given application may involve more than one stack, so the user interface to the operations must include a parameter that specifies which stack the indicated operation is to be performed on. Remember that an abstract data type permits the user of the ADT to define numerous instances or variables of the type and to perform any of the promised operations on an instance or variable of the type.

Along with the four operations defined above, we will find it useful to have two additional operations. The "define" operation will create an empty stack. This operation prepares the stack for all the other operations that are available. The second additional operation is the "makeempty" operation, which reinitializes an existing stack to an empty stack by removing all the elements contained in the stack.

The formal interface to the stack ADT along with the six operations identified above is given in the definition module of Listing 2.1.

Listing 2.1 Interface to Stack Abstract Data Type

```
DEFINITION MODULE stackadt;

(*  This module defines the public interface for the
    stack abstract data type.  It imports the type
    elementtype, which defines the type of elements to
    be stored in the stack.                                *)

FROM elements IMPORT
  (* type *) elementtype;

EXPORT QUALIFIED
  (* type *) stack,
  (* proc *) define, makeempty, empty, push, pop, topofstack;
```

```
TYPE stack (* depending on the implementation additional
              information may appear here *);


PROCEDURE define
        ( VAR s : stack                              (* out *) );
(* Creates an empty stack.  Must be used before any other
   stack operation.                                              *)


PROCEDURE makeempty
        ( VAR s : stack                              (* in/out *) );
(* Reinitializes an existing stack s to an empty stack by
   removing all elements contained in the stack.                 *)


PROCEDURE empty
        ( s : stack                                  (* in *) ) :
          BOOLEAN;
(* Returns true if the stack s contains no elements,
   otherwise returns false.                                      *)


PROCEDURE push
        ( VAR    s : stack                           (* in/out *);
              item : elementtype                     (* in *) );
(* Adds item to the top of stack s.                              *)


PROCEDURE pop
        ( VAR s    : stack                           (* in/out *);
          VAR item : elementtype                     (* out *) );
(* Removes item from the top of stack s.                         *)


PROCEDURE topofstack
        ( s    : stack                               (* in *) ) :
          elementtype;
(* Returns the item that is on the top of stack s without
   removing the item from the stack.                             *)


END stackadt.
```

One of the simplest examples that illustrates the use of a stack involves reversing the elements in an ordered list. The algorithm takes each successive item in the list and pushes it onto a stack. When the list is empty, the stack is popped repeatedly until it, too, is empty. Each item popped off the stack is placed in the list. The program module given in Listing 2.2 uses the operations

Listing 2.2 Test Program for Stack Abstract Data Type

```
MODULE stacktest;

   FROM stackadt IMPORT
     (* type *) stack,
     (* proc *) define, makeempty, empty, push, pop,
                topofstack;

   FROM elements IMPORT
     (* type *) elementtype;

   FROM InOut IMPORT
     (* var  *) EOL,
     (* proc *) WriteInt, WriteLn, Write, WriteString, Read;

   VAR
       name : stack;
       ch   : elementtype;

   BEGIN
     define( name );
     WriteLn;  WriteLn;
     WriteString( "Input your name:  " );
     Read( ch );
     WHILE ch # EOL DO
       (* On some implementations, use ORD(ch)# 10 *)
       push( name, ch);
       Read( ch );
     END(* while loop *);
     WriteLn;  WriteLn;
     WriteString( "The item at the top of the stack:  " );
     Write( topofstack( name ) );
     WriteLn;  WriteLn;
     WriteString( "Your name in reverse order:  " );
     WHILE NOT empty( name ) DO
       pop( name, ch );
       Write( ch );
     END(* while loop *);
     makeempty( name );
   END stacktest.
```

promised in the definition module for the stack ADT to reverse the characters in your name. The element type that is imported from elements is CHAR.

Other uses for a stack in computer science include converting infix expressions to postfix form, evaluating a postfix expression, processing subroutine calls and their returns, and syntax analysis. We will see examples of some of these applications in later sections of this book.

Definition of a Queue

A queue is an ordered collection of items in which the insertion of a new item takes place at one end, called the rear, while the removal of an existing item takes place at the other end, called the front. A queue is often referred to as a first-in, first-out (or FIFO) list.

The ticket lines that form at movie theaters, the customer service lines at banks, and the checkout lines at supermarkets are all examples of queues. When we arrive, we take our place at the rear of the queue and wait for all those in front of us to be served. When we finally arrive at the front of the queue, we are served and remove ourselves from the queue. If there are several lines to choose from, we examine the length of each queue and pick the one that is shortest. If there is no line at the ticket window, teller's cage, or checkout counter, then the queue is empty.

Figure 2.3*a* illustrates a queue containing four names. Hence, it has a length of 4. Mary is at the front of the queue and Erik is at the rear. Since items can be removed only from the front of the queue, when Mary is removed from the queue, Jim becomes the front. When Carol arrives, she is inserted at the rear of the queue. Finally, when Tom arrives, he is inserted behind Carol. Figure 2.3*b* illustrates the final configuration for this queue.

The preceding description references four basic operations on queues. One operation is the removal of the front item from the queue. We will name this operation "remove." Inserting an item, call it "insert", at the rear of the queue is a second operation. The third operation, "length", returns the number of items in the queue. Finally, if the queue contains no items, the "empty" operation returns true (otherwise it returns false).

A queue, like a stack, is conceptually a dynamic structure that is continually changing as items are added to the rear of the queue and removed from the front. A queue is also a type constructor, since different queue types can be

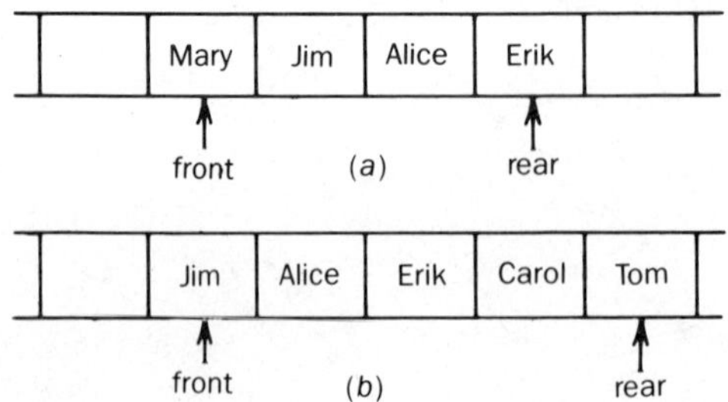

Figure 2.3 Illustration of a Queue

defined for different item types. As we did for the stack ADT, we will import the "elementtype" for the items in the queue from the module named elements.

Since a given problem may involve several queues, our formal interface to the operations must contain a parameter to indicate which queue to perform the desired operation on. Along with the four operations identified above, we specify two additional operations. The "define" operation creates an empty queue, thereby initializing it for the other available operations. The "makeempty" operation reinitializes an existing queue to the empty queue by removing all the elements contained in the queue.

The formal interface to the queue abstract data type is given in the definition module of Listing 2.3.

Listing 2.3 Interface to Queue Abstract Data Type

```
DEFINITION MODULE queueadt;

(* This module defines the public interface for the queue
   abstract data type.  The interfaces to the queue
   operations define, makeempty, empty, insert, remove, and
   length are defined. *)

FROM elements IMPORT
  (* type *) elementtype;

EXPORT QUALIFIED
  (* type *) queue,
  (* proc *) define, empty, makeempty, insert, remove,
             length;


TYPE queue (* Depending on the implementation, additional
              information may appear here. *);


PROCEDURE define
        ( VAR q : queue                         (* out *) );
(* Creates an empty queue.  Must be used before any other
   queue operation.                                        *)


PROCEDURE makeempty
        ( VAR q : queue                         (* in/out *) );
(* Reinitializes an existing queue q to an empty queue by
   removing all elements contained in the queue.           *)
```

```
PROCEDURE empty
      ( q : queue                                     (* in *) ) :
        BOOLEAN;
(* Returns true if the queue q contains no elements,
   otherwise returns false.                                    *)


PROCEDURE insert
      ( VAR    q : queue                              (* in/out *);
            item : elementtype                        (* in *) );
(* Adds item to the rear of queue q.                           *)


PROCEDURE remove
      ( VAR    q : queue                              (* in/out *);
        VAR item : elementtype                        (* out *) );
(* Removes item from the front of queue q.                     *)


PROCEDURE length
      ( q : queue                                     (* in *) ) :
        CARDINAL;
(* Returns the length of the queue.                            *)


END queueadt.
```

Queues arise in a number of applications in computer science, including the simulation of discrete events. We will see several examples that involve the use of queues in the next chapter. Listing 2.4 is presented now to show the use of the queue ADT. This program module performs queue operations on two different queues. The user selects the queue before performing an operation. The type of items is CHAR, which is imported from module elements.

Listing 2.4 Test Program for Queue Abstract Data Type

```
MODULE queuetest;

  FROM queueadt IMPORT
    (* type *) queue,
    (* proc *) define, empty, insert, remove, length;

  FROM elements IMPORT
    (* type *) elementtype;
```

```
FROM InOut IMPORT
  (* proc *) WriteInt, ReadInt, WriteLn, Write,
             WriteString, Read;

FROM Screen IMPORT
  (* proc *) HomeCursor, ClearScreen;

VAR a, b    : queue;
    k       : elementtype;
    choice  : CHAR;
    qname   : CHAR;
    valid   : BOOLEAN;
    done    : BOOLEAN;


PROCEDURE pause;
  VAR  ch : CHAR;
BEGIN
  WriteLn; WriteLn;
  WriteString ( "Hit any key to continue: " );
  Read( ch );
END pause;



PROCEDURE menu;
BEGIN
  ClearScreen;
  HomeCursor;
  WriteLn;
  WriteString( "The active queue is   " );
  Write( qname );
  WriteLn;
  WriteString( "The inactive queue is " );
  IF qname = 'a'
  THEN
    Write( 'b' )
  ELSE
    Write( 'a' )
  END (* if then *);
  WriteLn;  WriteLn;
  WriteString( "C: Change active queue." );
  WriteLn;
  WriteLn;
  WriteString( "I: Insert new object in active queue." );
  WriteLn;
  WriteLn;
  WriteString( "R: Remove object from active queue." );
  WriteLn;
  WriteLn;
```

```
  WriteString( "L: Length of active queue." );
  WriteLn;
  WriteLn;
  WriteString( "E: Exit program." );
  WriteLn;
  WriteLn;
  WriteString( "Enter appropriate choice: " );
  Read( choice );
  CASE choice OF
    'C' : IF qname = 'a' THEN
            qname := 'b'
          ELSE
            qname := 'a'
          END (* if then *);|
    'I' : WriteLn;  WriteLn;
          WriteString( "Enter item to be inserted: " );
          Read( k );
          CASE qname OF
            'a' : insert( a, k );|
            'b' : insert( b, k )
          END (* case *);
          pause;|
    'R' : WriteLn;  WriteLn;
          valid := FALSE;
          CASE qname OF
            'a' : IF NOT empty( a ) THEN
                    valid :=TRUE;
                    remove( a, k )
                  END (* if then *); |
            'b' : IF NOT empty( b ) THEN
                    valid := TRUE;
                    remove( b, k )
                  END (* if then *);
          END (* case *);
          IF valid THEN
            WriteString( "The item removed was: " );
            Write( k )
          END (* if then *);
          pause;|
    'L' : WriteLn;  WriteLn;
          WriteString( "The length of the queue is: " );
          CASE qname OF
            'a' : WriteInt( length( a ), 4 );|
            'b' : WriteInt( length( b ), 4 );
          END (* case *);
          pause;|
    'E' : done := TRUE;
  END (* case *);
END menu;
```

```
BEGIN
  define( a );
  define( b );
  qname := 'a';
  done := FALSE;
  REPEAT
    menu
  UNTIL done;
END queuetest.
```

2.2 The Stack and Queue Implemented Using Records and Arrays

In this section, we present an implementation for the stack and queue. Any implementation requires us to decide how to represent a stack or a queue using the data structures that exist in Modula-2. In this section, we examine one representation for the stack and the queue. In later sections in this chapter, we will consider two additional representations for these abstract data types.

An Implementation of the Stack Abstract Data Type

A stack is a list of items. An array in Modula-2 is also a list of items. Does this mean that we can declare a stack to simply be an array? The answer is "no," since a stack is fundamentally different from an array. An array is an object that is fixed in size, whereas a stack is a dynamic object whose size is continually changing as items are pushed onto the stack or popped off it.

Even though an array is not a stack, can it be the home of a stack? There is a problem here because an array is fixed in size and conceptually a stack may contain an arbitrary number of items. However, we can dimension the array large enough to accommodate the maximum size stack that is expected for the problem at hand. During the course of a computation, the stack will grow and shrink within the space reserved for it. We can let one end of the array represent the fixed bottom of the stack and let the top of the stack expand or contract within the array. Since we need to keep track of the top of the stack, we need a pointer to the array location that contains the top item in the stack.

Hence, an array can be the home of a stack if it is coupled to a pointer to the top of the stack. This suggests that we use a record containing an array of items and a pointer to the top of the stack. The following declarations accomplish this:

```
CONST
    stacksize = 100; (* Maximum number of elements in a
                        stack.                           *)
```

```
TYPE
    stack = RECORD
              storage : ARRAY [1..stacksize] OF elementtype;
              top     : [0..stacksize]
            END (* record *);
```

These declarations replace the single declaration "TYPE stack;" in the definition module for the stack abstract data type given in section 2.1. In this case, the stack is implemented as a transparent type, which means that the user of the stack has access to the underlying data structure. This is conceptually prohibited by the definition of an abstract data type, but the compiler cannot enforce this prohibition for transparent types.

A user's program that imports the type stack can declare multiple instances or objects of type stack with a declaration of the form;

```
VAR a, b : stack;
```

We still have a problem to solve before we can perform operations on the stacks a and b. That is, we must initialize the top of the stack to 0. In this implementation, we adopt the convention that this means that the stack is empty. The user can do this with the following statements;

```
a.top := 0;
b.top := 0;
```

However, this violates the concept of an abstract data type and results in the user's program becoming coupled to the implementation details for a stack. The purpose of the "define" operation identified in the formal interface to the stack ADT is to initialize the stack for the user without revealing the implementation details. Hence, the "define" operation must have the following form:

```
PROCEDURE define ( VAR s : stack        (* out *) );

BEGIN
  s.top := 0
END define;
```

The user's program would then contain the statements;

```
define( a );
define( b );
```

before any other stack operations are performed.

Listing 2.5, the implementation module for the stack ADT, is followed by a description of the procedures it contains.

The operations "makeempty" and "empty" could just as easily be performed in the user's program, but again this would make the user's program dependent on the implementation details. Modern software design advocates users' programs that are independent of the implementation details, because such programs are more comprehensible and easier to maintain.

We now consider the implementation details for the "pop" and "push" operations. Since we are using an array as the home of a stack, the maximum

Listing 2.5 Implementation of Stack Abstract Data Type

```
IMPLEMENTATION MODULE stackadt;

(*  This module is a static array implementation of the
    stack abstract data type.  It imports the type
    elementtype which defines the type of elements to be
    stored in the stack.                                  *)

  FROM InOut IMPORT
    (* proc *) WriteString, WriteLn;

  FROM elements IMPORT
    (* type *) elementtype;


  PROCEDURE define
          ( VAR s : stack                    (* out *) );

  BEGIN
    s.top := 0
  END define;


  PROCEDURE makeempty
          ( VAR s : stack                    (* in/out *) );

  BEGIN
    s.top := 0
  END makeempty;


  PROCEDURE empty
          ( s : stack                        (* in *) ) :
            BOOLEAN;

  BEGIN
    RETURN s.top = 0
  END empty;


  PROCEDURE stackfull
          ( s : stack                        (* in *) ) :
            BOOLEAN;

  BEGIN
    RETURN s.top = stacksize
  END stackfull;
```

```
PROCEDURE stackoverflow;
(* Error handling procedure:  message, recovery, abort.  *)
BEGIN
  WriteLn;  WriteLn;
  WriteString( "Stack overflow." );
  WriteLn;
  HALT
END stackoverflow;


PROCEDURE stackunderflow;
(* Error handling procedure:  message, recovery, abort.  *)
BEGIN
  WriteLn;  WriteLn;
  WriteString( "Stack underflow." );
  WriteLn;
  HALT
END stackunderflow;


PROCEDURE push
        ( VAR    s : stack                        (* in/out *);
              item : elementtype                  (* in *) );

BEGIN
  IF stackfull( s )
  THEN
    stackoverflow
  ELSE
    INC( s.top );
    s.storage[ s.top ] := item
  END (* if then *);
END push;


PROCEDURE pop
        ( VAR s    : stack                        (* in/out *);
          VAR item : elementtype                  (* out *) );

BEGIN
  IF empty( s )
  THEN
    stackunderflow
  ELSE
    item := s.storage[ s.top ];
    DEC( s.top )
  END(* if then *);
END pop;
```

```
  PROCEDURE topofstack
          ( s    : stack                              (* in *) ) :
            elementtype;

  BEGIN
    IF empty( s )
    THEN
      stackunderflow
    ELSE
      RETURN s.storage[ s.top ]
    END (* if then *)
  END topofstack;


END stackadt.
```

size of the stack is limited to the declared size of the array. Attempting to "push" an item onto a full stack is an illegal operation, which we must address in our implementation. The user of the stack ADT, however, thinks of the stack as capable of being arbitrarily large; hence the concept of a full stack does not exist. For this particular implementation, we must consider a full stack as a real possibility. Our solution is to include a private procedure, "stackfull", to recognize a full stack and another private error handling procedure, "stackoverflow", to handle an attempt to push an item onto a full stack.

Another illegal operation is an attempt to "pop" an empty stack. Our implementation calls an error procedure, "stackunderflow", to handle this event.

The error procedures "stackunderflow" and "stackoverflow" presented in this implementation print messages and halt the execution of the program. Each program that uses the stack ADT should tailor these error handling routines to perform an appropriate action for the problem at hand.

Notice that when we pop an item off the stack, we do not physically erase the item from the array. We simply decrement the pointer to the top of the stack so that logically the element just removed from the stack is no longer available.

The final operation specified in the formal interface to the stack ADT is "topofstack", which returns the top item in the stack without removing it from the stack. This is really not a primitive operation, since it can be decomposed into a "pop" operation followed by a "push" operation. In this implementation we chose to retrieve the top element directly. We must remember to check for an empty stack before we attempt the retrieve.

An Implementation of the Queue Abstract Data Type

Now let us develop the implementation details for the queue ADT. Since a queue, like a stack, is a structured list of items, let us consider an array as a possible home for a queue. The basic considerations are essentially identical to those for the stack. The major difference is that we need both a front and a rear pointer to indicate the indices in the array where the queue begins and ends. The following record declaration replaces the "TYPE queue;" declaration in the definition module for the queue ADT given in Listing 2.2.

```
CONST
    queuesize  = 20;
    queuespace = queuesize + 1;
    (* Allows for one blank space, which we use to
       distinguish a full queue from an empty queue.      *)
TYPE
    queue = RECORD
              storage     : ARRAY [0..queuesize] OF
                            elementtype;
              front, rear : [0..queuesize]
            END (* record  *);
```

The constant "queuespace" indicates the number of components in the storage array that will contain the items in the queue. The constant "queuesize" indicates the maximum number of items that can be in the queue at any given time. We do not permit "queuespace" to equal "queuesize" for a reason that will become apparent shortly. The imposition of a maximum queue size violates our notion of a queue, since conceptually a queue may contain an arbitrary number of items.

A first and obvious choice for the empty queue representation is to set both front and rear to the same value, say 0. However, when the first item is inserted into the queue, both the front and rear pointers will have the same value, since the single item in the queue is both the front item and the rear item. This means that we cannot distinguish the empty queue from the queue with one item. A solution to this dilemma is to initialize the queue so that rear is set to 0 and front is set to 1. The queue is then defined to be empty whenever the value for rear is less than the value for front. This solution eliminates storage position 0 as a possible location for a queue item.

With the preceding conventions, we can define the insert operation on queue, q, as follows:

```
INC( q.rear );
q.storage[ q.rear ] := item;
```

and the remove operation on queue, q, can be defined by:

```
item := q.storage[ q.front ];
INC( q.front );
```

The length of the queue is equal to q.rear − q.front + 1.

A queue, like a stack, is conceptually a dynamic structure whose size is continually changing as items are removed from and inserted into the queue. Let us examine this dynamic structure in detail by considering a queue with queuesize = 4. Figure 2.4*a* shows the initial configuration of the queue. If we

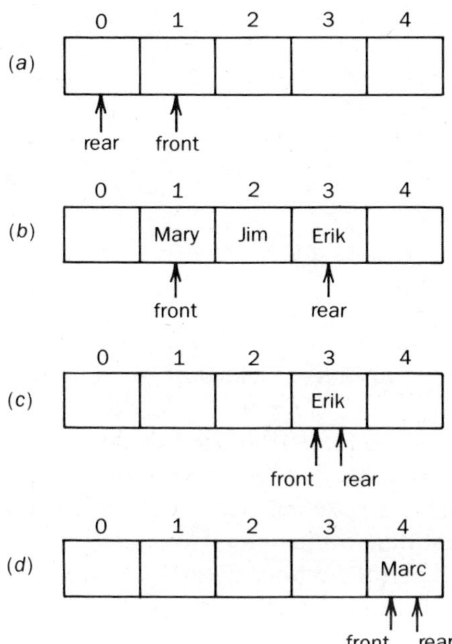

Figure 2.4 The Dynamic Behavior of a Queue

insert Mary, Jim, and Erik into the queue, then we have the representation given in Figure 2.4*b*. Suppose we now remove Mary and Jim, as illustrated in Figure 2.4*c*. Finally, we add Marc and remove Erik to get Figure 2.4*d*. Notice that the queue migrates through the storage array as we perform these operations. If we next remove Marc from the queue, we attempt to set q.front to the illegal value of 5 and we reach the absurd situation of having an empty queue into which we cannot insert a single item because we are at the boundary of our storage array. In this case, q.front = queuespace and an insert operation will cause an indexing error.

One solution to this problem is to modify the remove operation so that every time an element is removed from the queue, we shift all the items in the queue one position, thus ensuring that the front of the queue is always at storage position 1. Since front would always have a value of 1, we no longer need this pointer. The empty queue can be identified when rear = 0.

Although this solution seems reasonable, it has a major drawback if the queue is large. For example, if the queue contains 5000 items, thousands of items might have to be moved just to remove the item at the front of the queue. This could clearly be very inefficient.

A second solution to this problem is to visualize the queue as a circular array. That is, visualize bending the storage array into a circle so that the end of the storage array is now adjacent to the beginning of the storage array. Logically the zeroth position of the storage array immediately follows the last position, queuesize, of the storage array. This is illustrated in Figure 2.5. Now as the queue migrates through the storage array, we will permit it to migrate past the end of the storage array. Figure 2.6*a* shows the final configuration from

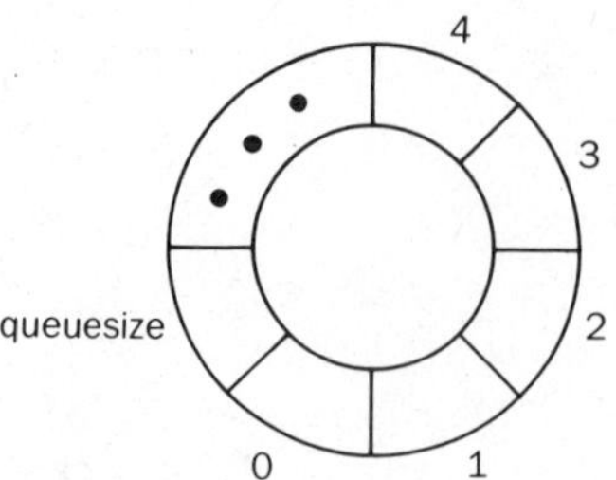

Figure 2.5 A Queue as a Circular Array

Figure 2.4*d*. Figure 2.6*b* illustrates the queue after the insertion of Tom and Ann.

Notice that the "rear < front?" test can no longer be used to determine whether the queue is empty. A solution is to adopt a new convention for the front and rear pointers to the queue. Suppose we define front to point to the storage space immediately preceding the first item in the queue and continue to let rear point to the last item in the queue. Then the empty queue is characterized by rear = front and the insert operation can be performed by:

```
IF rear = queuespace THEN
  rear := 0
ELSE
  INC( rear)
END (* if then else *);
storage[ rear ] := item
```

Using the MOD operation, the "IF THEN ELSE" statement can be replaced to obtain the following statements for the insert operation:

```
rear := (rear + 1) MOD queuespace;
storage[ rear ] := item;
```

Similarly, the remove operation can be defined by the following:

```
front := (front + 1) MOD queuespace;
item := storage[ rear ];
```

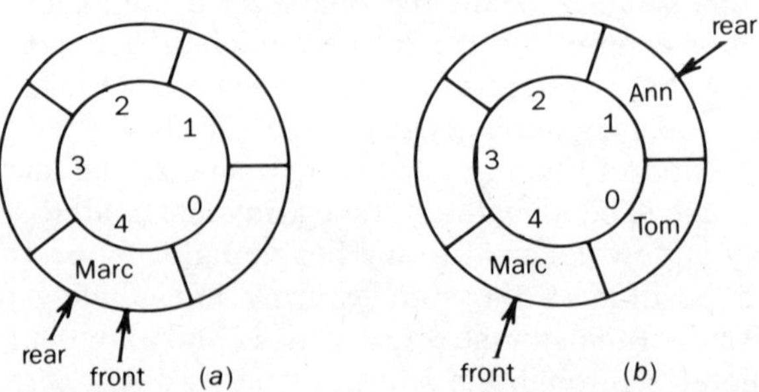

Figure 2.6 The Dynamic Behavior of a Circular Queue

Our implementation must check two illegal operations: an attempt to remove an item from an empty queue and an attempt to insert an item into a full queue. We previously indicated that the empty queue can be identified when front = rear, but this condition is also satisfied when the queue is full. We resolve this duality by adopting the conventions that one storage space will not be used to store queue items and that the full queue is identified when the front and rear pointers differ by 1 modulo the queuespace.

The implementation includes the private procedure "fullqueue" to determine whether the queue is full and two private error handling procedures: "queueoverflow" and "queueunderflow". The error procedures presented print messages and halt the execution of the program. These procedures should be tailored for a specific problem. Listing 2.6 presents the complete implementation details for the queue abstract data type.

Listing 2.6 Implementation of Queue Abstract Data Type

```
IMPLEMENTATION MODULE queueadt;

(*  This module is a static array implementation of the
    queue abstract data type.  It imports the type
    elementtype, which defines the type of elements to be
    stored in the queue.                                        *)

  FROM InOut IMPORT
    (* proc *) WriteString, WriteLn;

  FROM elements IMPORT
    (* type *) elementtype;


  PROCEDURE define
          ( VAR q : queue                           (* out *) );

  BEGIN
    WITH q DO
      front := queuesize;
      rear  := queuesize
    END (* with q *)
  END define;


  PROCEDURE makeempty
          ( VAR q : queue                           (* in/out *) );

  BEGIN
    define( q )
  END makeempty;
```

```
PROCEDURE empty
        ( q : queue                              (* in *) ) :
          BOOLEAN;

BEGIN
  WITH q DO
    RETURN front = rear
  END (* with q *)
END empty;


PROCEDURE fullqueue
        ( q : queue                              (* in *) ) :
          BOOLEAN;
BEGIN
  WITH q DO
    RETURN front = (rear + 1) MOD queuespace
  END (* with q *)
END fullqueue;


PROCEDURE queueoverflow;
(* Error handling procedure:  message, recovery, abort. *)
BEGIN
  WriteLn; WriteLn;
  WriteString( "Queue overflow." );
  HALT
END queueoverflow;


PROCEDURE queueunderflow;
(* Error handling procedure:  message, recovery, abort. *)
BEGIN
  WriteLn; WriteLn;
  WriteString( "Queue underflow." );
  HALT
END queueunderflow;


PROCEDURE insert
        ( VAR    q : queue                       (* in/out *);
              item : elementtype                 (* in *) );

BEGIN
  WITH q DO
    IF fullqueue( q ) THEN
      queueoverflow
    ELSE
      rear := (rear + 1) MOD queuespace;
      storage[rear] := item
```

```
      END (* if then *)
    END (* with q *)
  END insert;


  PROCEDURE remove
          ( VAR    q : queue                         (* in/out *);
            VAR item : elementtype                   (* out *) );

  BEGIN
    IF empty( q ) THEN
      queueunderflow
    ELSE
      WITH q DO
        front := (front + 1) MOD queuespace;
        item := storage[front]
      END (* with q *)
    END (* if then *)
  END remove;



  PROCEDURE length
          ( q : queue                                (* in *) ) :
            CARDINAL;

  BEGIN
    WITH q DO
      IF front <= rear THEN
        RETURN  rear - front
      ELSE
        RETURN queuespace - ( front - rear )
      END (* if then *)
    END (* with q *)
  END length;


END queueadt.
```

2.3 Review of Pointer Variables in Modula-2

In the preceding sections, we described the stack and queue as dynamic objects but we implemented them using the static array and record features that are available in Modula-2. In this section, we explore the dynamic storage allocation features of Modula-2. A second implementation for the stack and queue ADTs that utilizes these dynamic features is given in section 2.4.

Using a static array as the home for a stack or a queue has several major shortcomings. First, the number of items that can be pushed onto a stack or inserted into a queue is limited by the size of the array. This restriction violates our notions of stack and queue, since conceptually both can contain an arbitrary number of items. A second shortcoming is that once space has been allocated for objects of these types, it remains allocated until the active block is terminated.

Let us consider the second shortcoming in more detail. When a block containing the following declarations:

```
VAR
    a, b    :  stack;
    c, d, e :  queue;
```

becomes active, the compiler will have issued directives to reserve storage space for the stacks a and b to accommodate 100 items and space for the queues c, d, and e to accommodate 20 items. If the problem at hand involves only stacks that never contain more than 10 items or queues that never contain more than 5 items, computer memory space is wasted. On the other hand, we could reset the constants ''stacksize'' and ''queuesize'' to 10 and 5, respectively, so that very little memory space would be wasted on this problem. However, it is usually difficult to predict what these numbers should be for a given problem. If our estimate is too low, we risk the possibility of program termination due to stack or queue overflow. An estimate that turns out to be too high results in wasted computer memory space.

Before describing in detail the dynamic memory allocation features available in Modula-2, we will indicate how arrays and records are normally stored in computer memory. Since these types are fixed in size, the compiler can determine exactly how much memory to allocate. The compiler can then assign a variable or object of these types to a specific memory location. The memory locations that immediately precede or follow the array or record variable can be used for other variables, since the array or record cannot grow during program execution. If an array or record were permitted to grow during program execution, other variables stored in adjacent memory locations would have to be moved.

Usually only the starting address of the array or record needs to be saved, since the location of any item in the array or the location of any field in the record can be calculated as an offset from the starting address. The offset depends on the array subscript or the record field name. Such an address computation is dependent on the array or record being stored in consecutive memory locations. This type of storage scheme can be described as a fixed size, direct access storage scheme.

Dynamic storage allocation relaxes the requirement that items be stored in consecutive memory locations. Then growth of the dynamic structure can occur anywhere in computer memory where space is available. In such a situation, we can no longer find a specific item by calculating an offset from a starting location. Instead, we must save an indicator that tells us where the next data item is located. This indicator will be the memory address for the next data item. Such a storage scheme can be described as a varying size, sequential access storage scheme.

A memory address represents a low-level concept that might differ from one implementation or computer to the next. Modula-2 provides us with a high-level abstraction of this concept, called a pointer type. A pointer, like a stack and queue, is a type constructor because each pointer type is bound to another type called the base type. The base type may be any type that is already defined or predefined. The set of values for a variable of pointer type are memory addresses of objects of the base type. There is a predefined constant NIL that belongs to the set of values for every pointer type. It means that the pointer variable is not currently the address of an object of the base type.

Several examples of pointer declarations are:

```
TYPE nametype = ARRAY [0..10] OF CHAR;

TYPE namepointer = POINTER TO nametype;

TYPE infopointer = POINTER TO RECORD
                             name   : nametype;
                             age    : CARDINAL;
                             weight : CARDINAL
                          END;

VAR
     ptr1 : namepointer;
     ptr2 : infopointer;
```

Conceptually, one can visualize a pointer type as a template that can be placed at the memory address of an object of the base type. The template is very much like a window that describes what we see at this location. Figure 2.7 illustrates this concept for the preceding declarations.

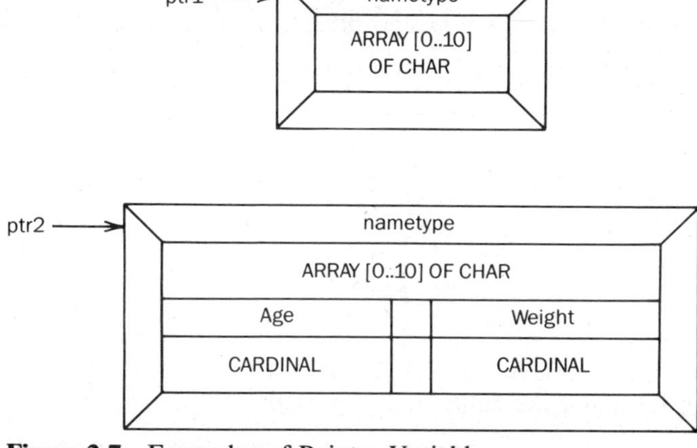

Figure 2.7 Examples of Pointer Variables

One operation defined on pointer types is the "dereferencing" operation. This unary operation is indicated using the operator symbol ^ after the operand. The operand must be a variable of pointer type. The value of a dereferenced pointer is the value of the object of the base type to which the pointer points. Using the preceding declarations, we could have the following:

```
ptr1^ = "Fred";
ptr2^.name = "Alice";
ptr2^.age = 19;
ptr2^.weight = 105;
```

It is an error to apply the dereferencing operation to a pointer variable whose value is NIL, since this value indicates that the pointer does not point to an object of the base type.

The dereferenced pointer variable ptr1^ is of type nametype; but since it is not declared with its own identifier, it is said to be an anonymous variable. An anonymous pointer variable can be accessed only via the pointer.

Since anonymous variables are not explicitly declared, they must be created in another manner. Modula-2 provides the operation NEW on pointer variables to create an anonymous pointer variable of the base type. The operation.

```
NEW( ptr1 );
```

allocates storage to hold one object of the base type and assigns the address of this allocated storage to ptr1. The created base type variable is dynamically allocated at execution time. It is anonymous and can be accessed only using the pointer coupled to the dereferencing operator.

Another operation is DISPOSE, which has a parameter of pointer type and deallocates or returns the storage of the base type that was previously allocated. The operation.

```
DISPOSE( ptr1 );
```

deallocates storage equivalent to one object of the base type and returns ptr1 undefined. Note that this is different from a pointer value of NIL.

For the example presented above, the following statements would allocate storage for the variables ptr1 and ptr2, assign values to the base type, and then deallocate storage:

```
NEW( ptr1 );
ptr1^ := "Fred";
NEW( ptr2 );
ptr2^.name   := "Alice";
ptr2^.age    := 19;
ptr2^.weight := 105;
DISPOSE( ptr1 );
DISPOSE( ptr2 );
```

The operations NEW and DISPOSE must be imported from a module called storage by using the following import list:

```
FROM Storage IMPORT ALLOCATE, DEALLOCATE;
```

The operations NEW and DISPOSE are translated by the Modula-2 compiler into invocations of the more primitive procedures ALLOCATE and DEALLOCATE.

Other operations on pointers include assignment and tests for inequality or equality. However, we must consider the meaning of these operations for dynamically allocated data. Consider the following statements:

```
TYPE
  integerptr = POINTER TO INTEGER;

VAR
  ptr1, ptr2 : integerptr;

NEW( ptr1 );
ptr1^ := 12;
NEW( ptr2 );
ptr2^ := 12;

IF ptr1 = ptr2 THEN ...

ptr2 := ptr1;
```

The "IF THEN" statement will be false because ptr1 and ptr2 point to two different memory locations. The value of the base variable in both cases is 12. So we cannot compare the values of the base variable by comparing the pointer variables that point to the same base type. The last statement results in ptr1 and ptr2 both pointing at the same base variable (i.e., 12). We now have one copy of the base variable but two pointers to that base variable: the assignment statement will not give us two copies of the base variable. Also notice that the assignment statement causes us to lose our pointer to the memory location to which ptr2 originally pointed. Hence, we can no longer deallocate this storage.

Record types in Modula-2 may contain one or more variant parts. An example of a record with a variant part is:

```
TYPE
   age = ( child, adult );
   data = RECORD
            name   : nametype;
            age    : CARDINAL;
            weight : CARDINAL;
            CASE member : age OF
              adult  : occupation : ARRAY [0..19] OF CHAR;
                       salary     : REAL; |
              child  : iq         : INTEGER
            END (* case *)
          END (* record *);

   ptr = POINTER TO data;

VAR
   v : ptr;
```

The variable member is referred to as a tag field of the record. A record can have more than one tag field. The statement:

```
NEW( v );
```

allocates storage for a record of type data. However, this record can be of two different sizes depending on whether member has the value adult or child. In the absence of any information to indicate which variant is intended, the NEW procedure will allocate storage to accommodate the maximum size of the base type.

This might be very wasteful of storage, so Modula-2 permits additional parameters to be used with the NEW and DISPOSE operation to indicate the variants desired. The additional parameters are values for the tag fields.

For example, if we know that the next variant needed has a tag field value of child, we can allocate precisely the storage needed using NEW with a second parameter supplying the value for the tag field:

```
NEW( v, child );
```

If we later wish to deallocate storage, we must specify the tag field so that the size of the block of storage can be determined. For example:

```
DISPOSE( v, child );
```

If we allocate variant records using tag fields, we must be careful to deallocate using tag fields. This poses no problem if we use the tag field of the record. For example, we can allocate storage by:

```
NEW( v, child );
v^.member := child;
```

The tag field is a record descriptor that can be assigned a value as part of the record. When we wish to deallocate, we can then use a statement of the form:

```
DISPOSE( v, v^.member );
```

In summary, arrays and records are said to be static because they remain fixed in size during the execution of the block of code in which they are declared. Pointer variables are dynamic because they can be created and destroyed during program execution. If a dynamic variable has as its base type a record that contains pointer variables, it is possible to build a chain of dynamic variables. This concept forms the basis for the implementation of the stack and the queue, as presented in the next section.

2.4 The Stack and Queue Implemented Dynamically

Dynamic data structures, although extremely versatile, pose potential problems for the programmer. We will examine some of these problems and their solutions in our implementation of the stack abstract data type. We will see these solutions in practice in many examples throughout this book.

Our implementation of the stack ADT will contain the following declaration in the definition module:

```
TYPE stack;
```

This statement declares a type identifier without defining the type. Such a Modula-2 type declaration is referred to as an opaque type, since a user of the type who has seen only the definition module cannot see or access its internal data structure representation.

When the compiler sees such a type declaration, it assumes that the type will be defined in the implementation module. However, the compiler must allocate storage for objects declared to be of opaque type. This implies that the compiler must know the underlying data structure used to represent the type. This is possible only if we completely define the representation for the type in the definition module or substantially restrict the representation for an opaque type. Most Modula-2 implementations restrict opaque types to be pointer types. The base type of the pointer type can be either imported by or defined in the implementation module. The base type can be any structure definable in Modula-2. This property, along with the ability to chain objects of the base type, permits us to define almost any arbitrary structures by appropriately defining the base type.

Thus, a variable of an opaque type is simply a pointer variable. Conceptually, the variable can hold a complicated structured value, since we can store such values by dynamically allocating a block of storage for a value and having the pointer contain the address of the block. This means that a value is physically stored as two parts: a statically allocated pointer and a dynamically allocated block of additional storage. Chaining such objects permits us to define complex data structures.

We will now examine three problems and their solutions associated with the use of opaque types. The first problem is the meaning of assignment and test for equality, the second is deallocation of dynamically allocated variables, and the third concerns bringing opaque types into existence.

The meaning of the assignment and test for equality or inequality of opaque types is identical to that described in section 2.3, since opaque types are pointer types. For example:

```
VAR a, b : stack;
b := a;
IF a # b THEN ...
```

The assignment statement is syntactically and semantically correct. It results in both a and b pointing to the block of storage that contains the stack a. It does not make a copy of a by assigning the stack items to b. The if statement is correct, but it compares two pointers rather than the contents of each stack. If the intent is to determine whether the contents of the two stacks are identical, then, this statement is not semantically correct. That is, an implementation of an abstract data type that involves opaque types must contain the operations of assignment and test for equality or inequality if we wish to perform such operations on objects of the ADT.

Another problem associated with opaque or pointer types is that dynamically allocated variables do not automatically get deallocated when the block of code in which they are declared terminates. This is in contrast to static variables for which storage is deallocated.

Termination of the block of code that contains the declarations given above will cause the deallocation of the variables a and b, whose values are addresses, but the base type to which a and b point will not be automatically deallocated. If the base type variables are not explicitly deallocated, a block of storage the size of the base type will remain allocated and unavailable for later use by the program. If we have chained objects of the base type, a substantial amount of storage may be lost for later use by the program. If this is done repeatedly, it is possible to allocate all the dynamic storage space that is available, resulting in program failure.

To address this problem, our implementation of an ADT will contain an operation to deallocate storage. We will typically call such an operation "makeempty"; however, "destroy" might be a more descriptive choice. The operation of "destroy" is semantically identical to "makeempty" because the intent is to empty the dynamically allocated structure and deallocate storage for later use. An argument could be made for the inclusion of both operations; however, we will use the "makeempty" operation exclusively.

As will be described later, the "define" operation cannot be used to perform the function of the "makeempty" operation. Any program that uses an ADT must be prepared to call "makeempty" before a block of code is terminated with a nonempty object of the ADT. If the termination is due to an error condition, failure to call "makeempty" will result in storage being lost, hence unavailable for later use by the program.

A third problem that arises in connection with dynamically allocated variables is that the declaration of variables of opaque type does not bring the variables into existence. In contrast, static variables are automatically brought into existence. For example, consider the following declarations that appear in a block of code:

```
VAR i, j : INTEGER;
    a, b : stack;
```

In the code that follows these declarations, the variables i and j exist and can be used immediately in assignment statements, expressions, or other Modula-2 program statements. In contrast, the variables a and b do not exist until they are brought into existence via a dynamic allocation statement such as NEW. Recall, however, that the compiler allocates storage for the address of both a and b, but the value of the address is undefined until storage is allocated or until a and b are assigned a value of NIL. Thus our implementation of an ADT must contain an operation to bring an object of the opaque type into existence. We will typically use an operation named "define" to do this.

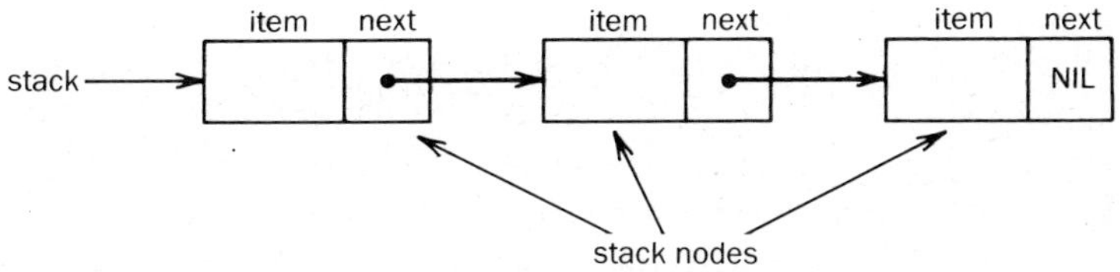

Figure 2.8 Dynamic Representation of a Stack

With this background, we are ready to implement the stack as an opaque type. We will use the following declarations to define the data structure representation for the stack:

```
TYPE
    stackptr   = POINTER TO stacknode;
    stacknode = RECORD
                   item  :  elementtype;
                   next  :  stackptr
                END(* record *);
    stack = stackptr;
```

Figure 2.8 illustrates how stacknodes can be chained together to represent a stack.

The "define" operation initializes the stack variable to a legal value that represents the empty stack. The appropriate value is NIL. Before we consider the "makeempty" operation, let us examine the "push" and "pop" operations. Figure 2.9 illustrates pushing an item onto a stack that already contains two items. Figure 2.10 illustrates popping one item off the stack.

Recall that in the static representation for the stack, we needed to check for stack underflow before a "pop" operation and stack overflow before a

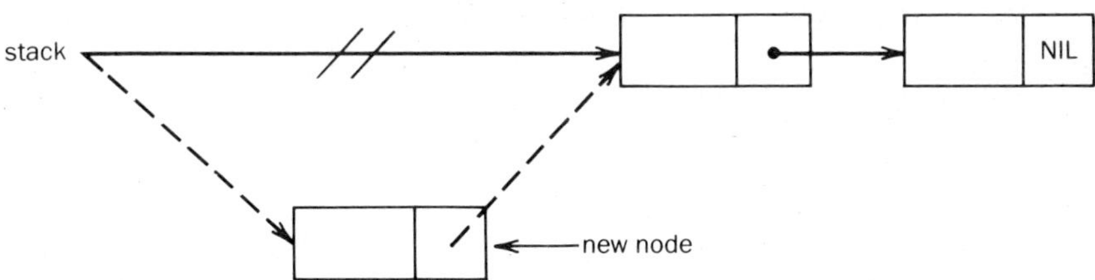

Figure 2.9 A Dynamic Stack with Three Elements

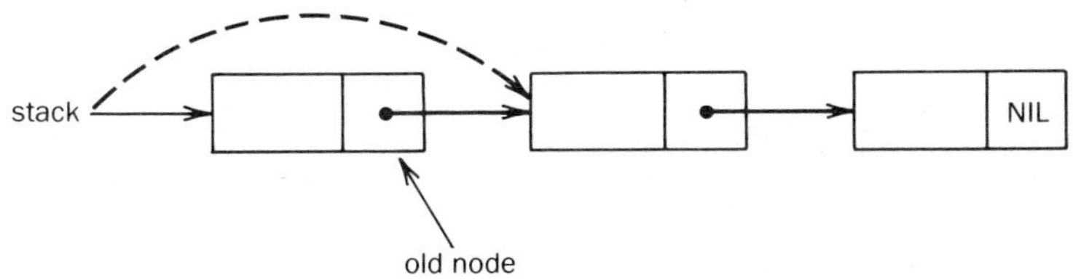

Figure 2.10 The Dynamic Stack of Figure 2.9 After One Pop Operation

"push" operation. For dynamic variables we no longer need to check for stack overflow, but we must still check for stack underflow. Clearly, it is possible to reach the situation in which all the computer memory that is available for dynamic storage allocation has been allocated. If this has occurred, an attempt to perform a "push" operation will usually cause the operating system to raise an error condition and terminate the program.

The "makeempty" operation deallocates all previously allocated stack nodes until the stack variable has a value of NIL. Note that a second call to "define" with a nonempty stack will also result in the assignment to the stack variable of the value NIL; all the previously allocated stack nodes will not be deallocated, however, and storage would be permanently lost.

The "empty" and "topofstack" operations are obvious from their implementation. Listing 2.7 presents the dynamic implementation of the stack ADT.

Listing 2.7 Dynamic Implementation of Stack Abstract Data Type

```
IMPLEMENTATION MODULE stackadt;

(*  This module is a dynamic implementation of the
    stack abstract data type.  It imports the type
    elementtype, which defines the type of elements
    to be stored in the stack.                              *)

  FROM InOut IMPORT
    (* proc *) WriteString, WriteLn;

  FROM Storage IMPORT
    (* proc *) ALLOCATE, DEALLOCATE;

  FROM elements IMPORT
    (* type *) elementtype;

  TYPE
      stackptr    = POINTER TO stacknode;

      stacknode   = RECORD
                      item  :  elementtype;
                      next  :  stackptr
                    END(* record *);

      stack = stackptr;


  PROCEDURE define
          ( VAR s : stack                           (* out *) );
```

```
BEGIN
  s := NIL
END define;


PROCEDURE makeempty
        ( VAR s : stack                          (* in/out *) );

VAR
  p : stackptr;
BEGIN
  WHILE s <> NIL DO
    p := s;
    s := s^.next;
    DISPOSE( p );
  END (* while loop *)
END makeempty;


PROCEDURE empty
        ( s : stack                              (* in *) ) :
          BOOLEAN;

BEGIN
  RETURN s = NIL
END empty;


PROCEDURE push
        ( VAR    s : stack                       (* in/out *);
              item : elementtype                 (* in *) );
VAR
  p : stackptr;
BEGIN
  NEW( p );
  p^.next := s;
  p^.item := item;
  s := p
END push;


PROCEDURE stackunderflow;
(* Error handling procedure:  message, recovery, abort. *)
BEGIN
  WriteLn;  WriteLn;
  WriteString( "Stack underflow." );
  WriteLn;
  HALT
END stackunderflow;
```

```
PROCEDURE pop
        ( VAR s    : stack                      (* in/out *);
          VAR item : elementtype                (* out *) );

VAR
  p : stackptr;
BEGIN
  IF empty( s )
  THEN
    stackunderflow
  ELSE
    p := s;
    item := s^.item;
    s := s^.next;
    DISPOSE( p );
  END (* if then *);
END pop;


PROCEDURE topofstack
        ( s     : stack                         (* in *) ) :
          elementtype;

BEGIN
  IF empty( s )
  THEN
    stackunderflow
  ELSE
    RETURN s^.item
  END (* if then *)
END topofstack;


END stackadt.
```

Note the relative simplicity of the implementation of these operations. The distinct advantage of this implementation over the static implementation is that computer memory space is not wasted. The stack variable contains precisely the amount of storage required to store the stack at any time. Each item in the stack, however, does require an additional field over the static implementation for the address of the next item in the stack. The disadvantage of this implementation is that it imposes more responsibility on the user to make sure that storage is deallocated.

Let us now turn our attention to implementing the queue as a dynamic structure. All the remarks made earlier pertaining to dynamic allocation and opaque types are still applicable. The definition module for the queue ADT will contain the declaration:

```
TYPE queue;
```

indicating that it will be implemented as an opaque type.

Before we can begin the implementation module for the queue ADT, we must determine the data structure or representation for the queue. Suppose we begin by considering the following declarations for the dynamic implementation of the queue ADT:

```
TYPE
  queueptr = POINTER TO queuenode;

  queuenode = RECORD
                storage :  elementtype;
                next    :  queueptr
              END;

  queue        = queueptr;
```

Let us also adopt the convention that queue points to the queue node at the rear of the queue. Figure 2.11 illustrates the empty queue and a queue with three elements. The "insert" operation is essentially equivalent to the "push" operation for the stack as previously described. The "remove" operation requires the taking of an item from the front of the queue. However, our representation does not give us direct access to the item at the front of the queue. We must traverse the entire queue, using the next field of the queue nodes to reach the front of the queue. For long queues, this seems like an unreasonable approach.

Let us now consider an alternative representation for the queue. Since a queue can be characterized by a pointer to the front of the queue and a pointer to the rear, let us associate a special node, called a header node, with each variable of queue type that contains a pointer to the front and rear of the queue. Then the "insert" and "remove" operations have direct access to the queue nodes on which the operation is to be performed. This suggests that the header node be a record with two pointers that point to the front and rear of the queue. Consider the following declarations:

```
TYPE queueptr   = POINTER TO queuenode;

     queuenode = RECORD
                   storage : elementtype;
                   next    : queueptr
                 END;
```

queue → NIL

queue → [| •]→[| •]→[| NIL]
rear ↑ (first node), front ↑ (last node)

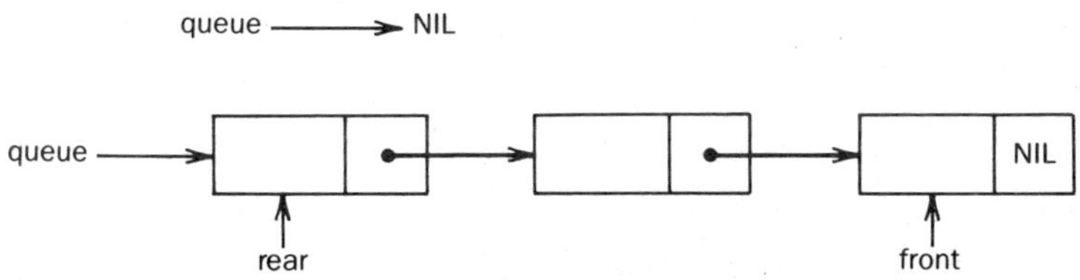

Figure 2.11 Examples of Queues

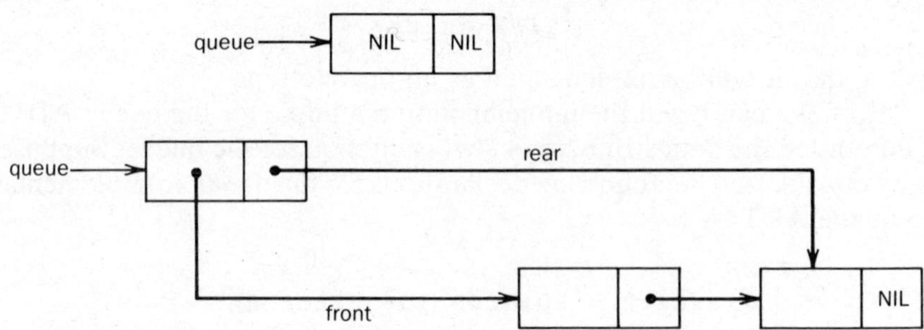

Figure 2.12 The Queue with a Header Node

```
queue           = POINTER TO RECORD
                     front : queueptr;
                     rear  : queueptr
                  END;
```

Figure 2.12 shows the empty queue and the queue with two nodes.

The "define" operation must allocate the header node and set the front and rear pointers to NIL to indicate the empty queue.

The "insert" operation allocates a queue node and sets the storage field to contain the item. If this is the first item inserted into the queue, we must set the front pointer of the header node to point to the new queue node. If the queue is not empty, we need to reset the next field of the last queue node to point to the new queue node. In both cases, we must also set the rear pointer of the header node to the new queue node which is now the last node in the queue. Figure 2.13 illustrates the insert operation.

The "remove" operation must verify that the operation is legal by checking whether the queue is empty. If it is not empty, the information contained in the storage field of the front queue node is transferred to the parameter named

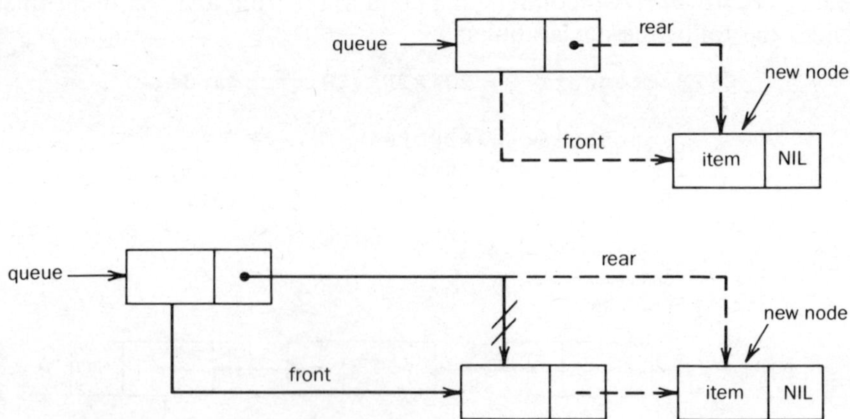

Figure 2.13 The Queue Insert Operation

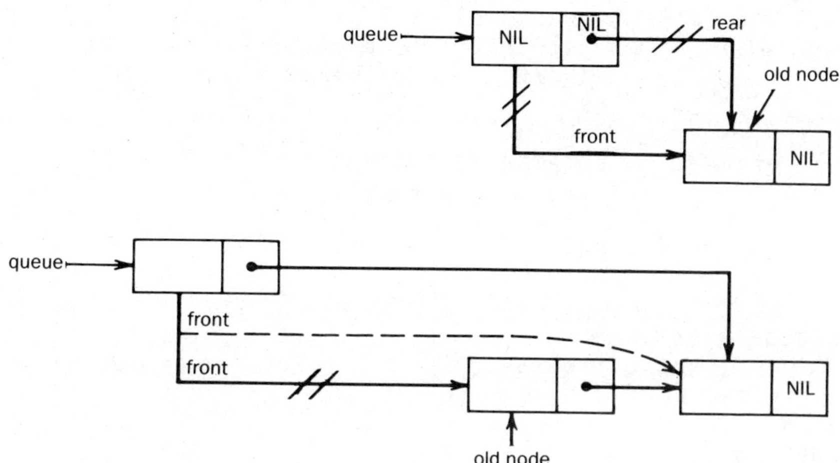

Figure 2.14 The Queue Remove Operation

item so that it can be returned to the calling program. The front pointer of the header node must be set to the next field of the current front queue node, since it will become the new front queue node. If this value is NIL, we are removing the only element that remains in the queue; therefore, we must also set the rear pointer of the header node to NIL. Finally, we deallocate the storage associated with the current front queue node. Figure 2.14 illustrates the remove operation.

If the queue is not empty, the "makeempty" operation deallocates the storage associated with each queue node in the queue. It also sets the front and rear pointers of the header node to NIL, which designates the empty queue.

The "length" operation simply traverses the queue, incrementing a counter for each queue node encountered. The implementation details are presented in Listing 2.8.

Listing 2.8 Dynamic Implementation of Queue Abstract Data Type

```
IMPLEMENTATION MODULE queueadt;

  FROM elements IMPORT
    (* type *) elementtype;

  FROM InOut IMPORT
    (* proc *) WriteString, WriteLn;

  FROM Storage IMPORT
    (* proc *) ALLOCATE, DEALLOCATE;

  TYPE queueptr  = POINTER TO queuenode;
```

```
    queuenode = RECORD
                  storage :  elementtype;
                  next    :  queueptr
                END;

    queue     = POINTER TO RECORD
                  front : queueptr;
                  rear  : queueptr
                END;


PROCEDURE define
        ( VAR q : queue                          (* out *) );

BEGIN
  NEW( q );
  q^.front := NIL;
  q^.rear  := NIL
END define;


PROCEDURE empty
        ( q : queue                              (* in *) ) :
          BOOLEAN;

BEGIN
  RETURN q^.front = NIL
END empty;


PROCEDURE makeempty
        ( VAR q : queue                          (* in/out *) );
  VAR nodetodelete, nextnode : queueptr;
BEGIN
  IF NOT empty( q )
  THEN
    nextnode := q^.front;
    WHILE nextnode <> NIL DO
      nodetodelete := nextnode;
      nextnode := nextnode^.next;
      DISPOSE( nodetodelete )
    END (* while loop *);
    q^.front := NIL;
    q^.rear  := NIL;
  END (* if then *)
END makeempty;


PROCEDURE insert
        ( VAR    q : queue                       (* in/out *);
              item : elementtype                 (* in *) );
```

```
    VAR queuenode : queueptr;
  BEGIN
    NEW ( queuenode );
    queuenode^.storage := item;
    queuenode^.next := NIL;
    IF empty ( q )
    THEN
      q^.front := queuenode
    ELSE
      q^.rear^.next := queuenode
    END (* if then *);
    q^.rear := queuenode
  END insert;


  PROCEDURE queueunderflow;
  (* Error handling procedure:  message, recovery, abort. *)
  BEGIN
    WriteLn; WriteLn;
    WriteString( "Queue underflow." );
    WriteLn;
    HALT
  END queueunderflow;


  PROCEDURE remove
          ( VAR    q : queue                       (* in/out *);
            VAR item : elementtype                 (* out *) );
    VAR queuenode : queueptr;
  BEGIN
    IF empty( q )
    THEN
      queueunderflow
    ELSE
      queuenode := q^.front;
      item := queuenode^.storage;
      q^.front := queuenode^.next;
      IF q^.front = NIL
      THEN
        q^.rear := NIL
      END (* if then *);
      DISPOSE ( queuenode )
    END (* if then *)
  END remove;


  PROCEDURE length
          ( q : queue                              (* in *) ) :
            CARDINAL;
    VAR queuenode : queueptr;
        count     : CARDINAL;
```

```
  BEGIN
    count := 0;
    queuenode := q^.front;
    WHILE queuenode <> NIL DO
      INC( count );
      queuenode := queuenode^.next
    END (* while loop *);
    RETURN count
  END length;


END queueadt.
```

A deque is a double-ended queue; that is, items can be inserted or deleted at either end. This being the case, it does not make sense to refer to one end of the deque as the front and the other as the rear. Rather, we tend to speak of the left and the right ends of the deque. The four basic operations are "removeleft", "removeright", "insertleft", and "insertright". Other operations include "define", "makeempty", "empty", and "length". The definition module for the deque ADT is given in Listing 2.9.

Listing 2.9 Interface to Deque Abstract Data Type

```
DEFINITION MODULE dequeadt;

   FROM  elements IMPORT
     (* type *) elementtype;

   EXPORT QUALIFIED
     (* type *) deque,
     (* proc *) define, empty, makeempty, insertleft,
                insertright, removeleft, removeright,
                length;


   TYPE deque;


   PROCEDURE define
           ( VAR d : deque                        (* out *) );


   PROCEDURE empty
           ( d : deque                            (* in *) :
             BOOLEAN;
```

```
    PROCEDURE makeempty
            ( VAR d : deque                           (* in/out *) );


    PROCEDURE insertleft
            ( VAR     d : deque                       (* in/out *);
                   item : elementtype                 (* in *) );


    PROCEDURE insertright
            ( VAR     d : deque                       (* in/out *);
                   item : elementtype                 (* in *) );


    PROCEDURE removeleft
            ( VAR     d : deque                       (* in/out *);
              VAR item : elementtype                  (* out *) );


    PROCEDURE removeright
            ( VAR     d : deque                       (* in/out *);
              VAR item : elementtype                  (* out *) );


    PROCEDURE length
            ( d : deque                               (* in *) ) :
              CARDINAL;

END dequeadt.
```

We leave the implementation details for the deque ADT for the exercises.

An input-restricted deque permits insertion of items at only one end, although items can be removed from both ends. An output-restricted deque permits insertion at both ends but removal at only one end.

2.5 The Generic Stack and Queue

The preceding versions of the stack and queue ADTs call for the recompilation of both the definition module and the implementation module whenever the element type is changed. This in turn implies that all client programs that use these abstract data types must also be recomplied. We also note that the client program can contain multiple objects of type stack or queue, but all must contain the same element type.

In this section, we will examine the features of Modula-2 that permit us to define and implement generic stacks and queues. A generic stack or queue is a stack or queue that contains items whose type is not specified in advance; rather, the structure or representation of the items that will be contained in the stack or queue is determined at execution time. Thus within an active block of code, we can define several variables of stack or queue type, each of which may contain items of different types.

The development of generic abstract data types requires the use of some low-level abstractions that are available in Modula-2. We briefly review these features before presenting the implementation of the generic stack ADT.

Review of Low-Level Abstractions

Every implementation of Modula-2 includes a module called SYSTEM, which exports several machine-dependent data types and operations, including the types BYTE, WORD, and ADDRESS and the operations ADR, SIZE, and TSIZE. We discuss only these types and operations from SYSTEM, since they are all we will need to implement generic ADTs.

Variables of type BYTE occupy exactly one byte of memory. The values for a variable of type WORD occupy exactly one word of memory. Since all computers do not have byte-addressable memory, the BYTE data type is not defined in all Modula-2 implementations. Also since all computers do not have the same word size, the size of an object of type WORD will vary from one computer to another.

A formal parameter of a procedure can be declared to be of type ARRAY OF BYTE or ARRAY OF WORD. This binds the actual parameter, which may be of any type and any size, to either an ARRAY OF BYTE or an ARRAY OF WORD. This feature of Modula-2 permits us to develop generic procedures that can perform a specific task on any kind of data object.

If item is of type ARRAY OF BYTE or ARRAY OF WORD, the subscript range is from 0 to HIGH(item). The number of bytes or words occupied by item is HIGH(item) + 1. Often in performing the low-level operations to implement a generic procedure; we need to know the size of a type or of a variable. Modula-2 provides this information via the SIZE and TSIZE procedures, which are exported from module SYSTEM.

The formal interfaces to SIZE and TSIZE are given by:

```
PROCEDURE SIZE( item : anytype (* in *) ) : CARDINAL;

PROCEDURE TSIZE( anytype (* in *) ) : CARDINAL;
```

The function procedure SIZE returns the size of its parameter, which is a variable of any type. For variant records, SIZE returns a value that allows for the largest possible field in each variant part. The function procedure TSIZE accepts a type identifier as a parameter and returns the size of objects or variables of that type. For variant records, additional parameters that specify the tag field values may be included.

Both these procedures return CARDINAL values that represent the size of the parameter in terms of memory storage units. This usually is given in bytes but on some computers the size is measured in words.

The ADDRESS type may be considered to be defined by the declaration.

```
TYPE ADDRESS = POINTER TO WORD;
```

This means that objects of ADDRESS type are compatible with all pointer types. Therefore, all the operations that can be performed on pointer types also can be performed on ADDRESS types. This includes the dereferencing operation.

The ADR procedure returns the machine address of its parameter, which must be a variable. The formal interface to the ADR function procedure is:

```
PROCEDURE ADR( item : anytype (* in *) ) : ADDRESS;
```

Recall from section 2.3 that the module storage exports the operations ALLOCATE and DEALLOCATE. The formal interfaces to these two procedures are:

```
PROCEDURE ALLOCATE( VAR p : ADDRESS; size : CARDINAL );

PROCEDURE DEALLOCATE( VAR p : ADDRESS; size : CARDINAL );
```

Let us now consider a simple example to illustrate the use of these two procedures. Suppose we have a pointer variable p that points to the base type, anytype. Then we can allocate storage using the statement:

```
ALLOCATE( p, TSIZE( anytype ) );
```

This statement is equivalent to the statement:

```
NEW( p );
```

The Modula-2 compiler actually translates the second statement into the first. Similarly, to deallocate storage, we can use the statement:

```
DEALLOCATE( p, TSIZE( anytype ) );
```

which is equivalent to the statement:

```
DISPOSE( p );
```

Again the Modula-2 compiler translates the latter statement into the former.

With this background, we are ready to present the definition module and implementation module for the generic stack abstract data type.

Generic Stack Abstract Data Type

In studying the definition module for the generic stack ADT given in Listing 2.10, note the use of the type ARRAY OF WORD in the parameter list for the "push" and "pop" operations. We also specify that the type stack is an opaque type.

Listing 2.10 Interface to Generic Stack Abstract Data Type

```
DEFINITION MODULE genericstack;

(*  This module defines the public interface for the
    generic stack abstract data type.  It imports
    the type WORD, which permits the type of elements
    to be stored in the stack to be bound to the type
    ARRAY OF WORD, thereby permitting generic elements
    to be stored in the stack.                                    *)

  FROM SYSTEM IMPORT
    (* type *) WORD;

  EXPORT QUALIFIED
    (* type *) stack,
    (* proc *) define, makeempty, empty, push, pop;


  TYPE stack;


  PROCEDURE define
        ( VAR s : stack                           (* out *) );
  (* Creates an empty stack. Must be used before any
     other stack operation.                                       *)


  PROCEDURE makeempty
        ( VAR s : stack                           (* in/out *) );
  (* Reinitializes an existing stack s to an empty stack
     by removing all elements contained in the stack.             *)


  PROCEDURE empty
        ( s : stack                               (* in *) ) :
          BOOLEAN;
  (* Returns true if the stack s contains no elements,
     otherwise returns false.                                     *)


  PROCEDURE push
        ( VAR s    : stack                        (* in/out *);
              item : ARRAY OF WORD                (* in     *) );
  (* Adds item to the top of stack s.                             *)
```

```
  PROCEDURE pop
          ( VAR    s : stack                         (* in/out *);
            VAR item : ARRAY OF WORD                 (* out *) );
  (* Removes item from the top of stack s.                     *)

END genericstack.
```

Notice that our interface to the generic stack ADT is identical to the interface presented earlier except that the operation "topofstack" is not included. Any program units that use the earlier versions of the stack ADT can use this version without modification, provided they do not use the "topofstack" operation.

Why have we excluded the "topofstack" operation? To be compatible with the earlier versions of the stack ADT, the interface to the generic version would have to have the form:

```
PROCEDURE topofstack( s : stack (* in *) ) : ARRAY OF WORD;
```

This statement is syntactically incorrect, since the type ARRAY OF WORD is not bound to any type. However, we can avoid this problem by defining this operation to be a procedure rather than a function with the following interface:

```
PROCEDURE topofstack(        s : stack         (* in *);
                      VAR item : ARRAY OF WORD (* out *) );
```

In this case, the type ARRAY OF WORD is bound to the type of item. We leave it as an exercise to implement the generic version of this operation.

Now let us work through the implementation details by considering several options for the representation of the stack opaque type. Since we do not know in advance the size of the items the stack will contain, we cannot define fixed size nodes for the items. Variant records cannot be used because we do not know the type of items. Our solution is to define nodes that contain two fields: a pointer to the next stack node and the address of the item. We will then use the ALLOCATE operation to allocate storage at that address to accommodate the item. The following declarations seem appropriate:

```
TYPE
    stackptr   = POINTER TO stacknode;

    stacknode  = RECORD
                   contents : ADDRESS
                   next     : stackptr;
                 END (* record *);

    stack      = stackptr;
```

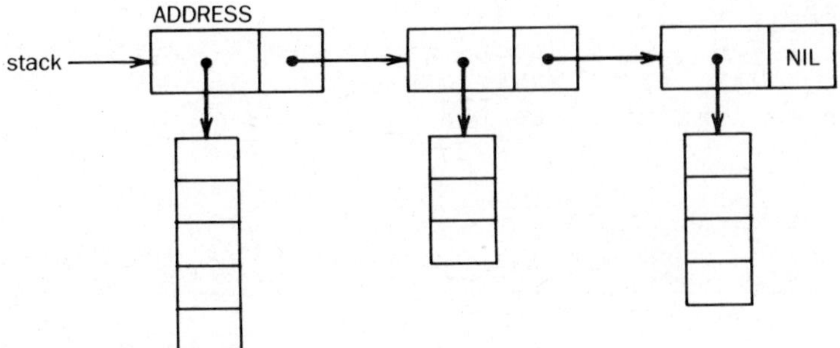

Figure 2.15 Generic Stack Representation

Conceptually, a generic stack containing three items is depicted in Figure 2.15.

Notice that this representation permits items of different size, and most likely of different types, to be placed in the same stack. It is not clear that many applications exist that require a stack with this much generality. Such generality also puts an extra burden on the user of the generic stack. For example, a "pop" operation must bind the returned type ARRAY OF WORD to a variable of a type defined in the user's program. If the returned item is not compatible with the size of the variable in the user's program, an execution error will occur.

We propose to make the generic stack more restrictive by requiring that all elements in the stack be of the same size. The user of the generic stack is not yet completely protected, since the elements can still be of different types as long as they are the same size. We do not know the size of the elements to be used with a given stack variable until we "push" the first item onto the stack. We need to save this size information to verify that later "push" operations are valid and to implement the "pop" operation.

These considerations suggest that we associate with each stack a header node that contains the size information along with a pointer to the rest of the stack. We propose the following declarations:

```
TYPE
    stack       = POINTER TO stackheader;

    stackptr    = POINTER TO stacknode;

    stackheader = RECORD
                    size   : CARDINAL;
                    next   : stackptr;
                  END (* record *);

    stacknode   = RECORD
                    contents : ADDRESS;
                    next     : stackptr;
                  END (* record *);
```

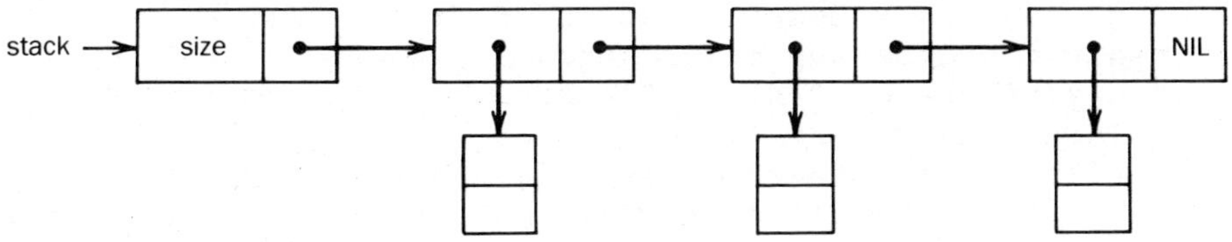

Figure 2.16 Generic Stack with Header Node

Figure 2.16 illustrates a generic stack containing three items of two words each.

We now consider the implementation details for the preceding declarations. The define operation must initialize the header node by assigning the size field a value of zero and the next field a value of NIL. We adopt the convention that the stack is empty if the next field of the header node is NIL.

Let us examine the "push" and "pop" operations in detail by presenting pseudo-code descriptions. The implementation details for the "makeempty" operation should then be apparent.

```
Procedure push ( s : stack; item : array of word)
  Allocate a new stack node
  Determine the size of item
  If the size field of the header node is zero
  Then
    Set the size field of the header node, since this is the
      first element on the stack
  Else
    If the size of the item is not the same as the size
      field of the header node
    Then
      Print an error message and halt execution of the
        program
    End If
  End If
  Allocate storage to accommodate the item
  Transfer the item to the allocated storage
  Set the next field of the new stack node to the value of
      the next field of the header node
  Set the next field of the header node to point to the new
      stack node
End push.

Procedure pop ( s : stack; item : array of word)
  If the stack is empty
  Then
    stack underflow
  Else
    Get the size of the elements from the header node
    Set a pointer to the top stack node
```

```
    Get the memory location of the item from the address
      field of the top stack node
    Transfer the contents of size successive memory
      locations to the item
    Deallocate the memory space that contained the item
    Set the next field of the header node to the next field
      of the top of stack node
    Deallocate the top of stack node
  End If
End pop.
```

Listing 2.11 presents the implementation details for the generic stack ADT. The reader should have little trouble understanding the implementation, which closely follows the pseudo-code algorithms presented above.

Listing 2.11 Implementation of Generic Stack Abstract Data Type

```
IMPLEMENTATION MODULE genericstack;

  FROM InOut IMPORT
    (* proc *) WriteLn, WriteString, WriteCard;

  FROM SYSTEM IMPORT
    (* type *) WORD, ADDRESS,
    (* proc *) TSIZE;

  FROM Storage IMPORT
    (* proc *) ALLOCATE, DEALLOCATE;

  TYPE
       stack       = POINTER TO stackheader;

       stackptr    = POINTER TO stacknode;

       stackheader = RECORD
                       size    : CARDINAL;
                       next    : stackptr;
                     END (* record *);

       stacknode   = RECORD
                       contents : ADDRESS;
                       next     : stackptr;
                     END (* record *);


  PROCEDURE define
        ( VAR s : stack                          (* out *) );
```

```
BEGIN
  NEW( s );
  s^.size := 0;
  s^.next := NIL;
END define;


PROCEDURE makeempty
        ( VAR s : stack                         (* in/out *) );


VAR
    node1 : stackptr;
    node2 : stackptr;
    size  : CARDINAL;


BEGIN
  size := s^.size;
  node1 := s^.next;
  WHILE node1 <> NIL DO
    node2 := node1;
    DEALLOCATE( node1^.contents, size );
    node1 := node1^.next;
    DISPOSE( node2 );
  END (* while loop *);
  s^.size := 0;
  s^.next := NIL;
END makeempty;


PROCEDURE empty
        ( s : stack                             (* in *) ) :
          BOOLEAN;


BEGIN
  RETURN s^.next = NIL;
END empty;


PROCEDURE push
        ( VAR s    : stack                      (* in/out *);
              item : ARRAY OF WORD              (* in     *) );


VAR
    size      : CARDINAL;
    newnode   : stackptr;
    wordcount : CARDINAL;
    location  : ADDRESS;
```

```
BEGIN
  NEW ( newnode );
  (* Calculate size of item in bytes. *)
  size := ( HIGH( item ) + 1 ) * TSIZE( WORD );
  IF s^.size = 0  (* This is first item on the stack.    *)
  THEN            (* Set size of items in header node.   *)
    s^.size := size;
  ELSIF  s^.size # size   (* This is not the first item on
                              the stack.               *)
  THEN            (* The size of item is not compatible. *)
    WriteLn;
    WriteString( "Error attempting to push an object of" );
    WriteString( " inconsistent size onto stack." );
    HALT;
  END (* if then *);
  ALLOCATE( newnode^.contents, size );
  location := newnode^.contents;
  FOR wordcount := 0 TO HIGH( item ) DO
    location^ := item[ wordcount ];
    INC( location, TSIZE( WORD ) );
  END (* for loop *);
  newnode^.next := s^.next;
  s^.next := newnode;
END push;


PROCEDURE stackunderflow;
(* Error handling procedure:  message, recovery, abort. *)
BEGIN
  WriteLn;  WriteLn;
  WriteString( "Error attempting to pop an empty stack." );
  WriteLn;
  HALT;
END stackunderflow;


PROCEDURE pop
        ( VAR s      : stack                 (* in/out *);
          VAR item   : ARRAY OF WORD         (* out    *) );

VAR
   size      : CARDINAL;
   oldnode   : stackptr;
   wordcount : CARDINAL;
   location  : ADDRESS;

BEGIN
  IF empty( s )
  THEN
    stackunderflow
```

```
    ELSE
      size     := s^.size;
      oldnode  := s^.next;
      location := oldnode^.contents;
      FOR wordcount := 0 TO size DIV TSIZE( WORD ) - 1 DO
        item[ wordcount ] := location^;
        INC( location, TSIZE( WORD ) );
      END (* for loop *);
      DEALLOCATE( oldnode^.contents, size );
      s^.next := oldnode^.next;
      DISPOSE( oldnode );
    END (* if then *)
  END pop;


END genericstack.
```

Let us next consider the generic queue ADT. Clearly, many of the considerations expressed above are applicable to the generic queue. An appropriate definition module for the generic queue is given as Listing 2.12.

Listing 2.12 Interface to Generic Queue Abstract Data Type

```
DEFINITION MODULE genericqueue;

(* This module defines the public interface for the generic
   queue abstract data type. It imports the type WORD,
   which permits the type of elements to be stored in the
   queue to be bound to the type ARRAY OF WORD, thereby
   permitting generic elements to be stored in the queue.  *)

FROM SYSTEM IMPORT
  (* type *) WORD;

EXPORT QUALIFIED
  (* type *) queue,
  (* proc *) define, empty, makeempty, insert, remove,
             length;

TYPE queue;


 PROCEDURE define
        ( VAR q : queue                          (* out *) );
 (* Creates an empty queue.  Must be used before any other
    queue operation.                                      *)
```

```
PROCEDURE makeempty
        ( VAR q : queue                        (* in/out *) );
(* Reinitializes an existing queue q to an empty queue
   by removing all elements contained in the queue.         *)


PROCEDURE empty
        ( q : queue                            (* in *) ) :
          BOOLEAN;
(* Returns true if the queue q contains no elements,
   otherwise returns false.                                 *)


PROCEDURE insert
        ( VAR    q : queue                     (* in/out *);
              item : ARRAY OF WORD             (* in *) );
(* Adds item to the rear of queue q.                        *)


PROCEDURE remove
        ( VAR    q : queue                     (* in/out *);
          VAR item : ARRRAY OF WORD            (* out *) );
(* Removes item from the front of queue q.                  *)


PROCEDURE length
        ( q : queue                            (* in *) ) :
          CARDINAL;
(* Returns the length of the queue.                         *)


END genericqueue.
```

The considerations pertaining to the generic stack that were discussed previously are applicable to the generic queue. Consider the following declarations:

```
TYPE
    queue       = POINTER TO queueheader;
    queueptr    = POINTER TO queuenode;
    queueheader = RECORD
                    front : queueptr;
                    size  : CARDINAL;
                    count : CARDINAL;
                  END (* record *);

    queuenode   = RECORD
                    contents : ADDRESS:
                    next     : queueptr
                  END (* record *);
```

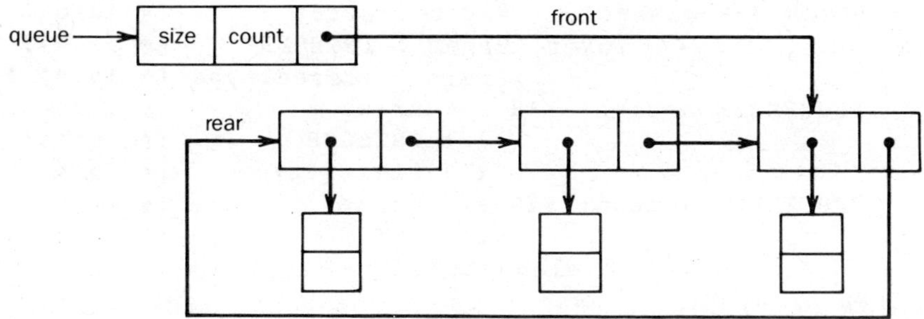

Figure 2.17 Generic Queue with Header Node

These declarations assume that the queue is to be implemented as a circular structure. That is, the front field of the queue header node points to the queue node at the front of the queue and the next field of queue node at the front points to the rear of the queue. Note that the header also contains the size of the elements contained in the queue and the count of the number of elements in the queue. Figure 2.17 illustrates a generic queue, based on the preceding declarations, that contains three elements of two words each. We leave the implementation details as an exercise.

Exercises

2.1 Suppose we have a computer language that has the stack data type but does not have the array data type. An array is characterized as an ordered list of items along with a dimension statement to indicate the size of the list by specifying the subscript range for the items. The fundamental operations include assignment of an item to a particular subscript location in the array and accessing an item from a particular subscript location in the array. Consider the following definition module for these operations:

```
DEFINITION MODULE arrayadt;
   FROM stackadt IMPORT
     (* type *) stack;
   FROM elements IMPORT
     (* type *) elementtype;
   EXPORT QUALIFIED
     (* type *) array,
     (* proc *) dimension, assign, access;
   TYPE array = RECORD
                   s   : stack;
                   l,u : INTEGER; (* lower and upper
                         subscripts *)
                END (* record *);
```

```
    PROCEDURE dimension( VAR a : array          (* in/out *);
                   lower, upper : INTEGER       (* in *);
                           init : elementtype (* in *) );
    PROCEDURE assign( VAR a : array             (* in/out *);
                          i : INTEGER           (* in *);
                          x : elementtype       (* in *) );
    PROCEDURE access( VAR a : array             (* in *);
                          i : INTEGER           (* in *) ) :
                  elementtype ;
  END arrayadt.
```

Implement these operations using the stack ADT. Write a test program to verify that your implementation is correct.

2.2 Implement the array ADT defined in exercise 2.1 as an opaque data type. As before, use only the stack in your implementation.

2.3 The stack ADT defined by Listings 2.1 and 2.5 prints an error message and halts execution when a stack overflow or stack underflow situation arises. Modify the interface to the "pop" and "push" operations so that they return an error flag to the user. This permits the user to perform corrective action. Test your implementation.

2.4 Using the stack ADT, develop and implement an algorithm to determine whether an input string of characters is of the form:

x y

where x is a string consisting of arbitrary characters and y is the reverse of x. For example, if x = "ABBDYCA" then y = "ACYDBBA".

2.5 Using the stack ADT, develop and implement an algorithm to determine whether an input string of characters is of the form:

a b c d ... z

where a, b, . . . , z are strings of the form x y defined in exercise 2.4.

2.6 Implement the stack ADT as an opaque type using the declarations:

```
CONST stacksize = 100;
TYPE stack = POINTER TO
       RECORD
          storage : ARRAY [1..stacksize] OF
                    elementtype;
          top     : [0..stacksize]
       END (* record *);
```

The implementation hides the internal representation of the stack from the user but has all the problems associated with using a fixed size array as the home of a stack.

2.7 Implement the queue ADT as an opaque type using the declarations:

```
CONST
    queuesize  = 20;
    queuespace = queuesize + 1;
```

```
TYPE queue = POINTER TO
        RECORD
          storage      : ARRAY [0..queuesize] OF
                           elementtype;
          front, rear : [0..queuesize]
        END (* record *);
```

Your implementation should be based on a circular queue representation for the storage array. This implementation hides the internal representation of the queue from the user.

2.8 Consider the queue to be represented as a circular dynamically allocated structure using the following declarations:

```
TYPE queueptr  = POINTER TO queuenode;
     queuenode = RECORD
                   storage : elementtype;
                   next    : queueptr
                 END;
     queue     = queueptr;
```

The queue can be conceptually visualized by Figure 2.18. Note that queue points to the item at the front of the queue and the next field of the front item points to the rear of the queue. Implement the queue operations promised in the definition module for the queue ADT presented in Listing 2.3.

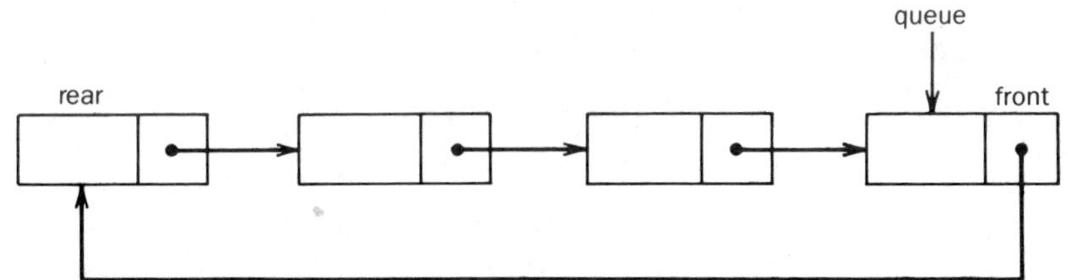

Figure 2.18 Queue for Exercise 2.8

2.9 Let us add another field to the header node of the queue that contains the length of the queue. Using the following declarations:

```
TYPE queueptr  = POINTER TO queuenode;
     queuenode = RECORD
                   storage : elementtype;
                   next    : queueptr
                 END;
     queue     = POINTER TO RECORD
                   front : queueptr;
                   count : CARDINAL;
                   rear  : queueptr
                 END;
```

implement all the operations defined in the definition module for the queue ADT in Listing 2.3. The "insert" and "remove" operations should update the count field to reflect the current length of the queue. The "length" operation should simply return the value of count.

2.10 In our operations on stacks we defined the operation "topofstack", which permits us to examine the top element of the stack before we pop it off the stack. In problems involving queues, it is sometimes necessary to examine the front element of the queue before removing it from the queue. Let us define the interface to this operation as follows:

```
PROCEDURE frontofqueue( q : queue (* in *) ) :
                                elementtype;
```

Implement and test this new operation for either the implementation presented in the text or for your implementations of exercises 2.7, 2.8 or 2.9.

2.11 Let us conceptually visualize the queue as in Figure 2.19. This is a variation of the implementation presented in section 2.4. Describe any problems associated with this different conceptualization.

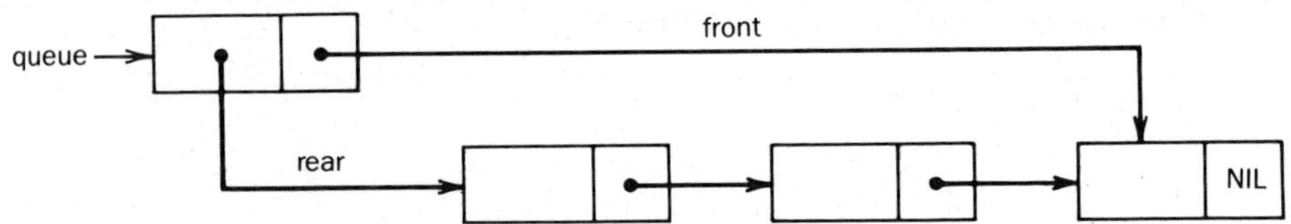

Figure 2.19 Queue for Exercise 2.11

2.12 Suppose that:

```
elementtype = stack;
```

for the queue ADT. That is, we have a queue of stacks. Describe any problems that might be associated with dynamic allocation. Implement and test the operations defined in the definition module for the queue ADT for a queue of stacks.

2.13 Suppose that:

```
elementtype = queue;
```

for the queue ADT. In this case, we have a queue of queues. Describe any problems associated with dynamic allocation and the recursive use of the queue type definition. Implement and test the operations defined in the definition module for the queue ADT for a queue of queues.

2.14 Define the interface to the operation "reverse", which repositions the elements in a queue so that the front of the queue becomes the rear, and vice versa. Implement the operation using the stack ADT.

2.15 For the deque ADT, implement the deque as a circular static array. The "TYPE deque;" declaration should be replaced by a declaration of the form:

```
TYPE
  deque   = RECORD
                storage      : ARRAY [0..dequesize] OF
                               elementtype;
                front, rear  : [0..dequesize]
              END (* record *);
```

where dequesize is a constant.

2.16 For the deque ADT, implement the deque as an opaque type using a header node that contains pointers to the front and rear of the deque.

2.17 For the deque ADT, implement the deque as an opaque type using a dynamically allocated circular structure as in exercise 2.8.

2.18 In the header node for the deque ADT of exercise 2.16, let us add a field that contains the length of the deque. Reimplement the deque using this new header node.

2.19 Describe how an input-restricted deque can be used to represent a stack. A queue. Describe how an output-restricted deque can be used to represent a stack. A queue.

2.20 Implement and test the procedure "topofstack" for the generic stack ADT.

2.21 Implement and test a version of the generic stack ADT that permits elements of different size and/or type to reside in the same stack.

2.22 Develop pseudo-code algorithms for the "insert" and "remove" operations for the generic queue ADT.

2.23 Implement and test the generic queue ADT.

2.24 Declare a queue header node and queuenodes so that a generic queue can contain elements of different sizes. Implement and test this version of the generic queue ADT.

2.25 Define the interface to the operation "frontofqueue" for the generic queue ADT. Implement and test this new operation.

3

Applications of Stack and Queue Abstractions

In Listing 2.2, we showed how a stack can be used to reverse a list of characters. In this chapter, we will show how a stack can be used to convert an algebraic expression from infix form to postfix form and how the resulting postfix form can be evaluated using a stack. We will also use the stack ADT to find a path through a maze and we will use both the stack and the queue ADTs to perform a discrete simulation of a simple computer system. Finally, we use the stack to implement an adaptive numerical integration algorithm. The exercises at the end of this chapter present many other examples of the use of the stack and queue.

3.1 Convert an Algebraic Expression from Infix Form to Postfix Form

Algebraic Expressions

A fundamental problem in computer science is the evaluation of algebraic expressions that can be expressed in a high-order language such as Modula-2. In this section, we develop algorithms that utilize the stack ADT to convert an algebraic expression from infix form to postfix form and to evaluate the resulting postfix form. Software to evaluate algebraic expressions is often incorporated into applications software such as spreadsheet software systems, statistical packages, and graphics/plotting software.

An algebraic expression is made up of operands, operators, and delimiters. Delimiters include parentheses, the assignment operation, :=, and the statement separator, ;. For example, the expression.

```
A / B - C * D + E
```

has five operands: A, B, C, D, and E; and four operators: /, −, ∗, and +. Even though these operands are all one-letter variables, operands can be any legal variable name or constant in a high-order programming language. In a strongly typed language such as Modula-2, the types of the operands must be consistent with the operations defined on them.

The meaning of the preceding expression depends on the order of the operations. By using parentheses, the order of evaluation can be specified:

(A / (B - C)) ∗ (D + E)

Alternatively, the order of evaluation can be specified by assigning the operators precedence. For example, if the precedence of the operators is:

∗, / have equal precedence
+, − have equal precedence
∗, / have higher precedence than +, −

and if we adopt the convention that expressions are evaluated from left to right, the preceding parentheses-free expression would be evaluated as follows:

((A / B) - (C ∗ D)) + E

This agrees with our usual concept of operator precedence from algebra, where the expression $A + B * C$ is evaluated as $A + (B * C)$ rather than as $(A + B) * C$.

Programming languages that allow algebraic expressions, including Modula-2, define a precedence for all operators. This permits the unambiguous evaluation of an expression regardless of whether parentheses are present in the expression. Table 3.1 presents the precedence of some of the operators in Modula-2. Operators at the same level in the table have the same precedence. Operators at the top of the table have the highest precedence.

Infix, Postfix, and Prefix Notation

Before developing our algorithms for evaluating algebraic expressions, we define infix, postfix, and prefix forms of algebraic expressions. For the moment, consider only binary operations, that is, operations that have two

TABLE 3.1 Operator Precedence in Modula-2

unary +	unary −	NOT				
∗	/	DIV	MOD	AND		
+	−	OR				
=	<>	#	<	<=	>	>=

TABLE 3.2 Infix, Postfix, and Prefix Examples

Infix	Postfix	Prefix
A + B	A B +	+ A B
A − B + C	A B − C +	− A + B C
A ∗ B / C	A B ∗ C /	∗ A / B C
A − B / C	A B C / −	− A / B C
A + B ∗ C − D / E	A B C ∗ + D E / −	+ A − ∗ B C / D E

operands. In the infix form of an algebraic expression, the operator is between its two operands. In postfix form the operator follows its two operands, and in prefix form the operator precedes its two operands. Some examples are given in Table 3.2.

The infix form is the usual form for algebraic expressions. However, the postfix and prefix forms are not unusual. Some hand calculators are based on postfix notation, since the operands are entered before the desired operation is performed. In section 1.2, we defined operations for complex numbers in Modula-2. To add or multiply the two complex numbers a and b to obtain the complex number c, we would use the following statements:

```
c := add( a, b);
c := mult( a, b );
```

These are examples of prefix notation, since the operator precedes the operands.

The preceding examples do not contain parentheses, so we used operator precedence to determine the postfix and prefix forms. In essence, to obtain the postfix and prefix forms we apply the precedence rules to determine which operation to perform next. We then write that operation, along with its two operands, in either postfix or prefix form. The result obtained after performing this single binary operation can be considered to be a single operand. We repeat this process until the entire algebraic expression is in the desired form. Table 3.3 contains parentheses to emphasize that the terms enclosed are treated as single operands:

TABLE 3.3 Infix-to-Postfix and -Prefix Conversion

Infix to Postfix	Infix to Prefix
A / B − C ∗ D + E	A / B − C ∗ D + E
(A B /) − C ∗ D + E	(/ A B) − C ∗ D + E
(A B /) − (C D ∗) + E	(/ A B) − (∗ C D) + E
(A B / C D ∗ −) + E	(− / A B ∗ C D) + E
A B / C D ∗ − E +	+ − / A B ∗ C D E

TABLE 3.4 Conversion of Infix Expressions with Parentheses

Infix to Postfix	Infix to Prefix
A / (B − C) * (D + E)	A / (B − C) * (D + E)
A / (B C −) * (D + E)	A / (− B C) * (D + E)
(A B C − /) * (D + E)	(/ A − B C) * (D + E)
(A B C − /) * (D E +)	(/ A − B C) * (+ D E)
A B C − / D E + *	* / A − B C + D E

What happens if we add parentheses to our original infix expression? Recall that parentheses can be used to override the default precedence. The expression within a matched pair of parentheses can be treated as a single operand that must be converted to the desired form. Consider Table 3.4.

Note that the postfix and prefix forms do not require parentheses. The postfix and prefix forms are unambiguous, parentheses-free representations for an infix expression containing parentheses. The order of the operations in the postfix and prefix forms determines the order of operations in evaluating the expression. Hence, the priority of the operators is no longer relevant. Also note that in all three forms the order of the variables (i.e., the operands) is the same.

Evaluation of a Postfix Expression

To evaluate a postfix expression, we need note only that each operator refers to the previous two operands in the expression. An operand may be the result of applying previous operators. To illustrate this, let us examine the steps involved in evaluating the postfix expression:

A B C − / D E + *

Each time we compute a value, we will store it in the variable, Ri, i >= 1. Recall that we evaluate the expression from left to right; thus the first operation we perform is B C − to obtain R1. The entire process can be summarized as follows:

Operation	*Postfix*
R1 ← B C −	A R1 / D E + *
R 2 ← A R1 /	R2 D E + *
R3 ← D E +	R2 R3 *
R4 ← R2 R3 *	R4

where R4 contains the value of the expression. Notice that the precedence of the operators is no longer important. As we scan from left to right, whenever we find an operator, we perform the indicated operation on the preceding two operands.

Suppose that each time we find the operand, we push its value onto a stack. Then whenever we find an operator, we will pop the top two operands from the stack and perform the indicated operation. The result of the operation will then be pushed onto the stack. When we have finished scanning the input expression from left to right, the single operand that remains in the stack is the value of the original expression.

This algorithm can be more precisely described as follows:

```
for each symbol in the postfix expression do
  if the symbol is an operand
  then
    push its value onto a real stack
  else
    pop opnd2 from the real stack
    pop opnd1 from the real stack
    perform the operation specified by the
      current symbol
    push the result on the real stack
  end if
end for
the value of the expression is the single value remaining on
      the stack
```

We illustrate the dynamic behavior of the real stack associated with this algorithm by considering the preceding prefix expression with the following values for the operands:

$$A = 8, \quad B = 2, \quad C = 4, \quad D = 3, \quad E = 9$$

Figure 3.1 shows the contents of the real stack after each execution of the for loop.

This algorithm does not verify that the postfix expression is free of errors. However the algorithm we develop for converting from infix to postfix should perform the necessary error checking on the input infix expression to guarantee that only valid postfix expressions are sent to the postfix evaluation algorithm.

The postfix expression is simply a string of characters. To perform the postfix evaluation algorithm, two other issues need to be addressed, namely: how to assign values to the operands and how to perform the arithmetic operation specified by a character in the postfix expression.

The assignment of values to the operands is facilitated by using a symbol table. Each unique operand in the original expression creates an entry in the

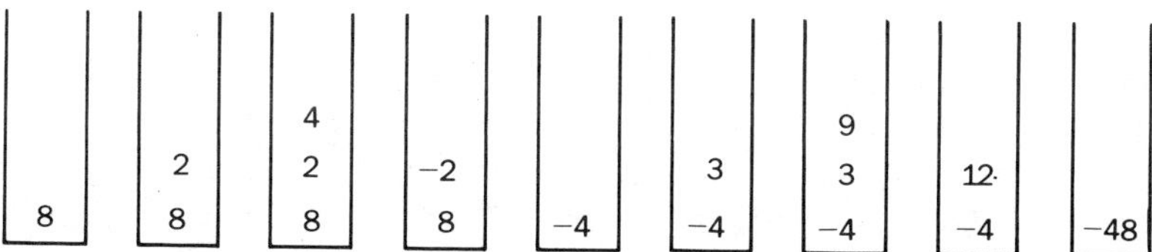

Figure 3.1 Evaluating a Postfix Expression Using a Stack

Operand	*Value*	*Operand*	*Address*
A	8	A	62100
B	2	B	62098
C	4	C	62096
D	3	D	62094
E	9	E	62092

Figure 3.2 Symbol Table

symbol table. Associated with each entry is a value. Each symbol has an address in the symbol table. In this simple example, the address is an index. However, the symbol table that is created by a compiler for the variables in your program will contain the address in computer memory at which the value of the variable is stored. The value of the variable is not stored in the symbol table. The symbol table for our problem and a corresponding portion of a symbol table that a compiler might generate are given in Figure 3.2.

The symbol table can be conceptualized as an object with two columns. The first contains the variable name and the second contains the corresponding value for the variable or the location in memory of the corresponding value. The index into the symbol table is the row subscript. For example, in Figure 3.2, if the index range is from 1 to 5, variable C corresponds to an index value of 3.

To evaluate a postfix expression, we scan the postfix expression and enter each unique operand into a symbol table. Then we assign a numerical value to each operand in the symbol table.

The second issue simply involves performing the operation denoted by a character on the values associated with two operands. This can be done as follows:

```
PROCEDURE result( symbol : CHAR; opnd1, opnd2 : REAL ) :
                  REAL;

BEGIN
   CASE symbol OF
      '+' : RETURN opnd1 + opnd2; |
      '+' : RETURN opnd1 - opnd2; |
      '*' : RETURN opnd1 * opnd2; |
      '/' : RETURN opnd1 / opnd2;
   END (* case *)
END result;
```

Converting an Infix Expression to Postfix Form

We have presented an algorithm for evaluating a postfix expression. Earlier, we described a method for converting an infix expression to either postfix or prefix form. We now formalize an algorithm for converting an infix expression to postfix form. When we have this algorithm in place, we will be able to take any infix expression, convert it to postfix form, and evaluate the resulting postfix expression. We leave it as an exercise to develop a similar algorithm for converting from infix to prefix form and evaluating the resulting prefix expression.

Our objective is to develop an algorithm that will convert an infix expression with parentheses to postfix form in one pass of the infix expression. We previously observed that the order of the operands is the same in infix and postfix. As we scan the infix expression from left to right, we will immediately pass all operands to the output string. As each operator or delimiter is encountered, it is either placed in a stack or sent directly to the output string. The choice depends on the precedence of the current operator symbol with the operator symbol on the top of the stack.

As a first step in the development of our algorithm, we will define a precedence function that returns TRUE if the precedence of operator1 is greater than or equal to the precedence of operator2 when operator1 appears to the left of operator2 in an infix expression. This means that the operation specified by operator1 should be performed on its operands before the operation specified by operator2. For example, in the expression A * B + C, the multiplication should be performed before the addition, since * has a higher precedence than + and the * appears to the left of the +. In this case, our precedence function should return a value of TRUE. For the expression A + B * C, the multiplication is still to be performed before the addition, since * has a higher precedence than +. In this case, our precedence function should return a value of FALSE because operator1 has a lower precedence than operator2.

For parentheses-free infix expression, our precedence function can be defined by:

```
PROCEDURE precedence( op1, op2 : CHAR ) : BOOLEAN;
BEGIN
  RETURN NOT( ( (op1 = '+') OR (op1 = '-') ) AND
        ( (op2 = '*') OR (op2 = '/') ) );
END precedence;
```

Since we are considering only the four operators +, −, *, and /, there are only 16 different combinations for the parameters op1 and op2 to the preceding precedence function. All but four of these combinations return a value of TRUE.

Our algorithm for parentheses-free infix expressions can be described as follows. The infix string is scanned from left to right. If the symbol is an operand, we immediately send it to the postfix string. If the symbol is an operator and the operator stack is not empty, and if the precedence of the operator at the top of the stack is greater than the current operator symbol, we pop the operator at the top of the stack and send it to the postfix string. We continue to compare the current operator symbol with the operator at the top of the stack until the stack is empty or until the precedence of the operator at the top of the stack is less than the current operator symbol. In either case, we add the current operator symbol to the stack. When we reach the end of the infix expression, we pop the remaining operators off the stack and send them to the postfix string.

The preceding description can be formalized as follows:

```
initialize an operator stack
for each symbol in the input string do
  if the symbol is an operand then
    add the symbol to the postfix string
  else
    while the operator stack is not empty and the
        precedence( topofstack( operator ), symbol ) do
      pop the operator stack, call the result topsymbol
      add topsymbol to postfix string
    end while
    push symbol onto operator stack
  end if
end for
while the operator stack is not empty do
  pop the operator stack, call the result topsymbol
  add topsymbol to postfix string
end while
```

We now consider what changes must be made to the precedence function and our algorithm to accommodate infix expressions containing parentheses. Each left parenthesis encountered opens the scope of a subexpression, which must be converted to postfix form. The corresponding right parenthesis closes the scope of the subexpression. Once the subexpression within the corresponding set of parentheses has been converted to postfix form, it can be treated as a single operand. The last pair of parentheses opened in an expression containing nested parentheses encloses the first subexpression to be transformed to postfix. This last in/first out behavior suggests that we continue to use a stack but allow it to contain both operators and parentheses.

When a left parenthesis is encountered in a valid infix expression, it opens the scope of a subexpression that must be converted to postfix form. We should insert the left parenthesis onto the stack, since all operators to the right are part of the subexpression until we encounter the corresponding right parenthesis that closes the scope of the subexpression. This can be achieved through the precedence function by defining the precedence of a left parenthesis to be less than any other operator, including another left parenthesis. That is, we define:

```
precedence( op1, '(' ) = FALSE
```

and

```
precedence( '(', op2 ) = FALSE if op2 # ')'
```

Note that if op1 is a right parenthesis, the infix expression is not correct. Also note that op2 can be a left parenthesis. When we encounter a right parenthesis, all operators in the stack up to the corresponding left parenthesis must be popped from the stack and sent to the postfix string. This can be achieved by setting:

```
precedence( op1, ')' ) = TRUE
```

We eventually encounter the corresponding left parenthesis. Since this indicates the end of the subexpression, we pop the left parenthesis off the stack and discard it as well as the corresponding right parenthesis, rather than sending them to the postfix string. We identify this situation by defining:

```
precedence( '(', ')' ) = TRUE
```

The definition of our precedence function is now given by:

```
PROCEDURE precedence( op1, op2 : CHAR ) : BOOLEAN;
BEGIN
  IF ( (op1 = '+') OR (op1 = '-') ) AND
     ( (op2 = '*') OR (op2 = '/') )

  THEN
    RETURN FALSE
  ELSIF ( ( op1 = '(' ) AND ( op2 # ')' )
          OR ( op2 = '(' )
  THEN
    RETURN FALSE
  ELSE
    RETURN TRUE
  END (* if then *);
END precedence;
```

Another description of the precedence function is that it compares the precedence of the operator at the top of the stack with the current scanned operator symbol in the infix expression. If the precedence function is assigned a value of false, the current scanned operator symbol should be pushed onto the operator stack. If true, the symbol at the top of the operator stack should be popped and sent to the postfix string.

The formal description of our preceding alogorithm modified to accept correct infix expressions with parentheses can be described by:

```
initialize an operator stack
for each symbol in the input string do
  if the symbol is an operand then
    add the symbol to the postfix string
  else
    while the operator stack is not empty and the
        precedence( topofstack( topsymbol ), symbol ) do
      pop the operator stack, call the result topsymbol
      if topsymbol = '(' and symbol = ')' then
        exit while loop
      end if
      if topsymbol # '(' then
        add topsymbol to postfix string
      end if
    end while
```

```
      if symbol # ')' then
         push symbol onto operator stack
   end for
   while the operator stack is not empty do
     pop the operator stack, call the result topsymbol
     if topsymbol # '(' then
        add topsymbol to postfix string
     end if
   end while
```

We illustrate this algorithm by considering the infix expression:

$$(A / (B - C)) * (D + E)$$

Table 3.5 shows the contents of the symbol, the operator stack, and the postfix string after scanning each symbol. The top of the operator stack is to the right.

The preceding algorithm does not contain any error checking to ensure that the infix string is correct. We leave this as an exercise.

The Postfix Abstract Data Type

Listing 3.1 presents a definition module that defines the type postfixtype as an ADT along with three operations. The operations convert an infix string into postfix, evaluate a postfix expression, and print a postfix expression.

A simple program that illustrates the use of this definition module is given in Listing 3.2

TABLE 3.5 Stepwise Infix-to-Postfix Conversion

Symbol	Operator Stack	Postfix String
(	(	
A	(	A
/	(/	A
(	(/ (	A
B	(/ (	A B
−	(/ (−	A B
C	(/ (−	A B C
)	(/	A B C −
)		A B C − /
*	*	A B C − /
(	* (	A B C − /
D	* (	A B C − / D
+	* (+	A B C − / D
E	* (+	A B C − / D E
)	*	A B C − / D E +
		A B C − / D E + *

Listing 3.1 Interface to Postfix Abstract Data Type: Math Expression

```
DEFINITION MODULE mathexpression;

  EXPORT QUALIFIED
    (* type *) postfixtype, string,
    (* proc *) evaluate,
    (* proc *) infixpostfix,
    (* proc *) writepostfix;


  TYPE postfixtype;
       string = ARRAY [0..79] OF CHAR;


  PROCEDURE infixpostfix
          ( infix : string                        (* in *) ) :
            postfixtype;
  (* Converts the infix input string into postfix form.    *)


  PROCEDURE evaluate
          ( postfix : postfixtype                 (* in *) ) :
            REAL;
  (* Requests values for the operands and calculates the
     value of the original infix expression.                *)


  PROCEDURE writepostfix
          ( postfix : postfixtype                 (* in *) );
  (* Prints the postfix form.                               *)

END mathexpression.
```

Finally, the implementation details are given in Listing 3.3. We need two stacks in the implementation, one containing operators in the infix to postfix algorithm and one containing real values of operands in the postfix evaluation algorithm. Because of this, we have chosen to use the generic stack ADT and to define two stacks, one containing characters and the other containing real numbers.

Listing 3.2 Sample Program Using Postfix Abstract Data Type

```
MODULE testmathexpression;

  FROM mathexpression IMPORT
    (* type *) postfixtype, string,
    (* proc *) infixpostfix, evaluate, writepostfix;

  FROM InOut IMPORT
    (* proc *) Read, WriteLn, WriteString, ReadString;

  FROM RealInOut IMPORT
    (* proc *) WriteReal;

  VAR
    expression : string;
    postfix    : postfixtype;
    value      : REAL;
    more, eval : BOOLEAN;
    char       : CHAR;

BEGIN
  more := TRUE;
  WHILE more DO
    WriteLn;  WriteLn;
    WriteString( "Enter an infix expression " );
    WriteLn;
    WriteString( ": " );
    ReadString( expression );
    WriteLn;  WriteLn;
    WriteString( "The postfix expression is " );
    WriteLn;
    WriteString( ": ");
    postfix := infixpostfix( expression );
    writepostfix( postfix );
    WriteLn;  WriteLn;
    WriteString( "Evaluate the expression (y/n) ? " );
    Read( char );
    IF ( char = 'y' ) OR ( char = 'Y' )
    THEN
      WriteLn;
      value := evaluate( postfix );
      WriteLn;
      WriteString( "The value of the expression is " );
      WriteLn;
      WriteString( ": " );
      WriteReal( value, 10 );
    END (* if then *);
```

```
    WriteLn;  WriteLn;
    WriteString( "Enter another expression (y/n) ? " );
    Read( char );
    IF ( char # 'y' ) AND ( char # 'Y' )
    THEN
      more := FALSE;
    END (* if then *);
  END (* while loop *);

END testmathexpression.
```

Listing 3.3 Implementation of Postfix Abstract Data Type

```
IMPLEMENTATION MODULE mathexpression;

  FROM Strings IMPORT
    Length;

  FROM Storage IMPORT
    ALLOCATE;

  FROM InOut IMPORT
    Write, WriteString, WriteLn;

  FROM RealInOut IMPORT
    ReadReal;

  FROM genericstack IMPORT
    (* type *) stack,
    (* proc *) define, makeempty, empty, push, pop;

  TYPE postfixtype = POINTER TO string;

  TYPE charset = SET OF CHAR;

  VAR
      allowable : charset;
      operand   : ARRAY[1..64] OF CHAR;
      value     : ARRAY[1..64] OF REAL;
```

```
PROCEDURE infixpostfix
      ( infix : string                       (* in *) ) :
        postfixtype;

VAR
   opstack               : stack;
   index1, index2        : INTEGER;
   symbol, topsymbol     : CHAR;
   postfix               : postfixtype;


  PROCEDURE precedence( op1, op2 : CHAR ) : BOOLEAN;
  BEGIN
    IF ( (op1 = '+') OR (op1 = '-') ) AND
       ( (op2 = '*') OR (op2 = '/') )
    THEN
      RETURN FALSE
    ELSIF ( (op1 = '(' ) AND (op2 # ')' ) ) OR (op2 = '(' )
    THEN
      RETURN FALSE
    ELSE
      RETURN TRUE
    END(* if then *);
  END precedence;

BEGIN (* infixpostfix *)
  define( opstack );
  NEW( postfix );
  index2 := 0;
  FOR index1 := 0 TO Length(infix) - 1 DO
    symbol := infix[index1];
    IF symbol IN allowable
    THEN
      postfix^[index2] := symbol;
      INC( index2 );
    ELSE
      LOOP
        IF empty( opstack )
        THEN
          EXIT;
        END (* if then *);
        (* The top symbol on the operator stack needs to
           be popped for use with the precedence function,
           since the generic stack ADT does not contain
           the operation topofstack.                     *)
        pop( opstack, topsymbol );
        IF NOT precedence( topsymbol, symbol )
```

```
          THEN (* Put top symbol back on the operator stack
                  if it should remain there due to
                  precedence.                                *)
            push( opstack, topsymbol );
            EXIT;
          END (* if then *);
          IF (topsymbol = '(' ) AND (symbol = ')' )
          THEN
            EXIT;
          END (* if then *);
          IF topsymbol # '(' THEN
            postfix^[index2] := topsymbol;
            INC( index2 );
          END (* if then *);
        END (* loop *);
        IF symbol # ')'
        THEN
          push( opstack, symbol );
        END (* if then *);
      END (* if then *);
    END (* for loop *);
    WHILE NOT empty( opstack ) DO
      pop( opstack, topsymbol );
      IF topsymbol # '(' THEN
        postfix^[index2] := topsymbol;
        INC( index2 );
      END (* if then *);
    END (* while loop *);
    postfix^[index2] := 0C; (* Terminate string. *)
    RETURN postfix;
  END infixpostfix;


  PROCEDURE evaluate
          ( postfix : postfixtype             (* in *) ) :
            REAL;

  VAR
      upper : CARDINAL;

    PROCEDURE scan;
    (* This procedure creates a symbol table.  Each unique
       operand encountered in the postfix expression results
       in an entry in the symbol table.                       *)

    VAR index,i,j : INTEGER;
        b         : BOOLEAN;
```

```
BEGIN
  FOR i := 1 TO 64 DO
    operand[i] := ' ';
  END (* for loop *);
  index := 1;
  (* Scan the postfix expression.  Insert each unique
     operand symbol into the symbol table.               *)
  FOR i:= 0 TO upper DO
    IF postfix^[i] IN allowable
    THEN (* Check to see if symbol is already in the
            symbol table.                                 *)
      b := FALSE;
      FOR j := 1 TO index DO
        IF postfix^[i] = operand[j]
        THEN
          b := TRUE;
        END (* if then *);
      END (* for loop *);
      IF NOT b  (* Symbol is not in symbol table.         *)
      THEN (* Add the symbol to the symbol table.         *)
        operand[index] := postfix^[i];
        INC( index )
      END (* if then *);
    END (* if then *);
  END (* for loop *);
END scan;


PROCEDURE assign;
(* This procedure assigns values to each operand in
   the symbol table.  The user is interactively
   requested to input the appropriate values.            *)

VAR
    index : CARDINAL;

BEGIN
  index := 1;
  WHILE (index <= 64) AND (operand[index] # ' ') DO
    WriteLn;
    WriteString( "Enter a value for " );
    Write( operand[index] );
    WriteString( " : ");
    ReadReal( value[index] );
    INC(index);
  END (* while loop *);
END assign;
```

```
    PROCEDURE result
            ( symbol: CHAR; opnd1, opnd2: REAL) :
              REAL;

    BEGIN
      CASE symbol OF
        '+': RETURN opnd1 + opnd2;
        '-': RETURN opnd1 - opnd2;
        '*': RETURN opnd1 * opnd2;
        '/': RETURN opnd1 / opnd2;
      END (* case *)
    END result;

  VAR
      opndstk : stack;
      i, j    : CARDINAL;
      symbol  : CHAR;
      rsymb   : REAL;
      opnd1   : REAL;
      opnd2   : REAL;
      answer  : REAL;

  BEGIN (* evaluate *)
    upper := Length( postfix^ ) - 1;
    scan;     (* Creates a table of all distinct operands.  *)
    assign;   (* Allows real values to be given to each
                 operand.                                   *)
    define( opndstk );
    FOR i:= 0 TO upper DO
      symbol:= postfix^[i];
      IF symbol IN allowable
      THEN
        j := 0;
        REPEAT
          INC (j);
        UNTIL postfix^[i] = operand[j];
        rsymb := value[j];
        push( opndstk, rsymb);
      ELSE   (* Symbol is an operator. *)
        pop( opndstk, opnd2 );
        pop( opndstk, opnd1 );
        answer := result( symbol, opnd1, opnd2 );
        push( opndstk, answer )
      END (* if then *);
    END (* for loop *);
    pop( opndstk, opnd1);
    RETURN opnd1;
  END evaluate;
```

```
PROCEDURE writepostfix
        ( postfix : postfixtype                    (* in *) );

VAR
  index : CARDINAL;

BEGIN
  index := 0;
  WHILE index < Length( postfix^ ) DO
    Write( postfix^[index] );
    INC( index )
  END (* while loop *)
END writepostfix;


BEGIN
  allowable := charset{'A'..'Z'} + charset{'a'..'z'};
    (* Some implementations may not support character sets of
      this size. *)
  END mathexpression.
```

3.2 A Maze Runner Example

Trying to find a path through a maze is a common puzzle that fascinates both children and adults. Experimental psychologists have used mazes to determine the learning curve of rats and mice.

In this section, we will develop a computer approach for finding a path through a maze. By defining a computer representation for a maze and determining the operations that must be performed on the maze, we come to the notion of the maze ADT, which we combine with the stack ADT. The algorithm we develop for finding a path through a maze may not perform as well as a rat would on its first attempt through the maze. It also may not find the shortest path through the maze. However, since we can save the path for later use, we have a distinct advantage over the rat, which may not be able to remember the path.

How should we represent the maze in the computer? An obvious simple representation of a maze is an array of 0's and 1's, where a 0 represents an open path and a 1 represents a wall. A type definition for a maze might be.

```
mazetype = ARRAY [1..xsize],[1..ysize] OF INTEGER;
```

where xsize and ysize are integer constants that define the size of the maze. An example of a maze is given in Figure 3.3.

At any point in the maze the rat must decide on which direction to go and then proceed in that direction a short distance until other paths or directions are visible. We can represent the position of the rat as a location in the maze, say

```
0 0 0 0 0 0 0 0 0 0
0 1 0 1 1 0 1 0 1 0
1 0 0 0 1 1 0 0 1 0
0 1 0 1 0 1 1 0 1 0
1 0 1 0 1 0 1 0 1 1
0 1 1 1 1 1 0 0 0 0
0 1 1 0 0 1 0 1 0 0
1 0 1 1 1 0 1 0 0 1
0 0 0 0 0 1 1 1 1 1
0 1 0 1 0 0 0 0 0 0
```

Figure 3.3 Example of a Maze

(x,y) where 1 ≤ x ≤ xsize and 1 ≤ y ≤ ysize. Now let us consider the moves that the rat can make. If we permit diagonal as well as horizontal and vertical moves, the rat can move in any one of eight directions, provided there is not a wall to obstruct the move. If we only consider vertical and horizontal moves, there are only four possible moves. In this example, we will consider the former case; all possible moves from the point (x,y) are shown in Figure 3.4.

If we define an 8 × 2 array, say movetable, with appropriate entries, a move can be made as follows:

```
x ← x + movetable[1, move]
y ← y + movetable[2, move]
```

where move has a value from 1 to 8. The move table has the following entries:

```
movetable[1, 1] := -1; movetable[1, 2] :=  0; (* north     *)
movetable[2, 1] := -1; movetable[2, 2] :=  1; (* northeast *)
movetable[3, 1] :=  0; movetable[3, 2] :=  1; (* east      *)
movetable[4, 1] :=  1; movetable[4, 2] :=  1; (* southeast *)
movetable[5, 1] :=  1; movetable[5, 2] :=  0; (* south     *)
movetable[6, 1] :=  1; movetable[6, 2] := -1; (* southwest *)
movetable[7, 1] :=  0; movetable[7, 2] := -1; (* west      *)
movetable[8, 1] := -1; movetable[8, 2] := -1; (* northwest *)
```

If the rat is currently at location (x,y), it can choose any of these eight adjacent positions, provided the maze contains a 0 in the position selected. If

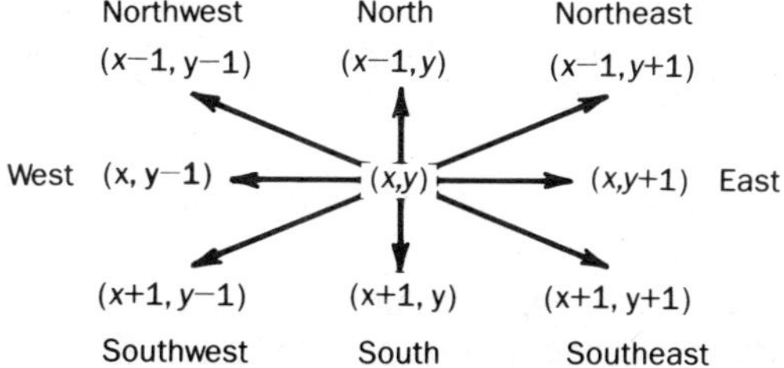

Figure 3.4 Moves from the Point (x,y)

```
1 1 1 1 1 1 1 1 1 1 1 1
1 0 0 0 0 0 0 0 0 0 0 1
1 0 1 0 1 1 0 1 0 1 0 1
1 1 0 0 0 1 1 0 0 1 0 1
1 0 1 0 1 0 1 1 0 1 0 1
1 1 0 1 0 1 0 1 0 1 1 1
1 0 1 1 1 1 1 0 0 0 0 1
1 0 1 1 0 0 1 0 1 0 0 1
1 1 0 1 1 1 0 1 0 0 1 1
1 0 0 0 0 0 1 1 1 1 1 1
1 0 1 0 1 0 0 0 0 0 0 1
1 1 1 1 1 1 1 1 1 1 1 1
```

Figure 3.5 Maze with a Boundary

the rat is at the edge of the maze, we must prevent it from leaving the maze by imposing a boundary around the maze. A simple way to do this is to add an extra row to the bottom and top of the maze and an extra column at the left and right side, assigning these positions a value of 1 to indicate a wall.

The modified type definition for the maze is now:

```
mazetype = ARRAY [0..xsize+1],[0..ysize+1] OF INTERGER;
```

and the maze has the structure shown in Figure 3.5.

We define a strategy for moving through the maze. At any point, we do not know which path is the best path to take. Since we can see only the nodes adjacent to the current point, we must select one of the adjacent nodes, move to that position, and reexamine our options at the new site. Our strategy at any node will be to look at all possible directions in which we can move—north, then northeast, then east, and so on, proceeding clockwise around the compass, such that the last direction is northwest. If we look in a given direction and there is no barrier, we make the move and save the current position and the direction of the move that was made to get there. If we proceed down a dead-end path, we can return to this position and try an alternate direction. This LIFO strategy suggests that we use a stack to save the position in the maze and the direction moved from that position.

We also need to devise a strategy to keep us from going down the same path twice or wandering around in circles. A technique for accomplishing this is to mark each position that we come to in the maze, so that we will know we have been there. We can either set up a another copy of the maze for marking purposes or mark the original maze, but we choose the latter approach because it does not require additional storage. If we set 0's to 1's in the maze as we arrive at legal positions, we will destroy the original maze. Instead, we choose to mark the locations that we arrive at with a -1. When we are finished, we can restore the original maze by changing all -1's back to 0's. (The original maze could also be restored by retrieving it from an input file.)

The strategy for running the maze can be described as follows:

```
initialize a path stack
get the maze information including the starting position and
      the ending position
display the maze
push the starting position and an initial move direction
      onto the path stack
while the path stack is not empty do
  pop the path stack to get a current position and the last
      move direction made from this position
  while there are more moves do
    make a move to a new position
    if the new position = ending position
    then
      push the current position onto the path stack
      push the ending position onto the path stack
      display the successful path and quit
    end if
    if the move to the new position is valid
    then
      mark the new position
      push the current position and the successful move
        direction onto the path stack
      set the current position equal to the new position and
        initialize the move direction
    end if
  end while
end while
indicate that no path can be found
```

An analysis of the preceding strategy leads to the objects identified in Table 3.6. The operations performed on the objects identified in Table 3.6 are presented in Table 3.7, which also identifies the name to be used in the corresponding software system.

Since the preceding strategy uses the stack ADT, we need to define the "elementtype" for the stack abstraction. The algorithm requires us to save in a

TABLE 3.6 Objects Used in the Maze Runner Strategy

Path stack
Maze
Position
Starting position
Ending position
Current position
New position

TABLE 3.7 Operations Used in the Maze Runner Strategy

Object	Operation	Program
Path stack	Initialize	define
	Push	push
	Empty	empty
	Pop	pop
	Display	printsuccessfulpath
Maze	Get maze information	getmazeinfo
	Display	printmaze
	Start position	startposition
	Ending position	endposition
Position	More moves	moremoves
	Make a move	makemove
	Equal	equal
	Move valid	movevalid
	Mark	mark
	Set	assign

stack each maze position that we successfully move to, along with the last direction we moved from the position. An appropriate elementtype definition is given in the following elements definition module.

```
DEFINITION MODULE elements;

  EXPORT QUALIFIED
    (* type *) elementtype;

  TYPE elementtype = RECORD
                       x         : INTEGER;
                       y         : INTEGER;
                       direction : [0..9]
                     END (* record *);
END elements.
```

We can then rename elementtype for the problem at hand by using the following Modula-2 statement:

```
TYPE positiontype = elementtype;
```

Every time we make a move, we must update the positiontype. We previously indicated how to update the position (x,y), but we must also update the direction field so that it contains the last move made.

The definition module for the maze abstract data type is given in Listing 3.4. The maze can be characterized by the number of rows and columns in the maze, the starting and ending positions, and an array of 0's and 1's that defines the maze. These quantities are all part of the record structure that defines the type mazetype.

Listing 3.4 Interface for Maze Abstract Data Type

```
DEFINITION MODULE mazeadt;

   FROM elements IMPORT
     (* type *) elementtype;

   FROM stackadt IMPORT
     (* type *) stack;

   EXPORT QUALIFIED
     (* type *) mazetype, positiontype,
     (* proc *) getmazeinfo, printmaze, startposition,
                endposition, assign, makemove, equal,
                moremoves, printsuccessfulpath,
                mark, movevalid;

   CONST xmax = 10;
         ymax = 10;

   TYPE
        positiontype = elementtype;

        mazetype = RECORD
                       numrows : INTEGER;
                       numcols : INTEGER;
                       start   : positiontype;
                       end     : positiontype;
                       maze    : ARRAY[0..xmax+1], [0..ymax+1]

                                  OF INTEGER
                   END (* record *);


   PROCEDURE getmazeinfo
          ( VAR m : mazetype                   (* out *) );
   (* This procedure reads the number of rows and the
      number of columns in the maze, the maze definition,
      and the start and end positions in the maze from a
      user defined file.                                    *)


   PROCEDURE printmaze
          ( m : mazetype                       (* in *) );
   (* This procedure prints the maze.                       *)


   PROCEDURE startposition
          ( m : mazetype                       (* in *) ) :
```

```
             positiontype;
(* This procedure returns the starting position for
   maze m.                                                *)


PROCEDURE endposition
          ( m : mazetype                      (* in *) ) :
            positiontype;
(* This procedure returns the ending position for
   maze m.                                                *)


PROCEDURE assign
          ( VAR p : positiontype              (* out *);
                q : positiontype              (* in *) );
(* This procedure assigns the position q to p and
   initializes the direction associated with
   position p.                                            *)


PROCEDURE makemove
          ( VAR p : positiontype              (* in/out *);
            VAR q : positiontype              (* out *) );
(* This procedure makes a move in the direction m from
   the maze position p to the maze position q.  The
   direction field associated with maze position p is
   updated to reflect the current direction moved.       *)


PROCEDURE equal
          ( p, q : positiontype               (* in *) ) :
            BOOLEAN;
(* This procedure returns true if maze positions p and
   q are equal, otherwise, it returns false.              *)


PROCEDURE moremoves
          ( p : positiontype                  (* in *) ) :
            BOOLEAN;
(* This procedure returns true if there are more moves
   to be considered otherwise returns false.              *)


PROCEDURE printsuccessfulpath
          ( VAR path : stack                  (* in/out *) );
(* This procedure prints the successful path contained
   in the path stack.  The procedure utilizes an
   auxiliary stack to reverse the path so that it is
   printed from the start position to the end
   position.                                              *)
```

```
  PROCEDURE mark
          ( VAR m : mazetype                     (* in/out *);
                p : positiontype                 (* in *) );
  (* This procedure marks the position p in maze m to
     indicate that this position has been successfully
     reached.                                            *)


  PROCEDURE movevalid
          ( m : mazetype                         (* in *);
            p : positiontype                     (* in *) ) :
            BOOLEAN;
  (* This procedure returns true if position p in maze m
     is a legal position and returns false otherwise.   *)

END mazeadt.
```

Using the stack ADT and the maze ADT, we can implement the strategy developed previously for running the maze. We can compile the program given in Listing 3.5 before implementing the operations promised in the definition module given in Listing 3.4.

Listing 3.5 The Maze Runner Software System

```
MODULE mazerunner;

  FROM stackadt IMPORT
    (* type *) stack,
    (* proc *) empty, pop, push, define;

  FROM InOut IMPORT
    (* proc *) WriteString, WriteLn;

  FROM mazeadt IMPORT
    (* type *) mazetype, positiontype,
    (* proc *) getmazeinfo, printmaze, startposition,
               endposition, assign, makemove, equal,
               moremoves, printsuccessfulpath,
               mark, movevalid;

  VAR
     path           : stack;
     maze           : mazetype;
     position       : positiontype;
     newposition    : positiontype;
```

```
BEGIN
  define( path );
  getmazeinfo( maze );
  printmaze( maze );
  push( path, startposition( maze ) );
  WHILE NOT empty( path ) DO
    pop( path, position );
    WHILE moremoves( position ) DO
      makemove( position, newposition );
      IF equal( newposition, endposition( maze ) )
      THEN
        push( path, position );
        push( path, newposition );
        printsuccessfulpath( path );
        HALT
      END (* if then *);
      IF movevalid( maze, newposition )
      THEN
        mark( maze, newposition );
        push( path, position );
        assign( position, newposition );
      END (* if then *);
    END (* while loop *);
  END (* while loop *);
  WriteLn;
  WriteString( "No path can be found." );
END mazerunner.
```

Notice how closely the program follows the informal strategy. Moreover, the program is independent of the details of the underlying data structures to represent the maze and the stack.

We now present the implementation details for the operations promised in Listing 3.4 for the maze ADT. Our only comment concerning the implementation relates to the operation printsuccessfulpath. When we have found a successful path, we print its maze coordinates from the starting point to the ending point. A minor complication arises, however, because the path is a stack, which means that popping items off the stack gives us the path in the reverse direction (i.e., from the ending point to the starting point). Since a stack can be used to reverse the elements in an ordered list, our implementation can define a temporary stack to reverse the elements in the path stack and then print the elements of the temporary stack.

Listing 3.6 presents the implementation details for the maze ADT.

Listing 3.6 Implementation of Maze Abstract Data Type

```
IMPLEMENTATION MODULE mazeadt;

  FROM elements IMPORT
    (* type *) elementtype;

  FROM stackadt IMPORT
    (* type *) stack,
    (* proc *) empty, pop, push, define;

  FROM InOut IMPORT
    (* proc *) OpenInput, CloseInput, ReadInt,
               WriteString, WriteLn, WriteCard,
               WriteInt;

  TYPE
     moveinfo = ARRAY[1..8], [1..2] OF INTEGER;
     movetype = [0..9];

  VAR
     movetable     : moveinfo;


   PROCEDURE getmazeinfo
          ( VAR m : mazetype                  (* out *) );
   VAR
       i, j : INTEGER;
   BEGIN
     WITH m DO
       OpenInput( "TEXT" );
       ReadInt( numrows );
       ReadInt( numcols );
       FOR i := 0 TO numrows + 1 DO
         FOR j := 0 TO numcols + 1 DO
           ReadInt( maze[i,j] )
         END (* for loop *);
       END (* for loop *);
       ReadInt( start.x );
       ReadInt( start.y );
       ReadInt( end.x );
       ReadInt( end.y );
       CloseInput;
       start.direction := 0;
       end.direction   := 0
     END (* with *)
   END getmazeinfo;
```

```
PROCEDURE printmaze
        ( m : mazetype                               (* in *) );
VAR
  i,j : INTEGER;
BEGIN
  WITH m DO
    FOR i := 1 TO numrows DO
      WriteLn;
      FOR j := 1 TO numcols DO
        WriteCard( maze[i,j], 3 )
      END (* for loop *);
    END (* for loop *)
  END (* with m *)
END printmaze;


PROCEDURE makemove
        ( VAR p : positiontype                       (* in/out *);
          VAR q : positiontype                       (* out *) );
  VAR m : movetype;
BEGIN
  m := p.direction + 1;
  q.x := p.x + movetable[m, 1];
  q.y := p.y + movetable[m, 2];
  q.direction := 0;
  p.direction := m
END makemove;


PROCEDURE startposition
        ( m : mazetype                               (* in *) ) :
          positiontype;
BEGIN
  RETURN m.start
END startposition;


PROCEDURE endposition
        ( m : mazetype                               (* in *) ) :
          positiontype;
BEGIN
  RETURN m.end
END endposition;


PROCEDURE assign
        ( VAR p : positiontype                       (* out *);
              q : positiontype                       (* in *) );
```

```
    BEGIN
      p.x := q.x;
      p.y := q.y;
      p.direction := q.direction
    END assign;


    PROCEDURE equal
            ( p, q : positiontype                (* in *) ) :
              BOOLEAN;
    BEGIN
      RETURN ( (p.x = q.x) AND (p.y = q.y) )
    END equal;


PROCEDURE getnextmove
        (  p   : positiontype;                   (* in  *);
        VAR m : movetype                         (* out *) );
    BEGIN
      m := p.direction + 1;
    END getnextmove;


    PROCEDURE moremoves
            ( p : positiontype                   (* in *) ) :
              BOOLEAN;
    BEGIN
      RETURN p.direction < 8
    END moremoves;


    PROCEDURE printsuccessfulpath
            ( VAR path : stack                   (* in/out *) );
      VAR
        reverse  : stack;
        position : positiontype;
    BEGIN
      define( reverse );
      WHILE NOT empty( path ) DO
        pop( path, position );
        push( reverse, position );
      END (* while loop *);
      WHILE NOT empty( reverse ) DO
        pop( reverse, position );
        WriteLn;
        WriteCard( position.x, 3 );
        WriteString( "   " );
        WriteCard( position.y, 3 );
```

```
    END (* while loop *);
  END printsuccessfulpath;


  PROCEDURE mark
          ( VAR m : mazetype                         (* in/out *);
                p : positiontype                     (* in *) );
  BEGIN
    WITH m DO
      maze[ p.x, p.y ] := -1
    END (* with m *)
  END mark;


  PROCEDURE movevalid
          ( m : mazetype                             (* in *);
            p : positiontype                         (* in *) ) :
            BOOLEAN;
   BEGIN
     WITH m DO
       RETURN maze[ p.x, p.y ] = 0
     END (* with m *)
   END movevalid;


BEGIN
  movetable[1,1]:= -1; movetable[1,2]:=  0; (* north     *)
  movetable[2,1]:= -1; movetable[2,2]:=  1; (* northeast *)
  movetable[3,1]:=  0; movetable[3,2]:=  1; (* east      *)
  movetable[4,1]:=  1; movetable[4,2]:=  1; (* southeast *)
  movetable[5,1]:=  1; movetable[5,2]:=  0; (* south     *)
  movetable[6,1]:=  1; movetable[6,2]:= -1; (* southwest *)
  movetable[7,1]:=  0; movetable[7,2]:= -1; (* west      *)
  movetable[8,1]:= -1; movetable[8,2]:= -1; (* northwest *)
END mazeadt.
```

3.3 Discrete Simulation of a Computer System

In this very simple example of a discrete simulation of a computer system, we use the stack and queue abstract data types. The system contains a card reader, a processor, and a line printer. At various times, jobs enter the system through the card reader and are placed at the rear of an input queue. When a job reaches the front of the input queue, it is a candidate for execution by the processor. Each job has an assigned priority that, in part, determines when it gets executed.

The processor executes a job for one unit of time and then determines what to do next. If the current job is finished, it is sent to the output queue to await its turn at the line printer. Otherwise, the current job is pushed onto the active job stack. Then the processor compares the priorities of the job at the front of the input queue and the job at the top of the active stack, selecting the one with the higher priority for execution during the next unit of time. A job remains in the processor only for the duration of its execution time.

When a job reaches the line printer, it remains there for the number of time units needed to print its output. The time in the printer will be consecutive time units, whereas the time in the processor may have periods of waiting in the active stack. Figure 3.6 shows how the system may be visualized.

A job consists of a number of descriptive parameters including the following:

Job number	Cardinal, range 1..500
Execution time	Cardinal, range 1..25
Printer time	Cardinal, range 1..25
Entry time	Cardinal, range 1..2000
Job priority	Character, range 'A' (low) .. 'Z' (high)

For every job, we will need to keep track of the execution time used so far and the printer time used so far. Thus several other descriptive parameters for a job are:

Executiontime used so far
Printertime used so far

The description of the computer system presented above indicates that jobs are the elements of the active job stack, the input queue, and the output queue. An element definition for use with the stack and queue abstract data types is:

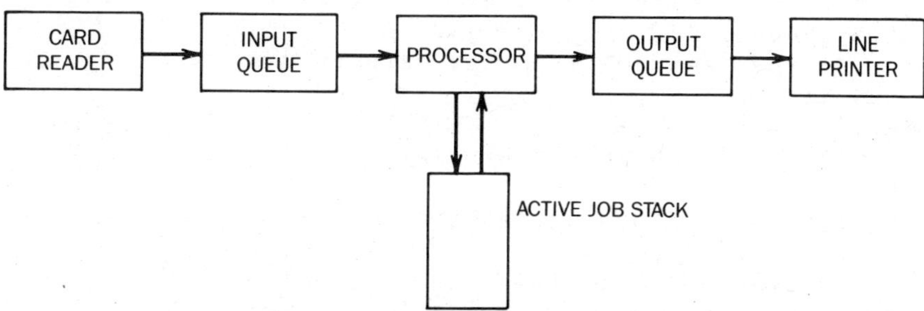

Figure 3.6 A Simple Computer System Simulation

```
DEFINITION MODULE elements;

  EXPORT QUALIFIED
     (* type *) elementtype;

  TYPE
    elementtype =
        RECORD
          jobnumber      : [1..500];
          executiontime : [1..25];
          printertime    : [1..25];
          entrytime      : [1..2000];
          jobpriority    : ['A'..'Z'];
                           (* A is high to Z low *)
          exectimeused  : CARDINAL;
          printtimeused : CARDINAL
        END (* record *);

END elements.
```

We can then rename elementtype for the problem at hand by using the following Modula-2 statement:

```
TYPE jobtype = elementtype;
```

The description of the computer system simulation can be formalized with the following pseudo-code description.

```
initially, set the time to 0
get the first job into the card reader
while all jobs are not done (including printing) do
  increment the time by one unit
  if there is a job in the card reader
  then
    if the time equals the entry time of the job in the
      reader
    then
      get the job in the reader and move it into the input
        queue
      get the next job into the card reader
    end if
  end if
  if there is a job in the processor
  then
    if that job is now finished
    then
      move the job into the output queue
    else
      push the job onto the active job stack
    end if
  end if
```

```
  select the next job for execution from either the input
      queue or the active job stack, depending on priority
  if there is a job in the printer
  then
    if that job is now finished
    then
      remove it from the system and print job statistics
    else
      continue printing the job
    end if
  end if
  if the printer is not active
  then
    select a new job from the print queue
  end if
end while
```

An analysis of this strategy suggests that we develop for our computer system an abstract model that performs a number of operations on jobs and has various attributes for determining the status of the card reader, processor, and printer. The strategy above is precise enough to accomplish this except for the statement "select the next job for execution from either the input queue or the active stack, depending on priority." We will denote this operation as "selectnextjob" and describe it more precisely as follows:

```
if the input queue and the active stack are not empty
then
  if the priority of the job at the top of the active stack
      is greater than the job at the front of the input
      queue
  then
    pop the job from the top of the active stack
    send the job to the processor
  else
    remove the job at the front of the input queue
    send the job to the processor
  end if
else if the input queue is not empty
then
    remove the job at the front of the input queue
    send the job to the processor
else if the active stack is not empty
then
    pop the job from the top of the active stack
    send the job to the processor
end if
```

From this analysis, we can construct Table 3.9.

We have carefully named the operations identified to reflect the informal strategy for the computer system simulation. Listing 3.7 defines the interface to these operations that support the computer system abstraction.

TABLE 3.9 Pseudo-code and Abstract Model Operations for the Simulation Algorithm

Pseudo-code Operation	Program Operation
Job into the card reader	jobtoreader
Jobs are done?	jobsdone
Job in the card reader?	readeractive
Entry time of the job in the reader	jobentrytime
Get the job in the reader	getreaderjob
Move job into the input queue	insert
Job in the processor?	processoractive
Processor job finished?	processorfinished
Move job into the output queue	insert
Push the job onto the active job stack	push
Select next job for execution	selectnextjob
Input queue empty?	empty
Active stack empty?	empty
Priority of job	priority
Send job to processor	jobtoprocessor
Remove job from input queue	remove
Pop job from active stack	pop
Job in the printer?	printeractive
Get printer job	getprinterjob
Printer job finished?	printerfinished
Print job statistics	printjobstatistics
Continue printing the job	jobtoprinter
Printer active?	printeractive

Listing 3.7 Interface to Computer System Abstraction

```
DEFINITION MODULE computersystem;

  FROM elements IMPORT
    (* type *) elementtype;

  EXPORT QUALIFIED
    (* proc *) jobtoreader, jobtoprocessor, jobtoprinter,
               getreaderjob, getprocessorjob, getprinterjob,
               readeractive, processorfinished,
               processoractive, printerfinished,
               printeractive, jobsdone, jobentrytime,
               priority, printjobstatistics;


  TYPE jobtype = elementtype;
```

```
PROCEDURE jobtoreader
        ( VAR j : jobtype                         (* in/out *) );
(* Gets a job j and places it in the reader.  Sets the
   reader to active.                                        *)


PROCEDURE jobtoprocessor
        ( VAR j : jobtype                         (* in/out *) );
(* Sends job j to the processor for one unit of time.
   Sets the processor to active.                            *)


PROCEDURE jobtoprinter
        ( VAR j : jobtype                         (* in/out *) );
(* Sends job j to the printer for one unit of time.  Sets
   the printer to active.                                   *)


PROCEDURE getreaderjob
        ( VAR j : jobtype                         (* in/out *) );
(* Gets job j from the reader and sets the reader to
   inactive.                                                *)


PROCEDURE getprocessorjob
        ( VAR j : jobtype                         (* in/out *) );
(* Gets job j from the processor and sets the processor
   to inactive.                                             *)


PROCEDURE getprinterjob
        ( VAR j : jobtype                         (* in/out *) );
(* Gets job j from the printer and sets the printer to
   inactive.                                                *)


PROCEDURE readeractive() :
          BOOLEAN;
(* Returns true if the reader is active, otherwise
   false.                                                   *)


PROCEDURE processorfinished
        ( j : jobtype                             (* in *) ) :
          BOOLEAN;
(* Returns true if job j has been in the processor for the
   number of units of time specified in the input,
   otherwise false.                                         *)
```

```
PROCEDURE processoractive() :
          BOOLEAN;
(* Returns true if the processor is active, otherwise
   false.                                                *)


PROCEDURE printerfinished
        ( j : jobtype                      (* in *) ) :
          BOOLEAN;
(* Returns true if job j has been in the printer for the
   number of units of time specified in the input,
   otherwise false.                                      *)


PROCEDURE printeractive() :
          BOOLEAN;
(* Returns true if the printer is active, otherwise
   false.                                                *)


PROCEDURE jobsdone() :
          BOOLEAN;
(* Returns true if the card reader, processor and printer
   are all inactive, otherwise false.                    *)


PROCEDURE jobentrytime
        ( j : jobtype                      (* in *) ) :
          CARDINAL;
(* Returns the job entry time for job j as specified in
   the input.                                            *)


PROCEDURE priority
        ( j : jobtype                      (* in *) ) :
          CHAR;
(* Returns the priority for job j as specified in the
   input.                                                *)


PROCEDURE printjobstatistics
        ( j    : jobtype                   (* in *);
          time : CARDINAL                  (* in *) );
(* For job j, prints the job number, entry time,
   completion time, and total wait time.                 *)


END computersystem.
```

The main program for the simulation is given in Listing 3.8. Since the stack and the queue ADTs have several operations with the same name, we import these operations from queueadt, giving direct visibility, and we import the stackadt rather than the specific operations, giving indirect visibility. To use an operation or type from stackadt, we must qualify it with a "stackadt." prefix. This is necessary because Modula-2 does not permit us to overload procedure names; that is, we cannot have two procedures with the same name but different parameters in the same scope.

Listing 3.8 Main Program Module for Computer System Simulation

```
MODULE computersystemsimulation;

  FROM elements IMPORT
    elementtype;

  FROM queueadt IMPORT
    (* type *) queue,
    (* proc *) insert, remove, length, define, frontofqueue,
               empty;

  IMPORT stackadt;

  FROM InOut IMPORT
    (* proc *) OpenInput, CloseInput, OpenOutput,
               CloseOutput;

  FROM computersystem IMPORT
    (* proc *) jobtoreader, jobtoprocessor, jobtoprinter,
               getreaderjob, getprocessorjob, getprinterjob,
               readeractive, processorfinished,
               processoractive, printerfinished,
               printeractive, jobsdone, jobentrytime,
               priority, printjobstatistics;

  TYPE jobtype = elementtype;

  VAR
    newjob, oldjob           : jobtype;
    printjob, readerjob      : jobtype;
    inputqueue, outputqueue  : queue;
    activestack              : stackadt.stack;
    time                     : CARDINAL;
```

```
  PROCEDURE selectnextjob
          ( VAR q : queue            (* in/out *);
            VAR s : stackadt.stack (* in/out *) );

VAR
    j : jobtype;
BEGIN
  IF NOT empty( q ) AND NOT stackadt.empty( s )
  THEN
    IF priority( stackadt.topofstack( s ) ) >=
       priority( frontofqueue( q ) )
    THEN
      stackadt.pop( s, j );
      jobtoprocessor( j )
    ELSE
      remove( q, j );
      jobtoprocessor( j )
    END (* if then *);
  ELSIF NOT empty( q )
  THEN
    remove(q, j );
    jobtoprocessor( j )
  ELSIF NOT stackadt.empty( s )
  THEN
    stackadt.pop( s, j );
    jobtoprocessor( j )
  END (* if then *);
END selectnextjob;


BEGIN
  OpenInput( "TEXT" ); (* Implementation dependent. *)
  OpenOutput( "TEXT");
  define( inputqueue );
  define( outputqueue );
  stackadt.define( activestack );
  time := 0;
  jobtoreader( readerjob );
  WHILE NOT jobsdone() DO
    INC( time );
    IF readeractive()
    THEN
      IF time = jobentrytime( readerjob )
      THEN
        getreaderjob( newjob );
        insert( inputqueue, newjob );
        jobtoreader( readerjob )
      END (* if then *);
    END (* if then *);
```

```
    IF processoractive()
    THEN
      getprocessorjob( oldjob );
      IF processorfinished( oldjob )
      THEN
        insert( outputqueue, oldjob )
      ELSE
        stackadt.push( activestack, oldjob )
      END (* if then *)
    END (* if then *);
    selectnextjob( inputqueue, activestack );
    IF printeractive()
    THEN
      getprinterjob( printjob );
      IF printerfinished( printjob )
      THEN
        printjobstatistics( printjob, time );
      ELSE
        jobtoprinter( printjob )
      END (* if then *);
    END (* if then *);
    IF NOT printeractive() AND NOT empty( outputqueue )
    THEN
      remove( outputqueue, printjob );
      jobtoprinter( printjob )
    END (* if then *);
  END (* while loop *);
  CloseInput;
  CloseOutput;
END computersystemsimulation.
```

Notice that the main procedure reads just like the strategy presented earlier in pseudo-code. Abstraction is the key that makes this possible. Readable code that mimics the real-world problem and uses the same terminology as the real-world problem should be your objective in problem solving in computer science.

Also notice that we have added the operation "frontofqueue" to our previously defined queue abstract data type. This operation permits us to examine the item at the front of the queue before removing it from the queue. Such an operation is often important in simulations involving queues.

We now present some input data and display the results produced by the program in Listing 3.8. For the input data of Table 3.10, the simulation results produced by the program of Listing 3.8 are given in Table 3.11.

For completeness, Listing 3.9 gives the implementation module for the computer system definition module presented above.

TABLE 3.10 Input Data for Listing 3.8

Job Number	Execution Time	Printer Time	Entry Time	Job Priority
1	5	6	1	A
2	1	2	2	D
3	10	1	4	B
4	4	4	5	A
5	3	12	7	C
6	8	3	9	B
7	2	5	10	D
8	9	9	12	A
9	6	2	13	B
10	5	4	15	A

TABLE 3.11 Simulation Results of Listing 3.8

Job Number	Entry Time	Completion Time	Total Wait Time
2	2	5	0
3	4	15	0
1	1	23	11
5	7	35	13
7	10	40	23
6	9	43	23
4	5	47	34
9	13	49	28
8	12	58	28
10	15	62	38

Listing 3.9 Implementation of Computer System Abstraction

```
IMPLEMENTATION MODULE computersystem;

  FROM InOut IMPORT
    (* var  *) Done, EOL,
    (* proc *) OpenInput, CloseInput, ReadInt, ReadCard,
               Read, WriteString, WriteLn, WriteCard,
               Write;

  TYPE computerstatus = RECORD
                          processoractive : BOOLEAN;
                          printeractive   : BOOLEAN;
                          readeractive    : BOOLEAN
                        END (* record *);
```

```
VAR
    computer     : computerstatus;
    processorjob : jobtype;
    printerjob   : jobtype;
    readerjob    : jobtype;
    heading      : BOOLEAN;


PROCEDURE jobtoreader
        ( VAR j : jobtype                          (* in/out *) );
VAR
    ch : CHAR;
BEGIN
   ReadCard( j.jobnumber );
   IF NOT Done THEN
     computer.readeractive := FALSE
   ELSE
     ReadCard( j.executiontime );
     ReadCard( j.printertime );
     ReadCard( j.entrytime );
     Read( j.jobpriority );
     (* Skip over blanks *)
     WHILE j.jobpriority = " " DO
       Read( j.jobpriority )
     END (* while loop *);
     (* Skip to next line *)
     Read( ch );
     WHILE ch <> EOL DO
       Read( ch )
     END (* while loop *);
     (* Initialize execution time used and print time
        used for this job. *)
     j.exectimeused  := 0;
     j.printtimeused := 0;
     computer.readeractive := TRUE;
     readerjob := j
   END (* if then *);
END jobtoreader;


PROCEDURE jobtoprocessor
        ( VAR j : jobtype                          (* in/out *) );
BEGIN
  processorjob := j;
  INC( processorjob.exectimeused );
  computer.processoractive := TRUE
END jobtoprocessor;


PROCEDURE jobtoprinter
        ( VAR j : jobtype                          (* in/out *) );
```

```
BEGIN
  printerjob := j;
  INC( printerjob.printtimeused );
  computer.printeractive := TRUE
END jobtoprinter;


PROCEDURE getreaderjob
        ( VAR j : jobtype                           (* in/out *) );
BEGIN
  j := readerjob;
  computer.readeractive := FALSE
END getreaderjob;


PROCEDURE getprocessorjob
        ( VAR j : jobtype                           (* in/out *) );
BEGIN
  j := processorjob;
  computer.processoractive := FALSE
END getprocessorjob;


PROCEDURE getprinterjob
        ( VAR j : jobtype                           (* in/out *) );
BEGIN
  j := printerjob;
  computer.printeractive := FALSE
END getprinterjob;


PROCEDURE readeractive() :
          BOOLEAN;
BEGIN
  RETURN computer.readeractive
END readeractive;


PROCEDURE processorfinished
        ( j : jobtype                               (* in *) ) :
          BOOLEAN;
BEGIN
  RETURN j.exectimeused = j.executiontime
END processorfinished;


PROCEDURE processoractive() :
          BOOLEAN;
BEGIN
  RETURN computer.processoractive
END processoractive;
```

```
PROCEDURE printerfinished
        ( j : jobtype                         (* in *) ) :
          BOOLEAN;
BEGIN
  RETURN j.printertime = j.printtimeused
END printerfinished;


PROCEDURE printeractive() :
          BOOLEAN;
BEGIN
  RETURN computer.printeractive
END printeractive;


PROCEDURE jobsdone() :
          BOOLEAN;
BEGIN
  RETURN  NOT (computer.processoractive OR
               computer.printeractive OR
               computer.readeractive)
END jobsdone;


PROCEDURE jobentrytime
        ( j : jobtype                         (* in *) ) :
          CARDINAL;
BEGIN
  RETURN j.entrytime
END jobentrytime;


PROCEDURE priority
        ( j : jobtype                         (* in *) ) :
          CHAR;
BEGIN
  RETURN j.jobpriority
END priority;


PROCEDURE printjobstatistics
        ( j    : jobtype                      (* in *);
          time : CARDINAL                     (* in *) );
BEGIN
  IF heading THEN
    WriteLn;
    WriteString( "Job Number    Entry Time   ");
                 Completion Time" );
    WriteString( "Total Wait Time" );
    WriteLn;
    heading := FALSE
```

```
    END (* if then *);
    WriteLn;
    WriteCard( j.jobnumber, 6 );
    WriteCard( j.entrytime, 15 );
    WriteCard( time, 15 );
    WriteCard( time - ( j.entrytime + j.executiontime
                + j.printertime ), 18 );
    computer.printeractive := FALSE
  END printjobstatistics;


BEGIN (* Initialization code *)
  computer.processoractive := FALSE;
  computer.printeractive   := FALSE;
  computer.readeractive    := FALSE;
  heading := TRUE;
END computersystem.
```

Notice that most of the procedures presented in Listing 3.9 are trivial. They are required to support the abstraction and the corresponding information hiding, since the underlying data structures are not visible to the user program given in Listing 3.8.

3.4 Adaptive Numerical Integration

The objective of numerical integration is to obtain an approximation for the value of the definite integral:

$$I = \int_a^b f(x)\,dx$$

In calculus, we learn that the value of the integral is given by:

$$I = F(b) - F(a)$$

where $F(x) = \int f(x)\,dx$ is the antiderivative of $f(x)$. For example, if $f(x) = \cos x$, the antiderivative is $f(x) = \sin x + c$, where c is an arbitrary constant of integration. The problem is to find an expression for $F(x)$ and then to evaluate it at the limits of integration. For specific forms of the integrand $f(x)$, there are rules for finding $F(x)$. In general, integration involves identifying the form of $f(x)$ and using the appropriate rule to find $F(x)$. However, this approach is not desirable for designing a computer program to calculate I because it requires the use of symbol manipulation. Our program would have to identify the form of $f(x)$ and then find the corresponding $F(x)$ from a large table of integrals contained within the program. Our program would fail often because rules that apply universally for an arbitrary $f(x)$ do not exist. That is, for the large numbers of integrands that commonly arise in practice, there is no corresponding rule for finding $F(x)$.

An alternative approach is to approximate the value of I numerically by using an m-point integration or quadrature rule:

$$Q_m = c_1 f(x_1) + c_2 f(x_2) + \cdots + c_m f(x_m) \tag{3.1}$$

where $a = x_1 \leq x_2 \leq \cdots \leq x_m = b$, and Q_m is simply a linear combination of the values of the integrand $f(x)$ at a collection of points called quadrature points. This is a much more viable approach to designing a computer program. Moreover, since quadrature rules are generally not restricted to specific forms of the integrand $f(x)$, they are better suited for general-purpose computer software. For these reasons, we compute an approximation for the value of I by means of the quadrature approach.

Most books on numerical analysis and numerical computing present a variety of quadrature rules. Our objective is to design and develop an adaptive quadrature algorithm that uses either the stack or the queue ADT. We will develop an adaptive quadrature algorithm later in this section. For now, we simply state that an adaptive quadrature algorithm is one that adapts itself to the behavior of the integrand $f(x)$ to obtain an approximation to the integral that is accurate to a specified accuracy.

To begin, let us define the user interface. A program to evaluate a definite integral normally needs no more than a function subprogram to evaluate the integrand $f(x)$, the limits of integration a and b, plus an error tolerance, eps. The error tolerance requests that the program return an answer whose absolute or relative error is less than eps. Listing 3.10 presents the user interface for adaptive numerical integration.

Listing 3.10 Interface for Adaptive Numerical Integration

```
DEFINITION MODULE adaptiveintegration;

  EXPORT QUALIFIED
    (* type *) function,
    (* proc *) integrate;

  TYPE function = PROCEDURE( REAL ) : REAL;
  (* This type definition specifies the form of the user-
     defined program that defines the integrand for use
     with the procedure integrate. Procedure types are
     covered in detail in section 4.1.2.                    *)


  PROCEDURE integrate
          (      a, b   : REAL
                 eps    : REAL
```

```
                f           : function              (* in *) ;
        VAR answer : REAL                  (* out *) );
  (* This procedure integrates the function f from a to b
     and returns an answer with an absolute error less than
     eps.                                                    *)

END adaptiveintegration.
```

The procedure integrate should attempt to compute as efficiently as possible a value for I that is accurate to within the specified tolerance. The design of such a procedure is in general not easy. We must decide what quadrature rule to use and then build around the rule an overall strategy that achieves the goals of efficiency and reliability. (In a "reliable" strategy, the approximate value of I returned by the procedure is guaranteed to have the accuracy requested by the user.) These two goals are virtually impossible to meet simultaneously.

One of the simplest quadrature rules is the trapezoid method. The trapezoid method is defined by (3.1) with $m = 2$, $c_1 = c_2 = h/2$, $x_1 = a$, and $x_2 = b$, where $h = b - a$. That is,

$$Q_2 = \frac{h}{2}\,[f(a) + f(b)] \tag{3.2}$$

The error, E, associated with the trapezoid method (3.2) is:

$$E = I - Q_2 = \frac{h^3 f''(z)}{12} \tag{3.3}$$

where z is in $[a,b]$. As illustrated in Figure 3.7, the trapezoid method cannot be expected to produce good results unless the integrand $f(x)$ is essentially a linear function. As a matter of fact, if $f(x)$ is linear, the error, E, is zero.

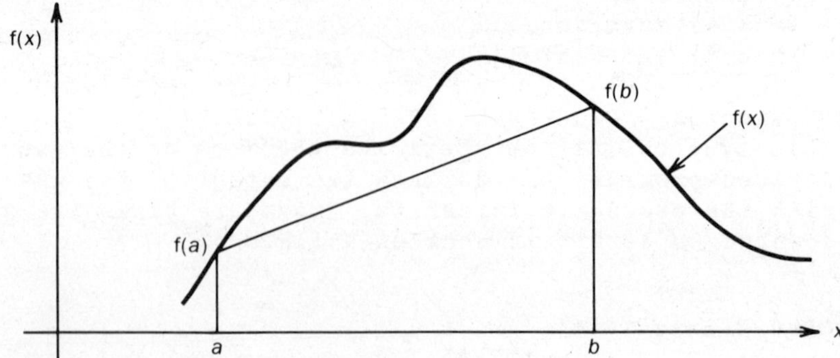

Figure 3.7 The Trapezoid Method

By considering a derivation of the trapezoid method, we can develop an approach for obtaining better methods. The trapezoid method can be derived by approximating $f(x)$ by a straight line connecting the points $(a, f(a))$ and $(b, f(b))$. We then approximate I by integrating the straight line or linear polynomial from a to b. To obtain better results, we could approximate $f(x)$ by a higher degree polynomial [obtained by evaluating $f(x)$ at an appropriate set of points] and then approximate I as the integral of the polynomial from a to b. For example, if we approximate $f(x)$ by a quadratic equation using the points a, $(a + b)/2$, and b, we obtain Simpson's method:

$$Q_3 = \frac{h}{3}[f(a) + 4f\left(\frac{a+b}{2}\right) + f(b)] \tag{3.4}$$

where $h = (b - a)/2$. The error, E, is given by:

$$E = I - Q_3 = \frac{h^5 f^{(iv)}(z)}{90} \tag{3.5}$$

where z is in $[a,b]$. Note that Simpson's method will be exact for cubic polynomials, since the fourth derivative of a cubic is zero; hence $E = 0$.

Rather than approximating the integrand $f(x)$ by higher degree polynomials, an alternative approach is to subdivide the interval $[a,b]$ into a number of smaller subintervals and then to apply a quadrature method over each subinterval. The approximation to I is determined as the sum of the approximations to the intergral over each subinterval. The resulting algorithms are referred to as composite quadrature methods.

We will now develop the composite trapezoid method, as illustrated In Figure 3.8, followed by the composite Simpson's method.

Let $h = (b - a)/n$, where n is the number of subintervals. Then using (3.2), the area of the ith subinterval is given by:

$$A_i = \frac{h}{2}[f(x_{i-1}) + f(x_i)] \tag{3.6}$$

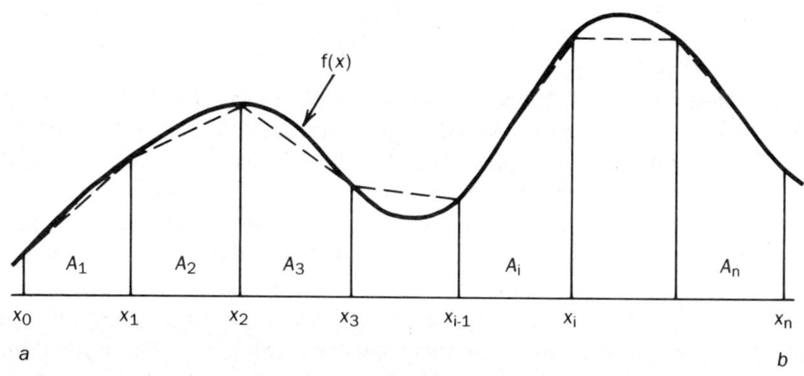

Figure 3.8 Composite Trapezoid Method

and our approximation to I using n trapezoids is given by:

$$\begin{aligned} T_n &= A_1 + A_2 + \ldots + A_n \\ &= \frac{h}{2}[f(x_0) + f(x_1)] + \frac{h}{2}[f(x_1) + f(x_2)] + \\ &\quad \ldots + \frac{h}{2}[f(x_{n-1}) + f(x_n)] \\ &= \frac{h}{2}[f(x_0) + 2f(x_1) + 2f(x_2) + \ldots + 2f(x_{n-1}) + f(x_n)] \end{aligned} \tag{3.7}$$

The accuracy of the resulting approximation to I depends on the number of trapezoids, n, that we use. A rapidly changing curve may require many trapezoids to obtain a specified accuracy. How large should n be? This question can be answered mathematically if we develop an expression for the error.

If we define $E_i = A_i - I$, where A_i is defined by (3.6) and

$$I_i = \int_{x_{i-1}}^{x_{-i}} f(x)\,dx = F(x_i) - F(x_{i-1}) \tag{3.8}$$

then by (3.3) we have:

$$E_i = \frac{h^3 f''(z_i)}{12} \tag{3.9}$$

where z_i is in $[x_{i-1}, x_i]$. If we define M to be the maximum absolute value of $f''(x)$ for x in $[a,b]$, then each $|E_i|$ is less than or equal to $h^3M/12$. If this error is assumed for all n trapezoids, the maximum total error, E_T, is:

$$E_T \le \frac{n\,h^3 M}{12} = \frac{(b-a)\,h^2\,M}{12} \tag{3.10}$$

The error formula (3.10) tells us that if we double the numer of trapezoids (i.e., make h half as large), the error E_T should be reduced by a factor of 4.

It is clear from (3.10) that the error of the composite trapezoid method can be controlled through the choice of h. For example, any h satisfying the inequality:

$$h^2 \le \frac{12}{(b-a)\,M}\,\text{eps} \tag{3.11}$$

will ensure that $E_T \le$ eps. However, this is not a very satisfactory method for choosing h. First, it requires a knowledge of a bound M on $|f''|$, which may be inconvenient or difficult to obtain. Second, the bound is usually very pessimistic, resulting in an h that is unnecessarily small. This makes the algorithm inefficient because extra evaluations of the integrand $f(x)$ will have to be done.

Let us now consider Figure 3.9 and develop the composite Simpson's method.

We will use the definition for h given previously but assume that n is a multiple of 2, since Simpson's method spans two intervals. The approximation

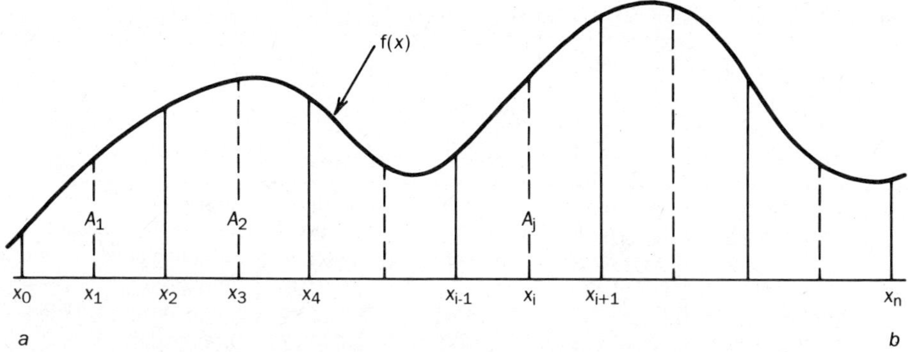

Figure 3.9 Composite Simpson's Method

to the integral over the interval $[x_{i-1}, x_{i+1}]$ is given by:

$$A_j = \frac{h}{3}[f(x_{i-1}) + 4f(x_i) + f(x_{i+1})] \tag{3.12}$$

where $j = 1, 2, \ldots, n/2$ and $i = 2j - 1$. Thus our approximation to I using Simpson's method $n/2$ times is given by:

$$\begin{aligned} S_n &= A_1 + A_2 + \ldots + A_{n/2} \\ &= \frac{h}{3}[f(x_0) + 4f(x_1) + f(x_2)] + \frac{h}{3}[f(x_2) + 4f(x_3) \\ &\quad + f(x_4)] + \ldots + \frac{h}{3}[f(x_{n-2}) + 4f(x_{n-1}) + f(x_n)] \\ &= \frac{h}{3}[f(x_0) + 4f(x_1) + 2f(x_2) + 4f(x_3) + \ldots \\ &\quad + 2f(x_{n-2}) + 4f(x_{n-1}) + f(x_n)] \end{aligned} \tag{3.13}$$

Using (3.5) we can derive an expression that bounds the error in a manner similar to that used for the composite trapezoid method. The resulting expression is:

$$E_S \leq \frac{(b - a)\, h^4 M}{180} \tag{3.14}$$

where M is the maximum value of $|f^{(iv)}(x)|$ on the interval $[a,b]$. In this case, if we reduce h by a factor of 2 the error, E_S, should be reduced by a factor of 16. For a given error tolerance, eps, we can ensure that $E_S \leq$ eps if h satisfies:

$$h^4 \leq \frac{180}{(b - a)M} \text{eps} \tag{3.15}$$

We now present some example numerical calculations to illustrate the behavior of these two algorithms.

TABLE 3.12 Integration Results for Example 1

	Trapezoid Method			Simpson's Method		
n	Integral	Error	Rate of Convergence	Integral	Error	Rate of Convergence
2	1.75393109	0.03564926		1.71886115	0.00057932	
4	1.72722190	0.00894008	1.9955	1.71831884	0.00003701	3.9682
8	1.72051859	0.00223676	1.9989	1.71828415	0.00000233	3.9920
16	1.71884113	0.00055930	1.9997	1.71828197	0.00000015	3.9980
32	1.71842166	0.00013983	1.9999	1.71828184	0.00000001	3.9995
64	1.71831679	0.00003496	2.0000	1.71828183	0.00000000	3.9999
128	1.71829057	0.00000874	2.0000	1.71828183	0.00000000	4.0000

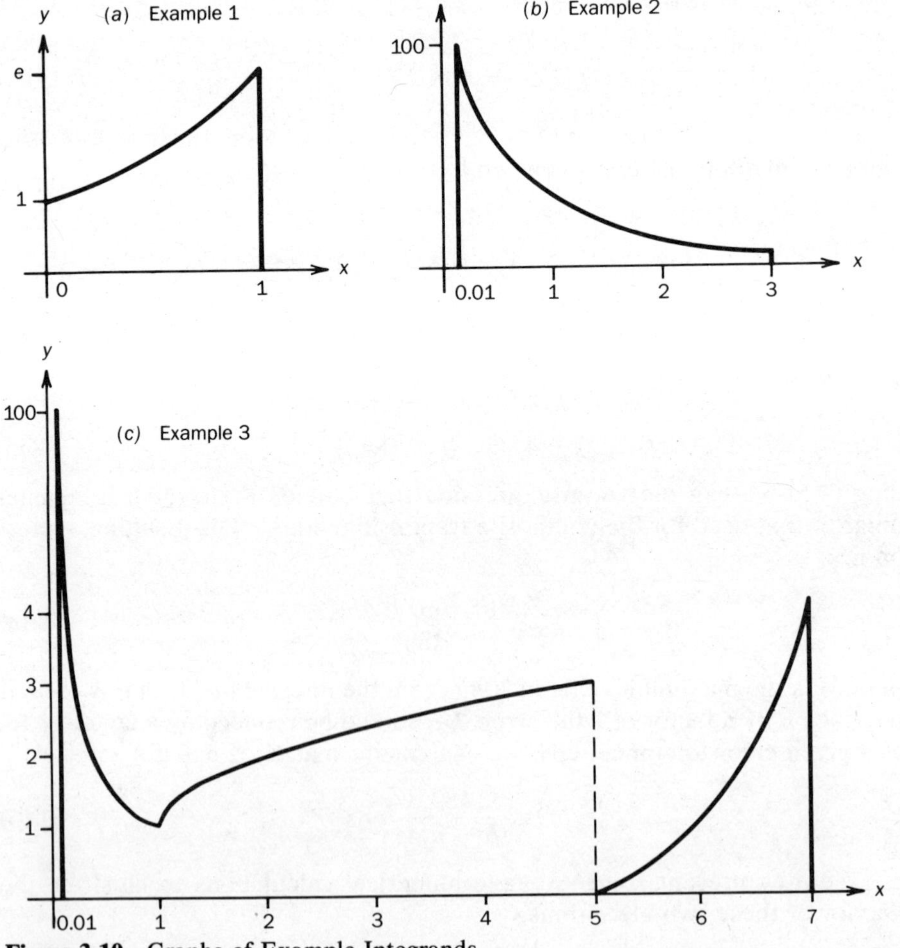

Figure 3.10 Graphs of Example Integrands

EXAMPLE 1

$$\int_0^1 e^x \, dx = e - 1 = 1.71828183$$

Table 3.12 presents the numerical results for Example 1, and Figure 3.10*a* graphs this simple integrand function. In the table, *n* refers to the number of intervals. The rate column shows the calculated rate of convergence. The theoretical rate of convergence for the composite trapezoid method is 2; that is, the error should be reduced by a factor of 4 when we double the number of intervals. For the composite Simpson's method the theoretical rate of convergence is 4.

EXAMPLE 2

$$\int_{0.01}^{3} \frac{1}{x \, dx} = \ln 3 - \ln 0.01 = 5.703782475$$

This example is much more difficult than Example 1 because of the behavior of the integrand near 0.01 (see Figure 3.10*b*). The results are presented in Table 3.13. Note that even when the number of intervals is very large, we still have not achieved much accuracy. Also notice that the theoretical rate of convergence is not attained until *n* becomes very large.

EXAMPLE 3

$$\int_{0.01}^{7} f(x) \, dx = 16.60517019$$

TABLE 3.13 Integration Results for Example 2

	Trapezoid Method			Simpson's Method		
n	Integral	Error	Rate of Conver-gence	Integral	Error	Rate of Conver-gence
2	75.99252215	70.28873967		51.32391842	45.62013595	
4	39.31491325	33.61113078	1.0644	27.08904362	21.38526114	1.0931
8	21.30303338	15.59925091	1.1075	15.29907342	9.59529095	1.1562
16	12.61183116	6.90804868	1.1751	9.71476375	4.01098128	1.2584
32	8.55460292	2.85082044	1.2769	7.20219350	1.49841103	1.4205
64	6.76952088	1.06573841	1.4195	6.17449354	0.47071107	1.6705
128	6.05629514	0.35251266	1.5961	5.81855322	0.11477074	2.0361
256	5.80690560	0.10312312	1.7733	5.72377575	0.01999328	2.5212
512	5.73135320	0.02757072	1.9032	5.70616906	0.00238659	3.0665
1024	5.71082904	0.00704656	1.9681	5.70398765	0.00020518	3.5400
2048	5.70555494	0.00177247	1.9912	5.70379691	0.00001444	3.8289
4096	5.70422629	0.00044382	1.9977	5.70378341	0.00000093	3.9497

where

$$f(x) = \begin{cases} 1/x & 0.01 \le x \le 1 \\ 1 + \sqrt{x - 1} & 1 < x \le 5 \\ (x - 5)^2 & 5 < x \le 7 \end{cases}$$

In this example we define $f(x)$ as the single function given above. That is, we do not split this integral into three separate problems. The puriest may argue that this function is not sufficiently differentiable to validate our theoretical results. We agree with this statement; however, $f(x)$ can be viewed as a ragged function that might occur in practice for which we need a value of the integral (see Figure 3.10*c*). The results presented in Table 3.14 indicate that the theoretical order of convergence is not attained and that even with very large n we still do not have very accurate results.

In the preceding examples, we used a uniform subdivision of the interval $[a,b]$. This is not necessarily the most efficient way of approximating the value of I. Consider the function $f(x)$ in Figure 3.11. Within the region marked I, the graph of the integrand $f(x)$ does not fluctuate very much, so h would not have to be very small to obtain good accuracy. However, it is clear that a much smaller h would be required to obtain good accuracy in the region marked II. The algorithms presented above can be modified easily to accommodate the use of unequal subdivisions of $[a,b]$. The error formulas (3.10) and (3.14) are still valid, with h replaced by $h = \max_i h_i$. However, we still must choose the subdivisions in advance.

It would be desirable to have an algorithm based on nonuniform subintervals that automatically "adapts" by choosing subintervals according to the behavior of the integrand $f(x)$. Algorithms that do this are called adaptive quadrature algorithms. A considerable amount of evidence has accumulated

TABLE 3.14 Integration Results for Example 3

	Trapezoid Method			Simpson's Method		
n	Integral	Error	Rate of Convergence	Integral	Error	Rate of Convergence
2	190.76660353	174.16143353	0.0000	133.19547137	116.59030137	0.0000
4	98.76314328	82.15797328	1.0840	68.09532320	51.49015320	1.1791
8	55.94808460	39.34291460	1.0623	41.67639837	25.07122837	1.0383
16	35.36689426	18.76172426	1.0683	28.50649748	11.90132748	1.0749
32	24.74706713	8.14189713	1.2044	21.20712475	4.60195475	1.3708
64	20.04700429	3.44183429	1.2422	18.48031667	1.87514667	1.2952
128	17.96830209	1.36313209	1.3363	17.27540136	0.67023136	1.4843
256	17.04188692	0.43671692	1.6422	16.73308187	0.12791187	2.3895
512	16.74243374	0.13726374	1.6697	16.64261601	0.03744601	1.7723
1024	16.65241937	0.04724937	1.5386	16.62241458	0.01724458	1.1187
2048	16.61965542	0.01448542	1.7057	16.60873411	0.00356411	2.2745
4096	16.60993697	0.00476697	1.6035	16.60669749	0.00152749	1.2224

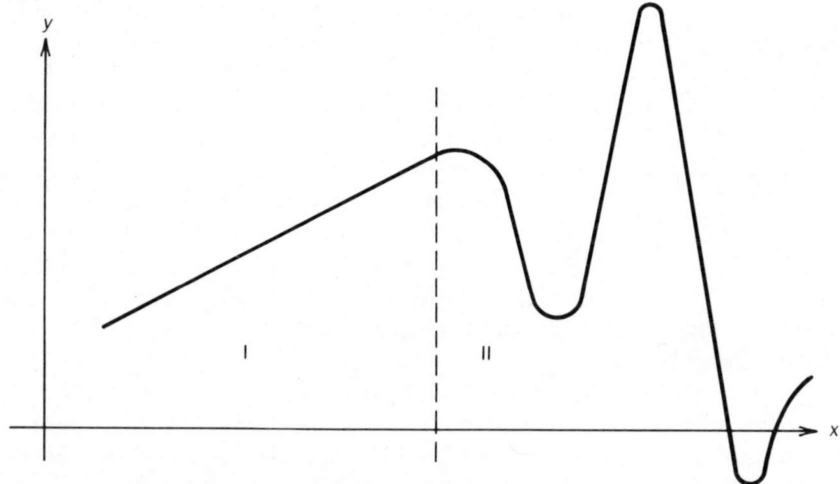

Figure 3.11 Integrand with Significantly Different Behavior in Regions I and II

to indicate that adaptive algorithms are substantially superior to nonadaptive ones.

The adaptive quadrature algorithm we now describe involves processing a collection of subintervals that must be organized into a data structure. Each data structure leads to a different algorithm and behavior. We will consider only two data structures: the stack and the queue.

The idea behind adaptive quadrature can be described as follows. Subdivide the interval $[a,b]$ by:

$$a = x_1 < x_2 < \cdots < x_N = b$$

and choose a basic quadrature method (not a composite method) to be used on each subinterval. To ensure that the adaptive algorithm begins with the original interval, choose N as 2. Now apply the quadrature method to each subinterval and place the subinterval end points and the corresponding approximate integral into a data structure. Select a subinterval from the data structure, and determine whether the corresponding approximate integral value is sufficiently accurate by subdividing the interval into two equal subintervals and applying the quadrature method to each half. If the sum of the values over the two half-intervals agrees sufficiently with that over the whole subinterval, we accept this value and continue. If not, we place both subinterval end points and corresponding integral values into our data structure. We repeat this process of selecting and processing subintervals until our data structure is empty (i.e., contains no more subintervals to be processed).

Each time a value of a subinterval is accepted, it is added to a running total that ultimately becomes the approximate value for I. It is possible for the length of a subinterval to become to small to permit further refinement within machine precision. This usually indicates trouble, such as a singularity in the integrand $f(x)$. In effect, an adaptive quadrature algorithm is a composite rule using variable subinterval sizes that are determined dynamically rather than being preassigned.

If we select a stack for our data structure, then we process the subintervals in a LIFO order. If we initialize the stack by pushing the subintervals onto the stack from right to left, the top of the stack contains the leftmost interval. The next interval to process is the one at the top of the stack, which is the leftmost subinterval that has not been accepted. If we do not accept this interval, the corresponding right and left subintervals are pushed onto the stack. Unfortunately, this strategy forces us to make a final, irrevocable decision to accept the leftmost interval before we have examined the integrand $f(x)$ in any detail over the entire interval.

Suppose we select a queue for our data structure and initialize it by inserting the initial subintervals into the queue from left to right. The front of the queue initially contains the leftmost subinterval. The next interval to process is the interval at the front of the queue. If we do not accept this interval, we insert the left and right subintervals into the queue. This places them at the rear of the queue, which means that they are not processed again until they arrive at the front of the queue (i.e., until all the subintervals in the queue have been processed). This approach does not entail the same problem as the stack data structure, but it may lead to potentially long queues.

Before we can implement this adaptive algorithm, we must determine the criteria for accepting a subinterval. We will assume that the user has specified that an absolute error of eps is desired. Let

A = calculated integral of $f(x)$ over the interval to be processed using some quadrature rule
B = calculated integral of $f(x)$ over the interval to be processed using some quadrature rule over two equal subintervals of the interval
I = exact integral over the interval to be processed

Then

$$I - A = Ch^{p+1}f^{(p)}(z) \tag{3.16}$$

where $p = 2$ for the trapezoid method, $p = 4$ for Simpson's method, C is a constant depending on the method, and z is a point in the interval being processed. Since B is calculated using an h half the size of that used in calculating A, we have:

$$\begin{aligned} I - B &= C\left(\frac{h}{2}\right)^{p+1} f^{(p)}(z_1) + C\left(\frac{h}{2}\right)^{p+1} f^{(p)}(z_2) \\ &= \frac{2C}{2^{p+1}}\, h^{p+1} f^{(p)}(z) \\ &= \frac{1}{2^p}\,(I - A) \end{aligned} \tag{3.17}$$

where we have assumed that $f^{(p)}$ has essentially the same value at z_1, z_2, and z.

Expression 3.17 can be rearranged to give:

$$B - I = \frac{A - B}{2^p - 1} \tag{3.18}$$

Since B should be a better approximation than A to the integral of $f(x)$ over the interval, we will use B in our running sum. Equation 3.18 gives us an estimate of the error in B in terms of A and B and p, which are known quantities.

If the length of the subinterval we are processing is h, this subinterval represents a fraction of the original interval $b - a$. If we attempt to uniformly distribute the error over the original interval, the accuracy that we should require for our approximation to the integral over this subinterval should be $h/(b - a)$ of the user-specified accuracy requirement. That is, we accept the interval if:

$$\frac{|A - B|}{2^p - 1} \leq \frac{h}{b - a} \text{eps} \tag{3.19}$$

We can make our adaptive algorithm slightly more efficient with very little additional work by employing Richardson's extrapolation, a technique for eliminating the first-order error terms. It is applicable if we know the order of the first-order error term and if we have used the same numerical procedure with different values for h to approximate the same quantity. Our processing of a subinterval involves all the quantities that we need to use Richardson's extrapolation. Specifically, we have the approximation A to the integral over the subinterval and the approximation B to the same quantity but calculated using an h half as large as that used in calculating A. By Richardson's extrapolation, the quantity:

$$\frac{2^p B - A}{2^p - 1} \tag{3.20}$$

is an approximation to I that is accurate to terms involving h^{p+2}. If we use the quantity (3.20) in our running sum instead of B, we need to modify our error test (3.19) by replacing p with $p + 2$ to reflect this more accurate approximation to I.

We are now ready to present the implementation details for our adaptive algorithm using the stack ADT. We leave the implementation involving the queue ADT as an exercise. Each node in the stack must contain a subinterval and the corresponding value for the integrand over the subinterval. The representation for a subinterval that we choose is simply the end points of that subinterval. We define the following element type for use by the stack ADT, where we designate this interval as [left, right] with a corresponding approximate integral value area.

```
DEFINITION MODULE elements;
   EXPORT QUALIFIED
   (* type *) elementtype;
```

```
TYPE
        elementtype = RECORD
                        left        : REAL;
                        right       : REAL;
                        area        : REAL
                      END (* record *);
END elements.
```

We will use Simpson's method with Richardson's extrapolation in our implementation, which begins with the initial interval $[a,b]$ and corresponding approximate value for the integral on the stack. Listing 3.11 gives the implementation details.

Listing 3.11 Adaptive Integration Implementation

```
IMPLEMENTATION MODULE adaptiveintegration;

  FROM elements IMPORT
    (* type *) elementtype;

  FROM stackadt IMPORT
    (* type *) stack,
    (* proc *) define, empty, pop, push;


  PROCEDURE integral
          ( a, b : REAL                           (* in *);
            f    : function                       (* in *) ) :
            REAL;
  (* This procedure integrates the function f from a to
     b using Simpson's method.                                 *)
  BEGIN
    RETURN  (b-a)/6.0 * ( f(a) + 4.0 * f((a+b)/2.0) + f(b) )
  END integral;


  PROCEDURE assignnode
          (     a, b, areavalue : REAL        (* in *);
            VAR node            : elementtype (* out *) );
  (* This procedure assigns the end points and corresponding
     approximate integral to a stack node element.             *)
  BEGIN
    WITH node DO
      left := a;
      right := b;
      area := areavalue
    END (* with *)
  END assignnode;
```

```
PROCEDURE integrate
        (     a, b    : REAL                    (* in *) ;
              eps     : REAL                    (* in *) ;
              f       : function                (* in *) ;
          VAR answer : REAL                     (* out *) );
(* This procedure implements adapative integration using
   a stack data structure to integrate the function f
   from a to b.  It returns an answer with absolute error
   less than eps.                                        *)

VAR
  arealeft, arearight : REAL;
  tol                 : REAL;
  intervalstack       : stack;
  p, q                : elementtype;

BEGIN
  answer := 0.0;
  tol := 63.0 * eps / (b - a);
  define( intervalstack );
  assignnode( a, b, integral( a, b, f ), p );
  push( intervalstack, p );
  WHILE NOT empty( intervalstack ) DO
    pop( intervalstack, p );
    WITH p DO
      arealeft := integral( left, (left+right)/2.0, f );
      arearight := integral( (left+right)/2.0, right, f );
      IF ABS( area - (arealeft + arearight ) ) <
              tol * (right - left)
      THEN
        answer := answer + ( 16.0 * (arealeft + arearight)

                                     - area ) / 15.0
      ELSE
        assignnode((left+right)/2.0, right, arearight, q);
        push( intervalstack, q );
        assignnode( left, (left+right)/2.0, arealeft, q );
        push( intervalstack, q );
      END (* if then *);
    END (* with *);
  END (* while loop *);
END integrate;

END adaptiveintegration.
```

We used this adaptive integration algorithm to integrate the three examples presented earlier. In all three cases, we set eps to 0.0001. The results are

TABLE 3.15 Adaptive Integration Results on Three Examples

Example	*n*	Answer	Error
1	1	1.71828269	.00000086
2	19	5.70383659	.00005411
3	147	16.60513765	.00003254

presented in Table 3.15. The column labeled *n* refers to the number of intervals processed and accepted. Recall that the processing of an accepted interval involves subdividing the interval and using the integration method over each half, followed by Richardson's extrapolation. Observe that the accuracy requested was attained.

Exercises

3.1 Convert the following infix expressions to postfix and prefix form:

(a) ((A + B) * C + D) / E

(b) A + (B * ((C + D / R + X) / C))

(c) A * (B − C * D) / E

3.2 Convert the following postfix expressions to infix forms:

(a) A B C D − / +

(b) A B C * D / E − *

(c) A B + A C − A D * A E / + * /

3.3 Convert the following prefix expressions to infix form:

(a) * / A − B + C D E

(b) + − / * A B C D E

(c) / * + / A B * A C − A D + A E

3.4 Develop an algorithm for converting an infix expression with parentheses to prefix form and evaluating the resulting expression. Code the definition and implementation modules and a write a main program to test your algorithms and their implementations. (*Hint*: Prefix expressions should be evaluated from right to left.)

3.5 Modify the algorithm for converting infix expressions to postfix form by adding the following specifications:

(a) Permit arbitrary blanks in the infix expression.

(b) Require every infix expression to be terminated by a semicolon. Produce a diagnostic message when this error (i.e., no terminal semicolon) is detected.

(c) Incorporate logic for detecting unmatched parentheses and produce appropriate diagnostic messages when errors are detected.

3.6 Suppose we define the symbol '$' to denote the exponentiation operation (i.e., 2 $ 4 = 16) and assign it a higher precedence than any other arithmetic operator (i.e., 3 * 2 $ 3 = 3 * (2 $ 3) = 24). Exponentiation is performed from right to left (i.e., 4 $ 2 $ 2 = 4 $ (2 $ 2) = 256). Modify the algorithm for converting infix expressions to postfix form to include exponentiation. Your solution should still require only one pass of the input infix string. Code and test your algorithm.

3.7 Modify the algorithm for evaluating a postfix expression so that it contains the exponentiation operation described in exercise 3.6. Code and test your algorithm.

3.8 Modify the algorithm for converting infix to postfix to include the operation of assignment.

3.9 Develop, code, and test an algorithm for converting from postfix form to fully parenthesized infix form. For example, * A B would be converted to (A * B) and A B C * + would be converted to (A + (B * C)).

3.10 The implementation given in Listing 3.3 uses the generic stack ADT. Modify this implementation so that it does not use the generic stack ADT.

3.11 For the maze given in Figure 3.5, display the path that the maze runner program will calculate.

3.12 Modify the maze runner program so that only four moves are possible from each point (north, east, south, and west). If a path can still be found in Figure 3.5, display the path.

3.13 The maze ADT defined in Listings 3.4 and 3.6 does not make type mazetype opaque to user programs. Modify the definition and implementation so that mazetype is opaque.

3.14 Modify the maze runner program so the maze is an array of BOOLEAN where TRUE represents an open path and FALSE represents a wall. The marking strategy to keep track of where we have been must be modified by using a second marking array of BOOLEAN.

3.15 Analyze the computing time for the maze runner program by examining the number of times the while loops will be executed. Note that the number of times that the outer while loop is executed depends on the given maze.

3.16 Modify the adaptive integration algorithm presented in Listing 3.11 that uses the stack ADT so that the integration method is the trapezoid method with Richardson's extrapolation. Solve Examples 1, 2, and 3.

3.17 Implement the adaptive integration algorithm using the queue ADT and solve Examples 1, 2, and 3:

(a) Using the trapezoid method.

(b) Using Simpson's method.

(c) Using the trapezoid method with Richardson's extrapolation.

(d) Using Simpson's method with Richardson's extrapolation.

3.18 Modify the implementation of the adaptive integration algorithm presented in Listing 3.11 so that the end points and area of each subinterval are printed when the subinterval is accepted. Use this modified algorithm to solve Example 3 and explain how the algorithm successfully integrates past a discontinuity.

3.19 Use an adaptive integration algorithm to integrate the function:

$$f(x) = x^{0.1}\,(1.2 - x)(1 - e^{20|x-1|})$$

from $x = 0$ to $x = 1$ using an eps $= 0.001$ and eps $= 0.0001$. The exact answer to six decimal places is 0.602297. Use the composite trapezoid and Simpson's methods and experimentally determine the number of intervals necessary to achieve roughly the same accuracy.

3.20 Use one of the adaptive algorithms described in the text to solve:

$$\int_0^{2\pi} (1 - \cos 32x)\,dx = 2\,\pi$$

The answer you get should be 0 rather than $2\,\pi$. Explain.

3.21 Try to use the adaptive integration algorithm on:

$$\int_{0.1}^{2.9} \frac{1}{(x-2)^2}\,dx$$

Print the end points and area of each subinterval when it is accepted. This problem has a singularity at $x = 2$.

3.22 Use the composite trapezoid and Simpson's methods to solve:

$$\int_0^1 \sqrt{x}\,dx = \frac{2}{3}$$

Calculate the observed order of convergence. It will not be the theoretical values, since the derivative of the integrand does not exist at 0.

3.23 Develop formulas for the composite trapezoid and composite Simpson's method similar to (3.7) and (3.13), respectively, that use unequal subintervals.

4

The List (Search Table) Abstraction and Some Implementations

4.1 The List (Search Table) as an Abstract Data Type

In Chapters 2 and 3, we presented the stack and the queue ADTs with several implementations. Both these structures permitted us to perform basic operations on the abstract data type without a knowledge of the type of elements in the structure. In this chapter, we discuss a more general structure called a list or search table. We will present the list as an abstract data type, but to perform some of the basic operations on the list, we need an ordering relation for the items in the list.

4.1.1 Fundamental List Operations

A list is a homogeneous, sequential access structure of varying size along with a number of operations. Two of the most fundamental operations are deletion and insertion, and their nature distinguishes the list from the stack and queue. The delete operation may be performed on any item in the list, and the insert operation may add an item anywhere in the list to achieve some logical ordering or structure to the list.

An array could conceptually be the home for a list. Since arrays are implemented as contiguous blocks of storage, this permits us to find an item given its index by a simple address computation. However, the delete and insert operations on an array have inherent problems. For example, the delete operation leaves unused space in the list unless the remaining items in the list are moved to occupy the vacated space. The insert operation may require the moving of many items in the list to make room for a new item.

In a list we do not require the storage to be contiguous. This causes us to lose the order of the items implied by contiguous storage but gives us freedom to insert or delete storage associated with the items in the list. To maintain the order of the items in the list, we will associate with each item the address of the next item. Each item in the list will be structured as a record so that we can combine the item with the address of the next item into a single entity. This record is usually referred to as a node. A list consists of a collection of linked nodes.

Figure 4.1 conceptually represents a linked list. Addresses are represented as arrows or pointers, since the exact addresses of the items in the list are not important. The boxes in the list are referred to as nodes. Each node contains two fields, an info field that contains the value of an item and a next field that contains the address of the next item. The entire linked list is accessed via a single external pointer, say list. The end of the list is represented by the nil pointer. The empty list is represented by the nil pointer.

How does one construct a linked list? First of all, we must have access to a source or pool of nodes. We define the operation "getnode" to be a function that returns the address of a new node to us from the node pool. Once we have a node, we would like to insert it at a specified place in the list. For example, if the item is to be inserted at the beginning of the list, an operation "insertfront" is desirable. If we wish to place the new item immediately after an existing item in the list, an "insertafter" operation would be our choice. Each of these operations requires the modification of address fields of certain nodes to reflect the insert operation.

To describe these list operations, we will need some notation for indicating the parts of a node. The notation we use is for describing algorithms only; it is not Modula-2 code.

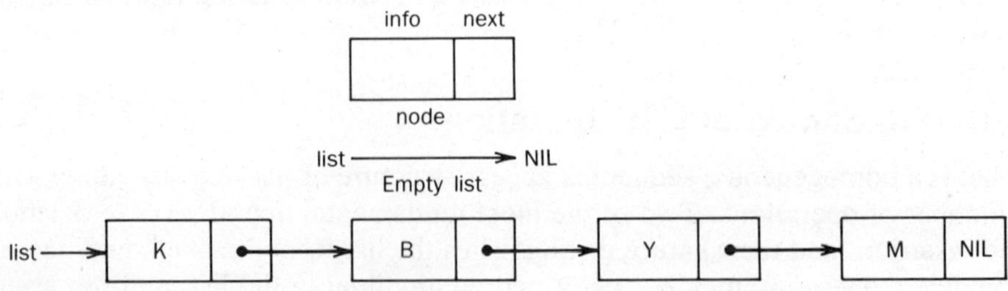

Figure 4.1 Diagram of a Linked List

list	An external pointer to the first node in a linked list
item	A user-defined element; the info field of each node in the linked list contains items
itemnode	A pointer to a list node with info field containing item
previousnode	A pointer to a list node with info field containing previousitem
previousitem	The info field of previousnode
newitem	An item to be inserted in the linked list
newnode	A pointer to a new node
oldnode	A pointer to a node to be removed from the linked list
currentnode	A pointer to a list node

Figure 4.2 illustrates the "insertfront" operation on the list of Figure 4.1. In this case, we insert the item 'N' into the list. The circled numbers in the figure correspond to the steps for the "insertfront" operation which is described as follows:

```
Procedure insertfront( list, item )
  newnode ←getnode
  set info field of newnode to item
  set next field of newnode to list
  set list to newnode
```

In Figure 4.3 we insert the item 'R' after the item 'B' in the list of Figure 4.1. A formal description of this operation is:

```
Procedure insertafter( list, previousitem, newitem )
   find previousnode that contains previousitem
   newnode ← getnode
   set info field of newnode to newitem
   set next field of newnode to next field of previousnode
   set next field of previousnode to newnode
```

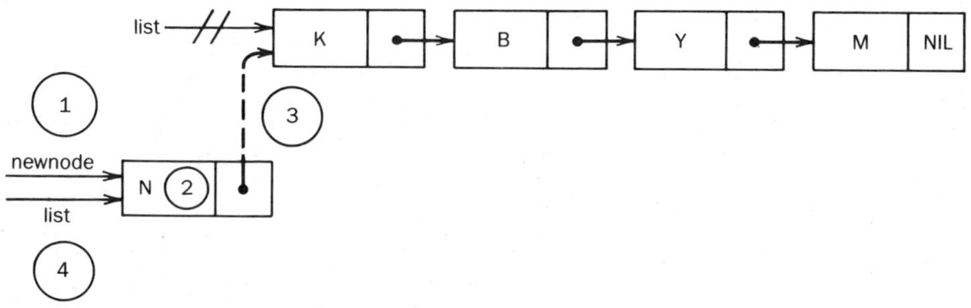

Figure 4.2 Insertion at the Front of a Linked List

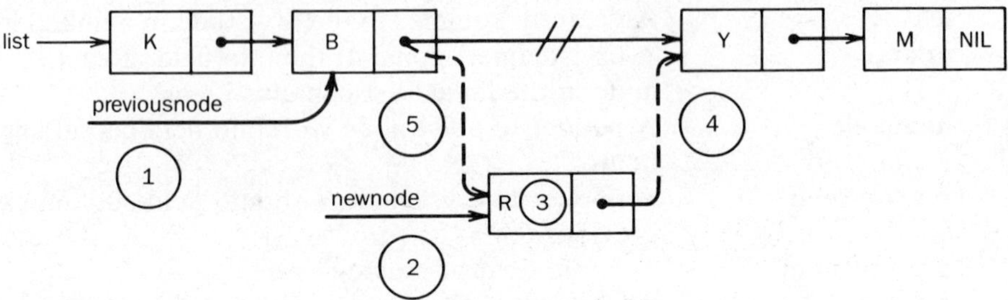

Figure 4.3 Insertion into a Linked List

Let us now consider the converse operations: "deletefront" and "deleteafter". As with the insert operations, each requires modification of the address fields of certain nodes to reflect the delete operation.

The "deletefront" operation illustrated in Figure 4.4 deletes the first node from the list of Figure 4.1. The delete operation results in an unused node. Since computers do not have an infinite amount of storage, only a finite number of nodes are available at any instant. To prevent this storage from being wasted, deleted nodes should be reused. We can accomplish this by returning the unused node to the node pool. We define the operation "freenode" to perform this task. The "deletefront" operation can be described by:

```
Procedure deletefront( list )
  set oldnode to list
  set list to the next field of oldnode
  freenode( oldnode )
```

The "deleteafter" operation deletes an item from the list that immediately follows a specified previous item. In Figure 4.5, we delete the item that follows item 'B' in the list of Figure 4.1. This operation can be described by:

```
Procedure deleteafter( list, previousitem )
  find previousnode that contains previousitem
  set oldnode to next field of previousnode
```

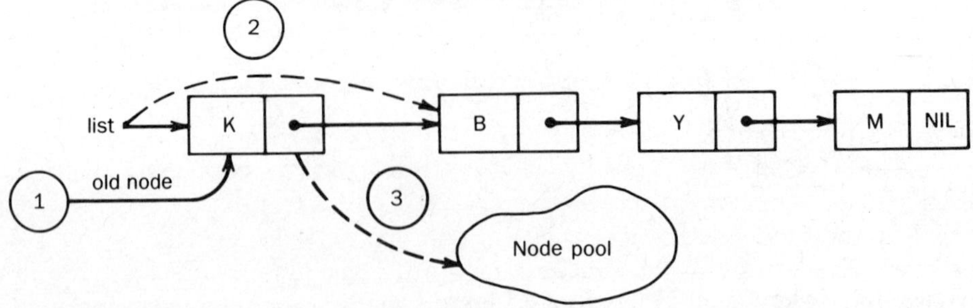

Figure 4.4 Deletion at the Front of a Linked List

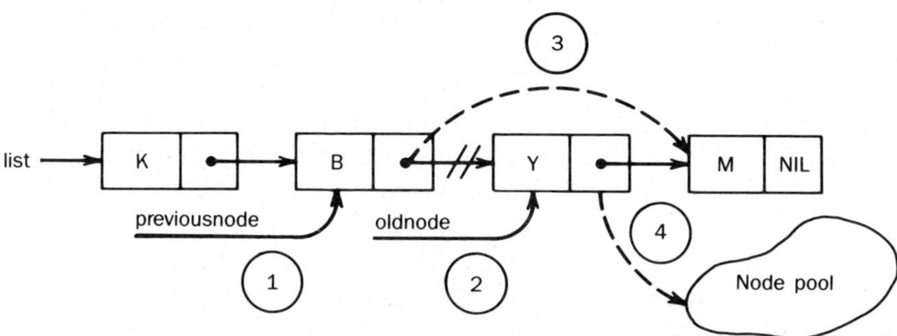

Figure 4.5 Deletion from a Linked List

```
set next field of previousnode to next field of oldnode
freenode( oldnode )
```

The operation "insertafter" requires us to find the node in the list that contains a specified item that we wish the new item to follow. The "deleteafter" operation requires us to find the node in the list that contains a specified item that precedes the item that is to be deleted from the list. The "insertafter" operation seems reasonable, but one must question why we chose the "deleteafter" operation rather than a delete operation that directly deletes a specified item from the list. It is easy to develop an algorithm that finds a node containing a specified item in the list and returns a pointer to that node. But as Figure 4.5 shows, it is the node before that node that actually changes its value. Unfortunately, there is no easy way to get from the node found back to the node to be changed. Thus, we use the "deleteafter" operation rather than a delete operation.

We now develop a search procedure to find a specified node in the list:

```
Procedure search( list, item, itemnode )
  set itemnode to list
  while next field of itemnode not equal to nil and item not
      equal to info field of itemnode do
    set itemnode to next field of itemnode
  end while
```

Note that the search procedure returns the nil pointer if the list is empty or if the item is not found in the list.

The items stored in a linked list are often records containing numerous data fields—for example, employee records, charge account records, and reservation records. Usually we would like the data that is stored in a list to be ordered based on some key field in the record. The examples cited above might be ordered by employee's last name, account number, or customer's last name, respectively.

This suggests that a useful operation on a list might be a "place" operation, which inserts a new item into the list based on an order relation defined for some key field in the record. To determine where to insert the new item, we must traverse the list and for each node encountered check whether the order relation is satisfied. If the order relation is satisfied, we can terminate the list traversal and insert the item into its proper place in the list. However, as indicated earlier, the insert operation requires a pointer to the previous node. This suggests that we use two pointers: one to the previous node and one to the current node. The info field of the current node is used in the order relation with the item to be inserted. The "place" operation can be described as follows:

```
Procedure place( list, item )
  set found to false
  set currentnode to list
  set previousnode to nil
  while currentnode not equal to nil and not found do
    if order relation between item and the info field of
      currentnode is satisfied
    then
      set found to true
    else
      set previousnode to currentnode
      set currentnode to the next field of currentnode
    end if
  if previousnode is nil
  then
    insertfront( list, item )
  else
    insertafter( list, previousitem, item )
  end if
```

It would also be convenient to be able to easily remove an item from a list. To achieve this, we define the "remove" operation to remove a specified item from the list. As with the place operation, we will need two pointers, since the delete operation requires a pointer to the previous node in addition to a pointer to the current node. In case the specified item is not found in the list, we return an indicator, found, with a value of false; otherwise, found is returned with a value of true.

The "remove" operation is defined by:

```
Procedure remove( list, item, found )
  set found to false
  set currentnode to list
  set previousnode to nil
  while currentnode not equal to nil and not found do
    if item is equal to currentnode info
    then
      set found to true
```

```
    else
      set previousnode to currentnode
      set currentnode to the next field of currentnode
    end if
  if found
  then
    if currentnode equal list
    then
      deletefront( list )
    else
      deleteafter( list, previousitem )
    end if
  end if
```

The two preceding operations permit us to update a list while maintaining an ordering of the list based on a key field in the records stored in the list.

Another fundamental operation we define for the list is the "display" operation, which traverses the list from beginning to end and processes each item in it. The actual processing is specified by the user of the list abstract data type. It may be simply printing information associated with each record in the list or updating each record. The "display" operation is specified by:

```
Procedure display( list )
   if the list is empty
   then
     indicate that the list is empty
   else
     set currentnode to list
     while currentnode is not equal to nil do
       process the info field of the currentnode
       set currentnode to the next field of currentnode
     end while
   end if
```

Other operations we define for the list ADT include "define", "empty", "erase", and "length". "Define" creates an empty list and must be used for each new list before any other list operations are performed. "Empty" returns true if the list is empty, otherwise false. "Erase" erases and reinitializes a list. Finally, "length" returns the number of items or records in the list.

We can define many other list operations. See the exercises for additional examples.

4.1.2 Procedure Types in Modula-2

The concept of a linked list is independent of the type of items or elements stored in the list. In this section, we address the question of how linked list operations can be implemented independent of the item type.

We assume that the items to be stored in a list are of type elementtype, which we import into the definition module and implementation module for the list ADT. This permits us to define and implement the ADT independent of the type of items in the list.

The "place" operation defined earlier uses a relation on the key field of the items that are stored in the list to determine where to insert an item into the list. The "search" and "remove" operations use a test for equality of two items. Finally, the "display" operation performs a user-defined operation on each item in the list.

Since we do not know in advance the type of items to be stored in the list, we cannot predefine an order relation or the meaning of equality for these items. If the items are restricted to types such as integers, reals, booleans, characters, or enumeration types, a natural ordering is implied and a test for equality can be accomplished by using the operators defined for these types in Modula-2. However, if the items are records consisting of a number of fields, an order relation or a test for equality does not follow in a natural manner and must be defined by the client module.

Modula-2 provides us with procedure types that enable us to resolve these issues and implement the list operations independent of the type of items in the list. Modula-2 views procedures as objects that can be assigned to variables. This means that a procedure declaration can be viewed as a special kind of constant declaration with the value of the constant being a procedure. The definition of a procedure type requires a specification of parameter types and binding mechanisms. If it is a function, the type of result must be specified. For example, the declaration:

```
TYPE equaltype = PROCEDURE ( elementtype, elementtype ):
                             BOOLEAN;
```

permits us to declare a variable of type equaltype, which is a function procedure with two parameters of type elementtype and returns a boolean value.

Procedure types can be used as parameters in procedures. For example, the following procedure declaration:

```
PROCEDURE deleteafter( VAR lst          : list;
                           previousitem : elementtype;
                           equal        : equaltype );
```

indicates that the parameter equal is a function procedure of type equaltype.

This powerful facility of Modula-2 permits us to implement the list operations independent of the items in the list. The two additional procedure types that we will need are defined by:

```
TYPE lessthantype = PROCEDURE ( elementtype, elementtype ):
                                BOOLEAN;
```

and

```
TYPE displaytype = PROCEDURE ( VAR elementtype );
```

The lessthantype defines the order relation for the list based on the element type that is stored in the list. Notice the binding mode specification in displaytype, which permits the user to write a procedure that displays the items in the list or performs an update operation on the items in the list.

The user of the list ADT must define procedures of types equaltype, lessthantype, and displaytype in a client module for the specific type of items to be contained in the list. An example is given in section 4.1.3.

4.1.3 Definition Module for Fundamental List Operations

In this section, we present the definition module for the list ADT. Notice that the only operation described above that requires a knowledge of pointer variables is the "search" operation. However, this operation is implemented as a private procedure that is required in the implementation of a number of the other operations. The significant point is that we are able to define an interface to list operations without a knowledge of the underlying data structure or the existence of pointers or addresses. The interfaces we define in Listing 4.1 perform operations at the item level rather than the pointer or address level. This is a level of abstraction higher than is usually found in descriptions of the linked list.

To illustrate the use of the list ADT we will consider a simple test program that defines a single list and performs place and remove operations on the items

Listing 4.1 Definition Module for Linked List

```
DEFINITION MODULE listadt;

  FROM elements IMPORT
    (* type *) elementtype;

  EXPORT QUALIFIED
    (* type *) list,
    (* proc *) define, empty, erase, length, ispresent,
               insertafter, deleteafter, insertfront,
               deletefront, place, remove, display;

  TYPE list;

  TYPE displaytype = PROCEDURE ( VAR elementtype );

  TYPE equaltype   = PROCEDURE ( elementtype, elementtype ):
                                 BOOLEAN;

  TYPE lessthantype= PROCEDURE ( elementtype, elementtype ):
                                 BOOLEAN;
```

```
PROCEDURE define
        ( VAR lst : list                          (* out *) );
  (* Create an empty list.  This procedure must be called
     for each new list prior to any other list
     operations.                                             *)


PROCEDURE empty
        ( lst : list                              (* in *)  ) :
          BOOLEAN;
  (* Returns true if the list is empty, otherwise false. *)


PROCEDURE erase
        ( VAR lst : list                          (* in/out *) );
  (* Erases and reinitializes a list.                        *)


PROCEDURE length
        ( lst : list                              (* in *) ) :
          CARDINAL;
  (* Returns the length of the list.                         *)


PROCEDURE ispresent
        ( lst  : list                             (* in *);
          item : elementtype                      (* in *);
         equal : equaltype                        (* in *) ):
          BOOLEAN;
  (* Returns true if item is present in the list.           *)


PROCEDURE insertafter
        ( VAR lst          : list                 (* in/out *);
              previousitem : elementtype          (* in *);
              newitem      : elementtype          (* in *);
              equal        : equaltype            (* in *) );
  (* Inserts into a list an item after a specified item
     in the list.                                            *)


PROCEDURE deleteafter
        ( VAR lst          : list                 (* in/out *);
              previousitem : elementtype          (* in *);
              equal        : equaltype            (* in *) );
  (* Deletes from a list an item after a specified item
     in the list.                                            *)


PROCEDURE insertfront
        ( VAR lst  : list                         (* in/out *);
```

```
             item : elementtype           (* in *) );
    (* Inserts at the front of a list a specified item.  *)


  PROCEDURE deletefront
        ( VAR lst  : list                 (* in/out *) );
    (* Deletes the item at the front of the list.         *)


  PROCEDURE place
        ( VAR lst      : list             (* in/out *);
              item     : elementtype      (* in *);
              equal    : equaltype        (* in *);
              lessthan : lessthantype     (* in *) );
    (* Places an item in a list so that the list is
       maintained as an ordered list.                     *)


  PROCEDURE remove
        ( VAR lst   : list                (* in/out *);
              item  : elementtype         (* in *);
              equal : equaltype           (* in *);
          VAR found : BOOLEAN             (* out *) );
    (* Removes from a list the specified item.  If the item
       is found and removed from the list, then found is
       returned as true, otherwise false.                 *)


  PROCEDURE display
        ( lst         : list              (* in *);
          displayproc : displaytype       (* in *)  );
    (* Displays or processes each item in the list.       *)

END listadt.
```

in the list based on a key field of the items. The program also uses the define, erase, length, and display operations.

In the test program we use the following definition for the items in the list:

```
DEFINITION MODULE elements;

  EXPORT QUALIFIED
    (* type *) elementtype;

  TYPE
       elementtype = RECORD
                       a : CHAR;
                       b : INTEGER
                     END;

END elements.
```

That is, the nodes in the list contain an info field of type elementtype.

We define the procedure lessthan to be a procedure of lessthantype, which defines the order relation for the list. The lessthan procedure uses the b field of elementtype as the key field to order the list in ascending order. The procedure equal of type equaltype defines two items in the list to be equal if their b fields, the key fields, are equal. The displayinfo procedure of type displaytype defines the processing that is to take place on the items in the list. In this example (Listing, 4.2), the processing is simply to print the contents of the item or record in the list.

Listing 4.2 Linked List Test Program

```
MODULE listtest;

  FROM elements IMPORT
    (* type *) elementtype;

  FROM InOut IMPORT
    (* proc *) WriteString, WriteLn, ReadInt, ReadString,
               Read, Write, WriteInt, WriteCard;

  FROM listadt IMPORT
    (* type *) list,
    (* proc *) define, erase, length,
               place, remove, display;

  VAR listofitems : list;
            item : elementtype;
            done : BOOLEAN;


  PROCEDURE printlength;
  BEGIN
    WriteLn;
    WriteString( "The current length of the list is " );
    WriteCard( length( listofitems ), 6 )
  END printlength;


  PROCEDURE displayinfo
          ( VAR info : elementtype (* in/out *) );
```

```
BEGIN
  WriteLn;
  Write( info.a );
  WriteString('  ');
  WriteInt( info.b, 4 )
END displayinfo;


PROCEDURE fetchinfo
        ( VAR info : elementtype                    (* out *) );
BEGIN
  Read( info.a );
  ReadInt( info.b )
END fetchinfo;


PROCEDURE equal
        ( p, q : elementtype                        (* in *) ) :
          BOOLEAN;
BEGIN
  RETURN p.b = q.b
END equal;


PROCEDURE lessthan
        ( p, q : elementtype                        (* in *) ) :
          BOOLEAN;
BEGIN
  RETURN p.b < q.b
END lessthan;


PROCEDURE add;
  VAR item : elementtype;
BEGIN
  WriteLn;   WriteLn;
  WriteString( "Enter information field for new record: ");
  fetchinfo( item );
  place( listofitems, item, equal, lessthan );
END add;


PROCEDURE delete;
  VAR found : BOOLEAN;
BEGIN
  WriteLn;   WriteLn;
  WriteString( "Enter item to key on for deletion: " );
  ReadInt( item.b );
  remove( listofitems, item, equal, found );
```

```
  IF NOT found THEN
    WriteLn;  WriteLn;
    WriteString( "Item entered was not found in list." );
  ELSE
    WriteLn;  WriteLn;
    WriteString( "We removed the item with key field" );
    WriteInt( item.b, 4 );
    WriteString( " from the records." );
  END (* if then *);
END delete;


PROCEDURE menu;
  VAR choice : INTEGER;
BEGIN
  WriteLn;  WriteLn;
  WriteString( "1: Add new record to list." );
  WriteLn;  WriteLn;
  WriteString( "2: Delete record from list." );
  WriteLn;  WriteLn;
  WriteString( "3: Print all records in list." );
  WriteLn;  WriteLn;
  WriteString( "4: Print length of list." );
  WriteLn;  WriteLn;
  WriteString( "5: Exit program." );
  WriteLn;  WriteLn;
  WriteString( "     Enter appropriate choice: " );
  ReadInt( choice );
  CASE choice OF
    1 : add;|
    2 : delete;|
    3 : display( listofitems, displayinfo );|
    4 : printlength;|
    5 : erase( listofitems );
        done := TRUE;
  END (* case *);
END menu;


BEGIN
  done := FALSE;
  define( listofitems );
  REPEAT
    menu
  UNTIL done;
END listtest.
```

4.1.4 Common Variants of the Linked List

Lists can be classified as singly linked or doubly linked, linearly linked or circularly linked, and with or without a header node. These list attributes are independent, resulting in eight common variants of the linked list. Each variant has advantages in certain situations. In this section, we briefly describe these variants. Later in this chapter, we will use some of these variants in our implementation of the list ADT.

The lists described so far in this chapter are singly linked, linearly linked lists with no header nodes. In section 4.1.1, we found that the inability to back up in a list influenced our design of the search, deleteafter, place, and remove operations. Another approach is to place two pointers in each node, one pointing to the next node in the list and the other pointing to the previous node in the list. This type of list structure, called a doubly linked list, is illustrated in Figure 4.6.

We pay a data storage price for such a structure, since each node is larger. Specifically, each node now contains an extra pointer field. Depending on the operation to be performed, we may also incur an execution speed penalty because of additional instructions required to manipulate the extra pointer field. However, the ability to move and search both ways in a list can simplify many operations, resulting in saving both execution time and program storage space.

Some operations may require us to treat the last node of the list differently from the others because the last node does not point to another node. If we permit the last node to point to the first node of the list, we have a circularly linked list (Figure 4.7). Exercise 2.8 used the queue as a special case of a circularly linked list. Note that the end of the circularly linked list can be recognized as the node that points to the same node as the list variable itself.

A circularly linked list may also be doubly linked, as shown in Figure 4.8.

Several of the operations defined in section 4.1.1 treat the front of the list as a special case. For example, insertfront and deletefront were specifically designed for the front of the list. Insertafter and deleteafter are not legal operations on the front of the list because both require a prior node. The empty list is also a special case, since it is a list with no nodes.

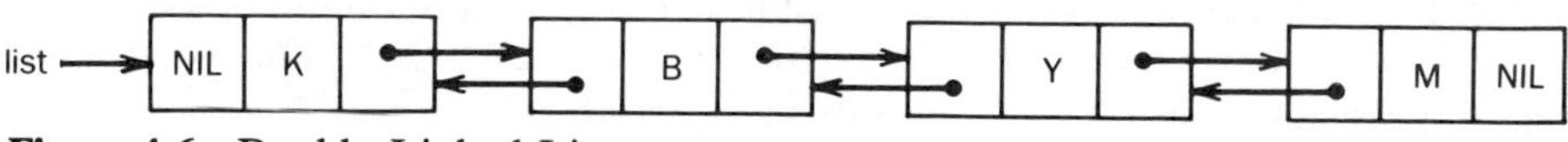

Figure 4.6 Doubly Linked List

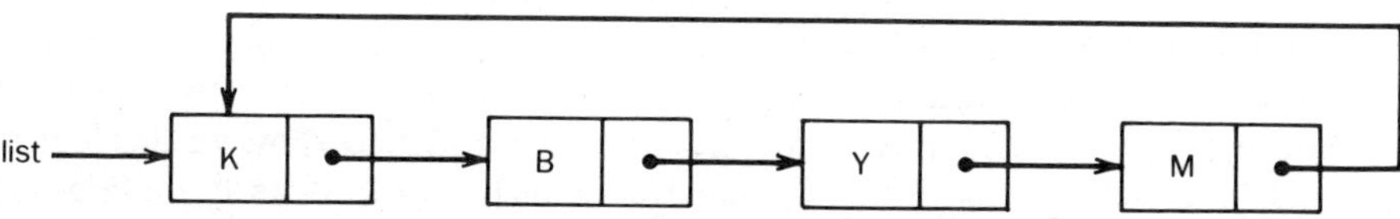

Figure 4.7 Singly Linked, Circularly Linked List

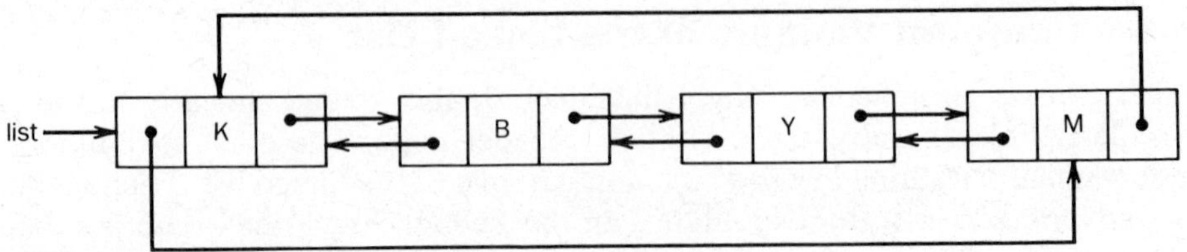

Figure 4.8 Doubly Linked, Circularly Linked List

The use of a header node or list header in a list is sometimes desirable to eliminate these special cases. A header node does not represent an item in the list and is always present even for the empty list. The information field of the header node may contain a special header value or may be undefined. For example, the header node could contain the number of items in the list. The insert and delete operations must then modify the header node to reflect the new number of items in the list after these operations are performed. The length operation would simply return this header value rather than traversing the entire list and counting the number of items encountered. The header node could also contain information relating to the size of the items in the list or a pointer to the last node in the list or a pointer to the current node in the list during a traversal process. As we will see below, the header node may be useful in simplifying various operations such as the search operation.

Figure 4.9 shows six lists with header nodes. In Figure 4.9*a*, a singly linked, circularly linked list, the info field of the header node is unused. Figures 4.9*b* and 4.9*c* present a singly linked list with a header node containing the number of items in the list. The empty list is no longer represented by a nil pointer, but is a list with a single header node. Figures 4.9*d* and 4.9*e* illustrate a doubly linked, circularly linked list with the header node containing the number of items in the list; Figure 4.9*d* is the representation for the empty list. Finally, Figure 4.9*f* shows a singly linked list with a header node containing a pointer to the last node in the list. Such a header node might be useful in the implementation of a queue.

If one is implementing a list with associated operations for a specific application, what variants should be used? No general answer can be given to such a question, since the choice of list variants depends on the operations required on the list. The software developer should determine the special cases that are difficult to handle and then choose the variant that makes the implementation of the operations as simple as possible.

Let us now consider some of the operations defined earlier and reexamine their implementation when a header node is used. The while loop of the search operation of section 4.1.1 requires the testing of two conditions each time around the loop: that the end of the list has not yet been reached and that the item has not yet been found. This algorithm can be speeded up if we can eliminate one of these tests. Specifically, we would like to remove the test for the end of the list by guaranteeing that the search will always be successful. This can be done by placing a copy of the item sought at the end of the list. If

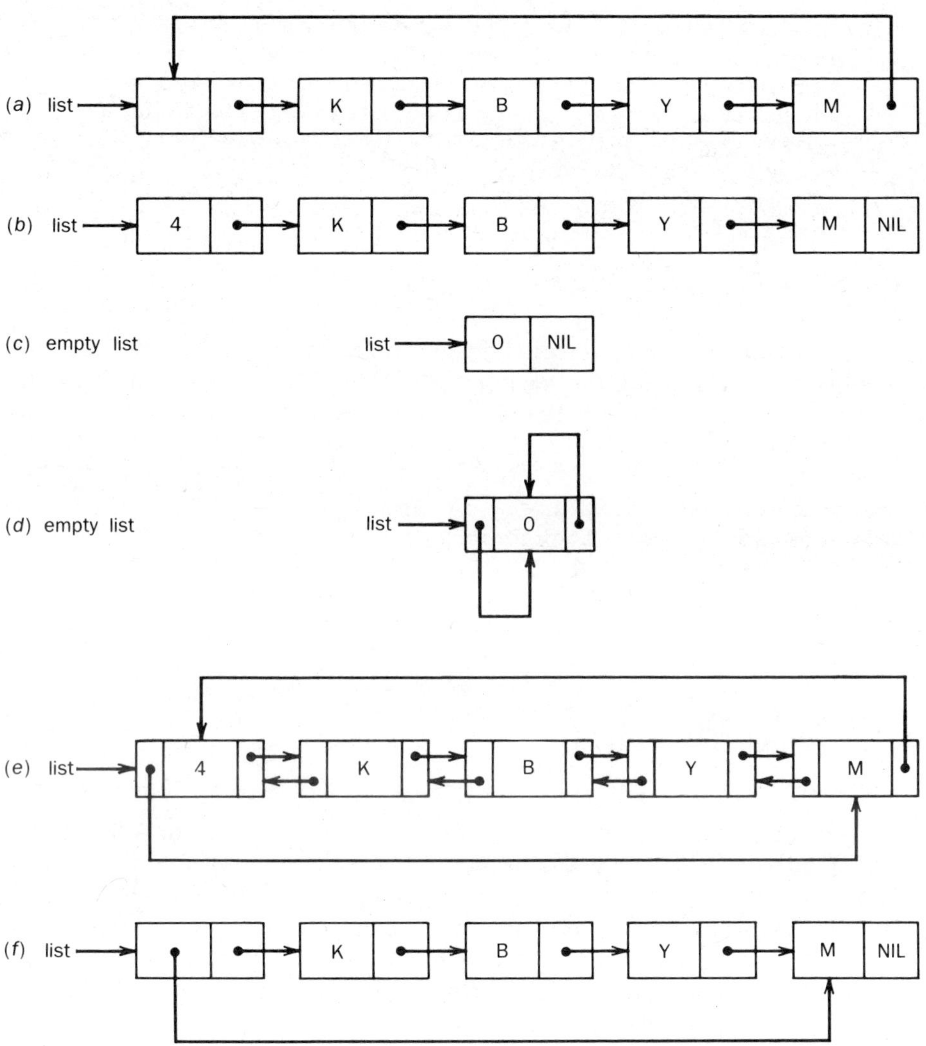

Figure 4.9 Lists with Header Nodes

the search is successful, we will find the item before we reach the end of the list; otherwise we will find the item at the end of the list. If we can distinguish these two cases, we will have a more efficient search algorithm.

Suppose we define a circularly linked list with a header node. The header node is conceptually at the end of the list, since it immediately follows the last node in the list. If we place the item sought in the info field of the header node, we can guarantee that the item sought will be in the list. We will begin our search at the node that immediately follows the header node. If we find the item in the header node, we will be able to distinguish this case, since the itemnode will have the same value as the list variable. The new search procedure is:

```
Procedure search( list, item, itemnode )
  set info field of header node to item
  set itemnode to the next field of the header node
  while item not equal to info field of itemnode do
    set itemnode to next field of itemnode
  end while
  if itemnode equals list
  then
    set itemnode to nil
end if
```

As a second example, we will consider deletion from a doubly linked list with a header node, using the search procedure just defined. Note that the algorithm presented does not treat deletion at the front or end of the list as special cases.

```
Procedure delete( list, item, itemnode )
  search( list, item, itemnode )
  if itemnode is not nil
  then
    set next field of the node that precedes itemnode to the
      next field of itemnode
    set previous field of the node that follows itemnode to
      the previous field of itemnode
    freenode( itemnode )
  end if
```

When using a linked list with a header node, we may need to define a new type of node to accommodate the header information that is different from the list nodes. For example, if the header node is to have an info field that contains the current length of the list, separate type declarations will be required for the header node and the list nodes. Alternatively, a variant record node declaration could be used. These options will be illustrated in the sections that follow.

4.2 The List Implemented as a Singly Linked List Using Arrays

Our first implementation of a list will be a singly linked list residing in an array of records. Each record will represent a node in the list and will contain two fields; an info field containing an item of type elementtype specified by the user and a field containing a pointer to the next node in the list. Specifically, we will use the following declarations:

```
CONST          nil = 0;
       numbernodes = 100;

TYPE nodepointer = [ 0..numbernodes ];
```

```
            node = RECORD
                     info : elementtype;
                     next : nodepointer;
                   END;

            list = nodepointer;

      VAR nodepool : ARRAY [ 1..numbernodes ] OF node;
```

As before, we assume that elementtype is imported from a module elements and that it has been appropriately defined by the user for the particular problem at hand.

Notice that we have explicitly defined the node pool to be an array of nodes. The getnode and freenode operations must be appropriately defined to get nodes from and to return nodes to this node pool. However, to do this we must somehow initialize the node pool. An obvious initialization is to make the node pool a linked list with an available pointer pointing to the first available node in the list. Figure 4.10 illustrates the initial configuration of the node pool for numbernodes = 10.

Let us now consider the getnode and freenode operations in more detail: the getnode operation removes the node at the front of the available list, and freenode returns a node to the front of the available list. These operations on the available list result in this list behaving like a stack.

Only one error condition can arise, namely: all the nodes are currently in use (hence it is impossible to allocate additional nodes). This situation, which arises when the available list is empty, is the result of insufficient storage allocation to the node pool.

The getnode and freenode operations can be described as follows:

```
Procedure getnode () : nodepointer;
  if available is empty
  then
    indicate that no nodes are available
  else
    set newnode to available
    set available to the next field of available
    return newnode
  end if
```

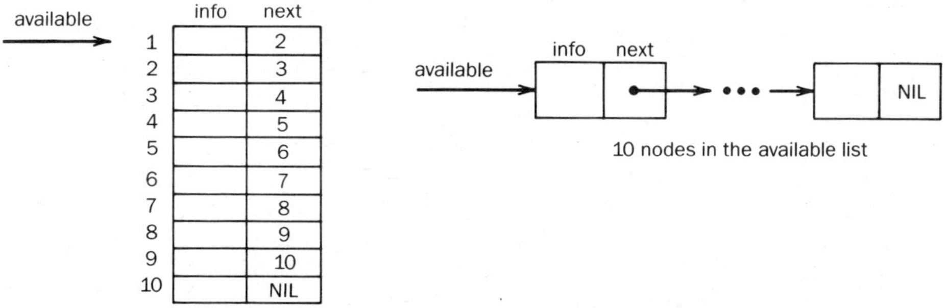

available →

	info	next
1		2
2		3
3		4
4		5
5		6
6		7
7		8
8		9
9		10
10		NIL

available → [info | next •] → ••• → [| NIL]

10 nodes in the available list

Figure 4.10 The Initial Node Pool

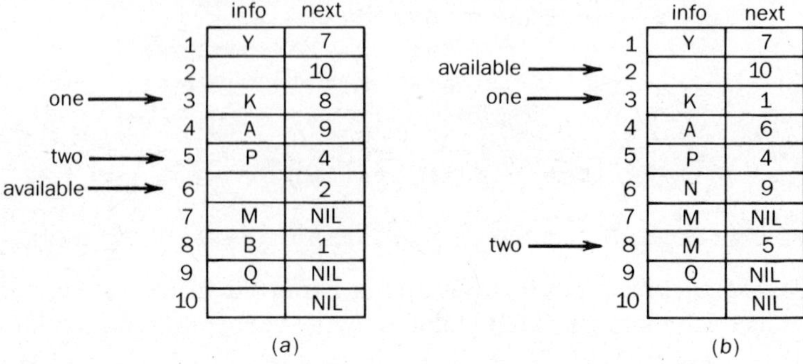

Figure 4.11 Several Lists Residing in a Common Node Pool

```
Procedure freenode( oldnode )
  set the next field of oldnode to available
  set available to oldnode
```

Our list implementation must permit the user of the list ADT to declare multiple objects of type list in the user's main program. Will the operations defined permit us to do this? The answer is yes, since each object of type list will have a unique pointer to the first node in the list and all the defined operations have a parameter to indicate which list the called operation is to be performed on. In Figure 4.11*a*, we illustrate two lists residing in the original node pool. Note that there is also a third list, the list of available nodes. Figure 4.11*b* illustrates these two lists after deletion of 'B' from list one and insertion of 'M' at the front of list two and 'N' after 'A' in list two. These operations are performed in the order described.

Finally, we present the complete implementation in Listing 4.3.

Listing 4.3 Implementation Module for Linked List Residing in an Array of Records

```
IMPLEMENTATION MODULE listadt;
  (* This module implements a singly-linked list that
     resides in an array of records data structure.          *)

  FROM elements IMPORT
    (* type *) elementtype;

  FROM InOut IMPORT
    (* proc *) WriteString, WriteLn;

  CONST nil = 0;
        numbernodes = 100;
```

```
TYPE nodepointer = [ 0..numbernodes ];

     node = RECORD
              info : elementtype;
              next : nodepointer
            END;

     list = nodepointer;

VAR
    nodepool  : ARRAY[ 1..numbernodes ] OF node;
    count     : CARDINAL;
    available : nodepointer;


PROCEDURE getnode () :
          nodepointer;
(* This procedure obtains a node from the node pool and
   returns a pointer to the node.                          *)
  VAR newnode : nodepointer;
BEGIN
  IF available = nil
  THEN
    WriteLn;
    WriteString( "No storage space available." );
    HALT
  ELSE
    newnode   := available;
    available := nodepool[ available ].next;
    RETURN newnode
  END (* if then *)
END getnode;


PROCEDURE freenode
          ( VAR oldnode : nodepointer      (* in/out *) );
(* This procedure returns oldnode to the node pool.        *)
BEGIN
  nodepool[ oldnode ].next := available;
  available := oldnode
END freenode;


PROCEDURE insertaftererror;
BEGIN
  WriteLn;
  WriteString( "Illegal insert after operation." );
  WriteLn;
  WriteString( "Item specified was not found in list." )
END insertaftererror;
```

```
PROCEDURE deleteaftererror;
BEGIN
  WriteLn;
  WriteString( "Illegal delete after operation." );
  WriteLn;
  WriteString( "Item specified was not found in list." )
END deleteaftererror;


PROCEDURE deletefronterror;
BEGIN
  WriteLn;
  WriteString( "Illegal delete front operation." );
  WriteLn;
  WriteString( "The list is empty." )
END deletefronterror;


PROCEDURE define
          ( VAR lst : list                         (* in/out *) );
BEGIN
  lst := nil
END define;


PROCEDURE empty
          ( lst : list                             (* in *) ) :
            BOOLEAN;
BEGIN
  RETURN lst = nil
END empty;


PROCEDURE erase
          ( VAR lst : list                         (* in/out *) );
  VAR nextnode, nodetodelete : nodepointer;
BEGIN
  nextnode := lst;
  WHILE nextnode <> nil DO
    nodetodelete := nextnode;
    nextnode := nodepool[ nextnode ].next;
    freenode( nodetodelete )
  END (* while loop *);
  lst := nil
END erase;


PROCEDURE length
          ( lst : list                             (* in *) ) :
            CARDINAL;
  VAR nextnode : nodepointer;
      count : CARDINAL;
```

```
BEGIN
  count := 0;
  nextnode := lst;
  WHILE nextnode <> nil DO
    count := count + 1;
    nextnode := nodepool[ nextnode ].next
  END (* while loop *);
  RETURN count
END length;


PROCEDURE search
         (     lst      : list               (* in *);
               item     : elementtype        (* in *);
           VAR itemnode : nodepointer        (* out *);
               equal    : equaltype          (* in *) );
  (* This procedure searches a list for a node that has
     the specified item.  It returns a pointer to the node
     if the item is found.  If the item is not found, then
     it returns a nil pointer.                             *)
BEGIN
  itemnode := lst;
  WHILE ( nodepool[ itemnode ].next <> nil ) AND
        ( NOT equal( item, nodepool[itemnode].info ) ) DO
    itemnode  := nodepool[ itemnode ].next
  END (* while loop *);
END search;


PROCEDURE ispresent
         ( lst  : list                        (* in *);
           item : elementtype                 (* in *);
           equal: equaltype                   (* in *) ) :
           BOOLEAN;
  VAR itemnode : nodepointer;
BEGIN
  search( lst, item, itemnode, equal );
  RETURN itemnode # NIL
END ispresent;


PROCEDURE insertafter
         ( VAR lst          : list        (* in/out *);
               previousitem : elementtype (* in *);
               newitem      : elementtype (* in *);
               equal        : equaltype   (* in *) );
  VAR previousnode, newnode : nodepointer;
BEGIN
  search( lst, previousitem, previousnode, equal );
  IF previousnode = nil THEN
    insertaftererror
  ELSE
```

```
    newnode := getnode();
    nodepool[newnode].info := newitem;
    nodepool[newnode].next := nodepool[previousnode].next;
    nodepool[previousnode ].next := newnode
  END (* if then *)
END insertafter;


PROCEDURE deleteafter
          ( VAR lst           : list        (* in/out *);
                previousitem : elementtype (* in *);
                equal        : equaltype   (* out *) );
  VAR previousnode, oldnode : nodepointer;
BEGIN
  search ( lst, previousitem, previousnode, equal );
  IF previousnode = nil THEN
  THEN
  ELSE
    oldnode := nodepool[ previousnode ].next;
    nodepool[previousnode].next := nodepool[oldnode].next;
    freenode( oldnode )
  END (* if then *)
END deleteafter;


PROCEDURE insertfront
          ( VAR lst  : list                 (* in/out *);
                item : elementtype          (* in *) );
  VAR newnode : nodepointer;
BEGIN
  newnode := getnode();
  nodepool[ newnode ].info := item;
  nodepool[ newnode ].next := lst;
  lst := newnode
END insertfront;


PROCEDURE deletefront
          ( VAR lst  : list                 (* in/out *) );
  VAR oldnode : nodepointer;
BEGIN
  IF empty ( lst ) THEN
    deletefronterror
  ELSE
    oldnode := lst;
    lst := nodepool[ oldnode ].next;
    freenode( oldnode )
  END (* if then *)
END deletefront;
```

```
PROCEDURE place
        ( VAR lst  : list                         (* in/out *);
              item : elementtype                  (* in *);
              equal : equaltype                   (* in *);
              lessthan : lessthantype             (* in *) );
  VAR found                          : BOOLEAN;
      currentnode, previousnode, newnode  : nodepointer;
BEGIN
  found        := FALSE;
  currentnode  := lst;
  previousnode := nil;
  WHILE ( currentnode <> nil ) AND ( NOT found ) DO
    IF lessthan( item, nodepool[ currentnode ].info )
    THEN
      found := TRUE
    ELSE
      previousnode := currentnode;
      currentnode  := nodepool[ currentnode ].next
    END (* if then *)
  END (* while loop *);
  IF previousnode = nil THEN
    insertfront( lst, item )
  ELSE
    newnode := getnode () ;
    nodepool[ newnode ].info := item;
    nodepool[ newnode ].next := currentnode;
    nodepool[ previousnode ].next := newnode;
  END (* if then *)
END place;


PROCEDURE remove
        ( VAR lst   : list                        (* in/out *);
              item  : elementtype                 (* in *);
              equal : equaltype                   (* in *);
          VAR found : BOOLEAN                     (* out *) );
  VAR currentnode, previousnode : nodepointer;
BEGIN
  found        := FALSE;
  previousnode := nil;
  currentnode  := lst;
  WHILE ( currentnode <> nil ) AND ( NOT found ) DO
    IF equal( item, nodepool[ currentnode ].info )
    THEN
      found := TRUE
    ELSE
      previousnode := currentnode;
      currentnode  := nodepool[ currentnode ].next
    END (* if then *)
```

```
    END (* while loop *);
    IF found THEN
      IF currentnode = lst THEN
        deletefront( lst )
      ELSE
        nodepool[ previousnode ].next := nodepool
          [ currentnode ].next;
        freenode( currentnode );
      END (* if then *)
    END (* if then *)
  END remove;


  PROCEDURE display
             (lst : list                          (* in *);
              displayproc : displaytype           (* in *) );
    VAR currentnode : nodepointer;
  BEGIN
    IF empty( lst ) THEN
      WriteLn;  WriteLn;
      WriteString( "The list is empty." )
    ELSE
      currentnode := lst;
      WHILE currentnode <> nil DO
        displayproc( nodepool[ currentnode ].info );
        currentnode := nodepool[ currentnode ].next
      END (* while loop *)
    END (* if then *)
  END display;

BEGIN
  (* The following code initializes the list of available
     nodes.  It is executed automatically prior to any
     other procedures defined in this module.                *)
  FOR count := 1 TO numbernodes - 1 DO
    nodepool[ count ].next := count + 1
  END (* for loop *);
  nodepool[ numbernodes ].next := nil;
  available := 1
END listadt.
```

4.3 The List Implemented as a Singly Linked List Using Pointer Variables

The dynamic allocation features of Modula-2 can be used to implement the list. As we will see, this totally different structure for the list has very little effect on the implementation details except for that dictated by the syntax of the language. The most significant changes occur in getnode and freenode.

When we use the dynamic features of Modula-2, we do not need to explicitly define the node pool as we did when the node pool was defined as an array of nodes. This is because the node pool automatically consists of all the available storage in the computer for dynamic variables. This storage area is sometimes referred to as the heap. Modula-2 provides us with the operations NEW and DISPOSE to get nodes from the heap and to return nodes to the heap. The getnode operation is now simply defined as:

```
Procedure getnode () : nodepointer
  NEW( newnode )
  return newnode
```

and freenode becomes:

```
Procedure freenode( oldnode )
  DISPOSE( oldnode )
```

It is possible that we will still run out of nodes by using up all the available memory in the heap. Our getnode procedure does not check for this possibility, so if this situation arises an execution error will occur, indicating that no more dynamic storage is available.

The complete implementation is presented in Listing 4.4. Note that the definition module that defines the interface to the operations for the list is unchanged for this new implementation.

Listing 4.4 Implementation Module for Linked List Using Dynamic Allocation

```
IMPLEMENTATION MODULE listadt;

  FROM elements IMPORT
    (* type *) elementtype;

  FROM InOut IMPORT
    (* proc *) WriteString, WriteLn;

  FROM Storage IMPORT
    (* proc *) ALLOCATE, DEALLOCATE;


  TYPE nodepointer = POINTER TO node;

       node = RECORD
                info : elementtype;
                next : nodepointer
              END;

       list = nodepointer;
```

```
PROCEDURE getnode () :
          nodepointer;
(* This procedure makes a node and returns a pointer to
   the node.                                           *)
  VAR newnode : nodepointer;
BEGIN
  NEW (newnode);
  RETURN newnode
END getnode;


PROCEDURE freenode
          ( VAR oldnode : nodepointer     (* in/out *) );
(* This procedure deallocates storage associated with
   oldnode.                                            *)
BEGIN
  DISPOSE (oldnode)
END freenode;


PROCEDURE insertaftererror;
BEGIN
  WriteLn;
  WriteString( "Illegal insert after operation." );
  WriteLn;
  WriteString( "Item specified was not found in list." )
END insertaftererror;


PROCEDURE deleteaftererror;
BEGIN
  WriteLn;
  WriteString( "Illegal delete after operation." );
  WriteLn;
  WriteString( "Item specified was not found in the list.")
END deleteaftererror;


PROCEDURE deletefronterror;
BEGIN
  WriteLn;
  WriteString( "Illegal delete front operation." );
  WriteLn;
  WriteString( "The list is empty." )
END deletefronterror;


PROCEDURE define
          ( VAR lst : list                  (* in/out *) );
BEGIN
  lst := NIL
END define;
```

```
PROCEDURE empty
          ( lst : list                          (* in *)   ) :
            BOOLEAN;
BEGIN
  RETURN lst = NIL
END empty;



PROCEDURE erase
          ( VAR lst : list                      (* in/out *) );
  VAR nextnode, nodetodelete : nodepointer;
BEGIN
  nextnode := lst;
  WHILE nextnode <> NIL DO
    nodetodelete := nextnode;
    nextnode := nextnode^.next;
    freenode( nodetodelete )
  END (* while loop *);
  lst := NIL
END erase;



PROCEDURE length
          ( lst : list                          (* in *) ) :
            CARDINAL;
  VAR nextnode : nodepointer;
          count : CARDINAL;
BEGIN
  count := 0;
  nextnode := lst;
  WHILE nextnode <> NIL DO
    count := count + 1;
    nextnode := nextnode^.next
  END (* while loop *);
  RETURN count
END length;



PROCEDURE search
          (     lst      : list                 (* in *);
                item     : elementtype          (* in *);
            VAR itemnode : nodepointer          (* out *);
                equal    : equaltype            (* in *) );
BEGIN
  itemnode := lst;
  WHILE ( itemnode <> NIL ) AND
        ( NOT equal( item, itemnode^.info ) ) DO
    itemnode := itemnode^.next
  END (* while loop *)
END search;
```

```
PROCEDURE ispresent
          ( lst  : list                           (* in *);
            item : elementtype                    (* in *);
           equal : equaltype                      (* in *) ):
            BOOLEAN;
  VAR itemnode : nodepointer;
BEGIN
  search( lst, item, itemnode, equal );
  RETURN itemnode # NIL
END ispresent;


PROCEDURE insertafter
          ( VAR lst          : list        (* in/out *);
                previousitem : elementtype (* in *);
                newitem      : elementtype (* in *);
                equal        : equaltype   (* in *)  );
  VAR previousnode, newnode : nodepointer;
BEGIN
  search ( lst, previousitem, previousnode, equal );
  IF previousnode = NIL
  THEN
    insertaftererror
  ELSE
    newnode := getnode();
    newnode^.info := newitem;
    newnode^.next := previousnode^.next;
    previousnode^.next := newnode
  END (* if then *)
END insertafter;


PROCEDURE deleteafter
          ( VAR lst          : list        (* in/out *);
                previousitem : elementtype (* in *);
                equal        : equaltype   (* in *) );
  VAR previousnode, oldnode : nodepointer;
BEGIN
  search ( lst, previousitem, previousnode, equal );
  IF previousnode = NIL
  THEN
    deleteaftererror
  ELSE
    oldnode := previousnode^.next;
    previousnode^.next := oldnode^.next;
    freenode( oldnode )
  END (* if then *)
END deleteafter;
```

```
PROCEDURE insertfront
          ( VAR lst  : list                      (* in/out *);
                item : elementtype               (* in *) );
  VAR newnode : nodepointer;
BEGIN
  newnode := getnode();
  newnode^.info := item;
  newnode^.next := lst;
  lst := newnode
END insertfront;


PROCEDURE deletefront
          ( VAR lst  : list                      (* in/out *) );
  VAR oldnode : nodepointer;
BEGIN
  IF empty (lst) THEN
    deletefronterror
  ELSE
    oldnode := lst;
    lst := oldnode^.next;
    freenode( oldnode )
  END (* if then *)
END deletefront;


PROCEDURE place
          ( VAR lst      : list                  (* in/out *);
                item     : elementtype           (* in *);
                equal    : equaltype             (* in *);
                lessthan : lessthantype          (* in *) );
  VAR found : BOOLEAN;
      currentnode, previousnode, newnode : nodepointer;
BEGIN
  found        := FALSE;
  currentnode  := lst;
  previousnode := NIL;
  WHILE (currentnode <> NIL) AND (NOT found) DO
    IF lessthan( item, currentnode^.info ) THEN
      found := TRUE
    ELSE
       previousnode := currentnode;
       currentnode  := currentnode^.next
     END (* if then *)
   END (* while loop *);
  IF previousnode = NIL THEN
    insertfront( lst, item )
  ELSE
    newnode := getnode();
    newnode ^.info := item;
```

```
    newnode^.next := currentnode
    previousnode^.next := newnode;
  END (* if then *)
END place;


PROCEDURE remove
          ( VAR lst   : list                      (* in/out *);
                item  : elementtype               (* in *);
                equal : equaltype                 (* in *);
            VAR found : BOOLEAN                   (* out *) );
  VAR currentnode, previousnode : nodepointer;
BEGIN
  found        := FALSE;
  previousnode := NIL;
  currentnode  := lst;
  WHILE (currentnode <> NIL) AND (NOT found) DO
    IF equal( item, currentnode^.info ) THEN
      found := TRUE
    ELSE
      previousnode := currentnode;
      currentnode  := currentnode^.next
    END (* if then *)
  END (* while loop *);
  IF found THEN
    IF currentnode = lst THEN
      deletefront( lst )
    ELSE
      previousnode^.next := currentnode^.next;
      freenode( currentnode );
    END (* if then *)
  END (* if then *)
END remove;


PROCEDURE display
          ( lst         : list                (* in *);
            displayproc : displaytype         (* in *) );
  VAR currentnode : nodepointer;
BEGIN
  IF empty( lst ) THEN
    WriteLn; WriteLn;
    WriteString( 'The list is empty.' )
  ELSE
    currentnode := lst;
    WHILE currentnode <> NIL DO
      displayproc( currentnode^.info );
      currentnode := currentnode^.next
    END (* while loop *)
```

```
    END (* if then *)
  END display;

END listadt.
```

4.4 The List Implemented as a Doubly Linked List Using Pointer Variables

In this section, we implement the list as a doubly linked circular list using dynamic allocation. Since a doubly linked list permits us to move in both directions in the list, we define the operations "insertbefore", "deletebefore", "insertrear", and "deleterear", which take advantage of this capability. Whereas the display traversed the list from beginning to end and performed a user-defined operation on each node as it was encountered, in this implementation, we use the "displayforward" and "displaybackward" operations, as defined below.

The interface to the doubly linked list implementation is identical to that defined in Listing 4.1 except for the new operations specified in the preceding paragraph. Listing 4.5 presents only the interface to these new operations.

Listing 4.5 Definition Module for Doubly Linked List

```
DEFINITION MODULE listadt;

  FROM elements IMPORT
    (* type *) elementtype;

  EXPORT QUALIFIED
    (* type *) list,
    (* proc *) define, empty, erase, length, ispresent,
               insertafter, insertbefore, deleteafter,
               deletebefore, insertfront, insertrear,
               deletefront, deleterear, place, remove,
               displayforward, displaybackward;

   (* The interface definition for all operations and types
      that are not explicitly defined below are identical to
      those given in Listing 4.1.                          *)


  PROCEDURE insertbefore
          ( VAR lst          : list        (* in/out *);
```

```
                nextitem     : elementtype (* in *);
                newitem      : elementtype (* in *);
                equal        : equaltype   (* in *) );
   (* Inserts into a list an item after a specified item
      in the list.                                        *)


 PROCEDURE deletebefore
           ( VAR lst         : list        (* in/out *);
                nextitem     : elementtype (* in *);
                equal        : equaltype   (* in *) );
   (* Deletes from a list an item after a specified item
      in the list.                                        *)


 PROCEDURE ispresent
           ( lst  : list                   (* in *);
             item : elementtype            (* in *);
            equal : equaltype              (* in *) ):
             BOOLEAN;
   (* Returns true if item is present in the list.        *)



 PROCEDURE insertrear
           ( VAR lst  : list               (* in/out *);
                 item : elementtype        (* in *) );
   (* Inserts at the rear of a list a specified item.     *)


 PROCEDURE deleterear
           ( VAR lst  : list               (* in/out *) );
   (* Deletes the item at the rear of the list.           *)


 PROCEDURE displayforward
           ( lst          : list           (* in *);
             displayproc : displaytype     (* in *)  );
   (* Displays or processes each item in the list.        *)


 PROCEDURE displaybackward
           ( lst          : list           (* in *);
             displayproc : displaytype     (* in *)  );
   (* Displays or processes each item in the list.        *)

END listadt.
```

Notice that the user interface gives no indication of the implementation details. In fact, the user interface is identical to the interface for the corresponding operations defined for a singly linked list.

Our implementation uses a header node that contains the current length of the list. This means that the info field of the header node contains a single variable of type CARDINAL, whereas the remaining nodes in the list contain an info field of type elementtype, which is imported and defined by the user. Our approach is to define a variant record structure that can accommodate nodes of both types. Specifically, we make the following declarations:

```
TYPE nodepointer = POINTER TO node;
     nodetype    = ( headernode, listnode );
     node = RECORD
              prior : nodepointer;
              CASE kind ; nodetype OF
                headernode : number : CARDINAL |
                listnode   : info   : elementtype
              END (* case *);
              next  : nodepointer
            END (* end *);
      list = nodepointer;
```

The empty list will consist of only a header node with a zero value for its number field. Figure 4.12 illustrates the empty list and a list with three nodes.

Our getnode operation needs to be able to get either a header node or a listnode. This is easily achieved by using a parameter in the call to getnode. Specifically, if k is of type nodetype then:

```
Procedure getnode ( k ) : nodepointer
  NEW ( newnode )
  set kind field of newnode to k
  return newnode
```

The freenode operation is identical to that defined in section 4.3.

Before proceeding with the implementation details, let us examine the

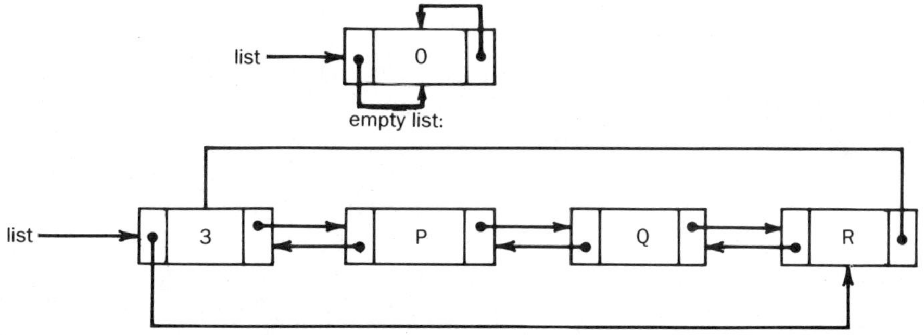

Figure 4.12 Doubly Linked List

insertafter and deleteafter operations. For a doubly linked list with a header node that contains the number of items in the list, we must set the necessary pointer fields and update the header node. The insertafter operation can be described as follows:

```
Procedure insertafter( list, prioritem, newitem )
  find priornode in the list that contains prioritem
  newnode ← getnode( listnode )
  set the info field of newnode to newitem
  set the prior field of newnode to priornode
  set the next field of newnode to the next field of
      priornode
  set the prior field of the node that immediately follows
      priornode to newnode
  set the next field of priornode to newnode
  update the length counter in the header node
```

The insertafter operation is illustrated in Figure 4.13, where we insert 'S' after 'Q'.

Let us now consider the deleteafter operation. A description of this operation is:

```
Procedure deleteafter ( list, prioritem )
  find priornode in the list that contains prioritem
  set oldnode to next field of priornode
  set next field of priornode to next field of oldnode
  set prior field of node following oldnode to priornode
  update the length counter in the header node
  freenode( oldnode )
```

This operation is illustrated in Figure 4.14, where we delete the node after the node that contains 'P'.

In Listing 4.6 we present the implementation details for the doubly linked circular list with a header node that contains the number of items in the list. Our

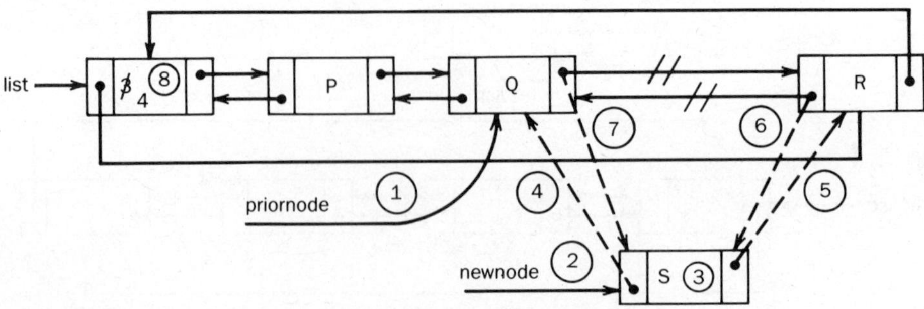

Figure 4.13 The Insertafter Operation in a Doubly Linked List

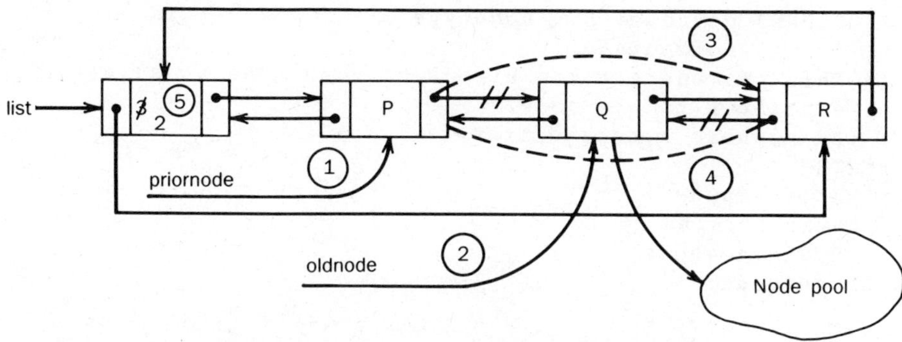

Figure 4.14 The Deleteafter Operation in a Doubly Linked List

implementation mimics the preceding implementations, hence may not take full advantage of the data structure used for the list.

Listing 4.6 Implementation of Doubly Linked List with Header Node

```
IMPLEMENTATION MODULE listadt;
  (* This module implements a doubly-linked list with
     a header node.  The header node contains the current
     length of the list.                                       *)

  FROM elements IMPORT
    (* type *) elementtype;

  FROM InOut IMPORT
    (* proc *) WriteString, WriteLn;

  FROM Storage IMPORT
    (* proc *) ALLOCATE, DEALLOCATE;


  TYPE nodepointer = POINTER TO node;

       nodetype    = ( headernode, listnode );

       node = RECORD
                prior : nodepointer;
                CASE kind : nodetype OF
                  headernode : number : CARDINAL |
                  listnode   : info   : elementtype
                END (* case *);
                next  : nodepointer
              END (* end *);

       list = nodepointer;
```

```
PROCEDURE getnode( k : nodetype              (* in *) ) :
          nodepointer;
(* This procedure makes a node of node type k and returns
   a pointer to the node.                                  *)
  VAR newnode : nodepointer;
BEGIN
  NEW( newnode );
  newnode^.kind := k;
  RETURN newnode
END getnode;


PROCEDURE freenode
          ( VAR oldnode : nodepointer      (* in/out *) );
(* This procedure deallocates storage associated with
   oldnode.                                                *)
BEGIN
  DISPOSE( oldnode )
END freenode;


PROCEDURE insertaftererror;
BEGIN
  WriteLn;
  WriteString( "Illegal insert after operation." );
  WriteLn;
  WriteString( "Item specified was not found in list." )
END insertaftererror;


PROCEDURE deleteaftererror;
BEGIN
  WriteLn;
  WriteString( "Illegal delete after operation." );
  WriteLn;
  WriteString( "Item specified was not found in list." )
END deleteaftererror;


PROCEDURE deletefronterror;
BEGIN
  WriteLn;
  WriteString( "Illegal delete front operation." );
  WriteLn;
  WriteString( "The list is empty." )
END deletefronterror;


PROCEDURE define
          ( VAR lst : list                 (* in/out *) );
```

```
BEGIN
  lst := getnode( headernode );
  lst^.prior  := lst;
  lst^.next   := lst;
  lst^.number := 0
END define;


PROCEDURE empty
          ( lst : list                         (* in *)   ) :
            BOOLEAN;
BEGIN
  RETURN lst^.number = 0;
END empty;


PROCEDURE erase
          ( VAR lst : list                     (* in/out *) );
  VAR nextnode, nodetodelete : nodepointer;
BEGIN
  nextnode := lst^.next;
  WHILE nextnode <> lst DO
    nodetodelete := nextnode;
    nextnode := nextnode^.next;
    DISPOSE( nodetodelete )
  END (* while loop *);
  DISPOSE( nextnode );
  define( lst )
END erase;


PROCEDURE length
          ( lst : list                         (* in *) ) :
            CARDINAL;
BEGIN
  RETURN lst^.number
END length;


PROCEDURE search
          (     lst      : list                (* in *);
                item     : elementtype         (* in *);
            VAR itemnode : nodepointer         (* out *);
                equal    : equaltype           (* in *) );
  (* This procedure searches a list for a node that has
     the specified item.  It returns a pointer to the node
     if the item is found.  If the item is not found and
     the list is not empty, then it returns a NIL pointer.
     If the list is empty, it returns a pointer to the
     header node in the list.                             *)
```

```
BEGIN
  itemnode := lst^.next;
  WHILE ( itemnode^.next <> lst ) AND
        ( NOT equal( item, itemnode^.info ) ) DO
    itemnode := itemnode^.next
  END (* while loop *);
END search;


PROCEDURE ispresent
          ( lst  : list                              (* in *);
            item : elementtype                       (* in *);
           equal : equaltype                         (* in *) ):
            BOOLEAN;
  VAR itemnode : nodepointer;
BEGIN
  search( lst, item, itemnode, equal );
  RETURN itemnode # NIL
END ispresent;


PROCEDURE insertafter
          ( VAR lst            : list            (* in/out *);
                prioritem      : elementtype     (* in *);
                newitem        : elementtype     (* in *);
                equal          : equaltype       (* in *) );
  VAR priornode, newnode : nodepointer;
BEGIN
  search ( lst, prioritem, priornode, equal );
  IF priornode = lst THEN
    insertaftererror
  ELSE
    newnode := getnode( listnode );
    newnode^.info  := newitem;
    newnode^.prior := priornode;
    newnode^.next  := priornode^.next;
    priornode^.next^.prior := newnode;
    priornode^.next := newnode;
    (* Update the length counter in the header node.     *)
    INC( lst^.number )
  END (* if then *)
END insertafter;


PROCEDURE insertbefore
          ( VAR lst            : list          (* in/out *);
                nextitem       : elementtype (* in *);
                newitem        : elementtype (* in *);
                equal          : equaltype   (* in *) );
```

```
BEGIN
  (* We leave the implementation of this procedure as an
     exercise.                                           *)
END insertbefore;


PROCEDURE deleteafter
          ( VAR lst       : list            (* in/out *);
                prioritem : elementtype     (* in *);
                equal     : equaltype       (* in *) );
  VAR priornode, oldnode : nodepointer;
BEGIN
  search ( lst, prioritem, priornode, equal );
  IF priornode = lst THEN
    deleteaftererror
  ELSE
    oldnode := priornode^.next;
    priornode^.next := oldnode^.next;
    priornode^.next^.prior := priornode;
    (* Update the length counter in the header node.    *)
    DEC( lst^.number );
    freenode( oldnode )
  END (* if then *)
END deleteafter;


PROCEDURE deletebefore
          ( VAR lst          : list        (* in/out *);
                nextitem     : elementtype (* in *);
                equal        : equaltype   (* in *) );
BEGIN
  (* We leave the implementation of this procedure as an
     exercise.                                           *)
END deletebefore;


PROCEDURE insertfront
          ( VAR lst  : list                 (* in/out *);
                item : elementtype          (* in *) );
   VAR newnode : nodepointer;
BEGIN
  newnode := getnode( listnode );
  newnode^.info  := item;
  newnode^.prior := lst;
  newnode^.next  := lst^.next;
  lst^.next^.prior := newnode;
  lst^.next := newnode;
  INC( lst^.number )
END insertfront;
```

```
PROCEDURE insertrear
         ( VAR lst  : list                      (* in/out *);
               item : elementtype               (* in *) );
BEGIN
  (* We leave the implementation of this procedure as an
     exercise.                                            *)
END insertrear;


PROCEDURE deletefront
         ( VAR lst  : list                      (* in/out *) );
  VAR oldnode : nodepointer;
BEGIN
  IF empty( lst ) THEN
    deletefronterror
  ELSE
    oldnode := lst^.next;
    lst^.next := oldnode^.next;
    lst^.next^.prior := lst;
    DEC( lst^.number );
    freenode(oldnode)
  END (* if then *)
END deletefront;


PROCEDURE deleterear
         ( VAR lst  : list                      (* in/out *) );
BEGIN
  (* We leave the implementation of this procedure as an
     exercise.                                            *)
END deleterear;


PROCEDURE place
         ( VAR lst      : list                  (* in/out *);
               item     : elementtype           (* in *);
               equal    : equaltype             (* in *);
               lessthan : lessthantype          (* in *) );
  VAR found : BOOLEAN;
      newnode, currentnode, priornode  : nodepointer;
BEGIN
  found       := FALSE;
  currentnode := lst^.next;
  priornode   := lst;
  WHILE (currentnode <> lst) AND (NOT found) DO
    IF lessthan( item, currentnode^.info ) THEN
      found := TRUE
    ELSE
      priornode    := currentnode;
      currentnode  := currentnode^.next
```

```
    END (* if then *)
  END (* while loop *);
  IF priornode = lst THEN
    insertfront( lst, item )
  ELSE
    newnode := getnode( listnode );
    newnode^.info  := item;
    newnode^.prior := priornode;
    newnode^. next := currentnode;
    currentnode^.next := newnode;
    priornode^.next := newnode;
    INC( lst^.number );
  END (* if then *)
END place;


PROCEDURE remove
         ( VAR lst   : list                    (* in/out *);
               item  : elementtype             (* in *);
               equal : equaltype               (* in *);
           VAR found : BOOLEAN                 (* out *) );
  VAR  currentnode, priornode : list;
BEGIN
  found        := FALSE;
  priornode    := lst;
  currentnode  := lst^.next;
  WHILE (currentnode <> lst) AND (NOT found) DO
    IF equal( item, currentnode^.info ) THEN
      found := TRUE
    ELSE
      priornode    := currentnode;
      currentnode  := currentnode^.next
    END (* if then *)
  END (* while loop *);
  IF found THEN
    IF currentnode = lst^.next THEN
      deletefront( lst )
    ELSE
      priornode^.next := currentnode^.next;
      currentnode^.next^.prior := priornode;
      DEC( lst^.number );
      freenode( currentnode );
    END (* if then *)
  END (* if then *)
END remove;


PROCEDURE displayforward
         ( lst          : list                 (* in *);
           displayproc : displaytype           (* in *)  );
```

```
  VAR currentnode : nodepointer;
BEGIN
  IF empty( lst ) THEN
    WriteLn; WriteLn;
    WriteString( 'The list is empty.' )
  ELSE
    currentnode := lst^.next;
    WHILE currentnode <> lst DO
      displayproc( currentnode^.info );
      currentnode := currentnode^.next
    END (* while loop *)
  END (* if then *)
END displayforward;


PROCEDURE displaybackward
         ( lst          : list              (* in *);
           displayproc : displaytype        (* in *)   );
  VAR currentnode : nodepointer;
BEGIN
  IF empty( lst ) THEN
    WriteLn; WriteLn;
    WriteString( 'The list is empty.' )
  ELSE
    currentnode := lst^.prior;
    WHILE currentnode <> lst DO
      displayproc( currentnode^.info );
      currentnode := currentnode^.prior
    END (* while loop *)
  END (* if then *)
END displaybackward;


END listadt.
```

4.5 The Generic List

In earlier implementations of the list, the user defined the elementtype in a definition module named elements. Our definition module for the list abstract data type imports elementtype, so it is necessary to recompile the definition module for each new elementtype definition. This recompilation of the definition module, of course, requires the recompilation of the implementation module for the list ADT. This is necessary to satisfy the recompilation order for Modula-2 programs, even though not a single line of code is modified in either the definition module or the implementation module for the list ADT.

The preceding implementations permit us to declare multiple objects of type list in the client or user program, but since only one elementtype is permitted, each list must consist of the same type of items. In some applications this is a severe restriction because lists containing items of different types are required.

In this section, we will implement the list to eliminate the need for recompilation for different elementtypes and to permit multiple lists defined in the user's program, with each list containing items of different types. Our implementation will cause us to lose strong type checking, which may or may not be a serious concern depending on the application. We emphasize, however, that no changes are required in the source code for the generic list ADT as we change the type of items stored in the list.

In our earlier implementations of the list ADT, we treated the info field of each node as a static item of type elementtype. To implement the generic list ADT, we need to generalize the info field of each node so that it is not associated with a static type declaration. The basic idea is to make the info field of each node a pointer to an item of the type that is to be stored in the list. But since a pointer variable is always associated with a base type, we cannot use pointer variables directly. Instead, we must use lower level features of Modula-2. An ADDRESS in Modula-2 is assignment compatible with a pointer but is not associated with any base type.

If we modify our interface definitions for the list ADT so that the parameters are addresses rather than objects of type elementtype, we can store and manipulate any type of items in the list depending on the data stored at the specific address. For this approach, the user of the generic list ADT must use pointer variables in the implementation of procedures of types displaytype, equaltype, and lessthantype, and the parameters in the calls to some of the procedures must be passed as addresses using the ADR function available in module SYSTEM of Modula-2. We will illustrate this with an example later.

The use of address parameters requires a different definition module. Listing 4.7 establishes as closely as possible the same user interface to the list ADT as that presented in Listing 4.1. The fundamental difference is that all parameters that were previously of type elementtype are now of type ADDRESS. We have also added to the define operation a parameter named item, which is of type "ARRAY OF WORD"; it is a sample item that is used to determine the size of the items to be stored in the list, as explained more fully in our description of the implementation of the generic list ADT.

Listing 4.7 Definition Module for Generic List Abstract Data Type

```
DEFINITION MODULE genericlistadt;

  FROM SYSTEM IMPORT
    (* type *) WORD, ADDRESS;
```

```
EXPORT QUALIFIED
  (* type *) list,
  (* proc *) define, empty, erase, length, ispresent,
             insertafter, deleteafter, insertfront,
             deletefront, place, remove, display;

TYPE list;

TYPE displaytype   = PROCEDURE ( ADDRESS );

TYPE equaltype     = PROCEDURE ( ADDRESS, ADDRESS ) :
                                 BOOLEAN;

TYPE lessthantype = PROCEDURE ( ADDRESS, ADDRESS ) :
                                 BOOLEAN;


PROCEDURE define
         ( VAR lst  : list                        (* in/out *);
               item : ARRAY OF WORD               (* in *)  );
  (* Create an empty list.  This procedure must be called
     for each new list prior to any other list operations.
     The sample item is used to determine the size of the
     elements that will be in the list.                    *)


PROCEDURE empty
         ( lst : list                             (* in *)   ) :
           BOOLEAN;
  (* Returns true if the list is empty, otherwise false.*)


PROCEDURE erase
         ( VAR lst : list                         (* in/out *) );
  (* Erases and reinitializes a list.                      *)


PROCEDURE length
         ( lst : list                             (* in *) ) :
           CARDINAL;
  (* Returns the length of the list.                       *)


PROCEDURE ispresent
         ( lst   : list                           (* in *);
           item  : ADDRESS                        (* in *);
          equal  : equaltype                      (* in *) ):
           BOOLEAN;
  (* Returns true if item is present in the list.          *)
```

```
PROCEDURE insertafter
         ( VAR lst          : list          (* in/out *);
               previousitem : ADDRESS       (* in *);
               newitem      : ADDRESS       (* in *);
               equal        : equaltype     (* in *) );
  (* Inserts into a list an item after a specified item
     in the list.                                         *)


PROCEDURE deleteafter
         ( VAR lst          : list          (* in/out *);
               previousitem : ADDRESS       (* in *);
               equal        : equaltype     (* in *) );
  (* Deletes from a list an item after a specified item
     in the list.  The item deleted is returned.          *)


PROCEDURE insertfront
         ( VAR lst  : list                  (* in/out *);
               item : ADDRESS               (* in *) );
   (* Inserts at the front of a list a specified item.   *)


PROCEDURE deletefront
         ( VAR lst  : list                  (* in/out *) );
   (* Deletes the item at the front of the list.         *)


PROCEDURE place
         ( VAR lst      : list              (* in/out *);
               item     : ADDRESS           (* in *);
               equal    : equaltype         (* in *);
               lessthan : lessthantype      (* in *) );
   (* Places an item in a list so that the list is
      maintained as an ordered list.                     *)


PROCEDURE remove
         ( VAR lst   : list                 (* in/out *);
               item  : ADDRESS              (* in *);
               equal : equaltype            (* in *);
           VAR found : BOOLEAN              (* out *) );
  (* Removes from a list the specified item.  If the item
     is found and removed from the list, then found is
     returned as true, otherwise false.                  *)


PROCEDURE display
         ( lst          : list              (* in *);
```

```
              displayproc : displaytype         (* in *)   );
    (* Displays or processes each item in the list.          *)

END genericlistadt.
```

Before proceeding with the implementation, let us consider a sample user program that uses the generic list ADT. Listing 4.8 uses the generic list and is a modification of the test program given in Listing 4.2.

Listing 4.8 Test Program for Generic List Abstract Data Type

```
MODULE listtest;

  FROM SYSTEM IMPORT
    (* type *) ADDRESS,
    (* proc *) ADR;

  FROM InOut IMPORT
    (* proc *) WriteString, WriteLn, ReadInt, ReadString,
               Read, Write, WriteInt, WriteCard;

  FROM genericlistadt IMPORT
    (* type *) list,
    (* proc *) define, erase, length,
               place, remove, display;

  TYPE
       elementtype = RECORD
                       a : CHAR;
                       b : INTEGER
                     END;


  VAR listofitems : list;
             item : elementtype;
             done : BOOLEAN;


  PROCEDURE printlength;
  BEGIN
    WriteLn;
    WriteString( "The current length of the list is " );
    WriteCard( length( listofitems ), 6 )
  END printlength;
```

```
PROCEDURE displayinfo
          (  p : ADDRESS                          (* in *) );
  VAR info : POINTER TO elementtype;
BEGIN
  info := p;
  WriteLn;
  Write( info^.a );
  WriteString('  ');
  WriteInt( info^.b, 4 )
END displayinfo;


PROCEDURE fetchinfo
          ( VAR info : elementtype                (* out *) );
BEGIN
  Read( info.a );
  ReadInt( info.b )
END fetchinfo;


PROCEDURE equal
          ( p, q : ADDRESS                        (* in *) ) :
            BOOLEAN;
  VAR x, y : POINTER TO elementtype;
BEGIN
    x := p;
    y := q;
    RETURN x^.b = y^.b
END equal;


PROCEDURE lessthan
          ( p, q : ADDRESS                        (* in *) ) :
            BOOLEAN;
  VAR x, y : POINTER TO elementtype;
BEGIN
    x := p;
    y := q;
    RETURN x^.b <= y^.b
END lessthan;


PROCEDURE add;
  VAR item : elementtype;
BEGIN
  WriteLn;   WriteLn;
  WriteString("Enter information field for new record: ");
  fetchinfo( item );
  place( listofitems, ADR( item ), equal, lessthan );
END add;
```

```
PROCEDURE delete;
  VAR found : BOOLEAN;
BEGIN
  WriteLn;   WriteLn;
  WriteString( "Enter item to key on for deletion: " );
  ReadInt( item.b );
  remove( listofitems, ADR( item ), equal, found );
  IF NOT found THEN
    WriteLn;  WriteLn;
    WriteString( "Item not found in list." );
  ELSE
    WriteLn;  WriteLn;
    WriteString( "We have removed item with key field " );
    WriteInt( item.b, 4 );
    WriteString( " from the records." );
  END (* if then *);
END delete;


PROCEDURE menu;
  VAR choice : INTEGER;
BEGIN
  WriteLn;  WriteLn;
  WriteString( "1: Add new record to list." );
  WriteLn;  WriteLn;
  WriteString( "2: Delete record from list." );
  WriteLn;  WriteLn;
  WriteString( "3: Print all records in list." );
  WriteLn;  WriteLn;
  WriteString( "4: Print length of list." );
  WriteLn;  WriteLn;
  WriteString( "5: Exit program." );
  WriteLn;  WriteLn;
  WriteString(      Enter appropriate choice: " );
  ReadInt( choice );
  CASE choice OF
    1 : add;|
    2 : delete;|
    3 : display( listofitems, displayinfo );|
    4 : printlength;|
    5 : erase( listofitems );
        done := TRUE;
  END (* case *);
END menu;


BEGIN
  done := FALSE;
  fetchinfo( item );
  define( listofitems, item );
```

```
    REPEAT
      menu
    UNTIL done;
  END listtest.
```

Notice the declaration of local variables of type "POINTER TO elementtype" in procedures equal, lessthan, and displayinfo, which are procedures of types equaltype, lessthantype, and displaytype, respectively. When these local variables are associated with a specific address, the data at that address can be interpreted as an elementtype.

There are two other things to note in our test program. First, the ADR function is used as a parameter in the calls to the "place" and "remove" operations. Second, in the main program we fetch a sample item so that we can pass it to the "define" operation. This is required for the implementation that we now describe.

Our implementation of the generic list ADT is a singly linked list with a header node that contains a size field whose CARDINAL value is the size of the items to be stored in the list. The size is a function of the number of computer words of memory that the item occupies. Each node in the list contains only two fields: an info field that contains the address of the item and a next field that contains a pointer to the next node in the list. Conceptually, the generic list can be viewed as illustrated in Figure 4.15. In this example, each item in the list occupies three computer words of storage.

A set of declarations for such a linked list is given by:

```
TYPE list        = POINTER TO listheader;

     nodepointer = POINTER TO node;

     listheader  = RECORD
                     size  : CARDINAL;
                     next  : nodepointer
                   END (* record *);
```

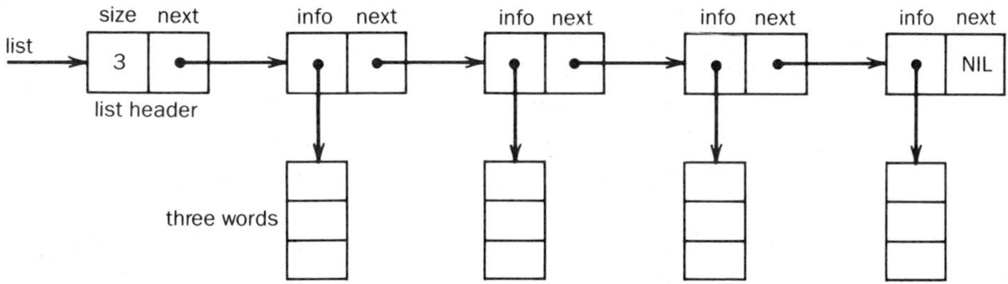

Figure 4.15 Generic List

```
node                = RECORD
                         info  : ADDRESS;
                         next : nodepointer
                      END;
```

Let us begin our implementation by considering the getnode operation, which not only needs to get a node but also must allocate storage for the item that is associated with the node, as indicated in Figure 4.15. Eventually, a specified item needs to be transferred to the allocated storage and the info field of the node set to the address of this allocated storage. We will define the getnode operation so that it performs both these operations.

The getnode operation has two parameters: one for the size of the item and the other for the address of the item that is to be associated with the new node. If newnode is a nodepointer, we can write down the following algorithm for getnode:

```
Procedure getnode( size, item )
  NEW( newnode )
  allocate size units of storage and set the info field of
     newnode to the address of the allocated storage
  transfer the item to the allocated storage one word at a
     time
  return newnode
```

The procedure freenode has two parameters: a parameter that indicates the size of the auxiliary storage that contains the item and a pointer to the node to be released, say oldnode. Freenode is described as follows:

```
Procedure freenode( size, oldnode )
  deallocate size units of storage at the address specified
     in the info field of oldnode
  DISPOSE( oldnode )
```

To allocate and deallocate storage as indicted, we use the ALLOCATE and DEALLOCATE procedures defined in module SYSTEM.

The define operation allocates the header node for the list and sets the size field of the header node to the size of the sample item. Once the size field has been set by define, it is not altered by any other operation. Our implementation requires that all items in the list be of the same size; however, we leave it as an exercise to trap this error and handle it appropriately.

The implementation of the other operations is similar to that presented for the dynamically allocated singly linked list given in Listing 4.4. As indicated earlier, the generic implementation loses strong type checking.

We present the complete implementation for the generic list ADT in Listing 4.9.

Listing 4.9 Implementation of Generic List Abstract Data Type

```
IMPLEMENTATION MODULE genericlistadt;

  FROM SYSTEM IMPORT
    (* type *) WORD, ADDRESS,
    (* proc *) TSIZE;

  FROM InOut IMPORT
    (* proc *) WriteString, WriteLn;

  FROM Storage IMPORT
    (* proc *) ALLOCATE, DEALLOCATE;


  TYPE list        = POINTER TO listheader;

       nodepointer = POINTER TO node;

       listheader  = RECORD
                       size  : CARDINAL;
                       next  : nodepointer
                     END (* record *);

       node        = RECORD
                       info : ADDRESS;
                       next : nodepointer
                     END;

  PROCEDURE getnode
            ( size : CARDINAL                    (* in *);
              item : ADDRESS                     (* in *) ) :
              nodepointer;
  (* This procedure makes a node, allocates size units of
     storage and stores the item in the allocated storage.
     It returns a pointer to the node.                       *)
  VAR
     newnode   : nodepointer;
     wordcount : CARDINAL;

  BEGIN
    NEW( newnode );
    ALLOCATE( newnode^.info, size * TSIZE( WORD ) );
    wordcount := 1;
    newnode^.info^ := item^;
    WHILE ( wordcount < size ) DO
      INC( newnode^.info, TSIZE( WORD ) );
      INC( item, TSIZE( WORD ) );
```

```
    newnode^.info^ := item^;
    INC( wordcount );
  END(* while loop *);
  DEC( newnode^.info, ( size - 1 ) * TSIZE( WORD ) );
  RETURN newnode;
END getnode;


PROCEDURE freenode
          (     size    : CARDINAL          (* in *);
            VAR oldnode : nodepointer       (* in/out *) );
(* This procedure deallocates oldnode and size units of
   storage associated with the item stored at the address
   specified in the info field of oldnode.                *)
BEGIN
  DEALLOCATE( oldnode^.info, size * TSIZE( WORD ) );
  DISPOSE (oldnode)
END freenode;


PROCEDURE insertaftererror;
BEGIN
  WriteLn;
  WriteString( "Illegal insert after operation." );
  WriteLn;
  WriteString( "Item specified was not found in list." )
END insertaftererror;


PROCEDURE deleteaftererror;
BEGIN
  WriteLn;
  WriteString( "Illegal delete after operation." );
  WriteLn;
  WriteString( "Item specified was not found in list." )
END deleteaftererror;


PROCEDURE deletefronterror;
BEGIN
  WriteLn;
  WriteString( "Illegal delete front operation." );
  WriteLn;
  WriteString( "The list is empty." )
END deletefronterror;


PROCEDURE define
          ( VAR lst  : list                 (* in/out *);
                item : ARRAY OF WORD        (* in *)   );
```

```
BEGIN
  NEW( lst );
  lst^.size := ( HIGH( item ) + 1 ); (* number of words  *)
  lst^.next := NIL
END define;


PROCEDURE empty
          ( lst : list                        (* in *)  ) :
            BOOLEAN;
BEGIN
  RETURN lst^.next = NIL
END empty;


PROCEDURE erase
          ( VAR lst : list                    (* in/out *) );
  VAR nextnode, nodetodelete : nodepointer;
BEGIN
  nextnode := lst^.next;
  WHILE nextnode <> NIL DO
    nodetodelete := nextnode;
    nextnode := nodetodelete^.next;
    freenode( lst^.size, nodetodelete )
  END (* while loop *);
  lst^.next := NIL
END erase;


PROCEDURE length
          ( lst : list                        (* in *) ) :
            CARDINAL;
  VAR nextnode : nodepointer;
        count : CARDINAL;
BEGIN
  count := 0;
  nextnode := lst^.next;
  WHILE nextnode <> NIL DO
    count := count + 1;
    nextnode := nextnode^.next
  END (* while loop *);
  RETURN count
END length;


PROCEDURE search
          (      lst      : list              (* in *);
                 item     : ADDRESS           (* in *);
             VAR itemnode : nodepointer       (* out *);
                 equal    : equaltype         (* in *) );
```

```
BEGIN
  itemnode := lst^.next;
  WHILE ( itemnode^.next <> NIL ) AND
        ( NOT equal( item, itemnode^.info ) ) DO
    itemnode := itemnode^.next
  END (* while loop *);
END search;


PROCEDURE ispresent
          ( lst  : list                       (* in *);
            item : ADDRESS                    (* in *);
            equal : equaltype                 (* in *) ):
            BOOLEAN;
  VAR itemnode : nodepointer;
BEGIN
  search( lst, item, itemnode, equal );
  RETURN itemnode # NIL
END ispresent;



PROCEDURE insertafter
          ( VAR lst          : list           (* in/out *);
                previousitem : ADDRESS        (* in *);
                newitem      : ADDRESS        (* in *);
                equal        : equaltype      (* in *)  );
  VAR previousnode, newnode : nodepointer;
      size : CARDINAL;
BEGIN
  search ( lst, previousitem, previousnode, equal );
  IF previousnode = NIL
  THEN
    insertaftererror
  ELSE
    newnode := getnode( lst^.size, newitem );
    newnode^.next := previousnode^.next;
    previousnode^.next := newnode
  END (* if then *)
END insertafter;


PROCEDURE deleteafter
          ( VAR lst          : list           (* in/out *);
                previousitem : ADDRESS        (* in *);
                equal        : equaltype      (* in *) );
  VAR previousnode, oldnode : nodepointer;
BEGIN
  search ( lst, previousitem, previousnode, equal );
  IF previousnode = NIL
```

```
    THEN
      deleteaftererror
    ELSE
      oldnode := previousnode^.next;
      previousnode^.next := oldnode^.next;
      freenode( lst^.size, oldnode )
    END (* if then *)
  END deleteafter;


  PROCEDURE insertfront
           ( VAR lst  : list                  (* in/out *);
                 item : ADDRESS               (* in *) );
    VAR newnode : nodepointer;
  BEGIN
    newnode := getnode( lst^.size, item );
    newnode^.next := lst^.next;
    lst^.next := newnode
  END insertfront;


  PROCEDURE deletefront
           ( VAR lst  : list                  (* in/out *) );
    VAR oldnode : nodepointer;
  BEGIN
    IF empty (lst)
    THEN
      deletefronterror
    ELSE
      oldnode := lst^.next;
      lst^.next := oldnode^.next;
      freenode( lst^.size, oldnode )
    END (* if then *)
  END deletefront;


  PROCEDURE place
           ( VAR lst       : list             (* in/out *);
                 item      : ADDRESS          (* in *);
                 equal     : equaltype        (* in *);
                 lessthan  : lessthantype     (* in *) );
    VAR found : BOOLEAN;
        currentnode, previousnode  : nodepointer;
  BEGIN
    found        := FALSE;
    currentnode  := lst^.next;
    previousnode := NIL;
    WHILE (currentnode <> NIL) AND (NOT found) DO
      IF lessthan( item, currentnode^.info ) THEN
        found := TRUE
```

```
    ELSE
       previousnode := currentnode;
       currentnode  := currentnode^.next
     END (* if then *)
   END (* while loop *);
  IF previousnode = NIL THEN
    insertfront( lst, item )
  ELSE
     newnode := getnode( list^.size, item );
     newnode^.next  := currentnode;
     previousnode^.next := newnode;
  END (* if then *)
END place;


PROCEDURE remove
          ( VAR lst   : list                  (* in/out *);
                item  : ADDRESS               (* in *);
                equal : equaltype             (* in *);
            VAR found : BOOLEAN               (* out *) );
  VAR currentnode, previousnode : nodepointer;
BEGIN
  found        := FALSE;
  previousnode := NIL;
  currentnode  := lst^.next;
  WHILE (currentnode <> NIL) AND (NOT found) DO
    IF equal( item, currentnode^.info ) THEN
      found := TRUE
    ELSE
      previousnode := currentnode;
      currentnode  := currentnode^.next
    END (* if then *)
  END (* while loop *);
  IF found THEN
    IF currentnode = lst^.next THEN
      deletefront( lst )
    ELSE
      previousnode^.next := currentnode^.next;
      freenode( lst^.size, currentnode );
    END (* if then *)
  END (* if then *)
END remove;


PROCEDURE display
          ( lst         : list                (* in *);
            displayproc : displaytype         (* in *) );
  VAR currentnode : nodepointer;
BEGIN
  IF empty( lst )
```

```
    THEN
      WriteLn; WriteLn;
      WriteString( 'The list is empty.' )
    ELSE
      currentnode := lst^.next;
      WHILE currentnode <> NIL DO
        displayproc( currentnode^.info );
        currentnode := currentnode^.next
      END (* while loop *)
    END (* if then *)
  END display;


END genericlistadt.
```

Exercises

4.1 Show how the singly linked list containing integers in the info field would be affected by the following sequence of operations:

```
insertafter( list, 13, 23 )
deleteafter( list,  6 )
```

where list = 5 and available = 3. *Note*: nil = 0.

	info	*next*
1		9
2	3	8
3		7
4	18	0
5	8	2
6	6	4
7		1
8	13	6
9		10
10		0

4.2 Consider the following pool of nodes, which contains list A and list B. Show how the following sequence of operations will affect the linked lists:

```
deleteafter( A, 13 )
insertfront( B, 5 )
insertafter( B, 8, 9)
insertafter( A, 4, 7)
deletefront( A )
```

where A = 2, B = 6, and available = 9.

	info	*next*
1	13	8
2	4	1
3		5
4	12	0
5		10
6	8	4
7	31	0
8	23	7
9		3
10		0

4.3 Consider insertion at the front of the circularly linked list shown in Figure 4.16*a*. We need to change the next field of the last node in the list so that it points to the new first node. This can be done only for a singly linked list by moving down the entire length of the list. We can eliminate this problem by adopting the convention that the list pointer points to the last node in the list rather than the first node. The first node in the list is the one pointed to by the next field of the last node, as in Figure 4.16*b*. Modify the implementation given in Listing 4.3 so that the list is a singly linked, circularly linked list using the preceding convention for the list pointer. With this convention, is it difficult to insert a node at the end of a circularly linked list? To delete a node at the end of a circularly linked list?

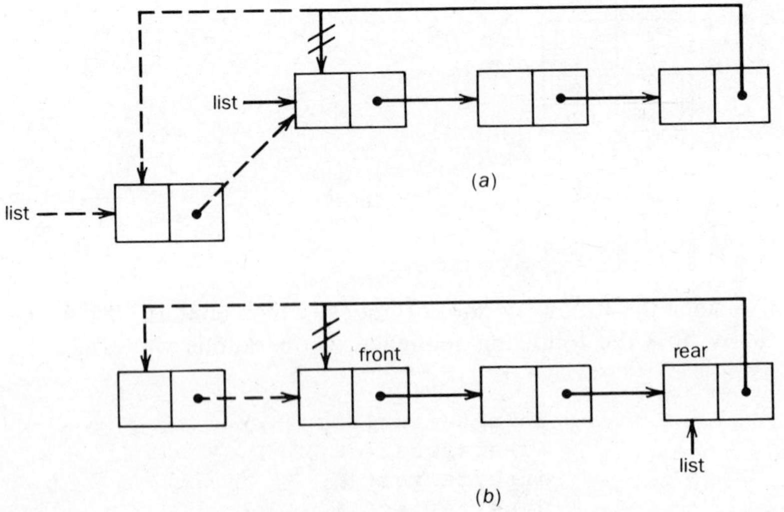

Figure 4.16 List for Exercise 4.3

4.4 Repeat exercise 4.3 for the implementation given in Listing 4.4.

4.5 Complete the implementation of the doubly linked list given in Listing 4.6 by implementing the ''insertbefore'', ''deletebefore'', ''insertrear'', and ''deleterear'' operations.

4.6 Implement the doubly linked list of Listing 4.6 so that it resides in an array of records.

4.7 Implement the operations for a queue defined in Listing 2.3 using a header node as illustrated in Figure 4.9*f*. That is, the header node contains a pointer to the rear of the queue.

4.8 Define elementtype to be a record containing three fields: the first field contains a word, the second the length of the word, and the third a count of the number of times the word appears in a given input text.

Choose a paragraph of moderate length to use as input. Isolate individual words and enter them into a list, maintaining the list in alphabetical order. For each new word encountered, a new node is created, the word field is set to the word currently being processed, the length field is set to the number of characters in the word, and the count field is set to one. If it is discovered that a word has already appeared in the input text, simply update the count field for the node that contains that word.

Upon completion of the processing of the input text, print the number of distinct words in the text and a table of all the words in the input text along with the number of times that each word appeared in the input text. Now make a second pass of the list and delete all nodes that contain words with a length less than or equal to 5. Print the table again.

4.9 Many other operations are possible and often desirable on a linked list. Define the interface and implement the following operations:

(a) Reverse the order of the elements in the list so the last item becomes the first, and so on.

(b) Combine two ordered lists into a single ordered list.

(c) Delete every *n*th element of the list.

(d) Insert an item at the rear of a list.

(e) Delete the item at the rear of a list.

(f) Make a copy of a list.

(g) Concatenate two lists.

These operations can be defined for any of the variants of a linked list.

4.10 Another approach to the implementation of a linked list is to define a number of simple, low-level operations on the nodes of a list independent of the underlying representation or data structure. Examples of such operations include:

```
PROCEDURE getinfo ( p : nodepointer ) : elementtype;
(* Returns the info field of the node p.                  *)

PROCEDURE writeinfo( VAR p : nodepointer; item :
                     elementtype );
(* Writes item to the info field of node p.               *)

PROCEDURE getnext( p : nodepointer ) : nodepointer;
(* Returns the next field of node p.                      *)

PROCEDURE writenext( VAR p : nodepointer; q :
                     nodepointer );
(* Writes q to the next field of node p.                  *)

PROCEDURE firstnode( lst : list ) : nodepointer;
(* Returns a pointer to the list node of list, lst.       *)

PROCEDURE endoflist( p: nodepointer ) : BOOLEAN;
(* Returns true if p does not point to a list node.       *)

PROCEDURE setnil( VAR p : nodepointer );
(* Sets p to the nil pointer.                             *)

PROCEDURE setlist( p : nodepointer ) : list;
(* Sets the nodepointer p to a list.                      *)
```

Implement the preceding operations either for a node pool as an array of records or using the dynamic allocation features of Modula-2. Then implement some of the operations defined for a singly linked list in Listing 4.1 or some of the operations defined in exercises 4.9 and show that the implementation will not change if we switch to the other node pool representation. Indicate both the benefits and the liabilities of this approach.

4.11 Determine what the following procedure does. This problem uses some of the low-level operations of exercise 4.10 for a singly linked list.

```
PROCEDURE what( VAR x : list );
  VAR p, q, r : nodepointer;
BEGIN
  p := firstnode( x );
  setnil( q );
  WHILE NOT endoflist( p ) DO
    r := q;
    q := p;
    p := getnext( p );
    writenext( q, r )
  END (* end while loop *);
  x := setlist( q )
END what;
```

4.12 Define lessthan, equal, and display procedures for the following element-type definition:

```
TYPE elementtype =
        RECORD
          lastname  : ARRAY [1..12] OF CHAR;
          firstname : ARRAY [1..12] OF CHAR;
          division  : ARRAY [1..12] OF CHAR;
          group     : ARRAY [1..12] OF CHAR;
          salary    : CARDINAL
        END (* record *);
```

The key field of the elementtype is the last name field. The display procedure should print last name, first name, and salary.

4.13 Modify the generic list implementation so that it will trap the error condition that arises if the user attempts to use elements of unequal size in the same list.

4.14 Modify the generic list implementation so that a single list can contain items of unequal size. *Hint*: Each node must contain a field that specifies the size of the item.

4.15 Why is strong type checking lost in the generic list ADT?

5

Applications of the List Abstraction

5.1 A Simple Course Registration System

In this section, we will develop a simple course registration system that uses the list and the queue ADTs from Chapter 2. The implementation will be independent of the data structures used in the implementation of the list and queue abstract data types.

The registration system is an interactive system that allows students to sign up for courses and to drop them. As each student registers, he or she is placed in course lists in alphabetical order by last name. There is a different course list for each course available. The enrollment in each course is limited to a specified capacity, and each course may have a different capacity. A student who registers for a course that is filled to capacity, is placed on a wait list. As students drop a course, the first student on the waiting list will be registered for the course. For simplicity, we do not permit students in the wait list for a course to drop that course, since they are not registered for it. At any time, we permit an alphabetical listing of the class roster to be printed, along with the number of students on the wait list for the course.

The preceding description of the course registration system suggests that for each course there is a specified enrollment capacity, an associated course list, and a wait list that funtions as a queue. We can declare the data structures for this software system as follows:

```
CONST maxnumbercourses = 50;

TYPE coursetype = RECORD
                      coursenumber : CARDINAL;
                      capacity     : CARDINAL;
```

```
                              courselist    : list;
                              waitlist      : queue
                            END (* record *);

    VAR courses : ARRAY [1 .. maxnumbercourses] OF
                  coursetype;
```

It is important to note that we must import the types list and queue from the list and queue ADTs, respectively. The variable courses is an array of records, with each record containing a list and a queue along with two fields that contain cardinal numbers.

The items that are to be placed in the course lists and wait lists are the students' names, so the following element type definition is used:

```
DEFINITION MODULE elements;

  EXPORT QUALIFIED
    (* type *) elementtype;

  TYPE
       string = ARRAY [ 0 .. 79 ] OF CHAR;

       elementtype = RECORD
                       lastname  : string;
                       firstname : string
                     END (* record *);

END elements.
```

Before proceeding further, let us consider some of the operations we need to define and implement. The basic operations are registering for classes, dropping classes, and printing the class rosters. We will also need a menu procedure, to permit interactive selection of the desired operations.

However, before we can do any of the basic operations, we need to get the course information (i.e., the number of courses, the course identifying numbers, and the capacity for each course). We define the procedure "getcourseinfo" to perform these tasks. We must also initialize or define each course list and each wait list, using the define operation from the list and queue ADTs. In the descriptions that follow, we assume that these variables have been defined globally:

```
VAR numbercourses : CARDINAL;
    index         : CARDINAL;
    done          : BOOLEAN;
```

A minor problem in using both the list and queue ADTs in the same applications program is that some of the operations defined for both ADTs have the same identifier names. Since Modula-2 does not permit "overloading" of identifier names, we use the qualified import for the queue. This avoids clashes of identical identifiers exported from different modules but requires us to qualify each queue operation or type definition with the definition module name (i.e., queueadt).

Assuming that we have all the course information and have defined the course list and the wait list, let us consider the registration process. We define the two operations getname and entercourse as follows:

```
PROCEDURE getname
        ( VAR name : elementtype                  (* out *) );
(* This procedure requests the student to enter his
   or her first name and last name and assigns the
   responses to the appropriate fields of name.         *)

PROCEDURE entercourse
        ( VAR index : CARDINAL          (* out *);
          VAR valid : BOOLEAN           (* out *) );
(* This procedure requests the student to enter a course
   number. It finds the index of the course in the variable
   courses such that courses[ index ] is equal to the
   course number entered. Valid is returned with the value
   TRUE if such an index is found, otherwise valid is
   returned with a value of FALSE.                      *)
```

After the student has entered his or her name, we want the student to be able to register for more than one class without reentering his or her name. This suggests the use of a while loop that terminates based on a response from the student that indicates whether the student wishes to register for another course. The procedure that defines the registration process is given by:

```
PROCEDURE register;
  VAR response    : CHAR;
      coursevalid : BOOLEAN;
      repeat      : BOOLEAN;
      name        : elementtype;
BEGIN
  getname( name );
  repeat := TRUE;
  WHILE repeat DO
    entercourse( index, coursevalid );
    WITH courses[ index ] DO
      IF NOT coursevalid
      THEN
        illegalcoursenumber
      ELSIF length( courselist ) = capacity
      THEN
        queueadt.insert( waitlist, name );
        notifywaitlist
      ELSE
        place( courselist, name, equal, lessthan );
        notifyregistered
      END (* if then *);
```

```
      END (* with *);
      WriteLn;
      WriteString( "Do you wish to register for " );
      WriteString( "another course (y/n)?" );
      Read( response );
      repeat := response = 'y'
    END (* while loop *);
  END register;
```

The procedures ‘‘illegalcoursenumber’’, ‘‘notifywaitlist’’, and ‘‘notifyregistered’’ simply tell the student that the course number entered was not valid, that the student has been placed on the wait list for the course, and that the student has successfully registered for the course, respectively. The use of the ‘‘place’’ operation from the list ADT requires that we define the procedures ‘‘equal’’ and ‘‘lessthan’’. We present these procedures later in this section.

Let us consider the issue of dropping courses using procedure drop, given as follows:

```
PROCEDURE drop;
  VAR response    : CHAR;
      found       : BOOLEAN;
      coursevalid : BOOLEAN;
      repeat      : BOOLEAN;
      name        : elementtype;
BEGIN
  getname( name );
  repeat := TRUE;
  WHILE repeat DO
    entercourse( index, coursevalid );
    IF NOT coursevalid
    THEN
      illegalcoursenumber
    ELSE
      WITH courses[ index ] DO
        remove( courselist, name, equal, found );
        IF found THEN
         notifydropped;
         IF NOT queueadt.empty( waitlist )
         THEN
           queueadt.remove( waitlist, name );
           place ( courselist, name, equal, lessthan )
         END (* if then *);
       END (* with *);
     END (* if then *);
    END (* if then *);
    WriteLn;
    WriteString( "Drop another course (y/n)?" );
    Read( response );
    repeat := response = "y"
```

```
 END (* while loop *);
END drop;
```

When we remove a student from the course list, we also remove the first student from the wait list if it is not empty and place the waiting student in the course list.

The final course registration operation is the printing of the class roster, given by:

```
PROCEDURE classroster;
  VAR response    : CHAR;
      coursevalid : BOOLEAN:
BEGIN
  entercourse( index, coursevalid );
  IF NOT coursevalid
  THEN
    illegalcoursenumber
  ELSE
    WITH courses[ index ] DO
      WriteLn;
      WriteString( "Classroll for course ");
      WriteCard ( coursenumber, 4 );
      display( courselist, printname );
      IF NOT queueadt.empty( waitlist )
      THEN
        WriteLn; WriteLn;
        WriteString( "Number of students on wait list is " );
        WriteCard   ( queueadt.length( waitlist ), 4 )
      END (* if then *);
    END (* with *);
  END (* if then *);
  (* The following statements create a pause. *)
  WriteLn;
  WriteString( "Hit spacebar to continue." );
  Read( response )
END classroster;
```

We note that the use of the display operation for the list ADT requires that we define the "printname" procedure of type displaytype.

Let us now consider the procedures "equal", "lessthan", and "printname" of types equaltype, lessthantype, and displaytype, respectively. These must be defined for use with the list ADT.

The "equal" procedure must compare two names to determine whether they are equal. We will compare only last names. First, we see whether they are the same length, since if they are not, they cannot be equal. If both names are of equal length, we compare them, character by character, to determine whether they are in fact equal.

Procedure "lessthan" is used to order the items in the list. Since we want that list to be ordered alphabetically, this procedure compares, character by character, two last names to determine which one comes first alphabetically. If one last name is shorter than the other, we compare only up to the length of the shorter name.

The course registration software system is presented in Listing 5.1.

Listing 5.1 Course Registration Software System

```
MODULE courseregistration;

  FROM InOut IMPORT
    (* proc *) WriteLn, WriteString, ReadString,
               WriteCard, ReadCard, Read;

  FROM Screen IMPORT
    (* proc *) HomeCursor, ClearScreen;

  FROM Strings IMPORT
    (* proc *) CompareStr, Length;

  FROM elements IMPORT
    (* type *) elementtype;

  FROM listadt IMPORT
    (* type *) list,
    (* proc *) define, place, remove, length, display,
               erase;

  IMPORT queueadt;

  CONST maxnumbercourses = 50;

  TYPE coursetype = RECORD
                      coursenumber : CARDINAL;
                      capacity     : CARDINAL;
                      courselist   : list;
                      waitlist     : queueadt.queue
                    END (* record *);

   VAR courses : ARRAY [1 .. maxnumbercourses] OF
                 coursetype;

       numbercourses : CARDINAL;
       index         : CARDINAL;
       done          : BOOLEAN;
```

```
PROCEDURE getcourseinfo;
BEGIN
  numbercourses := 3;
  courses[1].coursenumber := 110;
  courses[2].coursenumber := 120;
  courses[3].coursenumber := 220;
  courses[1].capacity     := 5;
  courses[2].capacity     := 4;
  courses[3].capacity     := 3
END getcourseinfo;


PROCEDURE entercourse
        ( VAR index : CARDINAL          (* out *);
          VAR valid : BOOLEAN           (* out *) );
  VAR number, i : CARDINAL;
BEGIN
  valid := FALSE;
  WriteLn;
  WriteString( "Enter course number: " );
  ReadCard( number );
  i := 1;
  REPEAT
    WITH courses[ i ] DO
      IF coursenumber = number
      THEN
        index := i;
        valid := TRUE;
      END (* if then *);
    END (* with *);
    INC(i);
  UNTIL valid OR ( i > numbercourses );
END entercourse;


PROCEDURE printname
        ( VAR name  : elementtype       (* in/out *) );
BEGIN
  WriteLn;
  WriteString( name.lastname );
  WriteString( ", " );
  WriteString( name.firstname )
END printname;


PROCEDURE getname
        ( VAR name : elementtype        (* out *) );
BEGIN
  WriteLn;
  WriteString( "Enter your first name : " );
```

```
    ReadString( name.firstname );
    WriteLn;
    WriteString( "Enter your last name  : " );
    ReadString( name.lastname )
  END getname;


  PROCEDURE equal
          ( nameone, nametwo : elementtype (* in *)  ) :
            BOOLEAN;
    VAR compare : INTEGER;
  BEGIN
    compare := CompareStr( nameone.lastname,
                            nametwo.lastname );
    (* CompareStr compares two strings and returns an
       integer value indicating the comparison result:
        -1 if the first string is less than the second
           string,
         0 if the first string equals the second string,
           and
         1 if the first string is greater than the second
           string.                                       *)
    IF compare <> 0
    THEN
      RETURN FALSE
    ELSE
      FOR index := 1 TO Length( nameone.lastname ) DO
        IF nameone.lastname[ index-1 ] <>
           nametwo.lastname[ index-1]
        THEN
          RETURN FALSE
        END (* if then *);
      END (* for loop *);
      RETURN TRUE
    END (* if then *);
  END equal;


  PROCEDURE lessthan
          ( nameone, nametwo : elementtype (* in *) ) :
            BOOLEAN;
    VAR upperlimit : CARDINAL;
        compare    : INTEGER;
  BEGIN
    compare := CompareStr( nameone.lastname,
                            nametwo.lastname );
    IF compare > 0
    THEN
      upperlimit := Length( nametwo.lastname )
```

```
    ELSE
      upperlimit := Length( nameone.lastname )
    END (* if then *);
    FOR index := 1 TO upperlimit DO
      IF nameone.lastname[ index-1 ] <
         nametwo.lastname[ index-1 ]
      THEN
        RETURN TRUE
      ELSIF nameone.lastname[ index-1 ] >
            nametwo.lastname[ index-1]
      THEN
        RETURN FALSE
      END (* if then *);
    END (* for loop *);
    RETURN Length( nameone.lastname ) <
           Length( nametwo.lastname );
  END lessthan;


  PROCEDURE illegalcoursenumber;
  BEGIN
    WriteLn;
    WriteString("The course number entered is not valid.")
  END illegalcoursenumber;


  PROCEDURE notifywaitlist;
  BEGIN
    WriteLn;
    WriteString( "The course entered is full. " );
    WriteLn;
    WriteString("You have been placed in the wait list. ")
  END notifywaitlist;


  PROCEDURE notifyregistered;
  BEGIN
    WriteLn;
    WriteString( "You have successfully registered for " );
    WriteString( "the course." );
  END notifyregistered;


  PROCEDURE notifydropped;
  BEGIN
    WriteLn;
    WriteString( "You have successfully dropped the " );
    WriteString( "course. " )
  END notifydropped;
```

```
PROCEDURE register;
  (* See program above. *)
END register;


PROCEDURE drop;
  (* See program above. *)
END drop;


PROCEDURE classroster;
  (* See program above. *)
END classroster;


PROCEDURE exit;
(* This procedure reinitializes all of the course lists
   and wait lists, thereby freeing the dynamic storage
   that was allocated and used for these lists.        *)
BEGIN
  FOR index := 1 TO numbercourses DO
    WITH courses[ index ] DO
      erase( courselist );
      queueadt.makeempty( waitlist )
    END (* with *);
  END (* for loop *);
  done := TRUE;
END exit;


PROCEDURE menu;
  VAR choice : CHAR;
BEGIN
  ClearScreen;
  HomeCursor;
  WriteString( "Course Registration System" );
  WriteLn; WriteLn;
  WriteString( "R : Register for courses." );
  WriteLn; WriteLn;
  WriteString( "D : Drop courses." );
  WriteLn; WriteLn;
  WriteString( "P : Print class roll." );
  WriteLn; WriteLn;
  WriteString( "E : Exit." );
  WriteLn; WriteLn;
  WriteString( "Enter appropriate choice: " );
  Read( choice );
  CASE choice OF
    'R' : register; |
    'D' : drop; |
```

```
        'P' : classroster; |
        'E' : exit
      END (* case *);
    END menu;


BEGIN
  done := FALSE;
  getcourseinfo;
  FOR index := 1 TO numbercourses DO
    WITH courses[ index ] DO
      define( courselist );
      queueadt.define( waitlist )
    END (* with *);
  END (* for loop *);
  REPEAT
    menu
  UNTIL done;
END courseregistration.
```

Note that in the main program, we initialize all the course lists and wait lists before using any other operations defined on the list and queue ADTs.

5.2 Long Integers

Integers are typically represented internally in the computer as single words, each containing either 16 or 32 bits. The specific representation depends on the hardware features of the computer. This places a potentially severe limitation on the range of integer values that can be assigned to integer variables. For example, with 16 bits we can represent only the integers from −32,768 to 32,767. With 32 bits the integer range is not nearly as restrictive: we can represent integers in the range from −2,147,483,648 to 2,147,483,647. However, for some applications even this range of values may be too limiting.

In this section, our objective is to develop an approach to long integers that permits us to represent and perform operations on integers that contain an arbitrary number of digits. Specifically, we define the long integer abstract data type and implement the operations make, add, and printlong. The make operation makes a long integer from a character string containing numeral characters, add returns the sum of two long integers, and printlong prints a long integer.

Our long integer is represented internally as a linked list. The implementation details will be addressed later in this section. We formalize the interface to the long integer operations in Listing 5.2.

Listing 5.2 Definition Module for Long Integer Abstract Data Type

```
DEFINITION MODULE longintegerarithmetic;

  FROM listadt IMPORT
    (* type *) list;

  EXPORT QUALIFIED
    (* type *) longinteger, string,
    (* proc *) make, add, printlong;

  TYPE longinteger = list;
       string = ARRAY [0..79] OF CHAR;

  PROCEDURE make
          ( s : string                        (* in *) ) :
            longinteger;
  (* This procedure takes a string s of integers with no
     blanks and converts it into longinteger form.          *)


  PROCEDURE add
          ( x, y : longinteger                (* in *) ) :
            longinteger;
  (* This procedure adds two longintegers and returns the
     result.                                                *)


  PROCEDURE printlong
          ( x : longinteger                   (* in *) );
  (* This procedure prints the longinteger x.               *)


END longintegerarithmetic.
```

Listing 5.3 illustrates the use of the long integer ADT by forming two long integers, adding them together, and printing the resulting sum.

The output from the preceding program is:

```
a =   123456789012345678901234567B9
b = 9876543210987654321
c = a + b = 1234567891111111111011111111110
```

When we add two integers together, we traverse the digits of each integer from right to left. Corresponding digits and a possible carry digit are summed. The carry digit comes from the sum of the preceding digits. Since the addition

Listing 5.3 The Use of the Long Integer Abstract Data Type

```
MODULE longintegertest;

  FROM longintegerarithmetic IMPORT
    (* type *) longinteger,
    (* proc *) add, make, printlong;

  FROM InOut IMPORT
    (* proc *) WriteLn, WriteString;

  VAR a, b, c : longinteger;

BEGIN

  a := make( '123456789012345678901234567890' );
  WriteLn;
  WriteString( 'a = ' );
  printlong( a );

  b := make( '98765432109876543210' );
  WriteLn;
  WriteString( 'b = ' );
  printlong( b );

  c := add( a, b );
  WriteLn;
  WriteString( 'c = a + b = ' );
  printlong( c );

END longintegertest.
```

operation is performed one digit at a time from right to left, this suggests that a long integer be represented as a linked list, having the least significant digit the first node and the most significant digit the last node. Such a representation is rather wasteful of storage, since each node contains only a single digit of our long integer. On a 16-bit computer we could allow each node to contain 4 digits of the long integer. The sum of two 4-digit numbers can be no larger than 19,998, which is significantly smaller than the largest integer that can be represented. This permits us to add the numbers in two corresponding nodes and determine the carry without exceeding the maximum integer size. Note that on a 16-bit computer we cannot allow 5 digits per node.

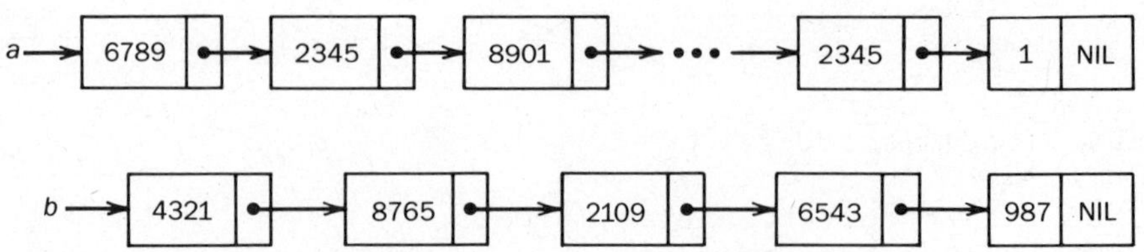

Figure 5.1 Linked List Representation of Long Integers

As an example, suppose that a, b, and c are variables of type longinteger and we wish to calculate c := a + b, where:

```
a = 1234567890123456789012345678 9
```

and

```
b = 98765432109876543 21
```

The linked-list representation for a and b with 4 digits per node is given in Figure 5.1.

Let us now consider how we make long integers. We cannot do it by simple assignment. Why? Our approach is to convert into a long integer a character string consisting of integer characters only. However, since we want our linked representation to contain the least significant digits first, we must extract four characters at a time, beginning with the last four characters in the string, convert the characters to an integer, and place them in the list. Each new node must be placed at the rear of the list, so we will define for a linked list the "insertrear" operation, which inserts an item at the rear of a linked list. If the list is empty, the "insertrear" operation inserts an item at the front of the list, since in this special case the front is also the rear. The interface for this operation is:

```
PROCEDURE insertrear
          ( VAR lst    : list            (* in/out *);
                item   : elementtype     (* in *) );
```

We now present the implementation details for the "make" operation. Our implementation of the long integer ADT is independent of the implementation used for the list ADT, since we use the low-level list operations defined previously (exercise 4.10.).

```
PROCEDURE make
        ( s : string                            (* in *) ) :
          longinteger;
  VAR x                  : longinteger;
      number, count  : CARDINAL;
      base, index    : CARDINAL;

  PROCEDURE int ( c : CHAR ) : CARDINAL;
  BEGIN
    RETURN ORD( c ) - ORD( '0' )
  END int;
```

```
BEGIN
  define( x );
  base := 1;
  number := 0;
  count := 0;
  FOR index := Length( s ) TO 1 BY -1 DO
    number := number + base * int( s[index -1] ) ;
    base := base * 10;
    count := count + 1;
    IF count = 4
    THEN
      insertrear( x, number );
      number := 0;
      base := 1;
      count := 0
    END (* if then *);
  END (* for loop *);
  IF count <> 0
  THEN
    insertrear( x, number );
  END (* if then *);
  RETURN x
END make;
```

The procedure int is a function that converts an integer represented as a character to an integer. Note how we build up the number for each node. As we move from right to left in the input string, we convert each character encountered to an integer using the int function. We simultaneously create the number:

```
number = s4 * 1000 + s3 * 100 + s2 * 10 + s1
```

using the four consecutive integers, s1, s2, s3, and s4 from the input string; number is then inserted at the rear of the list. We then reinitialize several variables so that we can create the next number from the input string. The last "IF" statement takes into account whether the input string was a multiple of 4.

We now develop an algorithm for adding two long integers together. When we add two integers together digit by digit from right to left, we obtain a total to the base 10. The corresponding digit in the sum is the total MOD 10 and the carry digit is the total DIV 10. Our linked list representation of a long integer contains 4 digit numbers. When we add two long integers together node by node, we are doing base 10,000 arithmetic. This means that the number that goes into the corresponding node of the sum is the total MOD 10,000 and the carry to the next node is total DIV 10,000. We must also take into account that the two long integers being summed may not be of the same length. When different lengths are involved, we must continue to add the nodes of the longer integer to the sum and account for the possibility of a carry from node to node. Even after we reach the end of both long integers, we must still determine whether there is a carry digit that requires another node to be inserted into the list for the sum. The complete implementation of this algorithm follows:

```
PROCEDURE add
        ( x, y : longinteger                    (* in *) ) :
          longinteger;

  CONST tenthousand = 10000;

  VAR carry, total, number : INTEGER;
      xnext, ynext, long   : nodepointer;
      sum                  : longinteger;

BEGIN
  define( sum );
  carry := 0;
  ynext := firstnode( x );
  ynext := firstnode( y );
  WHILE (NOT endoflist( xnext )) AND
        (NOT endoflist( ynext )) DO
    total  := getinfo( xnext ) + getinfo( ynext ) + carry;
    number := total MOD tenthousand;
    carry  := total DIV tenthousand;
    insertrear( sum, number );
    xnext  := getnext( xnext );
    ynext  := getnext( ynext )
  END (* while loop *);
  IF endoflist( xnext )
  THEN
    long := ynext
  ELSE
    long := xnext

  END (* if then *);
  WHILE NOT endoflist( long ) DO
    total  := getinfo( long ) + carry;
    number := total MOD tenthousand;
    carry  := total DIV tenthousand;
    insertrear( sum, number );
    long := getnext( long )
  END (* while loop *);
  IF carry <> 0 THEN
    insertrear( sum, carry )
  END (* if then *);
  RETURN sum
END add;
```

We next develop the implementation details for the "printlong" operation. To print an interger, we start with the most significant digits and print from left to right to the least significant digits. However, our linked-list representation has the least significant digits in the first node and the most significant digits in the last node. We must reverse the order of the list before we can print it. To do this we can use a stack. The "insertfront" operation is equivalent to the "push" operation defined for a stack. So we define a stack as a list and as we traverse the long integer list, we place each node in the stack list as it is encountered. Then we traverse the stack list and print each node as it is encountered. Finally, before terminating the printlong procedure, we erase the stack list.

There is still one minor problem. Any leading zeros contained by the number in a node will not be printed, resulting in a long integer output showing blanks where there should be zeros. To solve this problem, we determine the magnitude of the number and explicitly print the leading zeros if there are any. The first node in the stack list contains the most significant digits, and in this case we do not print the meaningless leading zeros, if any. The complete algorithm follows:

```
PROCEDURE printlong
        ( x : longinteger                                   (* in *) );
  VAR next       : nodepointer;
      stack      : list;
      value      : INTEGER;
      first      : BOOLEAN;
BEGIN
  define( stack );
  next := firstnode( x );
  first := TRUE;
  WHILE NOT endoflist( next ) DO
    insertfront( stack, getinfo( next ) );
    next := getnext( next );
  END (* while loop *);
  next := firstnode( stack );
  WHILE NOT endoflist( next ) DO
    value := getinfo( next );
    IF first
    THEN
      WriteInt( value, 4 )
    ELSIF value < 10
    THEN
      WriteString( '000' );
      WriteInt( value, 1 )
    ELSIF ( value >= 10 ) AND ( value < 100 )
    THEN
      WriteString( '00' );
      WriteInt( value, 2 )
    ELSIF ( value >= 100 ) AND ( value <1000 )
    THEN
      Write( "0" );
      WriteInt( value, 3 )
    ELSE
      WriteInt( value, 4 )
```

```
      END (* if then elsif *);
      next := getnext( next );
      first := FALSE
    END (* while loop *);
    erase( stack )
  END printlong;
```

This concludes the implementation of the long integer ADT as promised in Listing 5.2. One would expect that the performance of this implementation could be improved if we implement the list operations directly rather than using the list ADT. We leave this matter to the exercises. We used the list ADT to implement long integers to demonstrate that the long integer ADT can be implemented as a list without a knowledge of the underlying data structure for the list, provided the necessary low-level list operations are available.

A closer examination of the operations described above reveals that the "make" and "add" operations insert nodes only at the rear of the list. This suggests the desirability of a circularly linked list with a list pointer to the last item in the list. The "printlong" operation requires us to traverse the list in the reverse direction, which suggests a doubly linked list.

Now let us consider negative long integers. When we add a negative integer and a positive integer, we need to determine which is the larger in magnitude before we perform the operation (i.e., the subtraction). This is done by comparing the most significant digits first. However, with the preceding implementation we must traverse the list in reverse order. This suggests a doubly linked list. The compare operation can be improved if we know the number of nodes in the list representation. The list containing the most nodes is the integer of largest magnitude. We need to compare the numbers in each node only if the list representations are of equal length. A list with a header node containing the number of nodes would improve the compare operation. Finally, how do we indicate the sign of the long integer? If we have a header node, the sign of the number in the header node could be used to represent the sign of the long integer and the magnitude of the number in the header node the length of the long integer in terms of 4-digit nodes.

The preceding discussion indicates that the long integer ADT might be best implemented as a doubly linked, circularly linked list with a header node. We leave it as an exercise to implement the long integer ADT using this data structure.

5.3 Polynomial Arithmetic

The manipulation and evaluation of symbolic polynomials is a problem of interest in a number of application areas. By "symbolic polynomial" we mean the list of coefficients and exponents that define the polynomial. For example, the polynomial $p(x)$ given by:

$$p(x) = 2x^4 + 3x^2 - 1$$

is a symbolic polynomial of degree 4.

We would like to be able to perform a number of operations on symbolic polynomials: addition and multiplication of two polynomials, evaluation of a polynomial at a specified value of x, forming the derivative of the polynomial, and integrating the polynomial over a specified interval, to name a few.

Before we can proceed with the implementation of these operations, we must decide how to represent a symbolic polynomial in the computer. We consider the general nth- degree polynomial given by:

$$a_n x^n + a_{n-1} x^{n-1} + \cdot \cdot \cdot + a_1 x^1 + a_0$$

One representation is to use an ordered list in which the first item is the degree of the polynomial, followed by the $n + 1$ coefficients in order of decreasing exponent. In this case, a polynomial can be represented using a one-dimensional array of length $n + 2$:

$$(n, a_n, a_{n-1}, \ . \ . \ . \ , a_1, a_0)$$

This representation leads to simple algorithms for the operations specified above. Notice that we do not need to explicitly store the exponent of each term, since it can be determined by the position in the list and the degree of the polynomial.

The preceding representation does have a serious shortcoming in that for certain polynomials, a large amount of storage space is wasted. For example, the polynomial:

$$x^{1000} - 1$$

requires a vector of length 1002 with 999 entries having a value of 0. This wastefulness of storage forces us to consider another representation scheme, especially if we do not know in advance a bound for the degree of the polynomial or the number of nonzero terms in the polynomial.

The representation scheme we will adopt is a linked list in which each node contains the coefficient and exponent of the terms of the polynomial having nonzero coefficients. For example, in Figure 5.2 we show the linked-list representation of the polynomial $p(x)$ given above.

We will keep the polynomial as an ordered list with the terms of the polynomial stored in the order of decreasing exponent. We assume that no two terms have the same exponent and that no term has a zero coefficient.

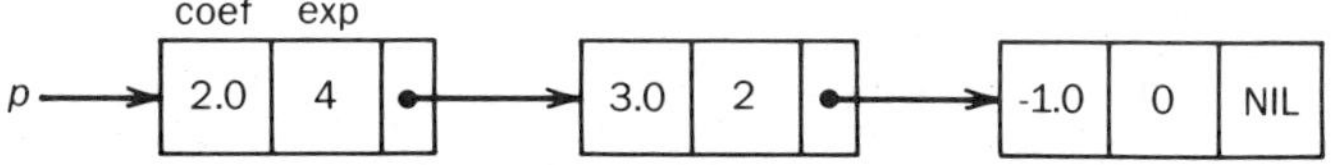

Figure 5.2 Linked List Representation of Polynomials

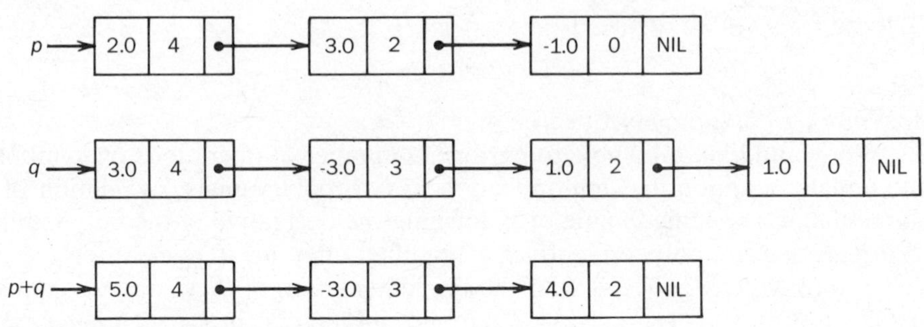

Figure 5.3 Polynomial Addition

Figure 5.3 illustrates the addition of two polynomials. The addition process is similar to merging two lists based on the exponent field, with the additional stipulation that when both polynomials have terms bearing the same exponent, the corresponding coefficients are added. If the resulting coefficient is zero, the term is not present in the polynomial sum.

The element type definition for use with the list ADT is given by:

```
DEFINITION MODULE elements;
   EXPORT QUALIFIED
     (* type *) elementtype;
   TYPE elementtype = RECORD
                        coef    : REAL;
                        exp     : CARDINAL
                      END (* record *);
END elements.
```

Listing 5.4 presents an interface definition to the polynomial abstract data type. We leave the implementation to the exercises.

Listing 5.4 Polynomial Abstract Data Type

```
DEFINITION MODULE polynomials;

  FROM listadt IMPORT
    (* type *) list;

  EXPORT QUALIFIED
    (* type *) polynomial,
    (* proc *) make, degree, add, subtract, multiply,
               evaluate, differentiate, integrate;

  TYPE polynomial;
```

```
PROCEDURE make
        ( VAR p : polynomial                    (* out *) );
(* This procedure makes the polynomial p from input
   consisting of coefficients and corresponding exponents
   for the terms in the symbolic polynomial.              *)


PROCEDURE degree
        ( p : polynomial                        (* in *) ) :
          CARDINAL;
(* This procedure returns the degree of the polynomial
   p.                                                     *)


PROCEDURE add
        ( p1, p2 : polynomial                   (* in *) ) :
          polynomial;
(* This procedure adds the two polynomials p1 and p2
   together to form the polynomial sum.                   *)


PROCEDURE subtract
        ( p1, p2 : polynomial                   (* in *) ) :
          polynomial;
(* This procedure subtracts the two polynomials p1 and
   p2 to form the polynomial p1 - p2.                     *)


PROCEDURE multiply
        ( p1, p2 : polynomial                   (* in *) ) :
          polynomial;
(* This procedure multiplies the two polynomials p1 and
   p2 to form the polynomial p1 * p2.                     *)


PROCEDURE evaluate
        ( p : polynomial                        (* in *);
          x : REAL                              (* in *) ) :
          REAL;
(* This procedure evaluates the polynomial p at the
   specified point x.                                     *)


PROCEDURE differentiate
        ( p : polynomial                        (* in *) ) :
          polynomial;
(* This procedure differentiates the polynomial p and
   returns the derivative, which is also a polynomial.    *)
```

```
  PROCEDURE integrate
          ( p : polynomial                          (* in *) ;
            a, b : REAL                             (* in *) ) :
            REAL;
  (* This procedure integrates the polynomial p from a to
     b and returns the result.                               *)

END polynomials.
```

Additional operations on polynomials we might also wish to define and implement include multiplying a polynomial by a scalar, finding all the roots of a polynomial (both real and complex), printing or displaying a polynomial, and dividing one polynomial by another to get two new polynomials (the quotient and the remainder). We leave the interface to these operations and their implementation as exercises.

5.4 Sparse Matrices

Linked lists can be used to implement sparse matrices—that is, tables or two-dimensional arrays with relatively few nonzero entries. Sparse matrices arise in mathematics, engineering, economics, and computer science problems. Figure 5.4 illustrates a 7 × 9 sparse matrix.

As another example, consider a table that contains company sales information. The rows of the table represent the sales staff, and the columns of represent the products sold by the company. Each entry indicates the number of items of a particular product sold by one of the salespeople. Since salespeople typically specialize in selling only a small range of products, we would expect the table to be sparse. Figure 5.5 illustrates this type of sparse matrix or table.

	1	2	3	4	5	6	7	8	9
1	0	3	0	0	0	0	11	0	0
2	5	0	0	0	−7	0	0	0	0
3	0	0	0	0	0	0	0	0	0
4	0	−4	0	0	0	0	0	0	13
5	0	0	0	0	0	0	0	10	0
6	0	0	0	0	0	0	0	0	0
7	0	0	−9	0	0	0	0	0	0

Figure 5.4 A Sparse Matrix

Employee \ Part	03	12	20	23	34	45	46	56	67	77	93
Adams	0	0	83	0	17	0	0	33	0	0	0
Baker	78	0	0	0	0	46	0	19	0	0	11
Fritz	0	65	0	0	0	0	0	39	0	9	0
Jones	0	0	0	86	67	0	0	0	19	0	0
Lamb	0	0	0	0	0	0	58	0	0	0	79
Morris	0	23	13	46	0	0	0	0	0	0	0
Parker	51	0	0	0	0	32	0	0	0	18	8
Smith	0	0	40	29	0	0	12	0	0	0	0
Wayne	0	0	0	0	0	0	0	0	121	0	0

Figure 5.5 A Sparse Table

Useful operations on sparse matrices include assignment of a value to a specified location, retrieving a value from a designated location, multiplying all entries in a specified row or column by a scalar, interchanging two rows, and adding a multiple of one row to another.

The simplest way to represent a sparse matrix is to use a two-dimensional array. If the sparse matrix contains m rows and n columns, then $m * n$ units of storage are required for the sparse matrix (where a ''unit of storage'' is the amount of space required to store one entry of the sparse matrix). This representation is certainly satisfactory for small matrices. If the matrix is large, however, the amount of storage required to store it in memory may exceed the capacity of the computer. For example, a 7×9 matrix requires 63 units of storage, but a 700×900 matrix requires 630,000 units of storage. However, if the matrix is both large and sparse, we should use a representation scheme that requires us to keep in memory only the nonzero entries.

The representation scheme we adopt is based on using linked allocation with eacn nonzero entry linked to the other nonzero entries. The simplest approach is to use the list ADT with the following elementtype definition:

```
TYPE elementtype = RECORD
                      row   : CARDINAL;
                      col   : CARDINAL;
                      entry : entrytype
                   END (* record *);
```

where entrytype defines the type of elements or items in the sparse matrix. In this representation, the entire sparse matrix is contained in a single linked list. The list begins with the first row of entries, followed immediately by the second row of entries, and so forth. The problem with this representation is that to access and entry in the ith row we must traverse the first $i - 1$ rows. Also, accessing the entries in the jth column requires us to traverse every entry in the list until we reach that column position in the last row. This is clearly an inefficient representation for a sparse matrix.

Another representation scheme is to keep a separate list for each row of the sparse matrix. This permits us to easily access a specified entry in the matrix by searching only the list associated with the specified row. However, the problem of accessing the entries in a specified column remains. If we keep a separate list for each column, the problem is transferred to accessing the entries in a specified row.

The solution is to keep each entry in the sparse matrix in two lists: a row list and a column list. We still need a method for accessing the first entry of each row or column list. One approach for an $m \times n$ sparse matrix is to define two arrays: one containing m pointers to the first entry in each row and the other containing n pointers to the first entry in each column. A second approach, which is the one we adopt, is to define header nodes for each row and column list. The header nodes can be recognized by a 0 in the row or column field. Furthermore, we will keep each row and column list as a circular list. So each row and column list is a linearly linked, circularly linked list with a header node.

The type of linked structure described for a sparse matrix is different from our previous list implementations, so we cannot use the list ADT directly. Instead, we must define our own operations for manipulating the dynamic lists that comprise a sparse matrix. The following declarations can be used to define the linked structure for representing a 700×900 sparse matrix containing entries of type entrytype.

```
CONST m = 700; (* The number of rows in the sparse matrix. *)
      n = 900; (* The number of columns in the sparse
                  matrix.                                 *)

TYPE rownum      = [0 .. m];
     colnum      = [0 .. n];
     nodepointer = POINTER TO node;
     node        = RECORD
                     row     : rownum;
                     col     : colnum;
                     entry   : elementtype;
                     nextrow : nodepointer;
                     nextcol : nodepointer
                   END (* record *);
```

The nextrow field of node points to the next entry in the same column and the nextcol field points to the next entry in the same row. We use type node for the header nodes for each row and column list. We also use a header node of type node to serve as a header node for the sparse matrix.

Figure 5.6 illustrates the sparse matrix given in Figure 5.4 using this linked allocation scheme. A similar linked allocation scheme can also be used to represent the sparse table of Figure 5.5.

We leave it as an exercise to develop the interface to the operations on sparse matrices and to implement the corresponding operations.

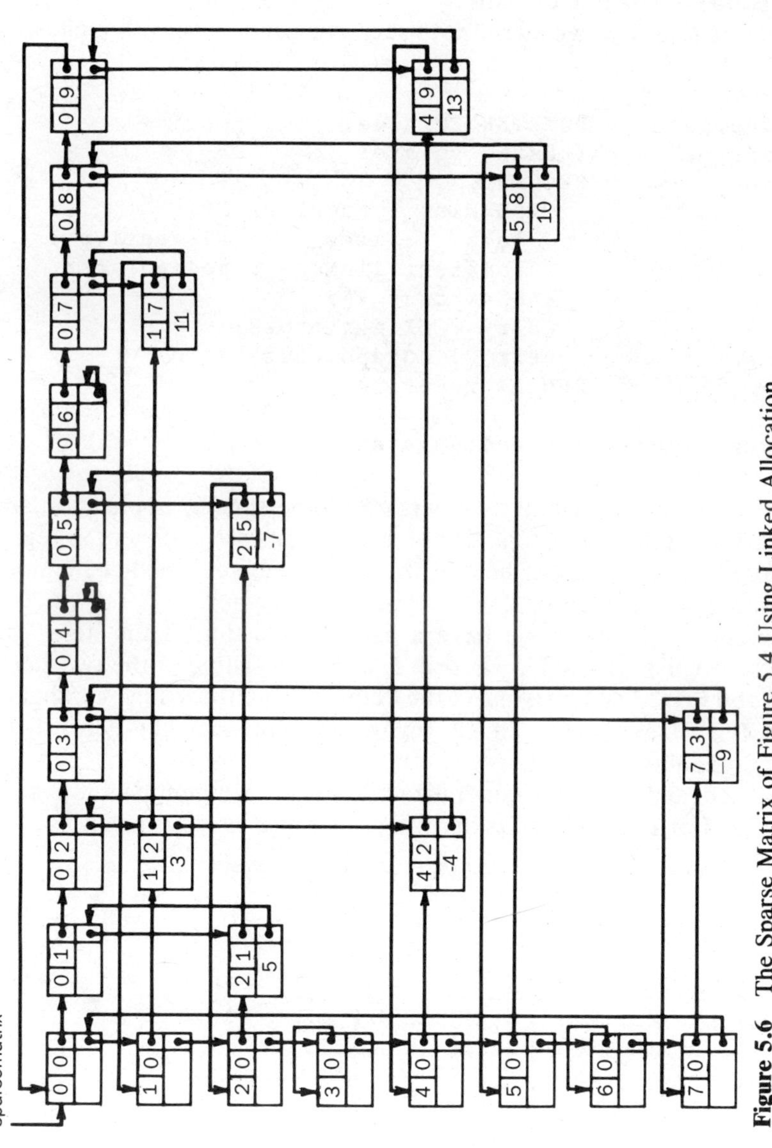

Figure 5.6 The Sparse Matrix of Figure 5.4 Using Linked Allocation

5.5 Generalized Lists

A generalized list is a list of finite length in which each node is either an item or a list. If a node is a list, the list is said to be a sublist of the original list. Each sublist can also be a generalized list.

The node structure for a generalized list can be defined using the following declarations:

```
TYPE nodepointer = POINTER TO node;
     nodetype    = ( data, pointer );
     node        = RECORD
                     CASE kind : nodetype OF
                       data    : item      : elementtype1 |
                       pointer: link       : nodepointer
                     END (* case *);
                     entry : elementtype2;
                     next  : nodepointer
                   END (* record *);

     generalizedlist = nodepointer;
```

where elementtype1 and elementtype2 depend on the specific application and are imported from module elements. These declarations are sufficient to represent any generalized list. The tag field of the node indicates whether the node contains a pointer to a sublist or data of type elementtype1.

As an example, suppose we have a list A consisting of the item "a" followed by the sublists B and C, where B is a list consisting of the two items "b" and "c" and C is a list consisting of the item "d" and the sublist C. That is, A = (a, B, C), B = (b, c), and C = (d, C). Figure 5.7, represents this generalized list using the preceding declarations.

One practical application of generalized lists is in representing multivariable polynomials. For example, consider the polynomial $p(x,y,z)$ given by:

$$p(x,y,z) = x^{10}y^3z^2 - 3x^6y^3z^2 + 5x^8yz^2 + x^4y^4z + 6x^2y^4z + xz + 10$$

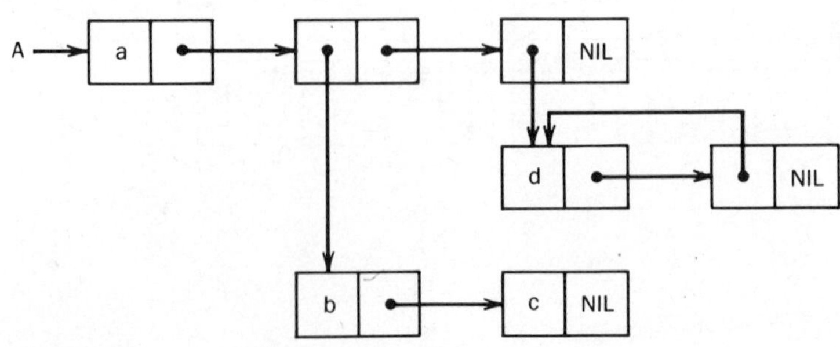

Figure 5.7 A Generalized List

This polynomial can be written as follows:

$$p(x,y,z) = A(x,y)z^2 + B(x,y)z + 10$$

where $A(x,y)$ and $B(x,y)$ are polynomials in the variables x and y. The polynomials A and B can be written as:

$$A(x,y) = C(x)y^3 + D(x)y$$

and

$$B(x,y) = E(x)y^4 + F(x)$$

where C, D, E, and F are polynomials in the variable x. Specifically,

$$C(x) = x^{10} - 3x^6 \qquad D(x) = 5x^8$$
$$E(x) = x^4 + 6x^2 \qquad F(x) = x$$

Every multivariable polynomial can be written in this manner.

We define the following node declaration for use in representing a multivariable polynomial. This slight modification of the node declaration above enables us to use the variable as a header node for each coefficient sublist rather than including the variable in every node of the generalized list.

```
TYPE nodepointer = POINTER TO node;
     nodetype    = ( variable, data, pointer );
     node        = RECORD
                     CASE kind : nodetype OF
                       variable : var      : CHAR |
                       data     : coef     : REAL |
                       pointer  : link     : nodepointer
                     END (* case *);
                     exp      : CARDINAL;
                     next     : nodepointer
                   END (* record *);
```

With this node declaration, the multivariable polynomial can be represented as in Figure 5.8. In practice, the variable field would probably contain a pointer to a symbol table containing the value of the variables that appear in the mutivariable polynomial.

Exercises

5.1 The course registration system defined the courses as a fixed size array of records. What problems, if any, are encountered in implementing courses as a linked list? Can we use the list ADT without modification?

5.2 Develop a charge account system. Customer accounts are kept in a list, with each item in the list containing a customer's name, the customer's account number, and the customer's current balance. Your system should permit the addition of new customers and the deletion of existing

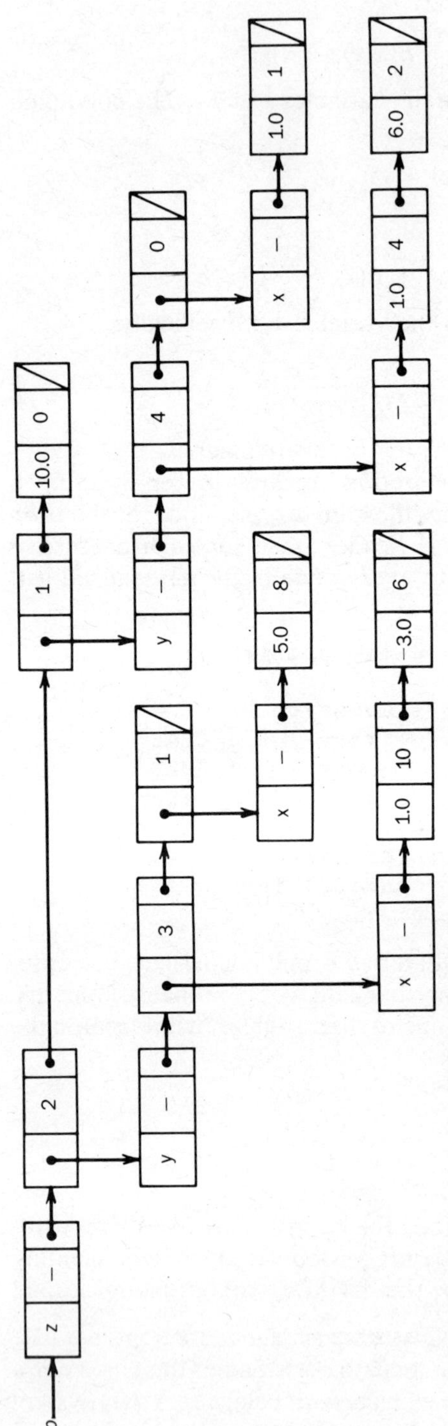

Figure 5.8 Generalized List Representation of a Multivariable Polynomial

customers. The customer list is ordered by increasing account numbers. Transactions contain the account number and an amount. If the amount is positive, it represents a charge and should be added to the customer's current balance. If the amount is negative, it represents a payment by the customer and should be subtracted from the current balance. Finally, the system should permit printing the accounts in ascending order of account number.

5.3 In an event-driven simulation, the events (operations on objects) are determined by data that is read in during the simulation. In a time-driven simulation, the events are determined by a clock (usually a counter in the program) and usually a random number generator. In an event-driven simulation, an event list is created, with each node in the event list representing a different possible event. Each node contains the time the event occurs, the type of event, and any other information associated with the event. The event list is usually ordered by the time for the next event. Redo the computer simulation presented in Chapter 3 using an event list.

5.4 Develop a program that implements the following hash sort algorithm. We wish to sort N numbers where we know that each number is in the range from 0 to 10,000. We define 10 bins as lists and place each number in its ordered position in each bin according to the following rule:

$$\begin{array}{l} 1 \ \ - \ \ 1000 \rightarrow \text{bin } 1 \\ 1001 - \ \ 2000 \rightarrow \text{bin } 2 \\ \ldots \\ 9001 - 10000 \rightarrow \text{bin } 10. \end{array}$$

Then the contents of each bin are printed, giving the sorted numbers.

5.5 Explain why we cannot use insertfront and insertafter operations in place of the insertrear operation in procedure make of the long integer implementation. Specifically, what logical error have we made if we initialize first to TRUE and replace the if statement in the for loop with the following?

```
IF count = 4
THEN
  insertfront( x, number );
  first := FALSE
ELSE
  insertafter( x, lastnumber, number, equal )
END (* if then *);
lastnumber := number;
```

5.6 Modify procedure printlong in the longinteger implementation so that it converts the long integer to a string of characters and prints the string of characters.

5.7 Implement the long integer ADT using a doubly linked, circularly linked list with a header node containing the sign of the long integer and the length of the list representation for the long integer.

5.8 Define the interface and implement the following additional operations for the long integer ADT:

(a) Subtract.

(b) Multiply.

(c) MOD.

(d) DIV.

(e) Comparison operations: lessthan, equal, greaterthan, notequal, greaterthanorequal.

5.9 Implement the operations for the polynomial ADT promised in the definition module given in Listing 5.4.

5.10 Define the interface and implement the following additional operations for the polynomial ADT:

(a) Print or display a polynomial.

(b) Divide one polynomial by another to get two new polynomials, the quotient and the remainder.

(c) Find all the roots of a polynomial (requires numerical algorithms).

(d) Display the polynomial in factored form (requires the results of part c).

5.11 Define the interface and implement the following operations for sparse matrices using the dynamic allocation scheme described in section 5.4. (Your interface should allow for multiple instances of sparse matrices: i.e., the sparse matrix on which the operation is to be performed must be a parameter for all the defined operations.)

(a) Assign an entry to a specified row and column location.

(b) Retrieve a value from a specified row and column location.

(c) Interchange two rows.

(d) Multiply all entries in a specified row by a scalar.

(e) Add a multiple of one row to another.

In parts d and e, we assume that multiple makes sense for the type of entries in the sparse matrix.

5.12 Rework exercise 5.11 using the array implementation of linked allocation.

5.13 Implement the string ADT using a linked list. Use the interface defined in Listing 1.4.

6

Review of Recursion

Because of the tremendous importance of recursion in many of the tree algorithms to be discussed in later chapters, we now review and illustrate the basic principles of recursion. We assume that the reader has had a brief introduction to recursion.

6.1 The Notion of Recursion

A recursive control structure is a generalization of an iterative control structure. An iterative control structure is distinguished by the characteristic that each iterative cycle (loop) must be completed before the next iterative cycle begins.

For a recursive control structure, a new iterative cycle may begin before the completion of the preceding iterative cycle. In this case the original iterative cycle is temporarily aborted and control is transferred to the new iterative cycle. This pattern may repeat itself many times, so that a chain of interrupted iterations is produced. The iterative cycles are serviced like a stack. That is, the first iterative cycle to be aborted is the last to be serviced. The last iterative cycle to be called is the first to be serviced.

In Modula-2, recursion may be initiated by having a subprogram (procedure or procedure function) call itself.

The operating system must save the values of all subprogram local variables and value parameters that were in force at the time of aborting an iterative cycle so that later, when control returns to the iterative cycle, the original values of the local variables and value parameters may be reinstated. This requires memory overhead. A stack structure is normally used internally and managed by the operating system as the recursion progresses. In addition to memory overhead, the operating system must save the location of the interruption, so that upon completion of the subsequent iteration(s), control can be transferred back to the appropriate statement in the original iteration.

In using recursion, it is the programmer's responsibility to avoid infinite loops. As an example of a recursion that produces an infinite loop, consider the following short and totally artificial program module.

```
MODULE test;
  TYPE realarray = ARRAY [ 1.. 1000 ] OF REAL;

  PROCEDURE recurse( a : realarray );
  BEGIN
    recurse( a );
  END recurse;

  VAR
    numbers : realarray;
BEGIN
  recurse( numbers );
END test.
```

Every time procedure recurse calls itself, a local copy of the array of 1000 real numbers is made and saved. Before long, a stack overflow run-time error occurs, aborting program execution. Perhaps we can be thankful that a stack overflow run-time error does occur, acting like a fuse in the system; otherwise the program would loop forever.

By modifying procedure recurse as shown below, we can avoid the infinite loop.

```
MODULE test;
  TYPE realarray = ARRAY [ 1.. 1000 ] OF REAL;

  PROCEDURE recurse( a : realarray; n : CARDINAL );
  BEGIN
    IF n > 0
    THEN
      recurse( a, n - 1 );
    END(* if then *);
  END recurse;

  VAR
     numbers : realarray;

BEGIN
  recurse( numbers, 3 );
END test.
```

In the modified program, the recursive procedure is protected by an alternative control structure (if then), so that when n is forced to zero after three iterations, the chain of new recursive calls ends and the existing iterative cycles may be completed.

In general, recursive procedures must be protected by an alternative control structure that ultimately limits the number of new recursive calls and avoids an infinite loop.

It is always possible to convert a recursive procedure to an iterative procedure. Often this conversion requires that the iterative procedure contain many more lines of code than the original recursive procedure. We will not discuss this issue in this book. The reader may wish to consult Tennenbaum (1981) for details concerning this conversion process.

A recursive solution to a problem is often more natural and requires less code than an iterative solution. Unless great care is exercised, a recursive solution may require significantly more memory overhead and run slower than the corresponding iterative solution.

In general, problems that naturally submit to a recursive solution possess two characteristics:

1. The solution of an instance of the problem may be expressed in terms of one or more smaller instances of the problem.
2. The smallest instance of the problem may be solved directly.

To illustrate these two characteristics, we consider the problem of finding the sum of the integers in an array, a. If we define *s(k)* as the sum of the integers over index values 1, . . . , *k*, we may write:

1. $s(k) = s(k - 1) + a[k]$
2. $s(1) = a[1]$

The first equation is an example of the solution of an instance of the problem being expressed in terms of one or more smaller instances of the problem. In the second equation, the smallest instance of the problem is solved directly.

Listing 6.1 presents a recursive procedure for finding the sum of the elements of an array.

Listing 6.1 A Recursive Procedure for Finding the Sum of Elements in an Array

```
TYPE intarray = ARRAY[ 1..500 ] OF INTEGER;

PROCEDURE sum
          ( VAR a     : intarray          (* in *);
                count : CARDINAL          (* in *) ) : INTEGER;

BEGIN
  IF count > 1
  THEN
    RETURN sum( a, count - 1 ) + a[ count ];
  ELSE
    RETURN a[ 1 ];
  END(* if then else *);
END sum;
```

We note that a pass-by-reference (VAR) parameter is used in procedure sum, even though we identify this parameter functionally to be an input parameter. Why? We do this to avoid the significant memory overhead that would be incurred if the array parameter *a* were a value parameter. Exactly *n* recursive calls to sum are required, each necessitating that copies of all local variables and value parameters be saved. By making the array parameter a reference parameter, we completely avoid this memory overhead problem.

Although we have solved the array summation problem using recursion, we recognize that because the single recursive call per iteration cycle occurs at the end of procedure sum, the recursion is an iteration in disguise. In this case, we may as well rewrite procedure sum iteratively, as given in Listing 6.2.

Listing 6.2 An Iterative Procedure for Finding the Sum of Elements in an Array

```
PROCEDURE sum
          ( VAR a     : intarray              (* in  *);
                size  : CARDINAL              (* in  *) ) :
INTEGER;

VAR
   index       : CARDINAL;
   runningsum  : CARDINAL;

BEGIN
  runningsum := 0;
  FOR index := 1 TO size DO
    runningsum := runningsum + a[ index ];
  END(* for loop *);
  RETURN runningsum;
END sum;
```

It may be of interest to note that a timing analysis comparing the execution time of recursive procedure sum, in Listing 6.1, with the iterative procedure sum, in Listing 6.2, reveals that the iterative version takes approximately 60 percent of the time the recursive version takes. These results are of course machine specific. We invite you to perform your own test.

6.2 Examples Illustrating Recursion

In this section we illustrate recursive procedures with a series of programs of increasing complexity.

6.2.1 Recursion Example 1: Binary Search of an Array

Suppose we have an array of objects, a, such that the objects are ordered from smallest to largest within the array. We wish to efficiently search the array to determine whether a given object—say, object key—is present. An efficient binary search procedure is presented in the main program module given in Listing 6.3.

Listing 6.3 Recursive Binary Search Procedure

```
MODULE testsearch;

  FROM InOut IMPORT
    (* proc *) WriteLn, WriteString, WriteCard;

  TYPE objects = ARRAY[ 1.. 1000 ] OF REAL;


  PROCEDURE search
            ( VAR a          : objects        (* in  *);
              low, high      : CARDINAL       (* in  *);
              key            : REAL           (* in  *);
              VAR position   : CARDINAL       (* out *) );

  VAR middle : CARDINAL;

  BEGIN
    IF low <= high
    THEN
      middle := ( low + high ) DIV 2;
      IF key = a[ middle ]
      THEN
        position := middle;
      ELSIF key < a[ middle ]
      THEN
        search( a, low, middle - 1, key, position )
      ELSE
        search( a, middle + 1, high, key, position );
      END(* if then *);
    ELSE
      position := 0;
    END(* if then *);
  END search;

VAR
   a    : objects;
```

```
  i   : CARDINAL;
  pos : CARDINAL;

BEGIN(* testsearch *)
  FOR i := 1 TO 1000 DO
    a[ i ] := FLOAT( i );
  END(* for loop *);
  search( a, 1, 1000, 499.0, pos );
  WriteLn;
  WriteString(" The location of 499.0 is ");
  WriteCard( pos, 1 );  (* The output will be 499 *)
  search( a, 1, 1000, 3050.0, pos );
  WriteLn;
  WriteString(" The location of 3050 is ");
  WriteCard( pos, 1 );  (* The output will be 0 *)
  search( a, 1, 1000, 1.0, pos );
  WriteLn;
  WriteString(" The location of 1.0 is ");
  WriteCard( pos, 1 );  (* The output will be 1 *)
  WriteLn;
END testsearch.
```

As with recursive procedure sum, in Listing 6.1, the recursive call in procedure search occurs in the last executable line in the procedure. This is the simplest type of recursion and, in fact, is identical to an iterative procedure.

The memory overhead associated with each recursive call is the memory required to save one real and four cardinal variables. In the worst case (the key not present), the number of recursive calls is approximately $\log_2 n$. See exercise 6.4. In exercise 6.5, we ask you to rewrite procedure as an iterative procedure.

6.2.2. Recursion Example 2: Computing *n* Factorial

Another very common example of a simple recursion, found in almost every introductory programming book, is computing $n!$ (n factorial), defined as $n \times (n - 1) \times \ldots \times 2 \times 1$. We display such a factorial procedure function in Listing 6.4.

Listing 6.4 Factorial Procedure Function Using Recursion

```
PROCEDURE factorial
          ( n : CARDINAL                (* in  *) ) : REAL;
```

```
BEGIN
  IF n > 0
  THEN
    RETURN FLOAT( n ) * factorial( n - 1 );
  ELSE
    RETURN 1.0;
  END(* if then *);
END factorial;
```

Do you see the two characteristics of a recursive problem, presented in section 6.1, displayed by procedure factorial? How many recursive calls will be required to evaluate $n!$? Why does procedure factorial return a real value rather than a cardinal or integer value? (Hint: What is the range of integer values?)

6.2.3 Recursion Example 3: Recursive Name Printer

In Listing 6.5, we present our last example of a simple recursion (recursive call is the last executable statement in the procedure).

Listing 6.5 Recursive Name Printer

```
MODULE namerecursion;

  FROM InOut IMPORT
    (* proc *) WriteLn, WriteString, Write;

  TYPE name = ARRAY[ 0 .. 9 ] OF CHAR;


  PROCEDURE writename
            (     n : name
              count : CARDINAL

  VAR
     index : CARDINAL;

  BEGIN
    IF count > 0
    THEN
      WriteLn;
      FOR index := 1 TO count DO
        Write(' ');
      END(* for loop *);
```

```
      WriteString( n );
      writename( n, count - 1 );
    END(* if then *);
  END writename;

BEGIN(* namerecursion *)
  writename( "MODULA-2", 10 );
END namerecursion.
```

Clearly, program module namerecursion writes out the string MODULA-2 10 times. Can you predict the format on the screen? See exercise 6.6.

6.2.4 Recursion Example 4: First Complex Recursion

The first three examples of recursion have been simple. In fact, all three examples could easily be rewritten as iterative procedures because the recursive call occurs at the end of each procedure.

We now introduce our first nontrivial recursive procedure in Listing 6.6.

Listing 6.6 First Complex Recursion

```
MODULE FirstComplexRecursion;

  FROM InOut IMPORT
    (* proc *) WriteLn, WriteString, WriteInt, ReadInt;

  PROCEDURE print
            ( n : INTEGER);

  BEGIN
    IF n # 0
    THEN
      WriteLn;
      WriteString(" Enter an integer: ");
      ReadInt( n );
      print( n );
      WriteLn;
      WriteInt( n, 1 );
    END(* if then *);
  END print;

BEGIN
  print( 1 );
END FirstComplexRecursion.
```

Suppose the input sequence is 5, 4, 3, 0. Can you predict the output of this program? We will trace the recursive logic of this program, step by step.

The first call to print, from the main program, sends a 1 to the parameter n. Because n # 0, we enter procedure print. After being prompted to enter an integer, we enter the number 5. Because n is a value parameter, its original value of 1 is immediately lost and the value 5 replaces it.

When print (with $n = 5$) is called, after a new interger has been entered from the keyboard, the execution of the first call to procedure print is temporarily aborted, the value $n = 5$ is saved on the recursive stack, and we enter print for the second time. After entering a new integer, 4, the initial value of $n = 5$ gives way to the next value, $n = 4$, just before print is called a third time. We enter print again, with $n = 4$, and replace this value with $n = 3$. We call print a fourth time. We enter print with $n = 3$, and replace n with the value 0. We call print a fifth time, sending in $n = 0$. We cannot reenter print, and the sequence of new calls to print stops.

The recursion returns to the line just below the last call to print, namely, the call when $n = 0$. The program prints out the value 0. Control then returns to the previous call to print, when $n = 3$, and the program prints out the value 3. Using the same logic, the remaining sequence of output consists of the integers 4 and 5.

The value 1, which triggered the recursion, is forever lost, having been replaced with the value 5 before the first recursive call was made. The correct sequence of numbers output is therefore: 0, 3, 4, 5. Did your output include a 1?

The added complexity to the recursion in Listing 6.6 is accounted for by the line of code under the recursive call. Whenever a recursive call occurs in the middle of a procedure, it is necessary to track the sometimes complex sequence of control transfers and keep track of the local and value parameter values that were in force just before the recursive call. When several recursive calls occur within the body of the same procedure, the tracking process becomes even more complex. We illustrate this in several examples.

6.2.5 Recursion Example 5: Second Complex Recursion

In the recursion presented in Listing 6.7, there are two recursive calls within procedure print.

Listing 6.7 Second Complex Recursion

```
MODULE SecondComplexRecursion;

  FROM InOut IMPORT
    (* proc *) WriteLn, WriteInt;
```

```
 PROCEDURE print
               ( n : INTEGER );

  BEGIN
    IF n # 0
    THEN
      print( n DIV 2 );
      WriteLn; WriteInt( n, 1 );
      print( n DIV 2 );
    END(* if then *);
  END print;

BEGIN
  print( 10 );
END SecondComplexRecursion.
```

Table 6.1 gives a step-by-step walk-through of SecondComplexRecursion.

It should be clear from Table 6.1 that there is some logical overhead associated with tracing a recursive procedure in which several recursive calls occur.

TABLE 6.1 Analysis of Listing 6.7: Second Complex Recursion

1. `print( n = 10 )`	We enter procedure print with $n = 10$.
2. `print( 5 )`	We recursively call print with $n = 5$.
3. `print( n = 5 )`	We enter procedure print with $n = 5$.
4. `print( 2 )`	We recursively call print with $n = 2$.
5. `print( n = 2 )`	We enter procedure print with $n = 2$.
6. `print( 1 )`	We recursively call print with $n = 1$.
7. `print( n = 1)`	We enter procedure print with $n = 1$.
8. `print( 0 )`	We recursively call print with $n = 0$. We enter print with $n = 0$ and then exit.
9. `output 1`	
10. `print( 0 )`	We recursively call print with $n = 0$. We enter print with $n = 0$ and then exit.
11. `output 2`	
12. `print( 1 )`	We recursively call print with $n = 1$.
13. `print( n = 1 )`	We repeat steps 8, 9, and 10 and output 1.
14. `output 5`	
15. `print( 2 )`	We recursively call print with $n = 2$.
16. `print( n = 2 )`	We repeat steps 6 to 13 and output 1, 2, 1.
17. `output 10`	
18. `print( 5 )`	We recursively call print with $n = 5$.
19. `print( n = 5 )`	We repeat steps 4 to 16 and output 1, 2, 1, 5, 1, 2, 1.

The output sequence: 1, 2, 1, 5, 1, 2, 1, 10, 1, 2, 1, 5, 1, 2, 1

6.2.6 Recursion Example 6: Third Complex Recursion

In the recursion presented in Listing 6.8, there is one recursive call within procedure whatisthis.

Listing 6.8 Third Complex Recursion

```
MODULE ThirdComplexRecursion;

  FROM InOut IMPORT
    (* proc *) WriteLn, WriteInt, WriteString;

  PROCEDURE whatisthis
            ( a, b : INTEGER );

  VAR c : INTEGER;

  BEGIN
    IF a > 0
    THEN
      c := a + b;
      a := a - 1;
      whatisthis( a, b );
      b := c;
      WriteLn; WriteString( " a = " ); WriteInt( a, 1 );
      WriteString( " b = " ); WriteInt( b, 1 );
    END(* if then *);
  END whatisthis;

BEGIN (* main program *)
  whatisthis( 5, 10 );
END ThirdComplexRecursion.
```

In Table 6.2, we walk through this recursion step by step.

6.2.7 Recursion Example 7: Permutations

The recursion in Listing 6.9 outputs every permutation of the original string of characters. In fact, procedure permute has important practical applications whenever it is necessary to generate a group of permutations on a set of objects. For example, suppose you wish to quickly generate 362,880 misspelled

TABLE 6.2 Analysis of Listing 6.8: Third Complex Recursion

	Trace	Comment
1.	`whatisthis( a = 5, b = 10)`	We enter whatisthis.
2.	`c = 15, a = 4`	
3.	`whatisthis( 4, 10 )`	We call whatisthis recursively.
4.	`  whatisthis( a = 4, b = 10)`	We enter whatisthis.
5.	`  c = 14, a = 3`	
6.	`  whatisthis( 3, 10 )`	We call whatisthis recursively.
7.	`    whatisthis( a = 3, b = 10 )`	We enter whatisthis.
8.	`    c = 13, a = 2`	No further comments.
9.	`    whatisthis( 2, 10 )`	
10.	`      whatisthis( a = 2, b = 10)`	
11.	`      c = 12, a = 1`	
12.	`      whatisthis( 1, 10 )`	
13.	`        whatisthis( a = 1, b = 10 )`	
14.	`        c = 11, a = 0`	
15.	`        whatisthis( 0, 10 )`	
16.	`        output a = 0, b = 11`	
17.	`      output a = 1, b = 12`	
18.	`    output a = 2, b = 13`	
19.	`  output a = 3, b = 14`	
20.	`output a = 4, b = 15`	

Listing 6.9 Permutations

```
MODULE permutations;

  FROM InOut IMPORT
    (* proc *) Write, WriteLn;

  TYPE string = ARRAY[ 1..20 ] OF CHAR;

  VAR
     number : CARDINAL;
     s      : string;


  PROCEDURE permute
            ( n     : CARDINAL (* in     *);
              VAR s : string   (* in/out *) );


  VAR
     temp : CHAR;
     i, j : CARDINAL;

  BEGIN
    IF n > 1
    THEN
      permute( n - 1, s );
```

```
      FOR i := n - 1 TO 1 BY -1 DO
        (* Interchange the elements in s[ n ] and s[ i ] *)
        temp := s[ n ];
        s[ n ] := s[ i ];
        s[ i ] := temp;
        permute( n - 1, s );
        (* Interchange the elements in s[ n ] and s[ i ] *)
        temp := s[ n ];
        s[ n ] := s[ i ];
        s[ i ] := temp;
      END(* for loop *);
    ELSE
      FOR j := 1 TO number DO
        Write( s[ j ] );
      END(* for loop *);
      WriteLn;
    END(* if then *);
  END permute;

BEGIN
  number := 3;
  s[ 1 ] := 'A';
  s[ 2 ] := 'B';
  s[ 3 ] := 'C';
  permute( 3, s );
END permutations.
```

words to test a spelling checker's speed in processing misspelled words. You would merely expand the original string, s, to include the letters A to I, change number from 3 to 9, and run the program. All 362,880 permutations of the characters from A to I would be generated and printed out.

The recursion in procedure permute is by far the most complex we have encountered because the recursive call occurs within a loop inside the recursive procedure. We present all the gory details in Table 6.3.

6.2.8 Recursion Example 8: Partitions of a Cardinal

This example of recursion and much of the discussion of it are taken with permission from Ford and Wiener (1985). We wish to determine how many partitions there are for a positive integer.

We define a partition of a cardinal number n as an expression of the form $a + b + c + \cdots + k$ that is equal to n. We will consider expressions that can be

TABLE 6.3 Analysis of Listing 6.9: Permutations

```
1.    permute( n = 3, s = [A,B,C] )
2.    permute( 2, s )
3.      permute( n = 2, s = [A,B,C] )
4.      permute( 1, s )
5.        permute( n = 1, s = [A,B,C] )
6.        output ABC
7.    i = i in FOR loop
8.    interchange s[2] with s[1] → s = [B,A,C]
9.    permute( 1, s )
10.     permute( n = 1, s = [B,A,C] )
11.     output BAC
12.   interchange s[2] with s[1] → s = [A,B,C]
        end FOR loop
13. i = 2 in FOR loop
14. interchange s[3] with s[2] → s = [A,C,B]
15. permute( 2, s )
16.   permute( n = 2, s = [A,C,B] )
17.   Repeat steps 4 to 12 and output ACB and CAB
        s is restored to [A,C,B]
18. interchange s[3] with s[2] → s = [A,B,C]
19. i = 1 in FOR loop
20. interchange s[3] with s[1] → s = [C,B,A]
21. permute( 2, s )
22.   permute( n = 2, s = [C,B,A] )
23.   Repeat steps 4 to 12 and output CBA and BCA
        s is restored to [C,B,A]
24. interchange s[3] with s[1] → s = [A,B,C]
      end FOR loop

The sequence of output is therefore: ABC
                                     BAC
                                     ACB
                                     CAB
                                     CBA
                                     BCA
```

derived from each other by rearranging the terms to be the same partition. As an example, the 11 partitions of the cardinal value 6 are:

6
5 + 1
4 + 2
4 + 1 + 1
3 + 3
3 + 2 + 1
3 + 1 + 1 + 1
2 + 2 + 2
2 + 2 + 1 + 1
2 + 1 + 1 + 1 + 1
1 + 1 + 1 + 1 + 1 + 1

If we agree to write partitions in the form shown above, with terms decreasing from left to right, we can make an important observation.

> A Partition of n that begins with the term k must have all other terms no greater than k and the sum of all other terms equal to $n - k$.

The number of partitions that begin with k equals the number of partitions of $n - k$, with the largest term at most k. If we compute this latter value for each possible $k = 1, 2, \ldots, n$, the sum of these values is the solution to our problem.

We will assume in Listing 6.10 that there is one partition of the integer zero. We will also assume that there are zero partitions of a negative integer. Also, if $n = 1$ or $k = 1$, there is only one partition possible.

Listing 6.10 Partitions of a Cardinal

```
MODULE Partition;

  FROM InOut IMPORT
    (* proc *) WriteLn, WriteString, WriteInt;

  PROCEDURE partition
          ( n : INTEGER (* number to be partitioned *);
            k : INTEGER (* largest first term        *) ) :
          INTEGER;

  VAR
      i     : INTEGER;
      count : INTEGER;

  BEGIN
    IF n < 0
    THEN
      RETURN 0;
    ELSIF ( n <= 1 ) OR ( k = 1 )
    THEN
      RETURN 1;
    ELSE
      count := 0;
      FOR i := 1 TO k DO
        count := count + partition( n - i, i );
      END(* for loop *);
      RETURN count;
    END(* if then *);
  END partition;

VAR number : INTEGER;

BEGIN
  FOR number := 1 TO 20 DO
```

```
    WriteLn;
    WriteString(" The number of partition of ");
    WriteInt( number,1 );
    WriteString(" equals ");
    WriteInt( partition( number, number ), 1 );
  END(* for loop *);
END Partition.
```

To better understand the recursion given in Listing 6.10, we will walk through an example when a call is made to partition (3, 3), as shown in Table 6.4.

TABLE 6.4 Analysis of Listing 6.10: Partitions

```
1.   partition( n = 3, k = 3 )
2.   count = 0
3.   i = 1
4.   count = 0 + partition( 2, 1 )
5.   partition( n = 2, k = 1 )
6.   count = 0
7.   i = 1
8.   count = 0 + partition( 1, 1 )
9.     partition( n = 1, i = 1 )
10.    RETURN 1
11.   RETURN 1
12. i = 2
13. count = 1 + partition( 1, 2 ) RETURN 1
14. i = 3
15. count = 2 + partition( 0, 3 ) RETURN 1
16. RETURN 3 as answer
```

Exercises

6.1 We indicated in section 6.1 that a recursive solution to a problem is often more natural and requires less code than an iterative solution. List five problems that should yield in a natural way to a recursive solution.

6.2 Write a recursive procedure for solving each of the five problems you listed in response to exercise 6.1.

6.3 For your computer, perform a careful timing analysis of the recursive and iterative programs given in Listings 6.1 and 6.2.

6.4 Prove that if a key is not present in an ordered array, a binary search of the array requires approximately $\log_2 n$ recursive calls.

6.5 Rewrite the binary search procedure given in Listing 6.3 using iteration. Do a careful timing analysis for your computer and compare execution times for recursion versus iteration.

6.6 What is the format for the output generated in Listing 6.5?

6.7 What is the output for the program in Listing 6.6 if the value parameter n is changed to a reference parameter, VAR n, in procedure print? Assume that other appropriate changes are made to the program, such as passing in a variable rather than a constant when print(1) is called from the main program.

6.8 What is the output for the program in Listing 6.7 if the value parameter n is changed to a reference parameter, VAR n, in procedure print? As in exercise 6.7, assume that other appropriate changes are made to the program.

6.9 Modify Listing 6.9 so that you generate all the permutations of the string "CANDY".

6.10 Write an iterative procedure for printing out the partitions of a cardinal number.

6.11 Write a recursive procedure to find the kth smallest element of an array z. *Hint:* Choose any element $z[j]$ and partition z into the elements smaller than, equal to, or greater than $z[j]$. See Horowitz, Ellis, and Sahni (1976).

6.12 Write a recursive procedure for finding the greatest common divisor of two integers a and b. The greatest common divisor, GCD, is defined as:

$$\begin{aligned} \text{GCD}(a, b) &= b && \text{if } b \leq a \text{ and } a \bmod b = 0 \\ \text{GCD}(a, b) &= \text{GCD}(b, a) && \text{if } a < b \\ \text{GCD}(a, b) &= \text{GCD}(b, a \bmod b) && \text{otherwise} \end{aligned}$$

6.13 Write a recursive procedure PAL that takes a pointer to a linked list of characters as input and returns the palindrome of the list (a new list twice as long as the first list: e.g., if list 1 = A B C, then list 2 = A B C C B A). A palindrome is a list that has the same sequence of elements when read from left to right and from right to left.

6.14 An important application of recursion occurs in numerical integration. Based on the material in section 3.4, develop a recursive algorithm using the trapezoid and Simpson quadrature rules.

7

Introduction to Binary Trees

7.1 Definition of a Tree

The tree is one of the most important nonlinear structures used for algorithm development in computer science. The important applications of trees include syntax checking, database management, searching, sorting, and game algorithms, to name a few. We will introduce tree concepts and some implementations in this chapter and examine applications of trees in Chapters 8 and 9.

Formally, a tree is a finite set of one or more nodes arranged so that:

1. There is a special node, the root node, that provides an entryway into the structure.
2. The remaining nodes, if any, are partitioned into $m \geq 0$ disjoint sets, each of which is a tree. The disjoint sets are called the subtrees of the root.

Note that this definition is recursive—we have defined a tree in terms of a tree.

Every node in a tree structure is the root node of subtrees. The degree of a node equals the number of subtrees associated with the node. A leaf node is a node of degree zero.

We define the level of the root node in a tree as 1. The root node's offspring, if any, are at level 2. Their offspring, if any, are at level 3, and so on.

How do we draw a tree? If we use terminology such as "bottom-up" analysis of a tree or "top-down" analysis, if we say that one node is "higher" than another, or if we refer to the "right" offspring of a node, then particular orientations of the tree are implied.

We will adhere to the almost universal convention of representing the root

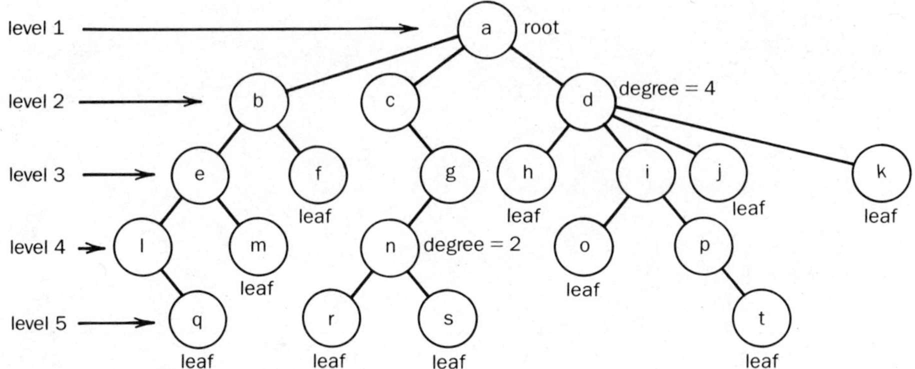

Figure 7.1 Tree with Five Levels

node as the apex or top node of the tree, with the subtrees of the root flowing "downward" from the root. We may then speak of the "depth" of a tree.

The tree in Figure 7.1 has five levels. Some nodes are labeled with the degree of the node; the leaf nodes and levels are also labeled.

The order of offspring nodes is important in most computer science applications. We will distinguish the trees depicted in Figures 7.2 and 7.3 as different trees because their orders of offspring are different. We will borrow from genealogy terms such as sibling, ancestor, and descendant to represent the relationships among the nodes of a (family) tree.

Finally, since we have defined trees, we should define a forest. A forest is formally defined as an ordered set of zero or more disjoint trees. Less formally, the nodes of a tree minus its root constitute a forest. We display a forest in Figure 7.4.

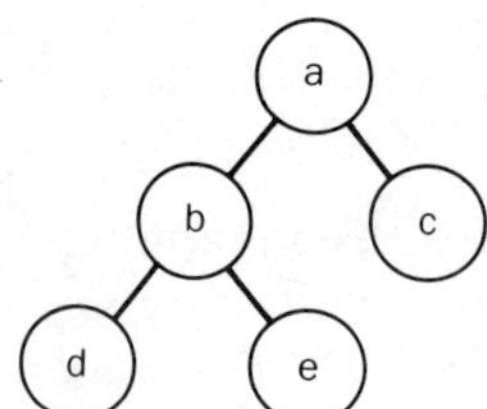

Figure 7.2 Tree Illustrating Order of Offspring

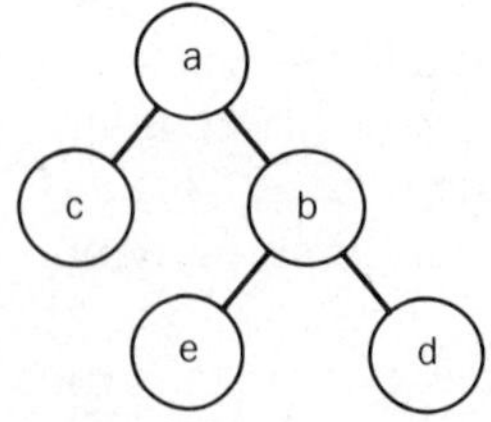

Figure 7.3 Another Tree Illustrating Order of Offspring

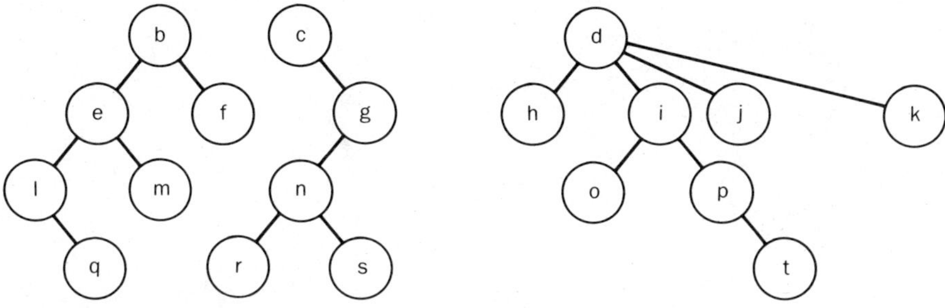

Figure 7.4 Forest

7.2 Definition of a Binary Tree

A binary tree is defined as a finite set of zero or more nodes arranged so that:

1. If there exists one or more nodes, there is a special node, the root node, that provides an entryway into the structure.

2. The remaining nodes, if any, are partitioned into two disjoint sets, and each of these sets is a tree. The disjoint sets are called the left and right subtrees of the root. Each node in a binary tree has either zero, one, or two children.

A binary tree is a tree in which we distinguish the left child from the right child. For example, the binary trees shown in Figure 7.5 are not the same.

A tree may always be represented as a binary tree. We link together all the siblings of each family (nodes at the same level within a family) and remove the vertical links except from a parent to the first child (going left to right). We illustrate this transformation in Figure 7.6. If we rotate the resulting structure by 45 degrees, we have a binary tree representation of the original tree.

Because of the transformation relating trees to binary trees, and because of the important applications of binary trees, we will focus on binary trees for the remainder of this chapter.

7.3 Some Operations on Binary Trees

Table 7.1 lists a set of operations common to all binary trees. In Chapter 8, we expand this set considerably and consider practical applications of binary trees.

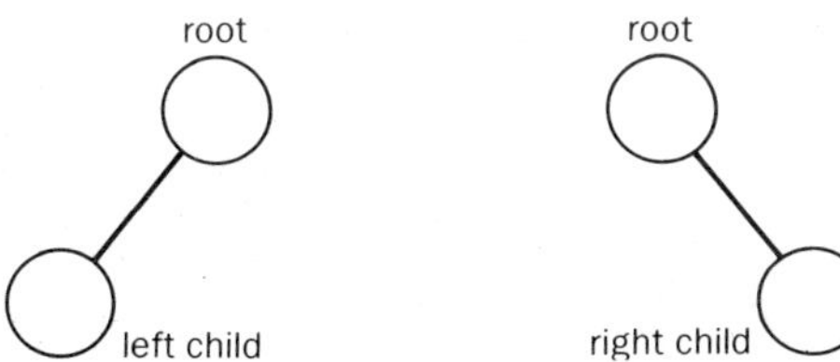

Figure 7.5 Two Different Binary Trees

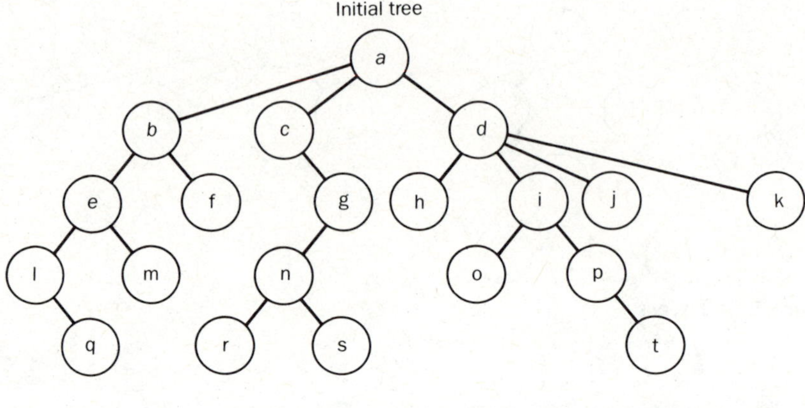

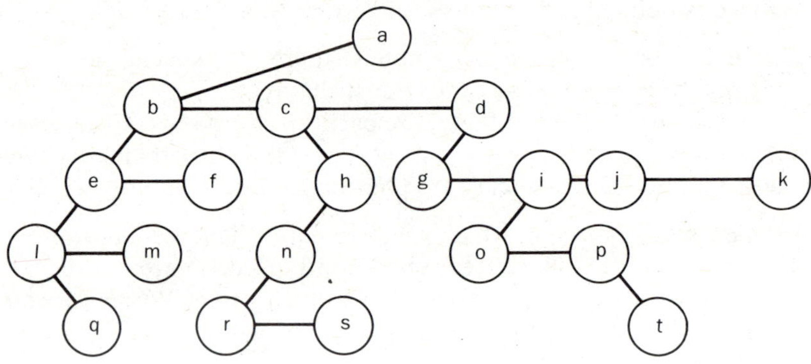

Figure 7.6 Transformation from Tree to Binary Tree

The precise interface presented in Listing 7.1 encapsulates the operations enumerated in Table 7.1.

We note the procedure parameters contained in procedures ispresent, addright, addleft, level, and parent. Like the interface to the list abstract data

TABLE 7.1 Basic Tree Operations

1. Define a tree.
2. Determine whether an item is present in a tree.
3. Add left child to a tree node with a specified item.
4. Add right child to a tree node with a specified item.
5. Determine whether a tree is empty.
6. Make a nonempty tree empty.
7. Determine the level of an item in a tree.
8. Determine the parent of an item in a tree.
9. Determine the youngest common ancestor (yca) of two items in a tree.

Listing 7.1 Interface to Basic Tree Operations

```
DEFINITION MODULE treeadt;

  FROM elements IMPORT
    (* type *) elementtype;

  EXPORT QUALIFIED
    (* type *) tree,
    (* proc *) define, ispresent, addleft, addright,
               isempty,
               makeempty, level, parent, yca,
               makeroot;

  TYPE tree;


  TYPE equaltype    = PROCEDURE( elementtype, elementtype ) :
                        BOOLEAN;


  PROCEDURE define
          ( VAR t          : tree              (* out  *) );
  (* This procedure must be used before any other tree
     operations are performed.                              *)


  PROCEDURE makeroot
          ( VAR t          : tree              (* out *);
                rootitem : elementtype       (* in  *);
  (* Returns the root node of a tree.                       *)


  PROCEDURE ispresent
          ( t              : tree                 (* in  *);
            item           : elementtype          (* in  *);
            equal          : equaltype            (* in  *) ):
            BOOLEAN;
  (* This procedure returns true if item is in the tree.   *)


  PROCEDURE addright
          (     t              : tree             (* in  *);
                parentitem     : elementtype      (* in  *);
                newitem        : elementtype      (* in  *);
                equal          : equaltype        (* in  *) );
  (* Adds a node containing newitem as the right child of
     parentitem.                                            *)
```

```
PROCEDURE addleft
          (      t                : tree           (* in  *);
                 parentitem       : elementtype    (* in  *);
                 newitem          : elementtype    (* in  *);
                 equal            : equaltype      (* in  *) );
(* Adds a node containing newitem as the left child of
   parentitem.                                            *)


PROCEDURE isempty
          (      t          : tree                 (* in  *) ) :
                 BOOLEAN;
(* Returns true if the tree does not contain any nodes.  *)


PROCEDURE makeempty
          ( VAR t          : tree               (* in/out *) );
(* Deallocates memory space by removing all nodes from the
   tree and returning the tree to a state equivalent to
   define.                                                *)


PROCEDURE level
          (      t          : tree            (* in     *);
                 item       : elementtype     (* in     *);
                 equal      : equaltype       (* in     *) ) :
                 CARDINAL;
(* Returns the level of the node containing item.  If item
   is not present, returns 0.                             *)


PROCEDURE parent
          (      t          : tree            (* in     *);
                 item       : elementtype     (* in     *);
                 equal      : equaltype       (* in     *) ) :
                 elementtype;
(* Returns the parent item of the node containing the
   input item.                                            *)


PROCEDURE yca
          (      t                : tree          (* in  *);
                 item1, item2     : elementtype   (* in  *);
                 equal            : equaltype     (* in  *) ) :
                 elementtype;
(* Returns the youngest common ancestor of two nodes
   containing item1 and item2.                            *)


END treeadt.
```

type presented earlier, the interface to the tree operations allows each tree node to contain an arbitrary object of type elementtype. The programmer using the tree operations in a client module must supply procedures that compare two objects of type elementtype, like the procedures used with lists.

We also note that the user of the tree abstract data type module never needs to "see" pointer variables and other low-level details of the tree implementation. The interface is given in terms of objects that are meaningful to a client program (i.e., items and comparison operations).

7.4 Implementations of Binary Trees

We will now examine two simple representations (data structures) of a binary tree. We mention the first in passing; the second is used in most of our applications.

7.4.1 Static Implementation of a Binary Tree

The array has been used to represent stacks, queues, and linked lists. We can also use it as a vehicle for housing a binary tree. Because the implementation details of type tree are hidden from any program unit that imports this type, however, none of the operations that are associated with an array (e.g., direct access of an array component) can be performed. Only the tree operations specified in the definition module may be performed.

The necessity to declare memory for an array statically (at compile time) forces the implementation module to limit the size of a tree that may be constructed in a program unit.

We map the index positions in an array to the positions of nodes in a binary tree as follows: the root node is assigned index position 1, the root's left child (even if it is empty) is assigned the position 2, the root's right child (even if it is empty) is assigned the position 3, the root's left child's left child (even if it is empty) is assigned the position 4, and so forth. In Figure 7.7, we display a binary tree and list the index positions associated with each node.

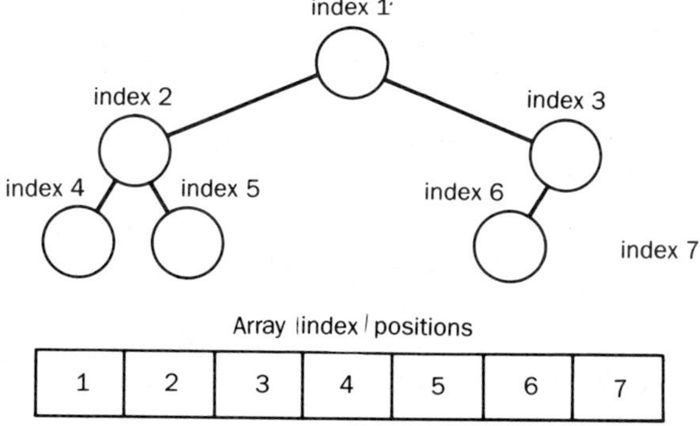

Figure 7.7 Association Between Array Index Positions and Binary Tree Nodes

A Modula-2 array representation of a binary tree containing items of type elementtype imported from module elements is:

```
TYPE tree = POINTER TO ARRAY [ 1 .. maxnodes ] OF
                    elementtype;
```

Please note the size constraint, maxnodes, required of an array representation. We use a pointer to an array because a pointer representation is required of all opaque types in Modula-2.

To move down such a tree, if child and parent represent index locations in the array, we use the relation:

```
leftchild  := 2 * parent
rightchild := 2 * parent + 1
```

To move up such a tree, if child and parent represent index locations in the array, we use the relation:

```
parent := child DIV 2.
```

7.4.2 Dynamic Implementation of a Binary Tree

Using pointer variables and dynamic allocation, a Modula-2 representation of a binary tree containing an item field is:

```
TYPE tree = POINTER TO node;

     node = RECORD
               item  : elementtype;
               left  : tree;
               right : tree;
            END(* record *);
```

Using this dynamic representation, nodes may be created or deleted at run time. Only the heap size of the host computer limits the number of nodes that may be created in a tree. We will use this dynamic tree representation or some small variation of it in implementing most tree algorithms.

7.5 Tree Traversal

In many algorithms based on binary trees, it is necessary to ''visit'' each node of a tree exactly once. The simplest application of tree traversal involves displaying the item contained in each node in a tree. Other applications of tree traversal involve deleting each node from a tree, searching a tree for some item, and other applications to be discussed later.

There are three basic algorithms for binary tree traversal: preorder, inorder, and postorder. We will present short recursive algorithms for all three types of traversal.

7.5.1 Preorder Traversal

The algorithm for preorder traversal is the following:

```
Algorithm PreorderTraversal( t : pointer to root (* in *) );
  if t is not empty
  then
    Visit( t )
    PreorderTraversal( leftchild ( t ) )
    PreorderTraversal( rightchild( t ) )
  end if

end Algorithm
```

We could reverse the last two steps and still have a preorder traversal from "right" to "left" instead of from "left" to "right".

We use the procedure Visit(t) to mean perform some operation on the node t (e.g., print out the item). Let us walk through an example and show that using a preorder traversal, we "Visit" each node once and only once. We will use the binary tree in Figure 7.8 to illustrate the three types of tree traversal. We interpret "visit" for our current purposes to mean "print out the item."

We begin the preorder traversal by visiting node A. Upon completion of the visit, the algorithm recursively calls itself with t pointing to node B. We visit node B. Then we visit node D. We next attempt to visit the left child of node D, which is NIL. We then are directed to visit the right child of node D, which is node H. We then visit node I. Then we attempt to visit node I's left and right children, which are both NIL. Control in the recursion then directs us to visit node J. We attempt to visit node J's left and right children, which are both NIL.

Having visited node D's left child and right child and B's left child, we continue by visiting node E. We attempt to visit node E's left and right child, which are both NIL. Having already visited node A and A's left child, we now visit node C. After C, we visit nodes F and K, in that order. After attempting to

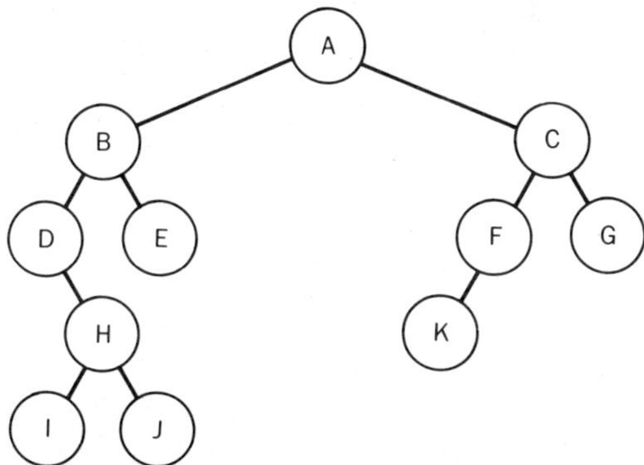

Figure 7.8 Tree Traversal

visit node K's left and right child and then node F's right child, which are all NIL, the recursion directs us to visit node G. The traversal terminates when we have attempted to visit node G's left and right children.

Thus, the output for the preorder traversal is:

A, B, D, H, I, J, E, C, F, K, G.

7.5.2 Inorder Traversal

The algorithm for inorder traversal is the following:

```
Algorithm InorderTraversal( t : pointer to root (* in *) );
  if t is not empty
  then
    InorderTraversal( leftchild ( t ) )
    Visit( t )
    InorderTraversal( rightchild( t ) )
  end if

end Algorithm
```

We could reverse the first and third steps and still have an inorder traversal from "right" to "left" instead of from "left" to "right."

Let us walk through another example and show that using an inorder traversal, we visit each node once and only once.

We begin by traversing (not visiting) the root node, node A. The traversal takes us down the tree through nodes B and D. At node D, we attempt to traverse to D's left child, which is NIL. We then visit node D. Then we traverse through nodes H and I. We next visit node I, after attempting to traverse I's left child, which is NIL. After attempting to visit node I's right child, we visit node H. Next we traverse to J, then visit J. Because we have already traversed node B and gone to its left child, we visit node B. After this we traverse, then visit, node E.

We ask the reader to complete this traversal and show that the sequence of remaining visits is: A, K, F, C, G.

The complete output for the inorder traversal is:

D, I, H, J, B, E, A, K, F, C, G.

7.5.3 Postorder Traversal

The algorithm for postorder traversal is the following:

```
Algorithm PostorderTraversal( t : pointer to root (* in *) );
  if t is not empty
  then
```

```
    PostorderTravseral( leftchild ( t ) )
    PostorderTravseral( rightchild( t ) )
    Visit( t )
  end if

end Algorithm
```

We could reverse steps 1 and 2 and still have an postorder traversal from "right" to "left" instead of from "left" to "right."

We leave it as an exercise for the reader to verify that the postorder traversal of the tree given in Figure 7.8 is:

I, J, H, D, E, B, K, F, G, C, A.

7.6 Implementation of Tree Operations

Listing 7.1 presented a definition module containing the Modula-2 interface for the ten basic tree operations given in Table 7.1. We now present the implementation of the tree operations in Listing 7.2.

Listing 7.2 Implementation of Tree Operations

```
IMPLEMENTATION MODULE treeadt;

  FROM Storage IMPORT
    (* proc *) ALLOCATE, DEALLOCATE;

  FROM Terminal IMPORT
    (* proc *) WriteLn, WriteString;

  FROM elements IMPORT
    (* type *) elementtype;

  TYPE tree = POINTER TO node;

       node = RECORD
                item  : elementtype;
                left  : tree;
                right : tree;
              END(* record *);


  PROCEDURE locate
            (      t          : tree              (* in  *);
                   item       : elementtype       (* in  *);
```

```
                 equal       : equaltype          (* in  *) ) :
            tree;
  (* This private procedure is invisible to client
     modules.                                               *)

  VAR
       found : BOOLEAN;
       ptr   : tree;


    PROCEDURE traverse
              (    t           : tree                (* in  *) );

    BEGIN
      IF ( t # NIL ) AND ( NOT found )
      THEN
        traverse( t^.left );
        traverse( t^.right );
        IF equal( item, t^.item )
        THEN
          found := TRUE;
          ptr   := t;
        END(* if then *);
      END(* if then *);
    END traverse;

  BEGIN (* locate *)
    found := FALSE;
    ptr := NIL;
    traverse( t );
    RETURN ptr;
  END locate;


  PROCEDURE define
            ( VAR t            : tree                (* out *) );

  BEGIN
    t := NIL;
  END define;


  PROCEDURE makeroot
            ( VAR t            : tree            (* out *);
                  rootitem     : elementtype     (* in  *) );

  VAR
       newnode : tree;

  BEGIN
    NEW( newnode );
```

```
  newnode^.left := NIL;
  newnode^.right := NIL;
  newnode^.item := rootitem;
  t := newnode;
END makeroot;


PROCEDURE ispresent
          ( t        : tree                (* in     *);
            item     : elementtype         (* in     *);
            equal    : equaltype           (* in     *) ) :
            BOOLEAN;
BEGIN
  RETURN locate( t, item, equal ) # NIL
END ispresent;


PROCEDURE inserterror;
BEGIN
  WriteLn;
  WriteString( "Illegal addleft or addright operation." )
END inserterror;


PROCEDURE addright
          (     t              : tree          (* in  *);
                parentitem     : elementtype   (* in  *);
                newitem        : elementtype   (* in  *);
                equal          : equaltype     (* in  *) );

VAR
    parent  : tree;
    newnode : tree;

BEGIN
  parent := locate( t, parentitem, equal );
  IF parent^.right # NIL
  THEN
    inserterror;
  ELSE
    NEW( newnode );
    newnode^.item := newitem;
    newnode^.left := NIL;
    newnode^.right := NIL;
    parent^.right := newnode
  END (* if then *);
END addright;
```

```
PROCEDURE addleft
          (     t                : tree            (* in  *);
                parentitem       : elementtype     (* in  *);
                newitem          : elementtype     (* in  *);
                equal            : equaltype       (* in  *));
VAR
    parent  : tree;
    newnode : tree;
BEGIN
  parent := locate( t, parentitem, equal );
  IF parent^.left # NIL
  THEN
    inserterror;
  ELSE
    NEW( newnode );
    newnode^.item  := newitem;
    newnode^.left  := NIL;
    newnode^.right := NIL;
    parent^.left   := newnode;
  END (* if then *);
END addleft;


PROCEDURE isempty
          (     t            : tree                 (* in   ) ):
          BOOLEAN;
BEGIN
  RETURN t = NIL;
END isempty;


PROCEDURE makeempty
          ( VAR t          : tree             (* in/out *) );

BEGIN
  IF NOT isempty( t )
  THEN
    makeempty( t^.left );
    makeempty( t^.right );
    DISPOSE( t );
  END(* if then *);
  + := NIL;
END makeempty;


PROCEDURE level
          (     t            : tree             (* in  *);
                item         : elementtype      (* in  *);
                equal        : equaltype        (* in  *) ) :
                CARDINAL;
(* See exercise 7.18. *)
```

```
VAR
    found : BOOLEAN;
    lev   : CARDINAL;  (* tracks the level of nodes *)


  PROCEDURE traverse
          (   t            : tree             (* in     *);
            VAR lev        : CARDINAL         (* in/out *) );


  BEGIN
    IF NOT isempty( t )
    THEN
      IF ( NOT found ) AND
      NOT ( isempty( t^.left ) AND isempty( t^.right ) )
      (* t is not a leaf node *)
      THEN
        INC( lev );
      END(* if then *);
      traverse( t^.left, lev );
      traverse( t^.right, lev );
      IF ( NOT found ) AND
         NOT ( isempty( t^.left ) AND isempty( t^.right ) )
      (* t is not a leaf node *)
      THEN
        DEC( lev );
      END(* if then *);
      IF equal( item, t^.item )
      THEN
        found := TRUE;
      END(* if then *);
    END(* if then *);
  END traverse;



BEGIN (* level *)
  IF NOT ispresent( t, item, equal )
  THEN
    RETURN 0;
  END(* if then *);
  found := FALSE;
  lev := 1;
  IF equal( item, t^.item )
  THEN
    RETURN 1;
  ELSE
    traverse( t, lev );
    RETURN lev;
  END(* if then *);
END level;
```

```
PROCEDURE parent
          (      t              : tree             (* in  *);
                 item           : elementtype      (* in  *);
                 equal          : equaltype        (* in  *) ):
          elementtype;

VAR
    found   : BOOLEAN;
    current : elementtype;


  PROCEDURE traverse
            (      t            : tree             (* in     *);
               VAR current      : elementtype      (* in/out *) );

  BEGIN
    IF ( NOT found ) AND ( NOT isempty( t ) )
    THEN
      IF ( ( t^.left # NIL ) AND
         ( equal( item, t^.left^.item ) ) ) OR
         ( ( t^.right # NIL ) AND
         ( equal( item, t^.right^.item ) ) )
      THEN
        found := TRUE;
        current := t^.item;
      END(* if then *);
      traverse( t^.left, current );
      traverse( t^.right, current );
    END(* if then *);
  END traverse;

BEGIN (* parent *)
  IF t # NIL THEN
    found := FALSE;
    IF equal( item, t^.item )
    THEN
    (* The parent of a rootnode is the rootnode.          *)
      RETURN t^.item;
    ELSE
      traverse( t, current );
      RETURN current;
    END(* if then *);
  END (* if then *);
END parent;


PROCEDURE yca
          (      t              : tree             (* in  *);
                 item1, item2   : elementtype      (* in  *);
                 equal          : equaltype        (* in  *) ):
                 elementtype;
```

```
  VAR
      node1, node2    : elementtype;
      level1, level2 : CARDINAL;

  BEGIN
    IF ( NOT ispresent( t, item1, equal ) ) OR
       ( NOT ispresent( t, item2, equal ) )
    THEN
      WriteLn;
      WriteString( "Illegal input in procedure yca." );
      HALT;
    END(* if then *);
    level1 := level( t, item1, equal );
    level2 := level( t, item2, equal );
    node1 := item1;
    node2 := item2;
    WHILE level1 > level2 DO
      node1 := parent( t, item1, equal );
      DEC( level1 );
    END(* while *);
    WHILE level2 > level1 DO
      node2 := parent( t, item2, equal );
      DEC( level2 );
    END(* while loop *);
    (* node1 and node2 are at the same level *)
    WHILE NOT equal( node1, node2 ) DO
      node1 := parent( t, node1, equal );
      node2 := parent( t, node2, equal );
    END(* while loop *);
    RETURN node1;
  END yca;


END treeadt.
```

The recursive and dynamic data structure presented in section 7.4.2 is used to represent the opaque data type, tree.

Function procedure locate, a private procedure, uses a postorder traversal of the tree to find a matchup between the external item and the node with the same internal item. Since the postorder traversal visits each node exactly once, if a matchup is to be found, this procedure will find it. If a matchup is not found, the pointer returned is NIL.

The first operation, define, sets the root node of the tree to NIL. In the absence of such a declaration, the root pointer to the tree is undefined.

Procedure makeemtpy displays another application of tree traversal. Using a postorder traversal, each and every node is visited and deleted. Why not

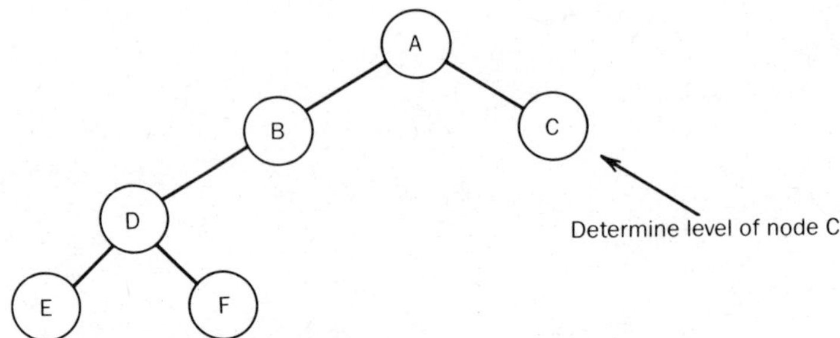

Figure 7.9 Level of Node in Tree

use a preorder or inorder traversal to accomplish node deletion? The final tree, after makeempty, is NIL.

To help explain the algorithm in the code for procedure level, we refer to Figure 7.9 and walk through this example.

Procedure level utilizes a postorder traversal. The variable lev is initially set to 1. We call the nested procedure traverse(pointer to A, 1). Because A is not empty, found is false, and A is not a leaf node, we increment lev to 2. We recursively call traverse(pointer to B, 2).

As before, because node B is not empty and is not a leaf node, and found is false, we increment lev to 3 and recursively call traverse(pointer to D, 3). Next we increment lev to 4, and call traverse(pointer to E, 4).

Because E is a leaf node, we do not increment lev, and it remains 4. We call traverse(NIL, 4) and then traverse(NIL, 4), each time no useful processing occurs. We do not decrement lev because E is a leaf node. We compare the key E to the key C and no matchup occurs. We exit the recursive call to E.

Control returns with t pointing to D. We call traverse(pointer to F, 4). As with leaf node E, no useful processing occurs and we exit from this recursive call without a matchup. Note that if a matchup had occurred for either node E or node F, the value of lev returned would have been 4, the correct level. Before exiting the recursive call to D, lev is decremented to 3 (node D is not a leaf node) and no matchup occurs. If a matchup had occurred, the value of lev returned would have been 3, the correct value.

Control returns with t pointing to B. We call traverse(NIL, 3). No useful processing occurs. Because node B is not a leaf node, lev is decremented to 2 before exiting this stage of recursion. Had a matchup occurred with node B, the value of lev returned would have been 2, which is correct.

Control returns with t pointing to C. Because C is a leaf node, lev is not incremented. After calls to traverse(NIL, 2) twice, lev is not decremented and a matchup is found. The correct value of 2 is returned for the level of node C.

Had there been additional nodes below node C, the recursion would have worked its way down and then back up the tree to node C. Once found is set to true, the value of lev is frozen and future recursive calls are cut off.

We urge the reader to walk through procedure parent and explain the tree traversal used.

We next examine the algorithm and Modula-2 implementation code for determining the youngest common ancestor between two nodes in a tree.

An informal strategy for locating the youngest common ancestor between two nodes of a tree is given as follows:

1. Locate the positions of the two tree nodes that correspond to the key values input to the procedure.
2. Compute the levels for each of the two descendant nodes.
3. If the levels are not the same, move up from child to parent, starting at the lower descendant node, to a node whose level is the same as the higher descendant node.
4. With both nodes now at the same level, move up from child to parent along the two branches until convergence to the same node occurs.
5. Output this final node.

We hope you agree that the implementation details presented for procedure yca are clear and follow the informal strategy given above. If we were to change the data structure of our tree, there would be no fallout effects at all on the client programs that use the treeadt because we have programmed using data abstraction.

Exercises

7.1 Compute the number of ancestors nodes in a binary tree for a given node a level k.

7.2 Write a Modula-2 procedure for determining whether a binary tree containing exactly $2^n - 1$ nodes is perfectly balanced.

7.3 List three applications outside computer science where a tree structure is useful. (*Hint*: One application involves your family ancestry.) For each application area, sketch a typical tree, labeling each node in terms of the variables relevant to the application area.

7.4 Can you deduce any relationship between the postorder traversal of a binary tree and the preorder traversal of its mirror image?

7.5 Find all binary trees such that the preorder and inorder traversals visit the nodes in exactly the same order.

7.6 Find all binary trees such that the preorder and postorder traversals visit the nodes in exactly the same order.

7.7 Find all binary trees such that the inorder and postorder traversals visit the nodes in exactly the same order.

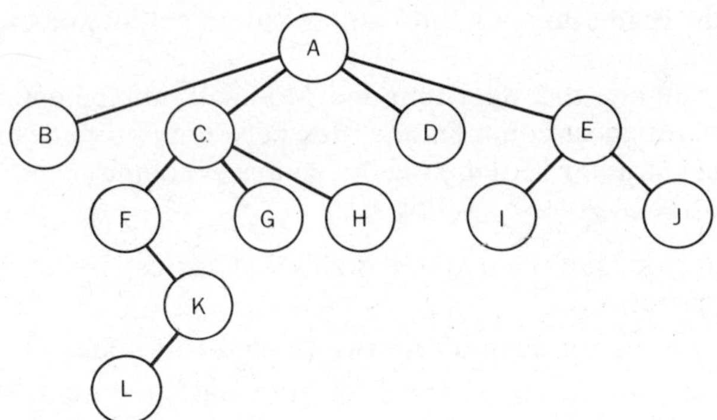

Figure 7.10 Tree for Exercise 7.11

7.8 Do the leaf nodes in a binary tree occur in the same order for preorder, inorder, and postorder traversals? If so, prove your contention?

7.9 Devise an algorithm for deleting a node from a binary tree. Implement and test your algorithm with a Modula-2 procedure.

7.10 Prove that if we are given the preorder and postorder traversals of a binary tree, the binary tree structure may be constructed. Write and test a Modula-2 procedure for accomplishing this.

7.11 Sketch the binary tree that results from transforming the tree shown in Figure 7.10 to a binary tree.

7.12 Why not use a preorder or inorder traversal to accomplish node deletion in procedure makeempty in section 7.6?

7.13 Write an alternative implementation to procedure level, given in section 7.7.

7.14 Write an alternative implementation to procedure parent, given in section 7.7.

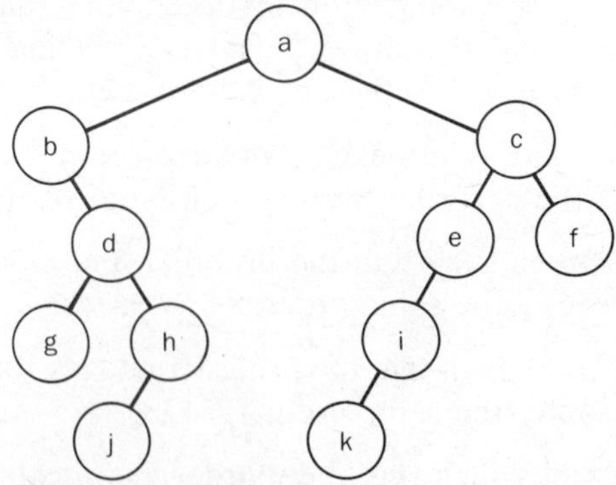

Figure 7.11 Tree for Exercise 7.17

7.15 Write a Modula-2 procedure copy. The interface is:

```
PROCEDURE copy
          (     t : tree     (* in  *);
            VAR c : tree     (* out *) );
(* Creates a tree, c, which is the same as t. *)
```

7.16 Write a Modula-2 procedure mirror. The interface is,

```
PROCEDURE mirror
         (     t : tree       (* in  *);
           VAR m : tree       (* out *) );
(* Creates a tree, m, which is the mirror image of t. *)
```

7.17 Determine the preorder, postorder, and inorder traversal of the tree shown in Figure 7.11.

7.18 Walk through the following procedure level. See procedure level on page 262.

```
PROCEDURE level
          (     t        : tree          (* in *);
                item     : elementtype   (* in *);
                equal    : equaltype     (* in *) ):
CARDINAL;
  VAR
      p : CARDINAL;
  PROCEDURE traverse
            (     ptr    : tree         (* in     *);
                  lev    : CARDINAL     (* in/out *) );
  BEGIN
    IF ptr # NIL
    THEN
      INC( lev );
      IF equal( ptr^.item, item )
      THEN
        p := lev;
      ELSE
        traverse( ptr^.left, lev );
        IF p = 0
        THEN
          traverse( ptr^.right, lev );
        END(* if then *);
      END(* if then *);
    END(* if then *);
  END traverse;
BEGIN (* level *)
  p := 0;
  traverse( t, p );
  RETURN p;
END level;
```

8

Applications of Binary Trees

A principal goal of this chapter, which presents several applications of binary trees, is to demonstrate the versatility and importance of the binary tree as an information structure. Our applications include the construction of an elementary search table, the removal of duplicates from a list, the sorting of a list, the computation of average path length in an elementary search tree, and the representation and evaluation of algebraic expressions.

We begin with some definitions relating to path length, both internal and external, for a binary tree. Although we will not delve deeply into the mathematical theory of binary trees nor follow up on many of the concepts introduced in this section, we believe that it is important for the reader to be aware of some of the basic definitions and mathematical relationships presented here.

8.1 Quantitative Relations Associated with Binary Trees

Suppose we are given a binary tree, such as the tree depicted in Figure 8.1. Each node shown is called an internal node. We may extend the tree and replace every empty subtree (nonexistent node) with an external node, shown with a square. Such a tree corresponding to the tree given in Figure 8.1 is shown in Figure 8.2. In exercise 8.1, we ask you to prove that an extended binary tree of n internal nodes contains $n + 1$ external nodes.

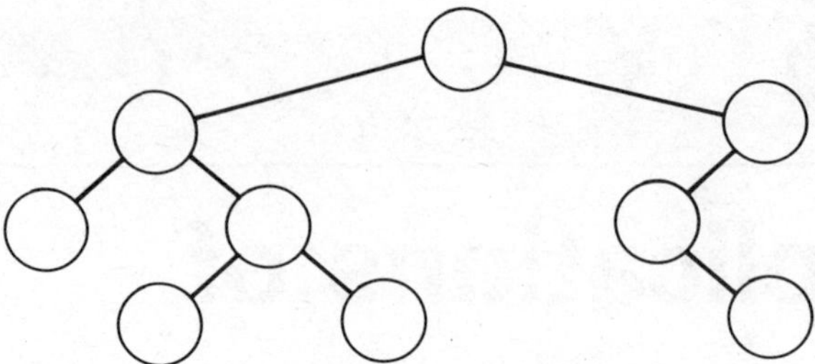

Figure 8.1 Binary Tree with Internal Nodes

We define the external path length, EPATH(T), of an extended binary tree T with n internal nodes as the sum of levels of all the external nodes.

We define the internal path length, IPATH(T), of a binary tree with n internal nodes as the sum of the levels of all the internal nodes. For the trees of Figures 8.1 and 8.2, the internal and external path lengths are 26 and 45, respectively.

Both the internal and external path lengths are important in evaluating the performance of algorithms that pertain to search trees. We introduce search trees in the next section.

We may define EPATH(T) and IPATH(T) recursively, using null to represent an empty tree or subtree. The recursive definitions are given by:

$$\text{IPATH(null)} = 0$$
$$\text{IPATH(T)} = \text{IPATH(left subtree)} + \text{IPATH(right subtree)} + n \quad (8.1)$$

$$\text{EPATH(null)} = 1$$
$$\text{EPATH(T)} = \text{EPATH(left subtree)} + \text{EPATH(right subtree)} + n + 1 \quad (8.2)$$

where n is the number of internal modes in T.

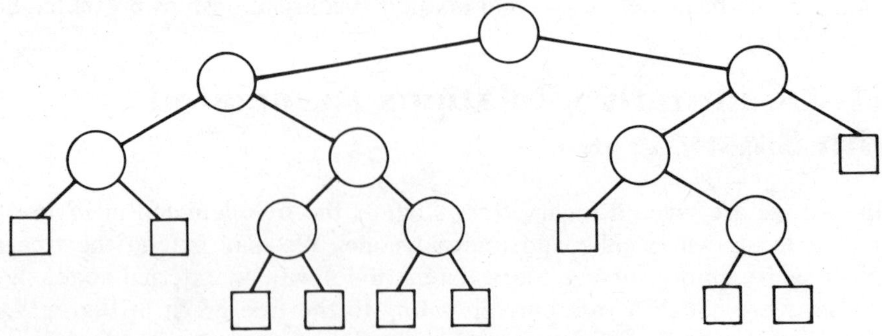

Figure 8.2 Binary Tree with Internal and External Nodes

Let us explain the IPATH recursion first. The left subtree and right subtree contain exactly $n - 1$ internal nodes. Adding an internal node in the form of a root or subroot above them increases the level of each internal node by 1. To this we must add the level of the root, which is 1.

To explain the EPATH recursion, we observe that EPATH(null) = 1 because an external node is a null node and any single node is at level 1. Next we observe that the left subtree and right subtree contain exactly $n + 1$ external nodes and that each of these nodes will have its level increased by 1 when we add the root or subroot.

Suppose we consider the difference between the external path length, EPATH, and the internal path length, IPATH. This difference is given by:

$$D(\mathrm{T}) = \mathrm{EPATH(T)} - \mathrm{IPATH(T)} \tag{8.3}$$

Using the recursions (8.1) and (8.2), we get:

$$\begin{aligned} D(\text{null}) &= 1 \\ D(\mathrm{T}) &= D(\text{left subtree}) + D(\text{right subtree}) + 1 \end{aligned} \tag{8.4}$$

For a tree with a single internal node (root node), we have:

$$\begin{aligned} D(\text{left subtree}) &= \text{EPATH(null)} - \text{IPATH(null)} = 1 \\ D(\text{right subtree}) &= \text{EPATH(null)} - \text{IPATH(null)} = 1 \end{aligned}$$

Therefore, $D(\mathrm{T}) = 3$.

For a two-node binary tree (assume root and left child), we write:

$$\begin{aligned} D(\text{left subtree}) &= 3 \\ D(\text{right subtree}) &= 1 \end{aligned}$$

Therefore, $D(\mathrm{T}) = 5$.

If we add a node to the two-node tree to form a three-node binary tree, two configurations are possible. For the first configuration we assume the root, with left child and another left child. For this tree.

$$\begin{aligned} D(\text{left subtree}) &= 5 \\ D(\text{right subtree}) &= 1 \end{aligned}$$

Therefore $D(\mathrm{T}) = 7$.

For the other configuration, a root and a left and right child, we get:

$$\begin{aligned} D(\text{left subtree}) &= 3 \\ D(\text{right subtree}) &= 3 \end{aligned}$$

Therefore $D(\mathrm{T}) = 7$.

We leave it to the reader (see exercise 8.2) to prove that for a binary tree of n internal nodes,

$$D(\mathrm{T}) = 2n + 1 \tag{8.5}$$

If follows from (8.5) that for a binary tree with n internal nodes:

$$\mathrm{EPATH(T)} = \mathrm{IPATH(T)} + 2n + 1 \tag{8.6}$$

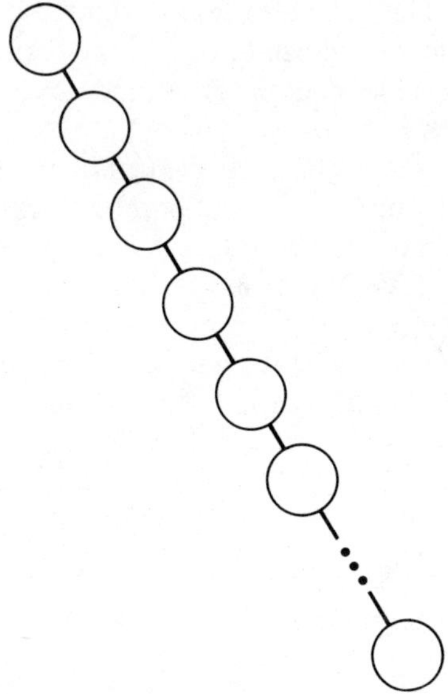

Figure 8.3 Tree Configuration with Maximum Path Length

What are the upper bounds of EPATH and IPATH for a tree with n internal nodes? The tree configuration that produces that largest EPATH and IPATH is shown in Figure 8.3. For such a tree:

$$\text{IPATH(T)} = n + (n - 1) + \ldots + 1 \tag{8.7}$$

This sum may be easily shown to equal $n(n + 1)/2$.

$$\text{IPATH(T)} = n(n + 1)/2 \tag{8.8}$$

$$\text{EPATH(T)} = \text{IPATH(T)} + 2n + 1 = (n^2 + 5n + 2)/2 \tag{8.9}$$

The lower bounds are more difficult. See Reingold and Hansen (1983), pp. 242, 243) and exercise 8.3.

8.2 Binary Search Trees

Binary search trees (henceforth called search trees) are an important subset of binary trees that support the abstraction of a search table. Search tables are important in compiler design, database management, file management, and other areas of computer science.

In a search tree, each node contains structured information. One field of such information, called the key field, contains a scalar quantity that has an associated order relation that forms the basis for ordering the information. If the order relation defines ascending order, the for each node in a search tree, the key field has a value greater than any of its left descendants and smaller than any of its right descendants.

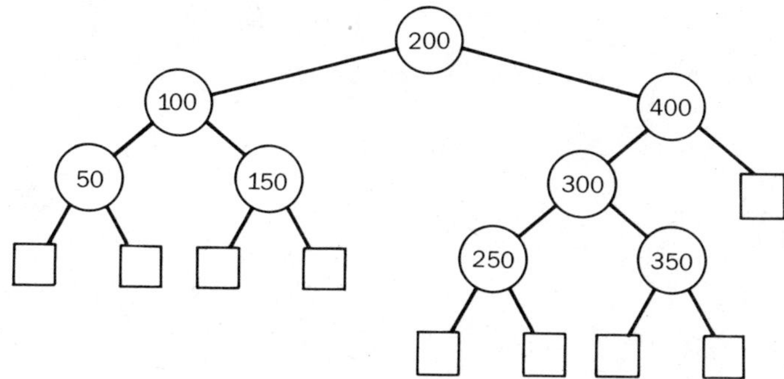

Figure 8.4 Binary Search Tree

In the search tree shown in Figure 8.4 each node contains exactly one information field, an integer key. We note that this definition disallows two nodes with identical keys to exist in the search tree.

8.2.1 Determining the Presence of a Key in a Search Tree

How do we search for a key in a search tree? Consider, for example, the search tree depicted in Figure 8.4. How do we search for key 350?

Informally, we compare 350 to the key of the root node, namely 200. Because 350 is greater than 200, we go to the right and compare 350 with key 400. Because 350 is less than 400 we go to the left and compare 350 to key 300. Because 350 is greater than 300 we go to the right and compare 350 with key 350. A matchup is found!

An algorithm for determining whether an item with a specified key field is present in a search tree is given next. We use the operators leftchild and rightchild without concern about the representational details of the search tree. We assume that each node of the tree contains a scalar information field called the key field of the node and that we have available the operation keyfield, which returns the key field of a node given a pointer to the node. The symbol nil is used to denote an empty subtree.

```
Algorithm ispresent( t    : pointer to root node (* in/out*);
                     item : elementtype          (* in *) )
  found ← false
  parent ← nil
  current ← t
  while ( current # nil ) and ( not found ) loop
    if key field of item = keyfield( current )
    then
      found ← true
```

```
      else
        parent ← current
        if key field of item < keyfield( current )
        then
          current ← leftchild( current )
        else
          current ← rightchild( current )
        end if
      end if
    end loop
    return found
  end ispresent
```

We may relate the efficiency of the search algorithm to the internal and external path lengths defined in the previous section. If we define S_n as the average number of comparison operations required for a successful search, and U_n as the average number of comparison operations required for an unsuccessful search, and if we assume that each node in the search tree has an equal probability of being accessed, we can write:

$$U_n = \frac{\text{sum of levels of the } n + 1 \text{ external nodes}}{n + 1} \tag{8.9}$$

$$U_n = \frac{\text{EPATH}}{n + 1} \tag{8.10}$$

$$S_n = \frac{\text{sum of the levels of the } n \text{ internal nodes}}{n} \tag{8.11}$$

$$S_n = \frac{\text{IPATH}}{n} \tag{8.12}$$

For the search tree of Figure 8.4:

$U_n = 39/9$
$S_n = 11/4$

8.2.2 Insertion into a Search Tree

How do we insert a node into a search tree? We present an algorithm for search tree insertion below.

```
Algorithm insert( t    : pointer to root node (* in/out *);
                  item : elementtype           (* in     *) )

  found ← false
  parent ← nil
  current ← t
  while ( current # nil ) and ( not found ) loop
    if key field of item = keyfield( current )
```

```
    then
      found ← true
    else
      parent ← current
      if key field of item < keyfield( current )
      then
        current ← leftchild( current )
      else
        current ← rightchild ( current )
      end if
    end if
  end loop
  if not found
  then
    if parent = nil
    then
      t ← makenode( item )
    else
      if key field of item < keyfield( parent )
      then
        addleft( parent, item )
      else
        addright( parent, item )
      end if
    end if
  end if
end insert
```

We walk through the algorithm using the small search tree depicted in Figure 8.5, assuming integer keys in each node.

We compare the key we wish to insert, which equals 125, to the root key, 200. The pointer parent is set to point to the root. The pointer current is reassigned to point to 100. Because the key is greater than 100, parent is set to 100 and current is set to 150. Because the left child of 150 is nil, parent is set to 150 and a node is added with key 125 as the left child of node 150.

We note that algorithm insertion always deposits the inserted node as a leaf node at the "bottom" of the tree. We also note that the number of compari-

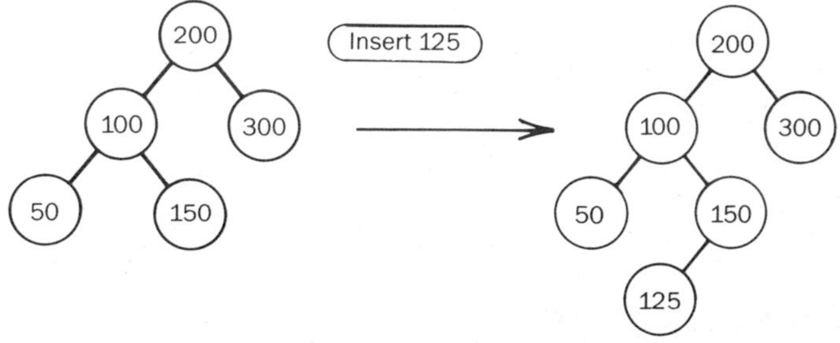

Figure 8.5 Insertion into a Search Tree

son opertions between the external or item key field and the internal key field is limited by the maximum number of levels currently in the tree. It is this property that makes the binary tree structure attractive in implementing search tables, particularly when such trees are nearly balanced.

8.2.3 Deletion from a Search Tree

Deletion from a binary search tree is complicated by the possibility that the node to be removed may not be a leaf node. We first dispense with two easy cases:

Case 1. The node to be removed is a leaf node.
Case 2. The node to be removed has only one child.

For case 1, the node may be removed directly with no further changes in the tree structure.

For case 2, the node is replaced by its one child with no further changes required in the tree structure. This type of deletion is identical to deletion from a linked list.

The third case, in which the node to be removed has two children, is the most difficult, In exercise 8.8, you are asked to prove that if such a node is replaced by its inorder successor, all the search tree properties are preserved.

The inorder successor of a given node in a tree is the node to be visited using the inorder traversal just after the given node. If we use the inorder traversal algorithm given in Chapter 7 (i.e., traverse left, visit, traverse right), it is easy to see that the inorder successor node cannot have a left child. If it did, the recursion would extend the path through this left child node. This is an important observation because we may replace the inorder successor node with its right child subtree (the inorder successor node itself is used to replace the deleted node). We could just as well have used the inorder successor going from right to left (traverse right, visit, traverse left).

We present an algorithm for deleting any node in a binary search tree.

```
Algorithm delete( t    : root node of tree     (* in out *);
                  item : elementtype           (* in     *) )
  previous ← nil
  present  ← t
  found    ← false
  (* Search for the external key and set present to point to
     key and previous to its parent.                        *)
  while ( present # nil ) and ( not found ) loop
    if keyfield( present ) = key field of item
    then
      found ← true
    else
      previous ← present
      if key field of item < keyfield( present )
      then
        present ← leftchild( present )
```

```
      else
        present ← rightchild( present )
      end if
    end if
    end loop
    if found
    then
    (* Set replace to point to the node that will
      replace present.                                        *)
      if leftchild( present ) = nil
      then
        replace ← rightchild( present )
      else
        if rightchild ( present ) = nil
        then
          replace ← leftchild( present )
        else (* Node present has two children; set replace
                to the inorder successor of present, and
                parent to the parent of replace. s is the
                child of replace.                             *)
          parent ← present
          replace ← rightchild( present )
          s ← leftchild( replace )
          while s # nil loop
            parent ← replace
            replace ← s
            s ← leftchild( replace )
          end loop
          if parent # present
          then
            leftchild( parent ) ← rightchild( replace )
            (* Remove node replace from its current position
               to take the place of node present.             *)
            rightchild( replace ) ← rightchild( present )
          end if
          leftchild( replace ) ← leftchild( present )
        end if
      end if
      if previous = nil
      then (* Node present was the root of the tree.          *)
        t ← replace
      else
        if present = leftchild( previous )
        then
          leftchild( previous ) ← replace
        else
          rightchild( previous ) ← replace
        end if
      end if
      freenode( present )
    end if
  end delete
```

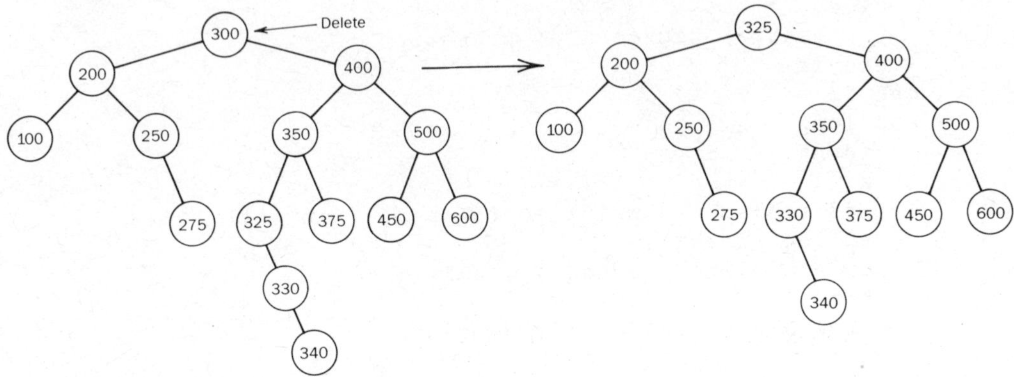

Figure 8.6 Deletion from a Search Tree

To illustrate algorithm delete, we will delete node 300 from the search true in Figure 8.6, each node of which contains an integer key.

Upon the completion of the first while loop, node present is pointing to 300 and node previous is pointing to nil. We trace the remaining steps in detail. We will use the notation t ← 300 to mean "node t is pointing to the node containing the key field 300."

```
parent ← 300
replace ← 400
s ← 350
while s # nil loop
  parent ← 400
  replace ← 350
  s ← 325
  parent ← 350
  replace ← 325
  s ← nil
end loop
since parent # 300
  leftchild( parent ) ← rightchild( 325 ) = 330
  (* We have replaced replace with its right child. *)
  rightchild( replace ) ← rightchild( 300 ) = 400
end if
leftchild( replace ) ← leftchild( present ) = 200
(* We have completed the installation of replace. *)
since previous = nil (* Present is a root node. *)
  t ← 325
end if
freenode( 300 )
```

In the next section we implement these procedures in Modula-2 for insertion and deletion in a search tree.

8.3 The Search Table Abstraction: A Search Tree

As we indicated in section 8.2, search tables are used in many application areas of computer science. For example, the symbol table of a compiler may use a search table abstraction. A spelling checker may use a search table for dictionary lookup. The basic kernels of many database systems employ a search table. In exercise 8.7, we ask you to identify and describe a dozen applications that utilize a search table.

What is a search table? Like any data abstraction, a search table is defined by the basic operations that one may perform on objects of type search table. These basic operations include define, delete, insert, display, and ispresent. This is a minimal set of operations required for a table and may be augmented in many applications. We will use a search tree to implement a search table.

You may wish to contrast the algorithm for searching presented above (algorithm ispresent) with the locate procedure given in Listing 7.2. Procedure locate makes no assumption about an order relationship among items contained in the tree nodes. The search algorithm, presented above, takes advantage of the search tree ordering relationship. It may be interesting to benchmark the search time using each procedure on a large search tree. The locate procedure is an algorithm of order n, whereas the search tree algorithm is $\log_2 (n)$, where n is the number of nodes.

In Listing 8.1 we display, using a definition module, the interface to a search table. We assume that each node in the table contains an arbitrary elementtype imported from module elements. Each client module that uses procedures insert, delete, ispresent, and display must define the operations of equal, lessthan, and display for objects of type elementtype.

When elementtype is redefined, in module elements, the recompilation requirements of Modula-2 dictate that definition module searchtable be recompiled because module searchtable imports elementtype from module elements. This necessitates the recompilation of the implementation module searchtable, as well as any client modules that import one or more components from searchtable. Although this required chain of recompilation may be tedious, the benefits of having a reusable search tree module may outweigh the liability of the recompilation overhead.

We note that not a single line of code must be modified in either the definition or implementation module searchtable when a change is made in elementtype. We also note that this approach to a search table (search tree) preserves strong type checking.

A shortcoming of this method is that only one elementtype may exist in a software system at a given time. A more advanced method for representing generic trees requires no recompilation when elementtype is changed and allows any number of elementtypes to coexist in the same system, but sacrifices strong type checking (see section 8.8).

Listing 8.1 Interface to Search Table Abstract Data Type

```
DEFINITION MODULE searchtable;

  FROM elements IMPORT
    (* type *) elementtype;

  EXPORT QUALIFIED
    (* type *) table,
    (* proc *) define,
    (* proc *) delete,
    (* proc *) insert,
    (* proc *) display,
    (* proc *) ispresent;

  TYPE table;

  TYPE equaltype    = PROCEDURE( elementtype, elementtype ):
                                 BOOLEAN;

  TYPE lessthantype = PROCEDURE( elementtype, elementtype ):
                                 BOOLEAN;

  TYPE displaytype  = PROCEDURE( VAR elementtype );


  PROCEDURE define
           ( VAR t     : table                (* out *) );
  (* This procedure must be used before any other
     procedure.                                          *)


  PROCEDURE delete
           ( VAR t     : table                (* in/out *);
             item      : elementtype          (* in     *);
             equal     : equaltype            (* in     *);
             lessthan  : lessthantype         (* in     *) );
  (* Removes the item from table t, if it is present.    *)


  PROCEDURE insert
           ( VAR t    : table                 (* in/out *);
             item     : elementtype           (* in     *);
             equal    : equaltype             (* in     *);
             lessthan : lessthantype          (* in     *) );
  (* Inserts the item into table t.                      *)


  PROCEDURE display
           ( t          : table               (* in     *);
```

```
            displayproc : displaytype      (* in     *) );
  (* Displays the item elements of the table in order.    *)


  PROCEDURE ispresent
          ( t          : table                    (* in     *);
            item       : elementtype              (* in     *);
            equal      : equaltype                (* in     *);
            lessthan   : lessthantype             (* in     *) ) :
            BOOLEAN;
  (* Returns true if item is present in table, otherwise
     false.                                                 *)

END searchtable.
```

In Listing 8.2, we present the implementation module for the search table.

Listing 8.2 Implementation of Search Tree Abstract Data Type

```
IMPLEMENTATION MODULE searchtable;

  FROM Storage IMPORT
    (* proc *) ALLOCATE, DEALLOCATE;

  FROM elements IMPORT
    (* type *) elementtype;

  TYPE table = POINTER TO node;

       node = RECORD
                info  : elementtype;
                left  : table;
                right : table;
              END(* record *);


  PROCEDURE addleft
          ( parent : table          (* out *);
            item   : elementtype    (* in *) );

  VAR
     newnode : table;

  BEGIN
    NEW( newnode );
```

```
  newnode^.info   := item;
  newnode^.left  := NIL;
  newnode^.right := NIL;
  parent^.left := newnode;
END addleft;


PROCEDURE addright
          ( parent : table          (* out *);
            item   : elementtype    (* in *) );

VAR
   newnode : table;

BEGIN
  NEW( newnode );
  newnode^.info   := item;
  newnode^.left  := NIL;
  newnode^.right := NIL;
  parent^.right  := newnode;
END addright;


PROCEDURE setleft
          ( parent : table        (* out *);
            node   : table        (* in *) );

BEGIN
  parent^.left := node;
END setleft;


PROCEDURE setright
          ( parent : table        (* out *);
            node   : table        (* in *)  );

BEGIN
  parent^.right := node;
END setright;


PROCEDURE makenode
          ( item : elementtype   (* in *) ) :
            table;

VAR newnode : table;

BEGIN
  NEW( newnode );
  newnode^.info := item;
  newnode^.left := NIL;
```

```
    newnode^.right := NIL;
    RETURN newnode;
  END makenode;


  PROCEDURE define
    ( VAR t     : table              (* out *) );
  BEGIN
    t := NIL;
  END define;


  PROCEDURE delete
          ( VAR t      : table                  (* in/out *);
            item       : elementtype            (* in      *);
            equal      : equaltype              (* in      *);
            lessthan   : lessthantype           (* in      *) );
  (* Uses the algorithm given in section 8.2.3.             *)


  VAR
      previous : table;
      present  : table;
      replace  : table;
      s        : table;
      parent   : table;
      found    : BOOLEAN;


  BEGIN
    previous := NIL;;
    present := t;
    found := FALSE;
    WHILE ( present # NIL ) AND ( NOT found ) DO
      IF equal( item, present^.info )
      THEN
        found := TRUE;
      ELSE
        previous := present;
        IF lessthan( item, present^.info )
        THEN
          present := present^.left;
        ELSE
          present := present^.right;
        END(* if then *);
      END(* if then *);
    END(* while loop *);
    IF found
    THEN
      IF present^.left = NIL
      THEN
        replace := present^.right;
```

```
    ELSE
      IF present^.right = NIL
      THEN
        replace := present^.left;
      ELSE
        parent := present;
        replace := present^.right;
        s := replace^.left;
        WHILE s # NIL DO
          parent := replace;
          replace := s;
          s := replace^.left;
        END(* while loop *);
        IF parent # present
        THEN
          setleft( parent, replace^.right );
          setright( replace, present^.right );
        END(* if then *);
        setleft( replace, present^.left );
      END(* if then *);
    END(* if then *);
    IF previous = NIL
    THEN
      t := replace;
    ELSE
      IF present = previous^.left
      THEN setleft( previous, replace );
      ELSE
        setright( previous, replace );
      END(* if then *);
    END(* if then *);
    DISPOSE( present );
  END(* if then *);
END delete;


PROCEDURE insert
          ( VAR t    : table                  (* in/out *);
            item     : elementtype            (* in     *);
            equal    : equaltype              (* in     *);
            lessthan : lessthantype           (* in     *) );
(* Uses the algorithm given in section 8.2.2.            *)


VAR
    found   : BOOLEAN;
    parent  : table;
    current : table;

BEGIN
  found := FALSE;
```

```
  parent := NIL;
  current  := t;
  WHILE ( current # NIL ) AND ( NOT found ) DO
    IF equal( current^.info, item )
    THEN
      found := TRUE;
    ELSE
      parent := current;
      IF lessthan( item, current^.info )
      THEN
        current := current^.left;
      ELSE
        current := current^.right;
      END(* if then *);
    END(* if then *);
  END(* while loop *);
  IF NOT found
  THEN
    IF parent = NIL
    THEN
      t := makenode( item );
    ELSE
      IF lessthan( item , parent^.info )
      THEN
        addleft( parent, item );
      ELSE
        addright( parent, item );
      END(* if then *);
    END(* if then *);
  END(* if then *);
END insert;


PROCEDURE display
          ( t           : table             (* in     *);
            displayproc : displaytype       (* in     *) ); ;

BEGIN
  IF t # NIL
  THEN
    display( t^.left, displayproc );
    displayproc( t^.info );
    display( t^.right, displayproc );
  END(* if then *);
END display;


PROCEDURE ispresent
          ( t         : table               (* in     *);
            item      : elementtype         (* in     *);
            equal     : equaltype           (* in     *);
```

```
            lessthan : lessthantype          (* in      *) ) :
            BOOLEAN;
  (* Uses the algorithm given in section 8.2.1.                  *)


  VAR
      current : table;
      found   : BOOLEAN;

  BEGIN
    current := t;
    found   := FALSE;
    WHILE ( current # NIL ) AND ( NOT found ) DO
      IF equal( item, current^.info )
      THEN
        found := TRUE;
      ELSE
        IF lessthan( item, current^.info )
        THEN
          current := current^.left;
        ELSE
          current := current^.right;
        END(* if then *);
      END(* if then *);
    END(* while loop *);
    RETURN found;
  END ispresent;


END searchtable.
```

Procedures addleft, addright, setleft, setright, and makenode in implementation module searchtable are not specified in the definition module searchtable. They are hidden (private) procedures, and their purpose is to support the main procedures whose interface are provided in the definition module.

The simple test program in Listing 8.3 assumes that elementtype is defined as follows:

```
DEFINITION MODULE elements;

  EXPORT QUALIFIED
    (* type *) elementtype;

  TYPE elementtype = RECORD
                       id    : INTEGER;
```

```
                        age  : CARDINAL;
                        name : ARRAY [ 0..9 ] OF CHAR;
                      END(* record *);

   END elements.
```

Note the simplicity, of procedures equalage, lessthanage, displayage, equalid, lessthanid, and displayid contained in the test program.

Listing 8.3 Test Program for Search Table Abstract Data Type

```
MODULE treetest;

  FROM searchtable IMPORT
    (* type *) table,
    (* proc *) insert, define, delete, ispresent, display;

  FROM elements IMPORT
    (* type *) elementtype;

  FROM InOut IMPORT
    (* proc *) WriteLn, WriteCard, WriteInt;

  PROCEDURE equalage
          ( item1, item2 : elementtype          (* in *) ):
            BOOLEAN;

  BEGIN
    RETURN item1.age = item2.age;
  END equalage;


  PROCEDURE lessthanage
          ( item1, item2 : elementtype          (* in *) ):
            BOOLEAN;

  BEGIN
    RETURN item1.age < item2.age;
  END lessthanage;


  PROCEDURE displayage
          ( VAR item : elementtype              (* in *) );

  BEGIN
    WriteLn; WriteCard( item.age, 1 );
  END displayage;
```

```
PROCEDURE equalid
          ( item1, item2 : elementtype            (* in *) ) :
            BOOLEAN;

BEGIN
  RETURN item1.id = item2.id;
END equalid;


PROCEDURE lessthanid
          ( item1, item2 : elementtype            (* in *) ) :
            BOOLEAN;

BEGIN
  RETURN item1.id < item2.id;
END lessthanid;


PROCEDURE displayid
          ( VAR item : elementtype                (* in *) );

BEGIN
  WriteLn; WriteInt( item.id, 1 );
END displayid;


VAR
    item1, item2, item3, item4 : elementtype;
    t1, t2                     : table;

BEGIN
  item1.id := -5;
  item1.age := 64;
  item1.name[ 0 ] := 'A';
  item1.name[ 1 ] := 'T';
  item2.id := 34;
  item2.age := 21;
  item2.name := item1.name;
  item3.id := 86;
  item3.age := 99;
  item3.name := item1.name;
  item4.id := -28;
  item4.age := 0;
  item4.name := item1.name;
  define( t1 );
  insert( t1, item1, equalage, lessthanage );
  insert( t1, item2, equalage, lessthanage );
  insert( t1, item3, equalage, lessthanage );
  insert( t1, item4, equalage, lessthanage );
  WriteLn; WriteLn;
```

```
  display( t1, displayage );
  WriteLn; WriteLn;
  display( t1, displayid );
  define( t2 );
  insert( t2, item1, equalid, lessthanid );
  insert( t2, item2, equalid, lessthanid );
  insert( t2, item3, equalid, lessthanid );
  insert( t2, item4, equalid, lessthanid );
  WriteLn; WriteLn;
  display( t2, displayid );
  WriteLn; WriteLn;
  delete( t1, item2, equalage, lessthanage );
  delete( t1, item3, equalage, lessthanage );
  display( t1, displayage );
END treetest.
```

In module treetest, we initialize items 1 through 4. We define table 1, t1, and insert the four items into the table, keying on age. We display table 1. We define table 2, t2, and insert the four items into the table, keying on id. We display table 2. We finally delete items 2 and 3 from table 1 and redisplay this table.

8.4 Removing Duplicates from a List and Sorting a List

A common and important problem in list manipulation is the removal of all duplicates from a list and the sorting of the list. For example, the creation of a textfile of English words to be used in the construction of a dictionary for a spelling checker program would probably involve several people typing the words into the textfile. It is likely that duplicate words would be typed into the file and we would want to remove any duplicates before building the dictionary file used in the spelling checker. Furthermore, before inserting the words into a dictionary file, it would be very important to sort the words (i.e., to alphabetize the list of words).

Listing 8.4 is a program that reads a list of words from a textfile, removes duplicates from the list, sorts the list, and dumps the sorted list to another textfile.

Our strategy is to construct a binary search tree from the list of words. This search tree, by definition, cannot accommodate duplicate keys (keys in this case are English words). After the search tree has been constructed, we perform an inorder traversal of the tree and dump the output to another textfile which will contain no duplicates and will be sorted.

The efficiency of this strategy is based on the observation that the number of comparison operations that must be performed during each insertion of a new word into the search tree is limited by the number of levels currently in the binary tree. If the tree is nearly balanced, its number of levels is approximately equal to the logarithm to the base 2 of the number of nodes (words) in the search tree.

In exercise 8.5, we ask you to construct a simpler "brute force" algorithm that removes duplicates from the textfile.

In module listmanipulations (Listing 8.4), we assume that the file of input words is called "INPUT" and the file of output sorted words with no duplicates is called "OUTPUT".

We caution the reader that the file I/O code used in this application is not standard. As with other programming languages, Modula-2 file commands are implementation dependent. It is expected that all Modula-2 installations will include a functionally similar set of basic file commands (see Ford and Wiener, 1985).

We note that procedure fetchword employs an in-out parameter, linepos. This parameter enables repeated calls to fetchword to start parsing from an interior position within a line. For the purposes of this application we have assumed that only the lower case and uppercase letters from a to z comprise legal words. We have not considered the complex issue of hyphenation.

Listing 8.4 List Manipulations: Removing Duplicates and Sorting

```
DEFINITION MODULE elements;

  EXPORT QUALIFIED
    (* type *) elementtype;

  TYPE elementtype = ARRAY[ 0..79 ] OF CHAR;

END elements.


MODULE listmanipulations;
(* This program removes duplicates from a list of words
   in file INPUT and sorts the list and deposits the
   result in file OUTPUT.                               *)

  FROM elements IMPORT
    (* type *) elementtype;

  FROM searchtable IMPORT
    (* type *) table,
    (* proc *) define, insert, display;
```

```
  FROM Strings IMPORT
    (* proc *) Length;

  FROM Files IMPORT
    (* type *) FILE, FileState,
    (* proc *) Open, Close, Create;

  FROM Texts IMPORT
    (* type *) TEXT, TextState,
    (* proc *) Connect, ReadLn, WriteString, WriteLn, EOT;

  TYPE linetype = ARRAY[ 0 .. 79 ] OF CHAR;
       setofchar = SET OF CHAR;

VAR
   inputfile  : FILE;
   outputfile : FILE;
   inputtext  : TEXT;
   outputtext : TEXT;
   fs         : FileState;
   ts         : TextState;
   line       : linetype;
   word       : elementtype;
   table      : table;
   linepos    : CARDINAL;


  PROCEDURE equalstring
            ( s1, s2       : elementtype       (* in *) ) :
              BOOLEAN;

  VAR
     index : CARDINAL;
     len1  : CARDINAL; (* length of s1 *)
     len2  : CARDINAL; (* length of s2 *)
     small : CARDINAL; (* smaller of len1 and len2 *)

  BEGIN
    len1 := Length(s1);
    len2 := Length(s2);
    IF len1 < len2
    THEN
      small := len1;
    ELSE
      small := len2;
    END(* if then *);
    index := 0;
```

```
    WHILE ( index <= small ) AND
          ( s1[ index ] = s2[ index ] ) DO
      INC(index);
    END(* while loop *);
    IF index <= small
    THEN
      RETURN s1[ index ] = s2[ index ];
    ELSE
      RETURN len1 = len2;
    END(* if then *);
  END equalstring;


  PROCEDURE lessthanstring
            ( s1, s2        : elementtype        (* in *) ) :
              BOOLEAN;

  VAR
     index : CARDINAL;
     len1  : CARDINAL; (* length of s1 *)
     len2  : CARDINAL; (* length of s2 *)
     small : CARDINAL; (* smaller of len1 and len2 *)

  BEGIN
    len1 := Length(s1);
    len2 := Length(s2);
    IF len1 < len2
    THEN
      small := len1;
    ELSE
      small := len2;
    END(* if then *);
    index := 0;
    WHILE ( index <= small ) AND
          ( s1[ index ] = s2[ index ] ) DO
      INC(index);
    END(* while loop *);
    IF index <= small
    THEN
      RETURN s1[ index ] < s2[ index ];
    ELSE
      RETURN len1 < len2;
    END(* if then *);
  END lessthanstring;


  PROCEDURE displaystring
            ( VAR s : elementtype                     (* out *) );
  BEGIN
    WriteString( outputtext, s );
```

```
    WriteLn( outputtext );
  END displaystring;


  PROCEDURE fetchword
           (line         : linetype        (* in     *);
            VAR linepos : CARDINAL        (* in out *) ) :
  elementtype;

  VAR
     word    : elementtype;
     length  : CARDINAL;
     start   : CARDINAL;

  BEGIN (* fetchword *)
    length := Length( line );
    (* Advance linepos to next legal character. *)
     WHILE NOT ( line[ linepos ] IN
                 setofchar{'a'..'z', 'A'..'Z'} ) DO
       INC( linepos );
       IF linepos = length + 1
       THEN
         RETURN ' ';
       END(* if then *);
     END(* while loop *);
     start := linepos;
     (* Advance linepos to next illegal character. *)
     WHILE line[ linepos ] IN
                 setofchar{'a'..'z', 'A'..'Z'} DO
       word[ linepos - start ] := line[ linepos ];
       INC( linepos );
       IF linepos = length + 1
       THEN
         RETURN ' ';
       END(* if then *);
     END(* while loop *);
     word[ linepos - start ] := 0C;
     RETURN word;
   END fetchword;


BEGIN (* listmanipulations *)
  (* We assume that the input file is called "INPUT.TEXT" on
     disk and the output file is called "OUTPUT.TEXT"
     on disk.                                              *)
  fs := Open( inputfile, "INPUT.TEXT" );
  fs := Create( outputfile, "OUTPUT.TEXT" );
  ts := Connect( inputtext, inputfile );
  ts := Connect( outputtext, outputfile );
  define( table );
```

```
  WHILE NOT EOT( inputtext ) DO
    ReadLn( inputtext, line );
    linepos := 0;
    LOOP
      word := fetchword(line, linepos);
      IF linepos = Length(line) + 1
      THEN
        EXIT; (* out of loop *)
      END(* if then *);
      insert( table, word, equalstring, lessthanstring );
    END(* loop *);
  END(* while loop *);
  fs := Close( inputfile );
  display( table, displaystring );
END listmanipulations.
```

Note the ease with which we have been able to use the search table module in removing duplicates and solving the sorting problem.

8.5 The Average Path Length for a Random Elementary Search Tree

The insertion and deletion procedures presented in section 8.2 for implementing a search table call for a computational complexity proportional to the number of levels in the search path required to locate the node to be inserted or deleted. Clearly, this search path is limited in length by the maximum depth of the search tree. If the elements inserted into a search tree are totally ordered (i.e., increasing or decreasing sequence of keys), the skewed worst-case structure depicted in Figure 8.3 would result; that is, the largest path length would equal the number of nodes in the tree. The best performance of the insertion and deletion algorithms occurs when the tree is perfectly or near perfectly balanced.

If the probability of access for the nodes in a search tree were unequal, it would be advantageous to move the frequently accessed nodes (high probability of access) to the top of the tree. This could be achieved by inserting those nodes before lower probability nodes. We explore this further in exercise 8.9.

How balanced is a typical elementary search tree (table)? To investigate this question, we will assume that each node in the tree enjoys equal probability of access, and furthermore, that the nodes are inserted in random order.

Suppose we wish to estimate the balance after creating a random search tree. Such a random search tree is obtained by constructing a tree using random keys (real number keys may be used in the simulation).

To perform the desired simulation experiment, it is necessary to modify the searchtable module and add a few lines of calibration code that computes the total path length of a search tree, while it is being built. We ask the reader to do this in exercise 8.16.

We compare the average path length obtained by simulation to the average path length of a perfectly balanced tree containing 2047 nodes. We may than obtain an estimate of how "balanced" a search tree is when matters are left to chance.

A perfectly balanced search tree with 2047 nodes has exactly 11 levels. The average internal path length of such a tree is defined as the sum of the internal path lengths divided by the number of nodes. The sum of internal path lengths is:

$$1 * 1 + 2 * 2 + 3 * 4 + 4 * 8 + 5 * 16 + 6 * 32 + 7 * 64 + 8 * 128 + 9 * 256 + 10 * 512 + 11 * 1024 = 20{,}481$$

where each factor is the internal path length times the number of nodes with that path length.

Therefore the average path length for the perfectly balanced tree is 20,481/2047 = 10.0054.

This result implies that on the average, about 10 comparison operations between the external key and internal key fields are needed to locate a random node in such a tree. Given that such a tree has only 11 levels, this suggests that most of the nodes reside near the bottom of the tree. This is indeed the case, as may be confirmed by sketching such a tree. (It will require several real trees to produce the paper to sketch such a binary tree!)

Our result of 10.0054 for the average path length represents a lower bound on what we may expect with an actual random search tree.

In constructing a simulation experiment, an additional procedure, pathlength, must be added to library module searchtable.

Our own simulation experiment yields an average path length of 13.75, which is about 37.5 percent greater than the average path length of a perfectly balanced search tree. One would therefore expect the computation time for the operations insert, delete, and ispresent for such an unbalanced random search tree to be about 37.5 percent greater than for a perfectly balanced tree with the same number of nodes.

Wirth (1976, pp. 213–214) uses a probabilistic model to derive the average path length for a random search tree. His results for a large tree, derived analytically, are the following:

average internal path length for random search tree =
1.386 * average path length for perfectly balanced tree

The simulation result of 1.375 is very close to this theoretical result.

We must caution the reader that the 38.6 percent penalty in computational effort is true, on average, only when the input keys used to build the search tree are truly random. In practice, there may be partial ordering of the input data used to construct the tree. In this case, the searching, insertion, and deletion performance of the tree may be many times worse than the performance of a perfectly balanced tree. Indeed, one may view the performance of a random search tree as a lower bound in actual practice.

In the next chapter we examine techniques for balancing a search tree during the insertion and deletion process as well as after an ordinary search tree is constructed. These methods are generally quite complex when compared to the operations introduced in this section for an elementary search tree. We have just seen the potential gains in performance that may be achieved by tree balancing. In some application areas this level of improvement may be very attractive.

8.6 The Representation of Algebraic Expressions Using Binary Trees

In Figures 8.7*a* and 8.7*b* we depict two binary trees (expression trees) that represents the algebraic expressions $(a + b) * c$ and $a + b * c$, respectively. If we were to perform a postorder traversal of each of these trees we would get:

`ab+c*` and `abc*+`

respectively. These are the postfix equivalents of the original infix expressions. Furthermore, if we were to perform a preorder traversal of each of the expression trees, we would obtain the correct prefix equivalents of the infix expressions. We ask the reader to do this as an exercise.

A third more complex expression tree is shown in Figure 8.8. Associated with this tree is the algebraic expression:

$$(a + b)/c * (d + e)$$

It is relatively easy to obtain an algebraic expression when given an expression tree. In this section we investigate the more difficult task of obtaining an expression tree when given an algebraic expression.

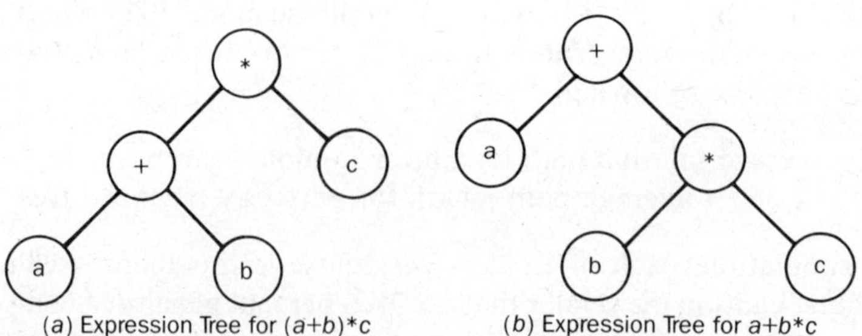

(*a*) Expression Tree for (*a*+*b*)**c* (*b*) Expression Tree for *a*+*b***c*

Figure 8.7 Examples of Expression Trees

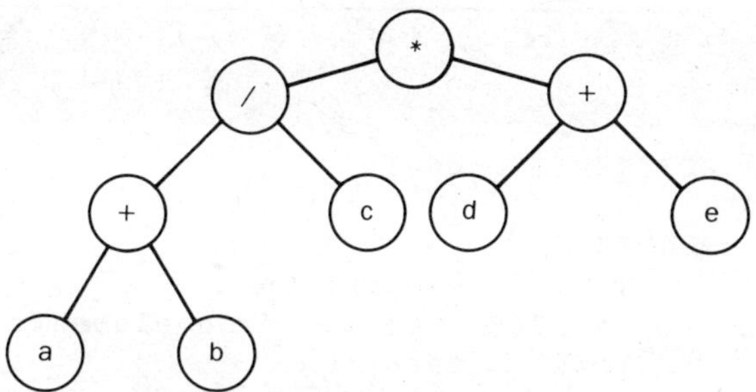

Figure 8.8 Expression Tree for $(a + b)/c * (d + e)$

We define the allowable set of operand symbols to be the set of uppercase and lowercase characters from A to Z. We define an operator symbol as a member of the set { +, −, *, /, $ }. The symbol $ is read "raised to the power."

Our general strategy is to form a skeletal tree composed only of operator keys (details later). Then we insert a set of leaf nodes, consisting of all the operand symbols, in the order in which they appear in the algebraic expression. We use a queue to store the operand symbols in the order in which they occur for later assignment into the tree.

A global cardinal variable, parencount, is used to track the cumulative number of left minus right parentheses encountered so far. Each operator node contains a cardinal field with the value of the parencount at the time the operator node is created. Because parentheses are not allowed in the expression tree, this parenthesis field is useful in determining the precedence between operators. See procedure precedence in Listing 8.5.

We embed the procedures given in Listing 8.5 and in Listing 8.6 (below) into the implementation module treeadt given in Chapter 7 to form definition and implementation modules for expression trees.

In Listing 8.5, we examine the procedure used to determine the algebraic precedence between two operators. This procedure plays a central role in forming expression trees. We must also add the private procedures,

```
PROCEDURE parenfield
          (     t             : tree     (* in *) ) : CARDINAL;

PROCEDURE setparen
          (     t             : tree     (* in *);
                parencount : CARDINAL (* in *) );
```

to the treeadt introduced in Chapter 7 so that we may access and assign the parenthesis field of each tree node outside this library module. We also augment the data structure for a tree node to that given in Listing 8.5.

We assume that module elements defines elementtype to be of type CHAR for this tree application. Thus the item field of each expression tree node contains a character.

Listing 8.5 Data Structure and Procedure Precedence for Expression Trees

```
TYPE tree = POINTER TO node;

     node = RECORD
                 item  : elementtype;
                 (* CHAR imported from elements *)
                 left  : tree;
                 right : tree;
                 paren : CARDINAL;
            END(* record *);


   PROCEDURE precedence
             ( op1    : tree      (* in *);
               op2    : CHAR      (* in *) ) : BOOLEAN;
  (* Returns true if op1 has precedence with respect to
     op2, otherwise returns false.                       *)

  BEGIN
    IF parenfield( op1 ) # parencount (* global variable *)
    THEN
        IF parenfield( op1 ) < parencount
        THEN
          RETURN FALSE;
        ELSE
          setparen( op1, parenfield( op1 ) - 1 );
          RETURN TRUE;
        END(* if then *);
      ELSE (* op1^.paren = parencount *)
        IF ( op1^.item = '+' ) OR
           ( op1^.item = '-' ) AND
           ( ( op2 = '*' ) OR ( op2 = '/' ) )
        THEN
          RETURN FALSE;
        ELSIF ( ( op1^.item = '+' ) OR
                ( op1^.item = '-' ) OR
                ( op1^.item = '*' ) OR
                ( op2 = '/' ) ) AND
                ( op2 = '$' )
        THEN
          RETURN FALSE;
        ELSE
          RETURN TRUE;
        END(* if then *);
      END(* if then *);
    END precedence;
```

Let us examine and explain the precedence function given in Listing 8.5 by examining the precedence between the operators + and * in the expression:

$$(a + b) * c$$

The operator + has a value of paren equal to 1 because the global variable parencount equals 1. When the operator * is encountered, the global value of parencount equals 0. Thus, the precedence of + with respect to * is TRUE because parent # parencount and parenfield(op1) is not less than parencount.

Let us examine the precedence between the operators * and + in the expression:

$$a * (b + c)$$

The operator * has a value of paren equal to 0 because the global variable parencount equals 0. When the operator + is encountered, the global value of parencount equals 1. Thus, the precedence of * with respect to * is FALSE because paren # parencount and op1^.paren is less than parencount. We note that normally the * operator would have a higher precedence than the operator +.

If parenfield(op1) = parencount, the usual tests for algebraic precedence are given (i.e., + and − have lower precedence than * and /, and +, −, *, and / have lower precedence than $).

We next examine the procedure for building an expression tree, given in Listing 8.6, procedure buildexpressiontree.

Listing 8.6 Procedure for Building an Expression Tree

```
PROCEDURE buildexpressiontree
        ( VAR t        : tree                (* out *);
          ch           : CHAR                (* in  *) );

VAR
    initial : tree;


  PROCEDURE newoperatornode
          ( first, tr : tree                 (* in *);
            ch        : CHAR                 (* in *) );

  VAR
     temp : tree;

    PROCEDURE precedence
            ( op1   : tree        (* in *);
              op2   : CHAR        (* in *) ) : BOOLEAN;

    BEGIN
      (* Code given in Listing 8.5. *)
    END precedence;
```

```
  BEGIN(* newoperatornode *)
    IF tr = NIL
    THEN (* Inserting first node. *)
      NEW( t );
      t^.item := ch;
      t^.left := NIL;
      t^.right := NIL;
      setparen( t, parencount );
    ELSE (* Inserting into existing tree. *)
      IF NOT precedence( tr, ch )
      THEN              (* ch of higher precedence than tr. *)
        IF tr^.right = NIL
        THEN
          addright( tr, ch, parencount );
          (* Note the slight change in procedure addright,
             namely the addition of the third parameter. *)
        ELSE
          first := tr;
          newoperatornode( first, tr^.right, ch );
        END(* if then *);
      ELSE              (* tr of higher precedence than ch. *)
        IF first = NIL
        THEN
          NEW( temp );
          temp^.item := ch;
          temp^.left := tr;
          temp^.right := NIL;
          setparen( temp, parencount );
          t := temp;
        ELSE
          NEW( temp );
          temp^.item := ch;
          temp^.left := tr;
          temp^.right := NIL;
          setparen( temp, parencount );
          first^.right := temp;
        END(* if then *);
      END(* if then *);
    END(* if then *);
  END newoperatornode;


BEGIN(* buildexpressiontree *)
  IF ch IN operand
  THEN
    queueadt.insert( q, ch );
  ELSIF ch = '('
  THEN
    INC( parencount );
```

```
    ELSIF ch = ')'
    THEN
      DEC( parencount );
    ELSIF ch IN operator
    THEN
      initial := NIL;
      newoperatornode( initial, t, ch );
    ELSE
      WriteLn; WriteLn;
      Write( CHR( 7 ) );
      WriteString(" Illegal character in expression. ");
      WriteLn;
      HALT;
    END(* if then *);
  END buildexpressiontree;
```

The main body of buildexpressiontree determines whether the input character, ch, is an operand, operator, or parenthesis. If ch is an operand, it is inserted into the queue. If ch is an operator, a new operator node is formed in the expression tree. If ch is a parenthesis, the global variable parencount is incremented or decremented.

Let us carefully examine the case when ch is an operator and procedure buildexpressiontree invokes procedure newoperatornode. The parameter named tr is initially set to point to the root of the expression tree.

The two basic cases are the following:

Case 1. ch of higher precedence than node tr.
Case 2. ch of lower precedence than node tr.

In the first case, a new node containing the operator ch is added to the right of node tr. In the second case, a new node is created that replaces the node containing tr and sets tr to be its left child. Note that the node of higher precedence is positioned closer to the bottom of the tree because expression evaluation occurs from bottom to top in the tree. In exercise 8.10, we ask you to justify the decision to create a new node to the right of tr when ch is of higher precedence then tr and to have tr positioned to the left of the new node containing ch when tr is of higher precedence than ch.

In Listing 8.7, we present the remaining procedures required for constructing an expression tree and converting infix expressions to prefix and postfix form. As an exercise, we ask you to explain the recursion used in procedure addoperands.

Listing 8.7 Remaining Procedures for Building Expression Trees

```
VAR
    operand     : setofchar;
    operator    : setofchar;
    parencount  : CARDINAL;
    q           : queueadt.queue;

  PROCEDURE addoperands
          ( t : tree          (* in *) );

    PROCEDURE checkandadd
            ( t : tree          (* in *) );

    VAR elem : CHAR;

    BEGIN
      IF t^.left = NIL
      THEN
        queueadt.remove( q, elem );
        addleft( t, elem, parencount );
      END(* if then *);
      IF t^.right = NIL
      THEN
        queueadt.remove( q, elem );
        addright( t, elem, 0 );
      END(* if then *);
    END checkandadd;

  BEGIN(* addoperands *)
    IF ( t # NIL ) AND ( NOT ( t^.item IN operand ) )
    THEN
      addoperands( t^.left );
      checkandadd( t );
      addoperands( t^.right );
    END(* if then *);
  END addoperands;


  PROCEDURE preorder
          ( t : tree          (* in *) );

  BEGIN
    IF t # NIL
    THEN
      Write( t^.item );
      preorder( t^.left );
      preorder( t^.right );
    END(* if then *);
  END preorder;
```

```
PROCEDURE postorder ( t : tree (* in *));

BEGIN
  IF t # NIL
  THEN
    postorder( t^.left );
    postorder( t^.right );
    Write( t^.item );
  END(* if then *);
END postorder;
```

Figures 8.9*a* and 8.9*b* display all the steps in building expression trees for the expressions $(a + b) * c$ and $a + b * c$.

8.7 Evaluation of Algebraic Expressions Using Expression Trees

The key to evaluating expression trees is the observation that each operator node has exactly two children. If we expand the data structure for a tree node to include a real field that represents the "value" of the node, we may first assign each operand node (leaf node) a value associated with the variable that the operand represents. By performing a postorder traversal on the expression tree, we may add values to each of the operator nodes as we move from the bottom of the tree to the top. Each operator node gets a value given by the result of applying the operator to the values of its children. We have limited our application to include only binary operators. The value of the root node will then become the value of the algebraic expression we are seeking.

As an exercise, we ask you to write and test the code for inputting values and evaluating an algebraic expression.

We note that a general tree structure may be used to represent expressions in which an operator has more than two operands. We pursue this in the exercises.

8.8 A Generic Search Table

This section may be skipped on a first reading of the book because it uses advanced low-level features of Modula-2.

The approach to generic data structures uses a more complex search tree data structure given in Figure 8.10.

Each generic tree contains a header node that stores the size, in number

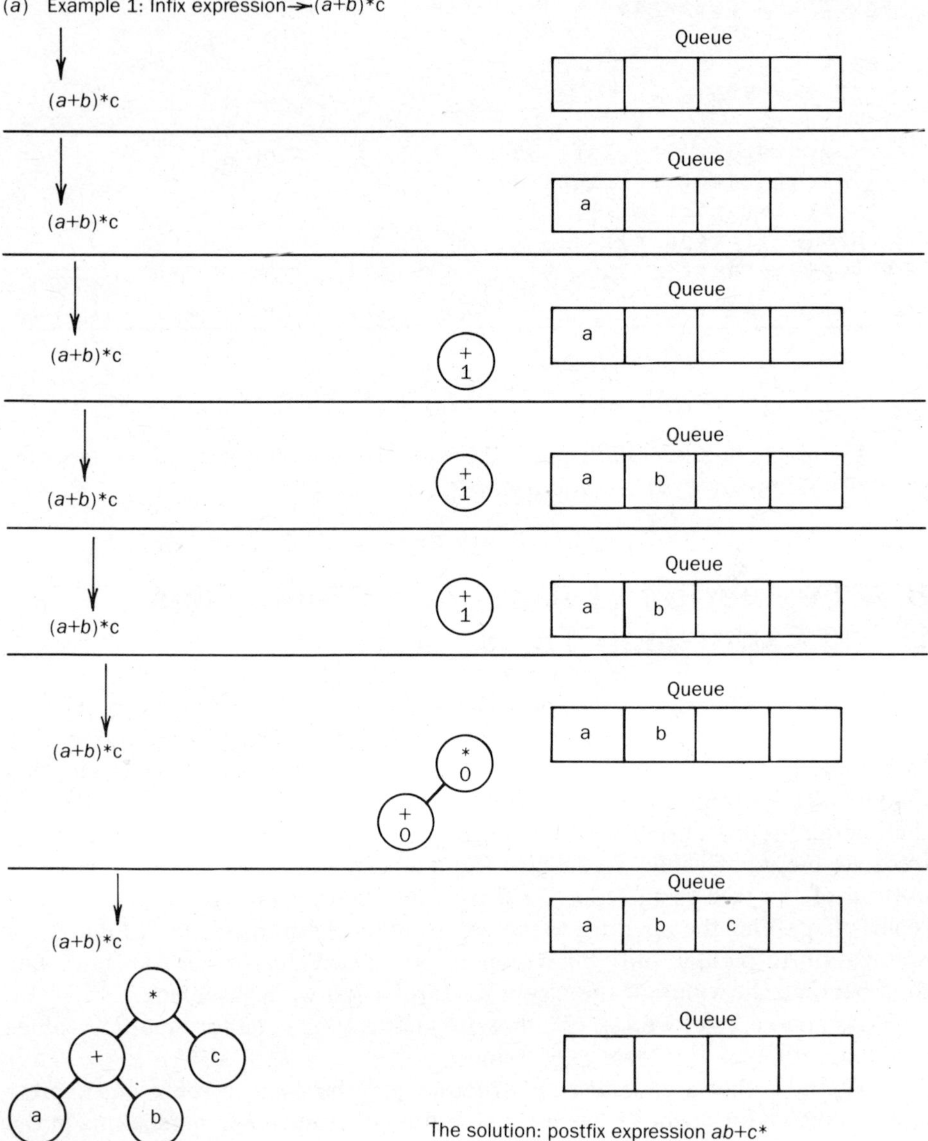

Figure 8.9 Expression Trees

of words, and a pointer to the root node of the search tree. It is necessary to store the size of the generic item because access to information is by way of the address of the information. A sample item is passed to procedure define to determine the size that is to be stored in the header node.

In Listing 8.8, we present the definition module generictreeadt, parts of the implementation module generictreeadt, and a test program. We again urge

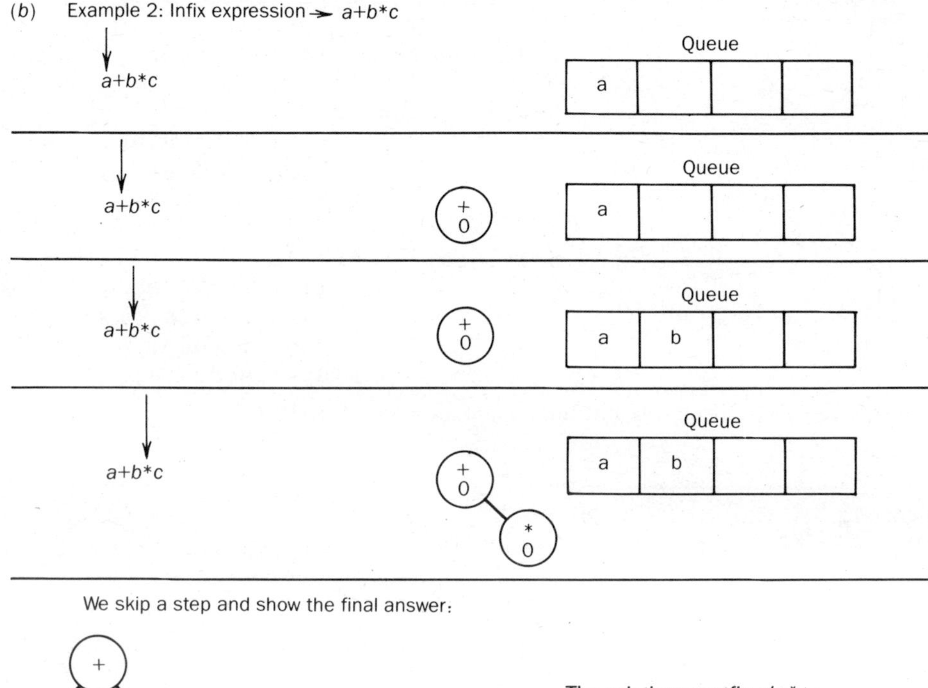

Figure 8.9 Expression Trees (continued)

the reader to study the test program carefully to see how easy it is to implement the procedure types equaltype and lessthantype.

Comparison of the Two Methods

The first method described in section 8.3 has several shortcomings. As you recall, a chain of recompilation must be performed each time a change is desired in the information structure for each node. The requirement to recompile module elements forces a recompilation of definition module searchtable, which forces a recompilation of implementation module searchtable and every other client module in the system. A client module is any module that imports one or more items from searchtable. In a large software system this recompilation overhead could be substantial.

A second shortcoming of the first method is that only a single information structure can be used within a software system for search trees. That is, only one module elements can exist at any given time, so that although there may be

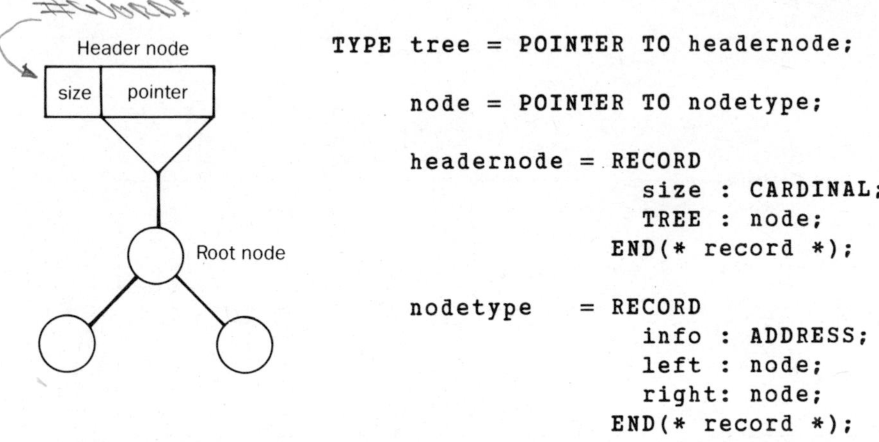


```
TYPE tree = POINTER TO headernode;

     node = POINTER TO nodetype;

     headernode = RECORD
                    size : CARDINAL;
                    TREE : node;
                  END(* record *);

     nodetype   = RECORD
                    info : ADDRESS;
                    left : node;
                    right: node;
                  END(* record *);
```

Figure 8.10 Data Structure and Implementation for Generic Search Tree

Listing 8.8 Interface, Implementation, and Test Program for a Generic Search Table Abstract Data Type

```
DEFINITION MODULE genericsearchtable;

  FROM SYSTEM IMPORT
    (* type *) WORD, ADDRESS;

  EXPORT QUALIFIED
    (* type *) tree,
    (* proc *) define,
    (* proc *) delete,
    (* proc *) insert,
    (* proc *) display,
    (* proc *) ispresent;

  TYPE tree;

  TYPE equaltype    = PROCEDURE( ADDRESS, ADDRESS ) :
                      BOOLEAN;

  TYPE lessthantype = PROCEDURE( ADDRESS, ADDRESS ) :
                      BOOLEAN;

  TYPE displaytype  = PROCEDURE( ADDRESS );

  PROCEDURE define
          ( VAR t    : tree             (* out *);
                item : ARRAY OF WORD    (* in *) );
  (* This procedure must be used before any other
     procedure.                                          *)
```

```
  PROCEDURE delete
           ( t          : tree                (* in *);
             item       : ADDRESS             (* in *);
             equal      : equaltype           (* in *);
             lessthan   : lessthantype        (* in *) );
  (* Removes the item from tree t, if it is present.          *)


  PROCEDURE insert
           ( t         : tree                 (* in *);
             item      : ADDRESS              (* in *);
             equal     : equaltype            (* in *);
             lessthan  : lessthantype         (* in *) );
  (* Inserts the item into tree t.                            *)


  PROCEDURE display
           ( t             : tree             (* in *);
             displayproc   : displaytype      (* in *) );
  (* Displays the item elements of the tree in order.         *)


  PROCEDURE ispresent
           ( t         : tree                 (* in *);
             item      : ADDRESS              (* in *);
             equal     : equaltype            (* in *);
             lessthan  : lessthantype         (* in *) ) :
             BOOLEAN;
  (* Returns true if item is present in tree, otherwise
     false.                                                   *)

END genericsearchtable.


IMPLEMENTATION MODULE genericsearchtable;

  FROM SYSTEM IMPORT
    (* type *) WORD, ADDRESS,
    (* proc *) TSIZE;

  FROM Storage IMPORT
    (* proc *) ALLOCATE, DEALLOCATE;

  TYPE tree = POINTER TO headernode;

       node = POINTER TO nodetype;

       headernode = RECORD
            size   : CARDINAL; (* Number of words of item. *)
            TREE   : node;     (* Points to search tree.   *)
          END(* record *);
```

```
    nodetype = RECORD
                  info  : ADDRESS;
                  left  : node;
                  right : node;
                END(* record *);


PROCEDURE makenode
         (      t    : tree    (* in *);
                item : ADDRESS (* in *) ) : node;

VAR
    newnode   : node;
    wordcount : CARDINAL;

BEGIN
  NEW( newnode );
  ALLOCATE( newnode^.info, t^.size * TSIZE( WORD ) );
  wordcount := 1;
  newnode^.info^ := item^;
  WHILE ( wordcount < t^.size ) DO
    INC( newnode^.info, TSIZE( WORD ) );
    INC( item, TSIZE( WORD ) );
    newnode^.info^ := item^;
    INC( wordcount );
  END(* while loop *);
  newnode^.left := NIL;
  newnode^.right := NIL;
  DEC( newnode^.info, ( t^.size - 1 ) * TSIZE( WORD ) );
  RETURN newnode;
END makenode;


PROCEDURE define
         ( VAR t    : tree            (* out *);
               item : ARRAY OF WORD (* in *) );
(* This procedure must be used before any other
   procedure.                                          *)

BEGIN
  NEW( t );
  t^.size := ( HIGH( item ) + 1 ); (* number of words *)
  t^.TREE := NIL;
END define;


PROCEDURE addleft
         (    t      : tree         (* in *);
              parent : node         (* in *);
              item   : ADDRESS      (* in *) );
```

```
BEGIN
  ..
END addleft;


PROCEDURE addright
          (   t      : tree          (* in *);
              parent : node          (* in *);
              item   : ADDRESS       (* in *) );

BEGIN
  ..
END addright;


PROCEDURE delete
          (   t          : tree               (* in *);
              item       : ADDRESS            (* in *);
              equal      : equaltype          (* in *);
              lessthan   : lessthantype       (* in *) );
(* Removes the item from tree t, if it is present.      *)

BEGIN
  ..
END delete;


PROCEDURE insert
          (   t         : tree            (* in *);
              item      : ADDRESS         (* in *);
              equal     : equaltype       (* in *);
              lessthan : lessthantype     (* in *) );
(*  Inserts the item into tree t.                       *)

VAR
    found   : BOOLEAN;
    parent  : node;
    current : node;

BEGIN
  found := FALSE;
  parent := NIL;
  current  := t^.TREE;
  WHILE ( current # NIL ) AND ( NOT found ) DO
    IF equal( current^.info, item )
    THEN
      found := TRUE;
    ELSE
      parent := current;
      IF lessthan( item, current^.info )
```

```
      THEN
        current := current^.left;
      ELSE
        current := current^.right;
      END(* if then *);
    END(* if then *);
  END(* while loop *);
  IF NOT found
  THEN
    IF parent = NIL
    THEN
      t^.TREE := makenode( t,  item );
    ELSE
      IF lessthan( item , parent^.info )
      THEN
        addleft( t, parent, item );
      ELSE
        addright(t, parent, item );
      END(* if then *);
    END(* if then *);
  END(* if then *);
END insert;


PROCEDURE display
          (      t             : tree              (* in *);
                 displayproc : displaytype       (* in *) );
(* Displays the item elements of the tree in order.      *)

  PROCEDURE print( NODE : node );

  BEGIN
    IF NODE # NIL
    THEN
      print( NODE^.left );
      displayproc( NODE^.info );
      print( NODE^.right );
    END(* if then *);
  END print;

VAR  NODE : node;

BEGIN(* display *)
  NODE := t^.TREE;
  print( NODE );
END display;


PROCEDURE ispresent
          (     t          : tree                      (* in *);
```

```
                 item      : ADDRESS              (* in *);
                 equal     : equaltype            (* in *);
                 lessthan  : lessthantype         (* in *) ) :
  BOOLEAN;
  (* Returns true if item is present in tree, otherwise
     false.                                                   *)

  BEGIN
    ...
  END ispresent;


END genericsearchtable.


MODULE treetest;

  FROM genericsearchtable IMPORT
    (* type *) tree,
    (* proc *) insert, define, delete, ispresent, display;

  FROM SYSTEM IMPORT
    (* type *) ADDRESS,
    (* proc *) ADR;

  FROM InOut IMPORT
    (* proc *) WriteLn, WriteCard, WriteInt, WriteString;

  TYPE elementtype = RECORD
                       id   : INTEGER;
                       age  : CARDINAL;
                       name : ARRAY[ 0..9 ] OF CHAR;
                     END(* record *);

  PROCEDURE equalage
           ( item1, item2 : ADDRESS (* in *) ) : BOOLEAN;

  VAR
      elementptr1 : POINTER TO elementtype;
      elementptr2 : POINTER TO elementtype;

  BEGIN
    elementptr1 := item1;
    elementptr2 := item2;
    RETURN elementptr1^.age = elementptr2^.age;
  END equalage;


  PROCEDURE lessthanage
           ( item1, item2 : ADDRESS (* in *) ) : BOOLEAN;
```

```
VAR
    elementptr1 : POINTER TO elementtype;
    elementptr2 : POINTER TO elementtype;

BEGIN
  elementptr1 := item1;
  elementptr2 := item2;
  RETURN elementptr1^.age < elementptr2^.age;
END lessthanage;


PROCEDURE displayage
          ( item : ADDRESS (* in *) );

VAR
    elementptr : POINTER TO elementtype;

BEGIN
  elementptr := item;
  WriteLn; WriteCard( elementptr^.age, 1 );
END displayage;


PROCEDURE equalid
          ( item1, item2 : ADDRESS (* in *) ) : BOOLEAN;

VAR elementptr1, elementptr2 : POINTER TO elementtype;

BEGIN
  elementptr1 := item1;
  elementptr2 := item2;
  RETURN elementptr1^.id = elementptr2^.id;
END equalid;


PROCEDURE lessthanid
          ( item1, item2 : ADDRESS (* in *) ) : BOOLEAN;

VAR elementptr1, elementptr2 : POINTER TO elementtype;

BEGIN
  elementptr1 := item1;
  elementptr2 := item2;
  RETURN elementptr1^.id < elementptr2^.id;
END lessthanid;

PROCEDURE displayid
          ( item : ADDRESS (* in *) );

VAR elementptr : POINTER TO elementtype;
```

```
  BEGIN
    elementptr := item;
    WriteLn; WriteInt( elementptr^.id, 1 );
  END displayid;


VAR
    item1, item2, item3, item4 : elementtype;
    t1, t2 : tree;

BEGIN
  ... (* Code to initialize item1, ..., item4. *)
  define( t1, item1 );
  insert( t1, ADR( item1 ), equalage, lessthanage );
  insert( t1, ADR( item2 ), equalage, lessthanage );
  insert( t1, ADR( item3 ), equalage, lessthanage );
  insert( t1, ADR( item4 ), equalage, lessthanage );
  WriteLn; WriteLn;
  display( t1, displayage );
  ... (* Additional code as before. *)
END treetest.
```

many trees importing an elementtype from module elements, there may only be one elementtype.

A strength of the first method is that strong type checking is preserved.

The second method has the shortcoming that strong type checking is suppressed in using module genericsearchtable. Serious trouble may result if a user fails to exercise care in calling procedures insert, delete, and ispresent.

The major strength of the second method is that no recompilation of genericsearchtable is ever required and thus no recompilation of client modules is required. Only the main driver program must be changed and recompiled if one wishes to change the information structure, elementtype. Furthermore, an unlimited number of information structures may coexist and be used in different trees that are constructed using genericsearchtable.

In some software development applications in which the information structure is defined early in the development process, it may be desirable to choose the first method over the second because of the benefits of preserving strong type checking. In our view, the second method comes closer to true generics because of its lack of limitations.

We must emphasize one property of both methods, namely: no changes in source code are required in either the definition module or the implementation module as one changes the base type stored in each node of the tree.

In comparing the performance of both methods, we used the record elementtype given in module elements. We timed 1500 insertions, then 1500 deletions using each method. The same array of random cardinals was used for the age field for insertion and deletion using both methods. The results are as follows:

First Method		*Second Method*	
Insertion time	22.78 time units	Insertion time	25.00 time units
Deletion time	17.47 time units	Deletion time	18.27 time units

It is evident that a small run-time penalty is incurred using the second method, but the difference in performance is not significant. The extra run-time overhead for the second method is probably due to the extra allocation or deallocation step required each time a new node is created or destroyed.

Exercises

8.1 Prove that an extended binary tree of n internal nodes contains $n + 1$ external nodes.

8.2 Prove that for a binary tree of n internal nodes,

$$D(\mathrm{T}) = 2n + 1$$

where $D(\mathrm{T}) = \mathrm{EPATH(T)} - \mathrm{IPATH(T)}$.

8.3 Prove that the minimum external path length for a binary tree is given by:

$$1 + (n + 1)\log_2(n + 1) + (n + 1)(2 - c - 2^{k-c})$$

where c is a very small constant and k is defined by Reingold and Hansen (1983, pp. 242, 243).

8.4 Develop a formula for the average number of successful searches in a binary search tree if the probability of access for node i is p_i.

8.5 Write a simple algorithm and then a procedure for removing duplicates from a list of real numbers. Compare the efficiency of your algorithm with the algorithm given in section 8.4.

8.6 Prove that an inorder traversal of a binary search tree always produces an ordered sequence of output.

8.7 Identify and describe a dozen applications that utilize a search table.

8.8 Prove that if a node to be deleted from a search tree is replaced by its inorder successor, all the search tree properties are preserved.

8.9 If the probabilities of access (i.e., combined frequency of searching, insertion, and deletion) for the nodes in a search tree were unequal, it would be advantageous to move the frequently accessed nodes (high probability of access) to the top of the tree. This could be achieved by inserting those nodes before lower probability nodes.

Create a sample search tree, carefully labeling the probability of access for each of its nodes. Compute the average internal path length for the original tree and for the tree constructed by inserting the nodes in the order from highest probability of access to lowest probability of access. Compare the two path lengths.

8.10 In procedure newoperatornode, in Listing 8.6, justify the decisions to create a new node to the right of tr when ch is of higher precedence than tr and to have tr positioned to the left of the new node containing ch when tr is of higher precedence than ch.

8.11 Explain the recursion used in procedure addoperands, in Listing 8.7.

8.12 A general tree structure may be used to represent more general mathematical expressions in which one or several operands may be associated with an operator. Generate a revised library module, expressiontree, that allows operators to have one or several operands. Test your new module with a revised test program.

8.13 Add to the expressiontree procedures so that one may evaluate an expression containing only one variable, say x, repeatedly for different values of x.

8.14 Generate 20 random search trees, each with 511 nodes, compute the minimum and maximum depths, and output these values. The minimum depth is defined as the level of the highest leaf node, and the maximum depth is defined as the level of the lowest leaf node.

8.15 Modify the search module searchtable, presented in section 8.3, to compute the total path length of the tree that is created.

8.16 After making suitable modifications to module searchtable, write a main driver program that allows you to simulate a random search tree with 2047 nodes. Output the average path length for this random tree. Repeat the experiment several times and output the average of the path lengths obtained.

8.17 Implement the algorithms in section 8.7 for evaluating an expression containing operators that may have more than two operands. You may have to use a general tree structure.

9

Balanced Trees

In this chapter we present algorithms for maintaining tree balance after insertions and deletions on a search tree. Part 1 focuses on trees maintained in fast memory (RAM), whereas in Part 2 we treat trees maintained in external storage, such as a disk.

PART 1: BALANCED TREES IN FAST MEMORY

Recall from section 8.5 that a search tree generated using random keys has an average path length approximately 38 percent greater than the path length of a perfectly or near perfectly balanced tree of the same size. This may not seem to provide sufficient motivation to investigate complex tree balancing algorithms. However, we must remember that in practice, it is rare to encounter a random sequence of input keys. Indeed, the further the input sequence deviates from total "randomness," the larger the average path length of the tree becomes. In worst case, the tree becomes a linked list (see Figure 8.3) with average path length potentially many times that of a perfectly or near perfectly balanced tree.

The tree balancing algorithms we shall present guarantee that after each insertion or deletion, the tree remains balanced. Clearly our trees cannot be perfectly balanced unless the number of nodes exactly equals $2^L - 1$, where L is the number of levels in the tree. This condition rarely holds. Thus we must define the concept of "near balance" or "close to perfectly balanced."

Before reading further, we challenge the reader to write down a definition of "near balance" that makes sense. Does your definition involve every node of the tree? Does it involve only the leaf nodes (e.g., some constraint on the deviation in levels of leaf nodes)? See exercise 9.1.

For your definition of balance to be useful, the user must be able to develop insertion and deletion algorithms that leave a tree in a state that satisfies your definition of balance.

9.1 AVL Trees: Height-Balanced Trees

In 1962 the Russian mathematicians G. M. Adelson-Velskii and E. M. Landis defined a workable definition of "near balance" for binary search trees and described procedures for insertion and deletion that maintain balance. Their tree balancing methods are called AVL algorithms and the trees generated are called AVL trees. A remarkable result is that under almost all conditions, the average path length of an AVL tree approximates that of a completely balanced binary search tree.

9.1.1 Definition of AVL Balance

An AVL tree is a binary search tree constructed such that for each node, the height of its right subtree differs from the height of its left subtree by at most 1. The balance factor or balance of a node is defined as the height of its right subtree minus the height of its left subtree. Thus for an AVL tree, the balance factor of each node is either 1, 0, or -1.

The height of a subtree is defined as the maximum depth from the subtree root node to the lowest level leaf node. This depth may be computed by subtracting the level of the "lowest" node in the subtree from the level of the subtree root node.

An AVL tree is called a "height-balanced" tree because each node is constrained in balance by the height of its subtrees. In section 9.2, we examine balancing algorithms based on weight rather than height.

Proper AVL trees and trees that fail the AVL test are displayed in Figures 9.1*a* and 9.1*b*, respectively.

9.1.2 AVL Insertion

A node that is inserted into an AVL tree may:

1. Cause the balance of a subtree root to go from -1 to 0 or from 1 to 0. In this case (Figure 9.2), the effect of the insertion is to create better balance in the tree. No rebalance is required.

2. Cause the balance of a subtree root to go from 0 to -1 or from 0 to 1. In this case (Figure 9.3), the effect of the insertion is to worsen the balance in the tree. No rebalance is required.

3. Cause the balance of a subtree root to go from -1 to -2 or from 1 to 2. In this case (Figure 9.4), the effect of the insertion is to destroy the AVL property of the tree. Rebalance is required.

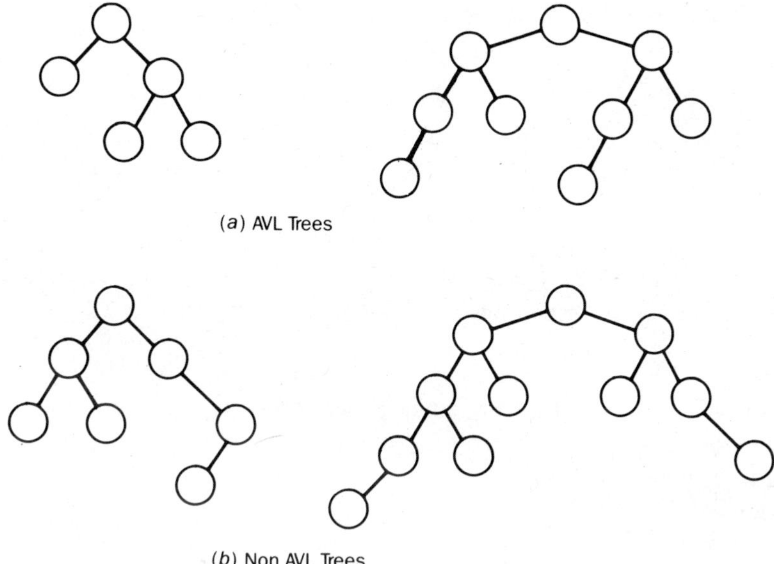

Figure 9.1 (*a*) AVL and (*b*) Non-AVL Trees

We examine the third condition more carefully. It can be shown that only two constellations of nodes call for rebalancing, and they require different techniques.

The first constellation (type 1) is revealed by the presence of a subtree node of balance 2(or −2) with a left or right child having a balance of 1(or −1), of the same sign as the parent node. A single rotation pivoting on the subtree node with balance 2 or −2 can always correct this imbalance.

The second constellation (type 2) is revealed by the presence of a subtree node of balance 2(or −2) with a left or right child having a balance of −1(or 1), of opposite sign from the parent node. A double rotation can always correct this imbalance. The first rotation uses the subtree node with balance 1 or −1 as the pivot node and the second rotation uses the subtree node with balance 2 or −2 as the pivot node. Examples of constellations of types 1 and 2 appear in Figures 9.5 and 9.6, respectively.

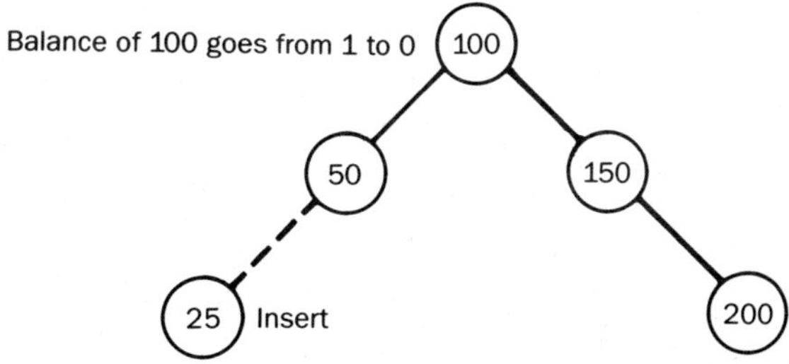

Figure 9.2 Insertion into AVL Tree—Better Balance

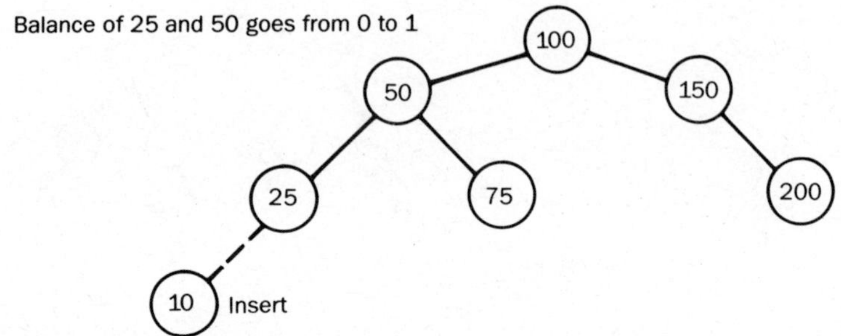

Figure 9.3 Insertion into AVL Tree—Worse Balance

Before we discuss the rebalance procedures for each type of constellation, let us digress to consider tree rotations. Table 9.1 presents algorithms for left and right rotations.

Figures 9.7 and 9.8, respectively, display a binary search tree left-rotated about node **a** and the same binary search tree right-rotated about node **a**.

As an exercise we ask you to prove that the search tree property is always preserved under the operations of left and right rotate.

To rebalance a type 1 constellation, we rotate on the node with balance 2 or -2 in a direction appropriate to restore balance, as illustrated in Figure 9.5: this tree contains a type 1 constellation because the node with key value 8 has a balance of -2, and the node with key value 4 has a balance of -1. We right rotate on node 8 and get the tree depicted in Figure 9.9.

To rebalance a type 2 constellation, we rotate on the node with a balance of 1 or -1 in a direction to restore balance. We follow this rotation with another rotation on the node with balance 2 or -2 in a direction opposite to the first rotation to restore balance, as illustrated in Figure 9.6: this tree contains a type 2 constellation because the node with key value 8 has a balance of -2, and the node with key value 4 has a balance of 1. We first left rotate on node 4 and then right rotate on node 8. These steps are shown in Figure 9.10.

Because the search tree property is preserved under left and right rotations, the methods just discussed for rebalancing an AVL tree after insertion produce another AVL tree.

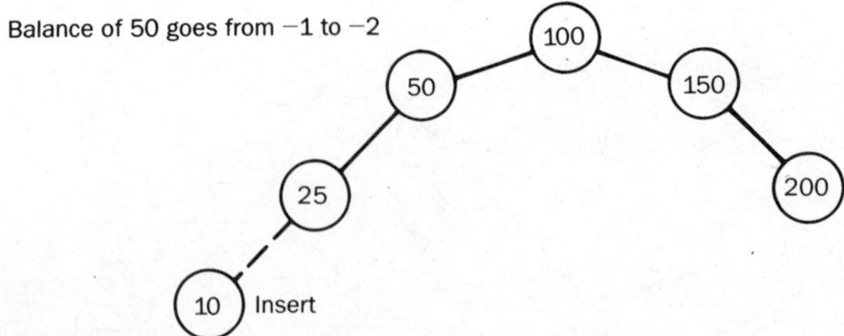

Figure 9.4 Insertion into AVL Tree—Rebalance Required

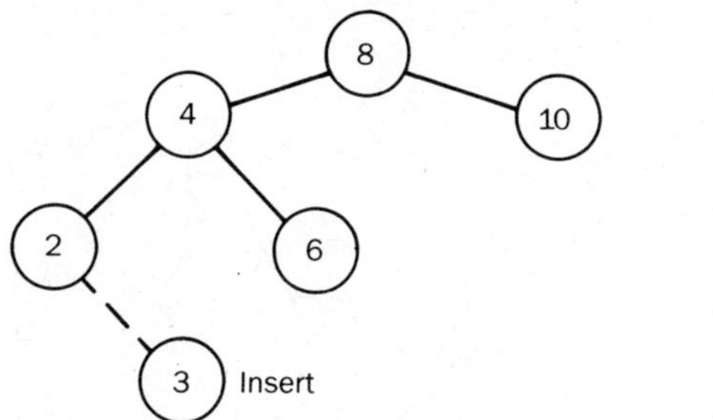

Figure 9.5 Type 1 Constellation

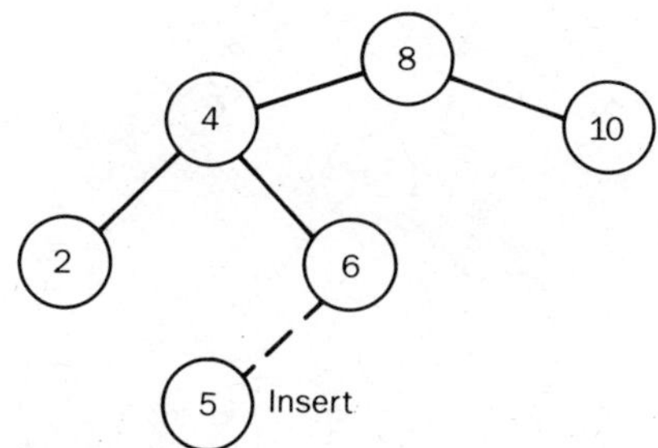

Figure 9.6 Type 2 Constellation

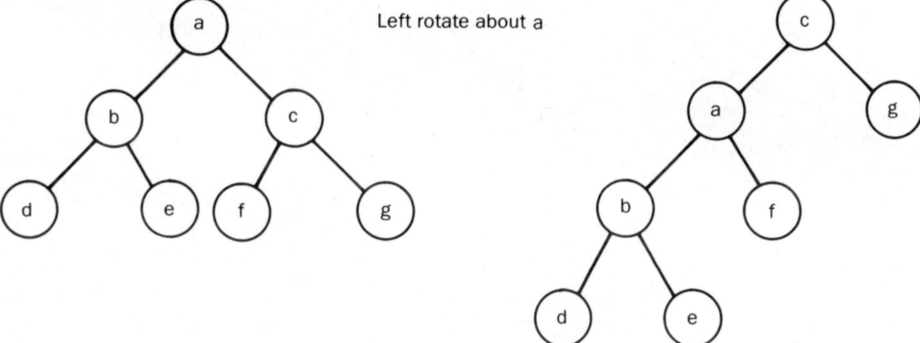

Figure 9.7 Left Rotation

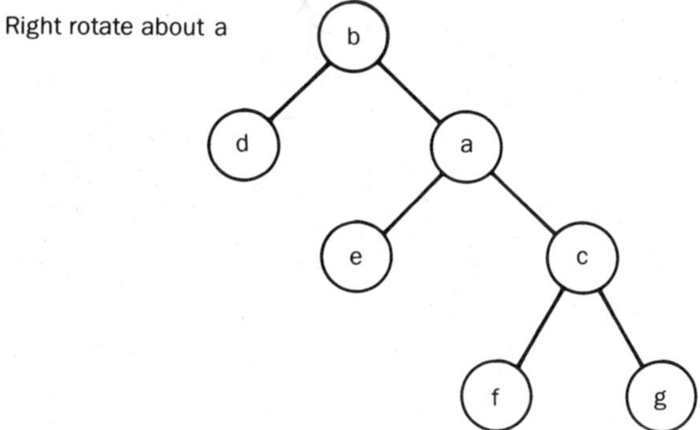

Figure 9.8 Right Rotation

TABLE 9.1 Left and Right Rotations

Algorithm leftrotate(p)	Algorithm rightrotate(p)
q←right(p) temp←left(q) left(q)←p right(p)←temp	q←left(p) temp←right(q) right(q)←p left(p)←temp

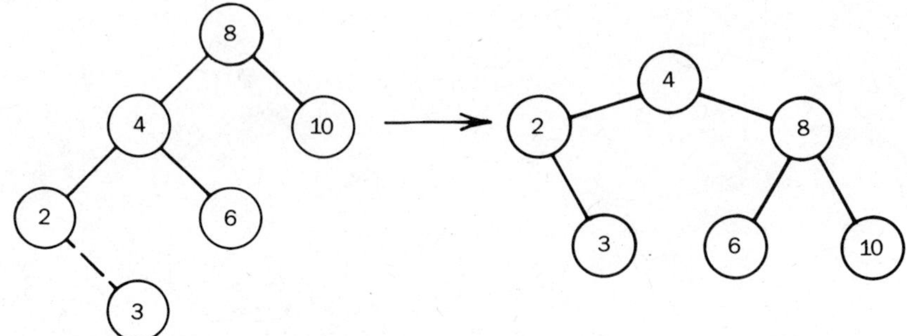

Figure 9.9 Type 1 Rotation to Restore Balance

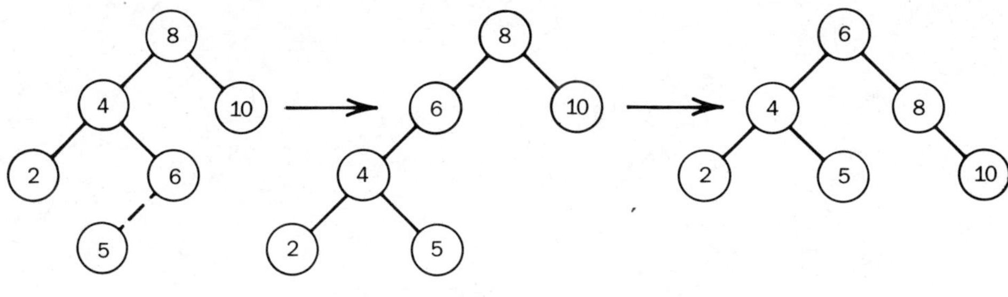

Figure 9.10 Type 2 Rotation to Restore Balance

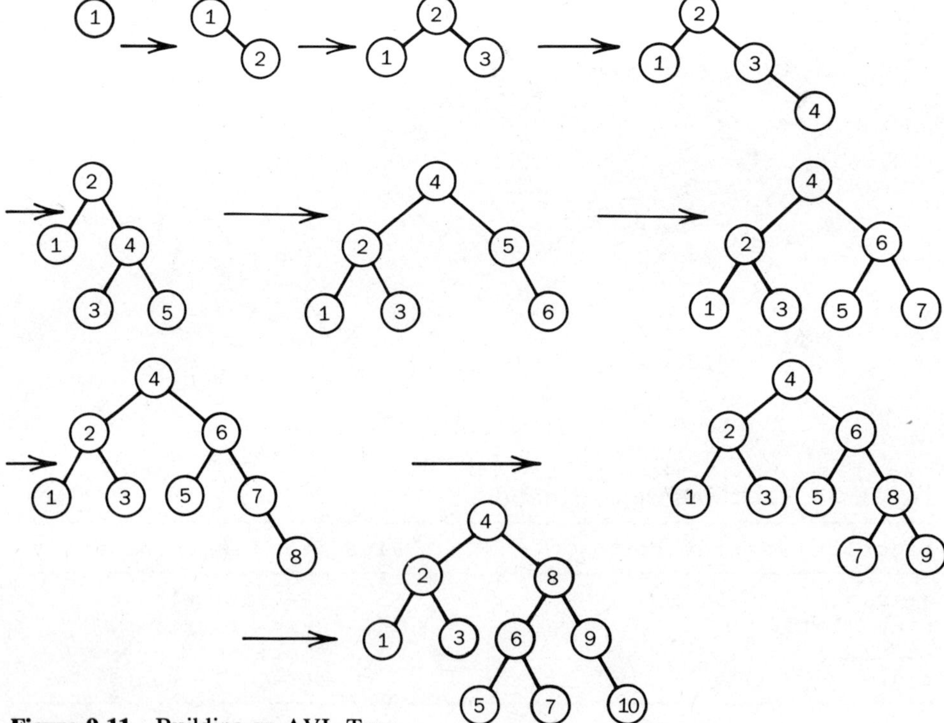

Figure 9.11 Building an AVL Tree

We illustrate the steps of building a small AVL tree, using the sequence of keys: 1, 2, . . . , 9, 10, in Figure 9.11.

9.1.3 Search Table Interface Revisited

Before discussing and displaying the implementation details for AVL insertion, let us look again at the search table as a data abstraction. In Listing 9.1, we display the interface to a search table.

Listing 9.1 Search Table Data Abstraction

```
DEFINITION MODULE table;

  FROM elements IMPORT
    (* type *) elementtype;

  EXPORT QUALIFIED
    (* type *) table,
    (* proc *) define, isempty, delete, insert, ispresent,
               makeempty, display;


  TYPE table;

  TYPE equaltype      = PROCEDURE( elementtype,elementtype ) :
                        BOOLEAN;

  TYPE lessthantype   = PROCEDURE( elementtype,elementtype ) :
                        BOOLEAN;

  TYPE displaytype    = PROCEDURE(  VAR elementtype   );


  PROCEDURE define
           ( VAR t           : table          (* out *) );
  (* Creates an empty table.                                *)


  PROCEDURE isempty
           (     t           : table          (* in    *) ) :
                 BOOLEAN;
  (* Returns true if table t is empty, otherwise false.    *)


  PROCEDURE ispresent
           (     t           : table           (* in    *);
                 item        : elementtype     (* in    *);
```

```
                    equal       : equaltype        (* in     *);
                    lessthan    : lessthantype     (* in     *) ) :
                    BOOLEAN;
  (* Returns true if item is in t, otherwise false.            *)


  PROCEDURE delete
            ( VAR t             : table            (* in/out *);
                  item          : elementtype      (* in     *);
                  equal         : equaltype        (* in     *);
                  lessthan      : lessthantype     (* in     *) );
  (* Removes the elementtype item in table t,
     if it is present.                                          *)


  PROCEDURE insert
            ( VAR t             : table            (* in/out *);
                  item          : elementtype      (* in     *);
                  equal         : equaltype        (* in     *);
                  lessthan      : lessthantype     (* in     *) );
  (* Inserts the elementtype item into table t.                 *)


  PROCEDURE makeempty
            ( VAR t             : table            (* in/out *) );
  (* This procedure removes table t from memory.                *)


  PROCEDURE display
            (     t             : table            (* in     *);
                  displayproc : displaytype        (* in     *) );
  (* Displays the elements of the table using displayproc. *)


END table.
```

As in Chapter 8, we write the search table abstraction in terms of items of type elementtype imported from the module elements. This requires the user of this library module to provide procedures for comparing two objects of type elementtype and to supply a procedure for displaying each item in the table.

9.1.4 Implementation of AVL Insertion

In Listing 9.2 we present the implementation details for AVL insertion.

Study Listing 9.2 carefully. We will walk through an example that exercises some but not all the branch paths in the algorithm. We leave it as an exercise for the reader to exercise the remaining branch paths.

Listing 9.2 Implementation Details for AVL Insertion

```
IMPLEMENTATION MODULE table;
(* This implementation uses AVL trees.                              *)

  FROM elements IMPORT
    (* type *) elementtype;

  FROM Storage IMPORT
    (* proc *) ALLOCATE, DEALLOCATE;

  FROM InOut IMPORT
    (* proc *) Write, WriteInt, WriteLn;


  CONST
        bell                = 7C;


  TYPE
        table               = POINTER TO node;

        node                = RECORD
                                key   : elementtype;
                                left  : table;
                                right : table;
                                bal   : [ -1..1 ];
                              END(* record *);


  PROCEDURE makenode
          ( VAR t         : table              (* out    *);
                item      : elementtype        (* in     *) );

  BEGIN
    NEW( t );
    t^.key := item;
    t^.left := NIL;
    t^.right := NIL;
    t^.bal := 0;
  END makenode;


  PROCEDURE insert
          ( VAR t           : table            (* in/out *);
                item        : elementtype      (* in     *);
                equal       : equaltype        (* in     *);
                lessthan    : lessthantype     (* in     *) );
```

```
VAR
      h                   : BOOLEAN;
(* Used to transmit information between recursive calls
   to AVLInsert and AVLDelete.  When the lowest level of
   the recursion is reached, and a node is inserted, h is
   set to true.                                        *)
PROCEDURE AVLInsert
          (     w         : elementtype     (* in     *);
             VAR p        : table           (* in/out *);
             VAR h        : BOOLEAN         (* in/out *) );

  VAR
        p1,
        p2                  : table;

BEGIN
  IF isempty( p )
  THEN
    h := TRUE;
    makenode( p, w );
  ELSIF lessthan( w, p^.key )
  THEN
    AVLInsert( w,  p^.left,  h );
    IF h
    THEN
      CASE p^.bal OF
        1 :
          p^.bal := 0;
          h := FALSE;
      | 0 :
          p^.bal := - 1;
      | -1 :
          p1 := p^.left;
          IF p1^.bal = - 1
          THEN
            (* single right rotation *)
            p^.left := p1^.right;
            p1^.right := p;
            p^.bal := 0;
            p := p1;
          ELSE
            (* left right rotation *)
            p2 := p1^.right;
            p1^.right := p2^.left;
            p2^.left := p1;
            p^.left := p2^.right;
            p2^.right := p;
            IF p2^.bal = - 1
            THEN
              p^.bal := 1
```

```
              ELSE
                p^.bal := 0;
              END(* if then *);
              IF p2^.bal = 1
              THEN
                p1^.bal := - 1
              ELSE
                p1^.bal := 0;
              END(* if then *);
              p := p2;
            END(* if then *);
            p^.bal := 0;
            h := FALSE;
        END(* case *);
      END(* if then *);
    ELSIF ( NOT equal( w, p^.key ) ) AND
          ( NOT lessthan( w, p^.key ) )
    THEN
      AVLInsert( w,  p^.right,  h );
      IF h
      THEN
        CASE p^.bal OF
          -1 :
            p^.bal := 0;
            h := FALSE;
        | 0 :
            p^.bal := 1;
        | 1 :
            p1 := p^.right;
            IF p1^.bal = 1
            THEN
              (* single left rotation *)
              p^.right := p1^.left;
              p1^.left := p;
              p^.bal := 0;
              p := p1;
            ELSE
              (* right left rotation *)
              p2 := p1^.left;
              p1^.left := p2^.right;
              p2^.right := p1;
              p^.right := p2^.left;
              p2^.left := p;
              IF p2^.bal = 1
              THEN
                p^.bal := - 1
              ELSE
                p^.bal := 0;
              END(* if then *);
              IF p2^.bal = - 1
```

```
                THEN
                  p1^.bal := 1
                ELSE
                  p1^.bal := 0;
                END(* if then *);
                p := p2;
              END(* if then *);
              p^.bal := 0;
              h := FALSE;
          END(* case *);
        ELSE
          h := FALSE;
        END(* if then *);
    ELSE
      h := FALSE;
    END(* if then *);
  END AVLInsert;

  BEGIN(* insert *)
    AVLInsert( item,  t,  h );
  END insert;
```

9.1.5 Example Illustrating the AVL Insertion Algorithm

We use the AVL tree given in Figure 9.6 and "walk" through the algorithm when key 5 is inserted.

The algorithm begins by a call to:

```
AVLInsert( 5, →8, h ), where →8 means "pointer to the node
      containing key 8".
```

Because the insertion key 5 is less than root key 8, a recursive call is made to:

```
AVLInsert( 5, →4, h )
```

Because the insertion key 5 is greater than node key 4, a recursive call is made to:

```
AVLInsert( 5, →6, h )
```

Because the insertion key 5 is less than node key 6, a recursive call is made to:

```
AVLInsert( 5, →NIL, h )
```

Because of the pointer to NIL, procedure makenode is called and h is assigned the value TRUE. Because the second parameter in the call to AVLInsert is p^.left, and it is a reference parameter, a link is forged between node 6 (the node with key value 6) and the new node 5. That is, the left child of node 6 is linked to node 5. Indeed, at the moment NEW(t) is called, in procedure makenode, the left child pointer of node 6 acquires the memory reference value of this new node (node 5). There is no explicit assignment connecting node 6 to node 5. The connection is forged implicitly.

The recursion returns to the line below:

```
AVLInsert( w, p^.left, h );
```

The pointer p is pointing to the node containing key 6. Because the current balance of node p is 0, the balance of this node is reassigned the value −1.

The recursion returns to the line below:

```
AVLInsert( w, p^.right, h );
```

The pointer p is pointing to the node containing key 4. Because the current balance of node p is 0, the balance of this node is reassigned the value 1.

The recursion returns to the line below:

```
AVLInsert( w, p^.left, h );
```

The pointer p is pointing to the root node containing key 8. Because the balance of node p is −1, p1 is assigned to point to node 4. Because the balance of p1 is not −1, the block of code with the leading comment "left right rotation" is used.

In exercise 9.4, you are asked to complete the walk-through of the code that performs left right rotation.

9.1.6 AVL Deletion

When a node is deleted from an AVL tree, this node may:

1. Have no children (i.e., be a leaf node).

2. Have one child.

3. Have two children.

In the first case, the leaf node is removed from the tree, and the tree rebalanced, if appropriate.

In the second case, the deleted node is replaced by its child. The tree is then rebalanced, if appropriate.

In the third case, the deleted node is replaced by its inorder successor, as with elementary search trees (see section 8.2.3). The tree is then rebalanced, if appropriate.

As with insertion, there are two constellations that necessitate rebalancing. Unfortunately, with AVL deletion, more than one rebalancing operation may be required. In fact, rebalancing may have to be performed on every node in the search path to the deleted node.

We illustrate this possibility by deleting node 200 in Figure 9.12*a*. The search path to node 200 includes the nodes 100 and 150. When nodc 200 is removed from the tree, a constellation of type 1 is formed with node 150 having a balance of -2 and node 125 having a balance of -1.

The rotational correction for this imbalance is shown in Figure 9.12*b*. This

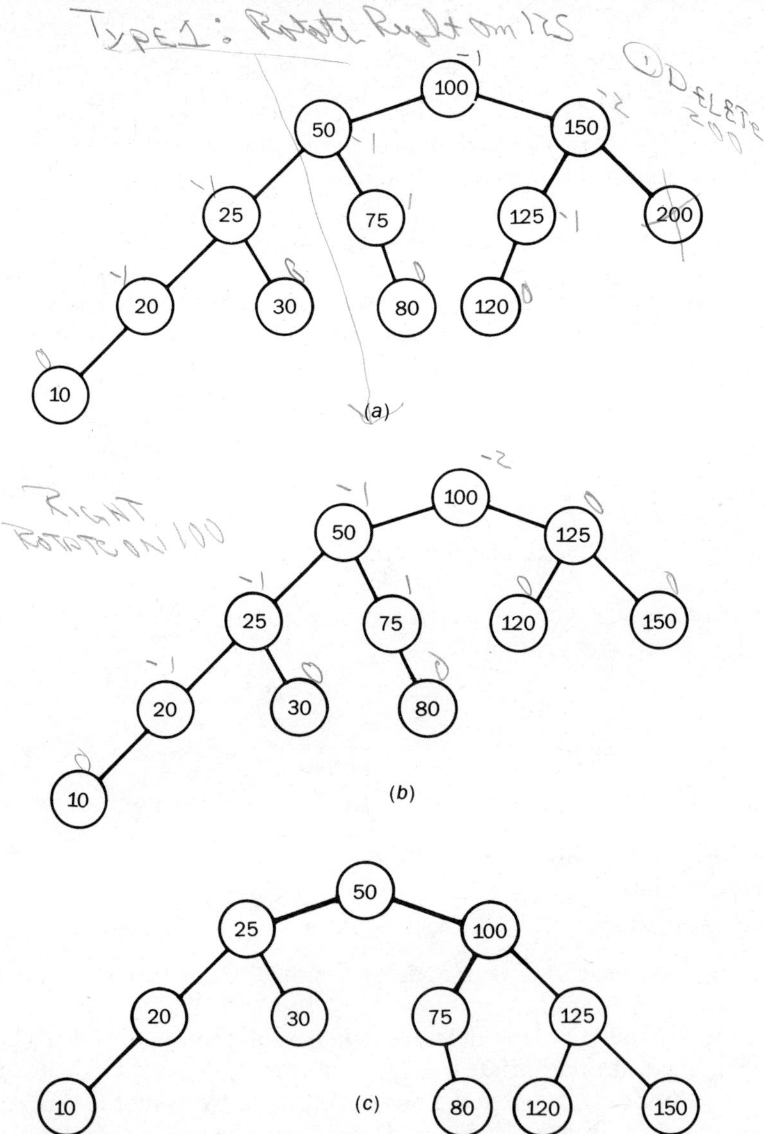

Figure 9.12 Deletion and Rotation in an AVL Tree

correction induces an imbalance (type 1 constellation) in node 100 (balance −2). Node 50 has a balance of −1. A final right rotation on node 100 corrects the imbalance and leads to the AVL tree shown in Figure 9.12*c*.

9.1.7 Implementation of AVL Deletion

In Listing 9.3, we present a procedure for AVL deletion.

Listing 9.3 AVL Deletion

```
PROCEDURE delete
   ( VAR t                  : table          (* in/out *);
         item               : elementtype    (* in     *);
         equal              : equaltype      (* in     *);
         lessthan           : lessthantype   (* in     *) );

  VAR
       h                     : BOOLEAN;

  PROCEDURE AVLDelete
     (      x                : elementtype    (* in     *);
        VAR p                : table          (* in/out *);
        VAR h                : BOOLEAN        (* in/out *) );

  VAR
      q,
      mark                 : table;

    PROCEDURE balance1
           ( VAR p           : table           (* in/out *);
             VAR h           : BOOLEAN         (* in/out *) );
    (* Rebalances left side of tree.                     *)

    VAR
          p1,
          p2                 : table;
          b1,
          b2                 : [ -1..1 ];

    BEGIN
      CASE p^.bal OF
        -1 :
          p^.bal := 0;
      | 0 :
```

```
        p^.bal := 1;
        h := FALSE;
    | 1 :
        p1 := p^.right;
        b1 := p1^.bal;
        IF b1 >= 0
        THEN (* single left rotate *)
          p^.right := p1^.left;
          p1^.left := p;
          IF b1 = 0
          THEN
            p^.bal := 1;
            p1^.bal := - 1;
            h := FALSE;
          ELSE (* double right left rotate *)
            p^.bal := 0;
            p1^.bal := 0;
          END(* if then *);
          p := p1;
        ELSE (* double right left rotate *)
          p2 := p1^.left;
          b2 := p2^.bal;
          p1^.left := p2^.right;
          p2^.right := p1;
          p^.right := p2^.left;
          p2^.left := p;
          IF b2 = 1
          THEN
            p^.bal := - 1
          ELSE
            p^.bal := 0;
          END(* if then *);
          IF b2 = - 1
          THEN
            p1^.bal := 1
          ELSE
            p1^.bal := 0;
          END(* if then *);
          p := p2;
          p2^.bal := 0;
        END(* if then *);
    END(* case *);
  END balance1;

  PROCEDURE balance2
          ( VAR p          : table              (* in/out *);
            VAR h          : BOOLEAN            (* in/out *) );
  (* Rebalances right side of tree.                        *)
    VAR
        p1,
        p2                 : table;
```

```
        b1,
        b2                      : [ -1..1 ];

  BEGIN
    CASE p^.bal OF
      1 :
        p^.bal := 0;
    | 0 :
        p^.bal := - 1;
        h := FALSE;
    | -1 :
        p1 := p^.left;
        b1 := p1^.bal;
        IF b1 <= 0
        THEN (* single right rotate *)
          p^.left := p1^.right;
          p1^.right := p;
          IF b1 = 0
          THEN
            p^.bal := - 1;
            p1^.bal := 1;
            h := FALSE;
          ELSE
            p^.bal := 0;
            p1^.bal := 0;
          END(* if then *);
          p := p1;
        ELSE (* double left right rotate *)
          p2 := p1^.right;
          b2 := p2^.bal;
          p1^.right := p2^.left;
          p2^.left := p1;
          p^.left := p2^.right;
          p2^.right := p;
          IF b2 = - 1
          THEN
            p^.bal := 1
          ELSE
            p^.bal := 0;
          END(* if then *);
          IF b2 = 1
          THEN
            p1^.bal := - 1
          ELSE
            p1^.bal := 0;
          END(* if then *);
          p := p2;
          p2^.bal := 0;
        END(* if then *);
    END(* case *);
  END balance2;
```

```
PROCEDURE del
          ( VAR r          : table             (* in/out *);
            VAR h          : BOOLEAN           (* in/out *) );
(* Marks node for deletion.                     *)

BEGIN
  IF NOT isempty( r^.right )
  THEN
    del( r^.right, h );
    IF h
    THEN
      balance2( r, h );
    END(* if then *);
  ELSE
    p^.key := r^.key;
    mark := r;
    r := r^.left;
    h := TRUE;
  END(* if then *);
  END del;


BEGIN(* AVLDelete *)
  IF isempty( p )
  THEN
    Write( bell );
    h := FALSE;
  ELSIF lessthan( x, p^.key )
  THEN
    AVLDelete( x,  p^.left,  h );
    IF h
    THEN
      balance1( p,  h );
    END(* if then *);
  ELSIF ( NOT equal( x, p^.key ) ) AND
        ( NOT lessthan( x, p^.key ) )
  THEN
    AVLDelete( x,  p^.right,  h );
    IF h
    THEN
      balance2( p,  h );
    END(* if then *);
  ELSE
    IF isempty( p^.right )
    THEN
      q := p;
      p := q^.left;
      h := TRUE;
      DISPOSE( q );
    ELSIF isempty( p^.left )
```

```
      THEN
        q := p;
        p := q^.right;
        h := TRUE;
        DISPOSE( q );
      ELSE
        del( p^.left,  h );
        IF h
        THEN
          balancel( p,  h );
        END(* if then *);
        DISPOSE( mark );
      END(* if then *);
    END(* if then *);
  END AVLDelete;


BEGIN(* delete *)
  AVLDelete( item,  t,  h );
END delete;
```

As an exercise, walk through the algorithm given in Listing 9.3 using the tree shown in Figure 9.12*a*.

How many rotations are required in inserting and deleting nodes from an AVL tree? One might think that more rotations are required for deletion because of the possible propagation effect discussed above. This is not the case. On the average for a random AVL tree, approximately half the insertions require rotational intervention, whereas about one-fifth of deletions require rotational intervention. Because the deletion interventions often require many more rotational corrections, the total numbers of rotations are about equal (see exercises 9.8 and 9.9).

The remaining procedures in the AVL implementation of the search table are identical to the elementary search table procedures given in Chapter 8 and are not repeated here.

9.2 Weight-Balanced Trees

As an alternative to the height-balanced AVL trees presented in section 9.1, we may achieve the same goals of reducing search time by creating a "balanced" tree if we consider weight balancing.

The important *ACM Communications* paper by Gaston Gonnet of the University of Waterloo (1983) forms the basis for our discussion of weight balance. We present a brief summary of Gonnet's results. The reader may consult the paper for further details.

The weight balance algorithm performs a single or double rotation on a node whenever such rotation can reduce the total internal path of the subtree associated with the node. Gonnet claims that using such a strategy, the worst internal path length on weight-balanced trees is never more than 5 percent worse than optimal and its height never more than 44 percent taller than optimal. This compares favorably with AVL trees, which are constrained to a worst case of 28 percent worse than optimal internal path length and the same 44 percent worst height.

A binary tree is internal-path balanced (IPB) if no single or double rotation on any of its nodes will decrease its internal path length. When an insertion or deletion is performed on an IPB tree, the only nodes that may fail the balance conditions are those in the path from the root to the new/deleted node (see exercise 9.12). To obtain balance after an insertion or deletion, we have to check the balance condition in the path from the root to the inserted/deleted node.

A consequence of the balance requirements is generally the need to perform many more rotations than are required for AVL trees. Thus weight-balanced trees are generally more expensive than AVL trees to build and maintain because of the extensive micromanagement required.

In Listing 9.4, we present several procedures for accomplishing weight-balanced tree insertion. We leave deletion as an exercise (see exercise 9.13).

Listing 9.4 Several Procedures for Insertion in a Weight-Balanced Tree

```
IMPLEMENTATION MODULE table;


  TYPE
        table                    = POINTER TO node;

        node                     = RECORD
                                     key    : elementtype;
                                     left   : table;
                                     right  : table;
                                     wt     : CARDINAL;
                                   END(* record *);


  PROCEDURE makenode
            ( VAR t             : table           (* out     *);
                  item          : elementtype     (* in      *) );

  BEGIN
    NEW( t );
    t^.key := item;
    t^.left := NIL;
```

```
    t^.right := NIL;
    t^.wt := 2;
  END makenode;


  PROCEDURE wt
            (      t          : table              (* in      *) ) :
                   CARDINAL;

  BEGIN
    IF isempty(  t  )
    THEN
      RETURN 1
    ELSE
      RETURN t^.wt;
    END(* if then *);
  END wt;


  PROCEDURE leftrotate
            ( VAR t           : table              (* in      *) );

    VAR
          temp        : table;


  BEGIN
    temp := t;
    t := t^.right;
    temp^.right := t^.left;
    t^.left := temp;
    t^.wt := temp^.wt;
    temp^.wt := wt( temp^.left ) + wt( temp^.right );
  END leftrotate;


  PROCEDURE rightrotate
            ( VAR t           : table              (* in      *) );

    VAR
          temp        : table;

  BEGIN
    temp := t;
    t := t^.left;
    temp^.left := t^.right;
    t^.right := temp;
    t^.wt := temp^.wt;
    temp^.wt := wt( temp^.right ) + wt( temp^.left );
  END rightrotate;
```

```
PROCEDURE checkrotations
          ( VAR t         : table           (* in/out *) );

  VAR
        wl,
        wr          : CARDINAL;

BEGIN
  IF NOT isempty( t )
  THEN
    wl := wt( t^.left );
    wr := wt( t^.right );
    IF wr > wl
    THEN
      (* left rotation needed *)
      IF wt( t^.right^.right ) > wl
      THEN
        leftrotate( t );
        checkrotations( t^.left );
      ELSIF wt( t^.right^.left ) > wl
      THEN
        rightrotate( t^.right );
        leftrotate( t );
        checkrotations( t^.left );
        checkrotations( t^.right );
      END(* if then *);
    ELSIF wl > wr
    THEN
      (* right rotation needed *)
      IF wt( t^.left^.left ) > wr
      THEN
        rightrotate( t );
        checkrotations( t^.right );
      ELSIF wt( t^.left^.right ) > wr
      THEN
        leftrotate( t^.left );
        rightrotate( t );
        checkrotations( t^.left );
        checkrotations( t^.right );
      END(* if then *);
    END(* if then *);
  END(* if then *);
END checkrotations;


PROCEDURE insert
          ( VAR t         : table           (* in/out *);
                item      : elementtype     (* in     *);
                equal     : equaltype       (* in     *);
                lessthan  : lessthantype    (* in     *) );
```

```
  BEGIN
    IF isempty( t )
    THEN
      makenode( t,  item );
    ELSIF equal( t^.key,  item )
    THEN
      Write( bell );
    ELSE
      IF lessthan( item, t^.key )
      THEN
        insert( t^.left, item );
      ELSE
        insert( t^.right, item );
      END(* if then *);
      t^.wt := wt( t^.left ) + wt( t^.right );
      checkrotations( t );
    END(* if then *);
  END insert;

  ...

END table.
```

We note the new data structure that includes a wt field used for each node of the tree:

```
node = RECORD
         key   : elementtype;
         left  : table;
         right : table;
         wt    : CARDINAL;
       END(* record *);
```

In procedures makenode and wt we assign a weight of 1 to a NIL pointer. In exercise 9.15 we ask you to walk through recursive procedure checkrotations and insert and build a weight-balanced tree.

Please note that we have retained the same interface to the search table abstraction in procedure insert. Any modules that may be dependent on module table would not have to be modified or recompiled if our implementation of the search table were changed from an AVL tree to a weight-balanced tree. This is one of the major benefits of data abstraction. The remaining procedures (define, ispresent, display, and makeempty), are the same as displayed in the elementary search tree implementation in Chapter 8.

9.3 Global Tree Rebalancing

Suppose that from the elementary search tree procedures given in Chapter 8, we have built a search tree that is not balanced. We would like to be able to create a balanced tree from it without having to rebuild from scratch. In this section, we consider a method, based on a paper by Chang and Iyengar (1984), for globally rebalancing any binary tree. For details, consult this paper.

We present the highlights of the algorithm in the Modula-2 procedure globalbalance given in Listing 9.5.

Listing 9.5 Procedure for Globally Rebalancing a Binary Tree

```
PROCEDURE globalbalance
          ( VAR root : table              (* in/out *) );
(* Takes a pointer to a binary search tree as input and
   returns a pointer to a balanced binary search tree
   as output.                                            *)

CONST maxnodes = 3000;

VAR
    link    : ARRAY[ 1 .. maxnodes ] OF table;
    (* Used to store pointers to ordered list of nodes.   *)

    n       : CARDINAL; (* number of nodes in tree *)
    m       : CARDINAL; (* median node in tree     *)
    ansl    : table;
    ansr    : table;


  PROCEDURE traverse
            (     t : table                (* in     *) );

  BEGIN
    IF NOT isempty( t )
    THEN
      traverse( t^.left );
      INC(n);
      link[ n ] := t;
      traverse( t^.right );
    END(* if then *);
  END traverse;


  PROCEDURE grow
            (    low, high : CARDINAL   (* in     *) );
```

```
  VAR
     mid       : CARDINAL;
     tl        : table;
     tr        : table;

  BEGIN
    IF low > high
    THEN
      ansl := NIL;
      ansr := NIL;
    ELSIF low = high
    THEN
      ansl := link[ low ];
      ansr := link[ low + m ];
      ansl^.left  := NIL;
      ansl^.right := NIL;
      ansr^.left  := NIL;
      ansr^.right := NIL;
    ELSE (* low < high *)
      mid := ( low + high ) DIV 2;
      tl := link[ mid ];
      tr := link[ mid + m ];
      grow( low, mid-1 );
      tl^.left := ansl;
      tr^.left := ansr;
      grow( mid + 1, high );
      tl^.right := ansl;
      tr^.right := ansr;
      ansl := tl;
      ansr := tr;
    END(* if then *);
  END grow;

BEGIN (* globalbalance *)
  n := 0;
  traverse( root );
  IF n <= 2
  THEN
    RETURN;
  END(* if then *);
  m := ( n + 1 ) DIV 2;
  root := link[ m ];
  IF n = 2 * m
  THEN
    INC( m );
    grow( 1, m - 2 );
    link[ m ]^.left  := NIL;
    link[ m ]^.right := NIL;
    link[ m + 1 ]^.left := link[ m ];
  ELSE
```

```
    grow( 1, m - 1 );
  END(* if then *);
  root^.left   := ansl;
  root^.right := ansr;
END globalbalance;
```

We will walk through procedure globalbalance and rebalance the tree shown in Figure 9.13, where the letters designate memory references. The first step in the global rebalance algorithm is to traverse the tree and store pointers to the inorder elements in an array called link.

Tracing the algorithm in procedure globalbalance yields:

```
m = 4
root = B
m = 5 ( since n is even )
grow( 1, 3 )
mid = 2
tl = G
tr = C
  grow( 1, 1 )
  ansl = H
  ansr = A
  left( H ) = right( H ) = NIL
  left( A ) = right( A ) = NIL
left( G ) = H
left( C ) = A
  grow( 3, 3 )
  ansl = D
  ansr = F
```

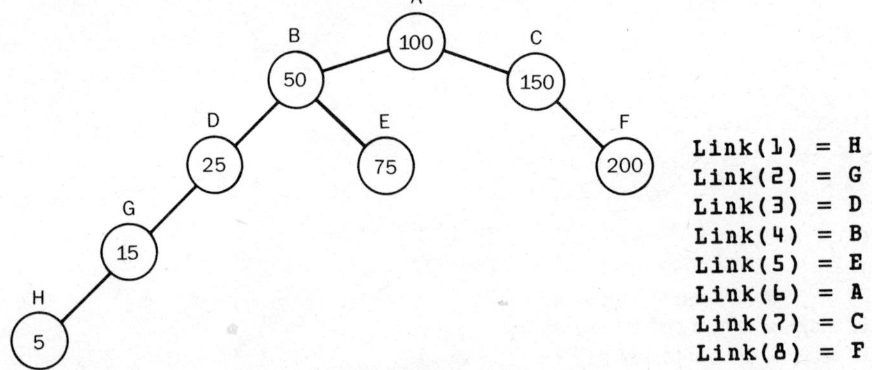

Figure 9.13 Tree to Illustrate Global Rebalance

```
    left( D ) = right( D ) = NIL
    left( F ) = right( F ) = NIL
  right( G ) = D
  right( C ) = F
  ansl = G
  ansr = C
  left( E ) = right ( E ) = NIL
  left( A ) = E
  left( B ) = G
  right( B ) = C
```

In Figure 9.14 we show the rebalanced tree resulting from the application of procedure globalbalance.

In exercise 9.17 we ask you to explain the rationale for the global rebalance algorithm given in Listing 9.5.

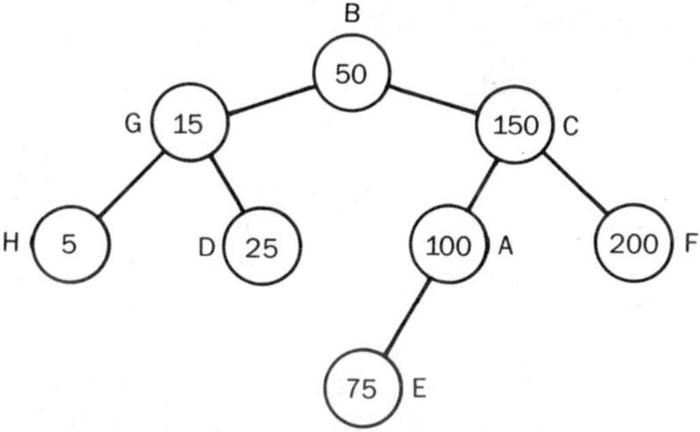

Figure 9.14 Tree of Figure 9.13 After Global Rebalance

PART 2: BALANCED TREES USING SECONDARY STORAGE: B-TREES

Thus far, we have considered tree structures that are constructed in RAM (random access memory). In file management and database applications, it is useful to store tree structures on secondary storage. As an example, consider a huge AVL tree with 1,000,000 nodes, each containing an integer key, which may be an index to another still larger file. On many computers it would be very difficult, if not impossible, to store the entire AVL tree in memory (RAM). Suppose such a tree is constructed on disk. A nearly balanced binary tree with 1,000,000 nodes contains 20 levels. Therefore a search, insertion, or deletion in such a disk-based tree might involve as many as 20 disk accesses.

Disk accesses are very slow compared to RAM accesses. On some machines disk accesses are measured in tenths of a second, whereas RAM accesses are measured in microseconds. A goal of any disk-based tree algorithm is to reduce to an absolute minimum the number of disk accesses.

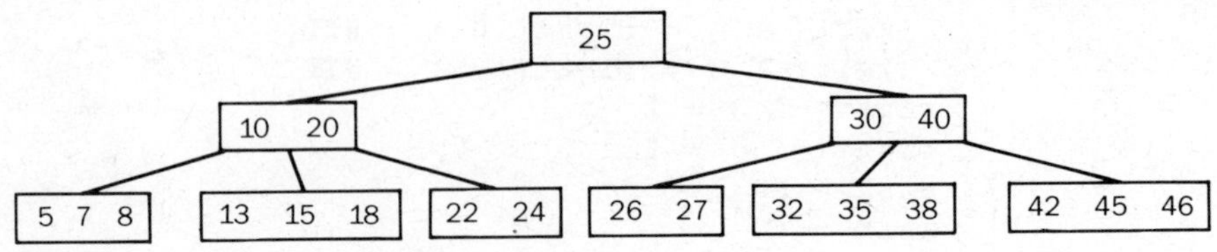

Figure 9.15 B Tree of Order 2 with Three Levels

B-trees introduced in 1970, are designed specifically to reduce secondary storage accesses. A B-tree consists of a set of pages, each page containing an ordered set of keys, usually implemented as an array of keys.

9.4 Definition of B-Tree

A B tree of order n has the following properties:

1. Every page consists of at most $2n$ keys.
2. Every page except the root page contains at least n keys.
3. Every page has a pointer to a left descendent page and every key has a pointer to a right descendent page.
4. All leaf pages are at the same level.

The B-tree in Figure 9.15 is of order 2 and contains three levels. Each page, represented in Figure 9.15 as a box, is stored in a file block on disk. The left descendant of the root page is the page containing the keys 10 and 20. The pointer to this page is a cardinal containing the disk file block number of the page. The key value 25 has a pointer (cardinal representing the file block) to its right descendent page, namely, the page containing the keys 30 and 40.

The page containing 10 and 20 has a pointer to its left descendant page containing keys 5, 7, and 8. Key 10 points to its right descendant page containing the keys 13, 15, and 18. Key 20 points to its right descendant page containing the keys 22 and 24. A similar configuration exists for the page containing 30 and 40.

Have you noticed how the leaf page keys are interleaved between the keys of the parent page? This is true in general. The B-tree structure generalizes the search tree property defined earlier for binary trees. All keys in pages that are to the left of a given page are smaller, and all keys in pages that are to the right of a given page are larger than the keys in the given page.

9.5 Informal Algorithm for B-Tree Insertion

How do we insert keys into a B-tree? Figure 9.16 illustrates the insertion of the keys 20, 40, 10, 30, 15, 35, 7, 26, 18, 22, 5, 42, 13, 46, 27, 8, 32, 38, 24, 45, and 25 into a B-tree of order 2.

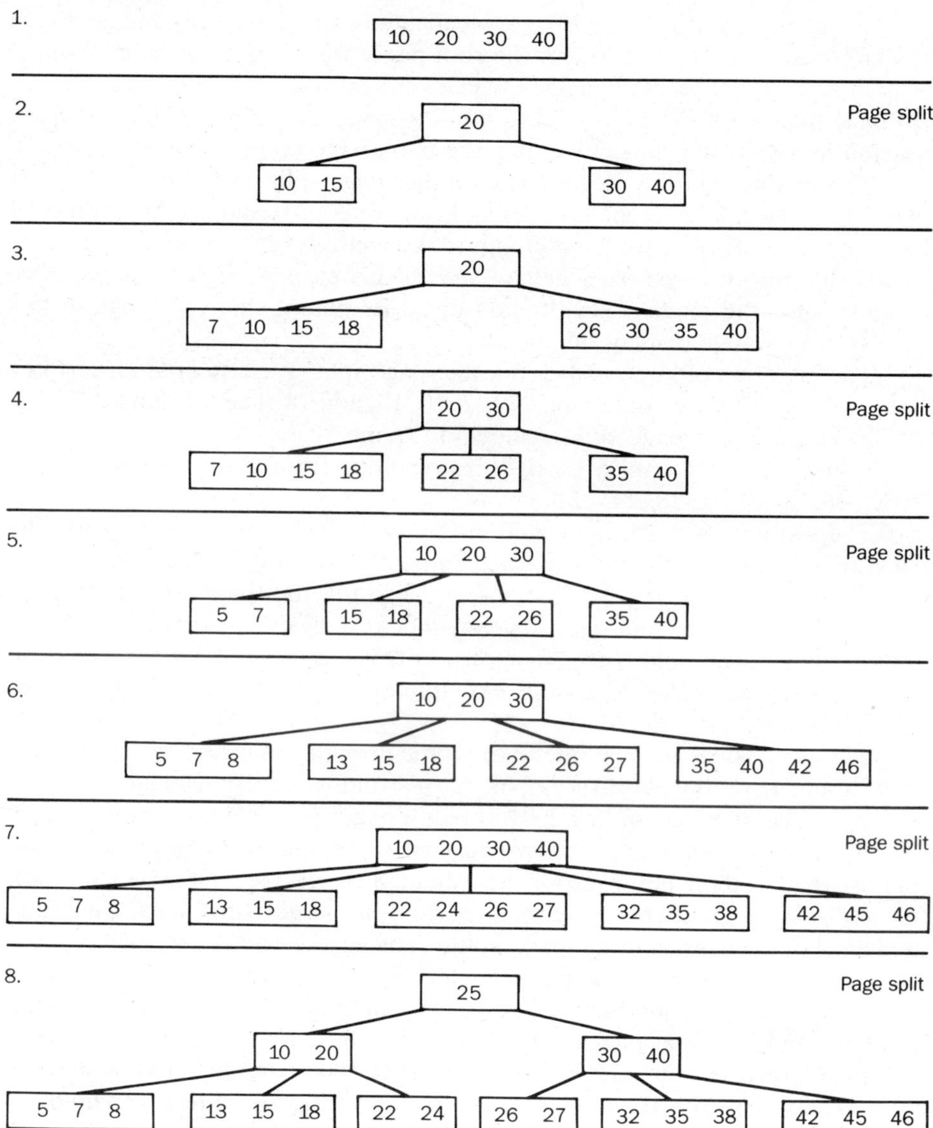

Figure 9.16 Insertion into a B-Tree

Keys 20, 40, 10, and 30 form a full root page, shown as frame 1 in Figure 9.16. Note the reordering of the four keys from smallest to largest within the root page. Key 15 cannot fit into the root page, so a page split operation occurs. The median value key among the keys 10, 15, 20, 30 and 40 sifts up to its parent page. In this case such a parent page does not exist, so it must be created. Key 20 is deposited in a new root page. The left descendent page of the new root page contains the keys 10 and 15 and the right descendent page of key 20 contains the keys 30 and 40. This is shown in frame 2.

To insert key 35 into the B-tree, we locate this key in the root page. Since it is larger than the largest key of the root page, we go to the page containing keys 30 and 40. We locate key 35 between keys 30 and 40. Because we are in a leaf page that is not full, we insert 35 into this page. The keys 7, 26, and 18 are inserted in a similar manner, yielding the B-tree shown in frame 3.

The insertion of key 22 requires another page split. We attempt to insert key 22 into the full leaf page containing keys 26, 30, 35, and 40. Regardless of the order of the B-tree, we must compute the median key among $2n + 1$ keys, an odd number of keys. The median key in this case is 30. This is a simple computation—the median key 30 sifts up to its parent, the root page in this case. In frame 4 we display this result.

The insertion of key 5 causes another page split. We attempt to insert key 5 into the full leaf page containing keys 7, 10, 15, and 18. The median key is key 10. The result of the page split is shown in frame 5.

Frames 6 and 7 display the B-trees resulting from the insertion of keys, 42, 13, 46, 27, 8, 32, 38, 24, and 45.

The last key, key 25, is located in the root page between 20 and 30. The key is then located in the full leaf page containing the keys 22, 24, 26, and 27. The median key is 25. It sifts up to its parent, a full root page. A second page split is induced by the root page. The median key, again 25, sifts up to form a new root page. The final B-tree is shown in frame 8 of Figure 9.16.

It should be evident from this example that B-trees grow upward whenever a root page must be split.

Let us consider the arithmetic of B-tree growth, taking a worst-case scenario. Suppose we have a B-tree of order 1000 and we insert 2000 keys into the root page. The insertion of key 2001 causes a page split. We now have a single key in the new root page and two leaf pages, each containing 1000 keys. Suppose that 1000 further insertions end up in the largest leaf page (worst case). The addition of another key earmarked for this largest leaf page (insertion number 3002) causes another page split, causing the root page to have two keys, and leaving three root pages, each with 1000 keys. If this pattern of worst-case insertion continues, we will eventually have the root page filled with 2000 keys and 2001 leaf pages, each with 1000 keys.

In worst case, our 2-level B-tree of order 1000 contains $2001 \times 1000 + 2000 = 2{,}003{,}000$ keys. It would have taken an AVL tree of 21 levels to hold the same number of keys.

The worst-case, 3-level B-tree of order 1000 contains 2000 keys in its root page and has 2001 pages, each containing 1000 keys; and each of these 2001 level-2 pages has 1001 children pages, each containing 1000 keys. The total number of keys in such a worst-case, 3-level B-tree of order 1000 is: $2000 + 2001 \times 1000 + 2001 \times 1001 \times 1000 = 2{,}005{,}004{,}000$. It would take 31 levels in an AVL tree to represent the keys ($> 2 \times 10^9$) contained in a B-tree of order 3 that requires only three levels.

It is clear that a B-tree provides tremendous leverage compared to AVL trees in reducing the number of levels in the tree.

9.6 Informal Algorithm for B-Tree Deletion

We state some guidelines for B-tree deletion and then informally illustrate the algorithm with an example.

Some Guidelines for B-Tree Deletion

1. If the key being deleted is in a leaf page, delete the key from the leaf page.

2. If the key being deleted is not in a leaf page use a right-to-left traversal to replace the key being deleted with its inorder successor, which is in a leaf page.

3. If the number of keys remaining in a leaf page is less than n, the order of the B tree, perform either a balance operation (exchange of keys with adjacent leaf page) or a merge operation (resulting in the removal of a page).

4. Try first to perform either an exchange or a merge operation with the right adjacent leaf page or, if this is not possible, with the left adjacent leaf page. An exchange or merge with the left adjacent leaf page is justified only when the key-deficient leaf page does not share a common ancestor key with the right adjacent leaf page.

5. A balance with the right (left) adjacent leaf page is justified whenever the sum of the keys on the two pages plus the common ancestor key is equal or greater than $2n + 1$.

6. A merge with the right (left) adjacent leaf page is justified whenever the sum of the keys on the two pages plus the common ancestor key is equal or less than $2n$.

The common ancestor key of two pages is the key in the common parent page with one of the two pages to its left and the other to its right.

For example, in Figure 9.15, the common ancestor key of the page containing 32, 35, and 38 and the page containing 42, 45, and 46 is key 40. The common ancestor key of the page containing 5, 7, and 8 and the page containing 13, 15, and 18 is key 10. We note that the page containing 22 and 24 does not have a right adjacent page, and the page containing 26 and 27 does not have a left adjacent page.

In Figure 9.17 we informally illustrate the algorithm for B-tree deletion. In case of deletion requiring balance (Figure 9.17*a*), we identify the page containing keys 38, 42, and 46 as the right adjacent page. With key 24 removed, there are $2n + 1 = 5$ keys remaining. Thus an exchange operation may be performed producing the second B-tree in Figure 9.17*a*.

In the second case (Figure 9.17*b*) we again identify the page containing the keys 42 and 46 as the right adjacent page. With key 24 removed, there are 4 $< 2n + 1$ keys remaining. Thus a merge operation may be performed, removing one page from the B-tree and resulting in the second tree in Figure 9.17*b*.

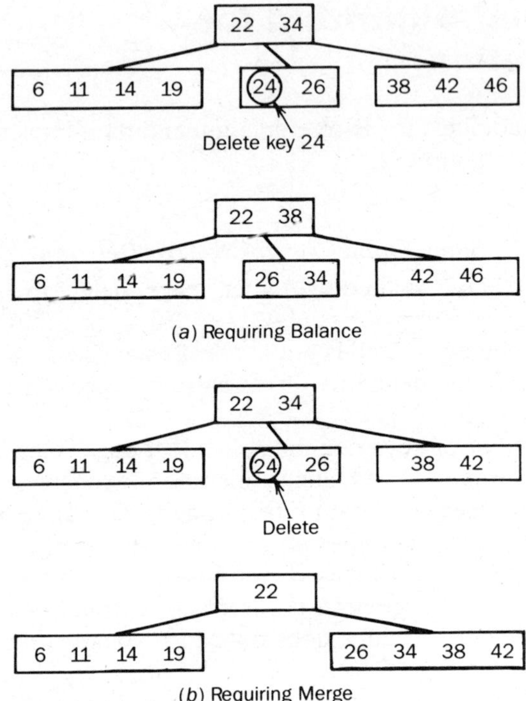

Figure 9.17 Deletions from a B-Tree

In Figure 9.18 we present a slightly more complex example of B-tree deletion. We wish to delete key 25 from the root page (Figure 9.18*a*). We replace key 25 by its inorder successor going right to left, which is key 24. Because the leaf page originally containing key 24 is now deficient by 1, our first thought would be to balance or merge it with its right adjacent leaf page. We cannot do this, however, because there is no right adjacent leaf page. We instead merge with the left adjacent leaf page. The keys that we must work with in the merge are 13, 15, 20, and 22. The B-tree that results is shown in Figure 9.18*b*.

We find that the page that contains key 10 is deficient by one key (as a result of the previous merge operation). We must perform another merge with its right adjacent page (the page containing keys 30 and 40). The final B tree is shown in Figure 9.18*c*.

9.7 Interface to the B-Tree Module

In Listing 9.6 we present the interface to the B-tree module.

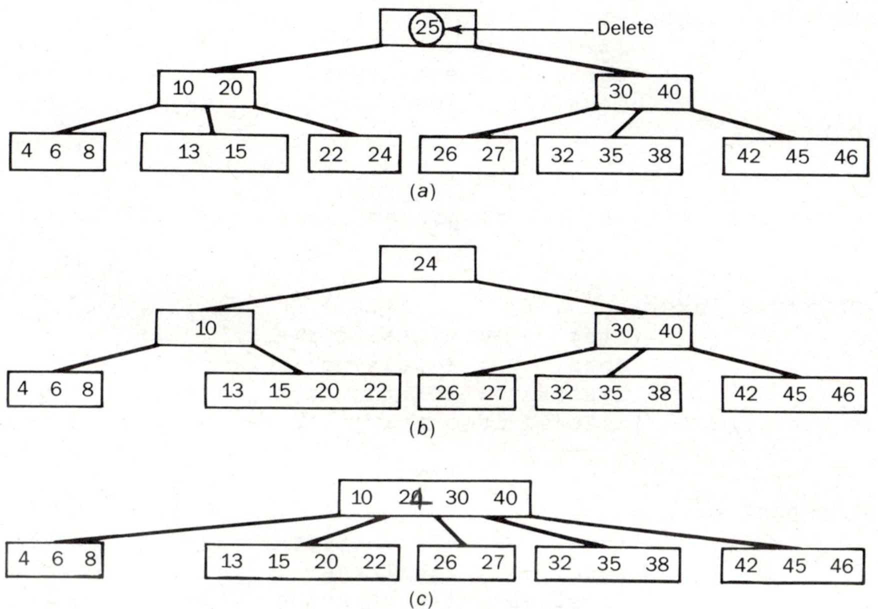

Figure 9.18 Deletion of Root Node Key from a B-Tree

Listing 9.6 Definition Module for B-Tree

```
DEFINITION MODULE Btree;
(* This module provides the interface to a single B-tree
   file stored on disk. The name assigned to the B-tree
   file is    "BTREE".                                  *)

  FROM elements IMPORT
    (* type *) elementtype;

  EXPORT QUALIFIED
    (* proc *) ispresent, insert, delete, display, save;

  TYPE

       equaltype    = PROCEDURE( elementtype, elementtype ) :
                                 BOOLEAN;

       lessthantype = PROCEDURE( elementtype, elementtype ):
                                 BOOLEAN;

       displaytype  = PROCEDURE( VAR elementtype );
```

```
  PROCEDURE ispresent
           (      item     : elementtype      (* in      *);
                  equal    : equaltype        (* in      *);
                  lessthan : lessthantype     (* in      *) ) :
  BOOLEAN;

  (* Returns true if item is present, otherwise false. *)

  PROCEDURE insert
           (      item     : elementtype      (* in      *);
                  equal    : equaltype        (* in      *);
                  lessthan : lessthantype     (* in      *) );
  (* The item is inserted into a page of the B-tree.   *)

  PROCEDURE delete
           (      item     : elementtype      (* in      *);
                  equal    : equaltype        (* in      *);
                  lessthan : lessthantype     (* in      *) );

  (* The item is deleted from a page of the B-tree if
     it is present.                                      *)

  PROCEDURE display
           (      displayproc : displaytype  (* in  *) );
  (* The B-tree is displayed either on the screen or on
     a printer.                                          *)

  PROCEDURE save;
  (* The B-tree file is updated and closed.              *)

END Btree.
```

As with tree modules presented earlier, the B-tree module requires the programmer writing a client module to define the operations of equal, lessthan, and display for objects of type elementtype. The interface given in Listing 9.6 assumes the presence on disk of a single B-tree file called "BTREE". We leave it as an exercise for the reader to modify the interface and implementation to allow many B-tree files to coexist and to be individually accessed.

9.8 Data Structure for B-Tree

In Listing 9.7 we present the beginning of the B-tree implementation including the data structure for the B-tree.

Examination of the data structure for the B-tree given in Listing 9.7 reveals that each page is defined as a record with three fields. The first field contains the number of keys in the page, the second contains a pointer to the

Listing 9.7 B-Tree Data Structure and Beginning of Implementation

```
IMPLEMENTATION MODULE Btree;

  FROM elements IMPORT
    (* type  *) elementtype,
    (* const *) initialvalue;

  FROM FileSystem IMPORT
    (* proc *) Lookup, Close, File, WriteNBytes, ReadNBytes,
               SetPos, SetRead, SetWrite, Response,
               SetModify, Length;

  FROM SYSTEM IMPORT
    (* proc *) TSIZE, ADR, SIZE;

  FROM util IMPORT
    (* proc *) centermessage;

  FROM screen IMPORT
    (* proc *) clrscreen;

  FROM InOut IMPORT
    (* proc *) WriteLn, Write, WriteString, WriteCard;


  CONST
        orderofbtree = 2; (* very important parameter.     *)
        (* This is the only parameter that must be changed
           to implement a B-tree of any order.             *)
        minpagesize         = orderofbtree;
        maxpages            = 5000;
        maxpagesize         = 2 * minpagesize;

  TYPE

        pagepointer         = [  0 .. maxpages  ];
        (* 0 represents the NIL pointer.      *)
```

```
TYPE

    item    =    RECORD
                   info           : elementtype;
                   successorpage : pagepointer;
                   duplicates     : CARDINAL;
                 END(* record *);

TYPE

    page    =    RECORD
                   numberkeys : [ 0 .. maxpagesize ];
                   leftchild  : pagepointer;
                   pagedata   : ARRAY[ 1 .. maxpagesize ]
                                OF item;
                 END(* record *);

------------------------------------------------------------

DEFINITION MODULE elements;

  EXPORT QUALIFIED
    (* type  *) elementtype,
    (* const *) initialvalue;

  TYPE elementtype = RECORD
                       lastname  : ARRAY[ 0..19 ] OF CHAR;
                       firstname : ARRAY[ 0..19 ] OF CHAR;
                       idnumber  : REAL;
                     END(* record *);

  VAR initialvalue : elementtype;

END elements.

------------------------------------------------------------

IMPLEMENTATION MODULE elements;

BEGIN
  initialvalue.idnumber := 1.0E-33;
END elements.
```

left descendant of the page (0 points to NIL), and the third contains an array of objects, each of type item. Each item is itself a record consisting of info (type elementtype), a successorpage (pointer to right descendant), and the number of duplicates of the given item in the tree.

9.9 Support Procedures in B-Tree Implementation

In Listing 9.8, we present procedures that are needed by those given in the definition module given in Listing 9.6. Some of the support procedures are implementation specific and would have to be rewritten for a different Modula-2 implementation.

Listing 9.8 Support Procedures in B-Tree Implementation

```
PROCEDURE getnextpage
          ( VAR nextpointer   : pagepointer    (* out *) );


BEGIN
  nextpointer := nextarray[  0   ];
  IF nextpointer = 0
  THEN
    WriteLn;
    Write( CHR( 7 ) );
    WriteString( " B tree file overflow." );
    HALT;
  END(* if then *);
  nextarray[  0   ] := nextarray[  nextarray[  0   ]  ];
END getnextpage;


PROCEDURE dispose
          (      ptr      : pagepointer      (* in *) );


BEGIN
  nextarray[  ptr   ] := nextarray[  0   ];
  nextarray[  0   ] := ptr;
END dispose;


PROCEDURE writepage
          (      ptr      : pagepointer      (* in     *);
                 p        : page             (* in     *) );
```

```
VAR
    h, l              : CARDINAL;
    high, low         : CARDINAL;
    written           : CARDINAL;

BEGIN
  IF ptr >= 1
  THEN (* File pointer is low + 65535 * high.          *)
    low := ( ( ptr - 1 ) * pagesize ) MOD 65535;
    high := ( ( ptr - 1 ) * pagesize ) DIV 65535;
    Length( btree, h, l ); (* Size of B-tree file.    *)
    IF low = l
    THEN
      SetWrite( btree );
    ELSE
      SetModify( btree );
    END(* if then *);
    SetPos(  btree,  high, low  );
    WriteNBytes(  btree, ADR( p ), pagesize, written  );
  END(* if then *);
END writepage;


PROCEDURE getpage
          (     ptr  : pagepointer       (* in  *);
             VAR p    : page              (* out *) );
(* The Logitech implementation [1984] sets a byte offset of
   high * 65535 + low bytes in procedure SetPos.             *)

VAR
    high, low         : CARDINAL;

BEGIN
  IF ptr >= 1
  THEN
    low := ( ( ptr - 1 ) * pagesize ) MOD 65535;
    high := ( ( ptr - 1 ) * pagesize ) DIV 65535;
    SetRead( btree );
    SetPos(  btree,  high, low  );
    ReadNBytes(  btree, ADR( p ), pagesize, read  );
  END(* if then *);
END getpage;


PROCEDURE getcurrentpage
          (     ptr      : pagepointer      (* in *) );

BEGIN
  IF ptr = rootpointer
  THEN
    currentpage := rootpage;
```

```
  ELSE
    getpage(  ptr,   currentpage  );
  END(* if then *);
END getcurrentpage;
```

Procedures getnextpage and dispose use ordinary linked-list operations to maintain a stack of available file block numbers. The list is initially configured so that the page numbers are issued in numerical order (page 1, page 2, . . .). When a deletion from the B-tree occurs, the number of the deleted page is placed at the beginning of the linked list of available file blocks so that the file space for this file block will be reused before a new file block is allocated.

This implementation does not perform true garbage collection of deleted pages from the disk file (i.e., deleted pages are not purged from disk), but instead reuses the disk space of deleted pages before allocating new space.

The procedures writepage and getpage are implementation specific. The code presented here reflects file module procedures available in the Logitech (1984) implementation of Modula-2. The variable pagesize is assumed to have been assigned TSIZE(page).

9.10 B-Tree Insertion

In Listing 9.9 we present the implementation of B-tree insertion.

Listing 9.9 B-Tree Insertion

```
PROCEDURE insert
         (      inputitem : elementtype   (* in *);
                equal     : equaltype     (* in *);
                lessthan  : lessthantype  (* in *) );
  VAR
        u                 : item;
        h, split          : BOOLEAN;
  PROCEDURE search
          (      inputitem : elementtype (* in  *);
                 ptr       : pagepointer (* in  *);
             VAR h         : BOOLEAN     (* out *);
             VAR v         : item        (* out *) );
  VAR
         k, left, right    : CARDINAL;
         q                 : pagepointer;
         u                 : item;

   PROCEDURE insertion;
```

```
VAR
      key                    : CARDINAL;
      nextpagepointer        : pagepointer;
      newpage                : page;
      newroot                : BOOLEAN;

BEGIN
  getcurrentpage(  ptr  );
  WITH currentpage DO
    IF numberkeys < maxpagesize THEN
      (* no need to split page *)
      split := FALSE;
      INC( numberkeys );
      h := FALSE; (* b tree will not grow vertically *)
      (* Move all keys to the right of the insertion point
         to the right by 1.                                   *)
      FOR key := numberkeys TO right + 2 BY - 1 DO
        pagedata[  key  ] := pagedata[  key - 1  ];
      END(* for loop *);
      (* insert new key *)
      pagedata[  right + 1  ] := u;
      IF ptr = rootpointer THEN
        rootpage := currentpage;
      END(* if then *);
      writepage(  ptr,  currentpage  );
    ELSE
      (* Page is full; split it and assign emerging item
         to v.                                                *)
      split := TRUE;
      getnextpage(  nextpointer  );
      nextpagepointer := nextpointer;
      IF right <= minpagesize THEN
        IF right = minpagesize THEN
          v := u;
        ELSE
          v := pagedata[  minpagesize  ];
          IF minpagesize >= right + 2 THEN
            FOR key := minpagesize TO right + 2 BY - 1 DO
              pagedata[  key  ] := pagedata[  key - 1  ];
            END(* for loop *);
          END(* if then *);
          pagedata[  right + 1  ] := u;
        END(* if then *);
        FOR key := 1 TO minpagesize DO
          newpage.pagedata[  key  ] :=
          pagedata[  key + minpagesize  ];
        END(* for loop *);
      ELSE
        (* insert u in the right page *)
        right := right - minpagesize;
```

```
        v := pagedata[  minpagesize + 1  ];
        FOR key := 1 TO right - 1 DO
          newpage.pagedata[  key  ] :=
          pagedata[ key + minpagesize + 1 ];
        END(* for loop *);
        newpage.pagedata[  right  ] := u;
        IF right + 1 <= minpagesize THEN
          FOR key := right + 1 TO minpagesize DO
            newpage.pagedata[  key  ] :=
            pagedata[  key + minpagesize  ];
          END(* for loop *);
        END(* if then *);
      END(* if then *);
      numberkeys := minpagesize;
      writepage(  ptr,  currentpage  );
      IF ptr = rootpointer THEN
        rootpage := currentpage;
      END(* if then *);
      newpage.numberkeys := minpagesize;
      newpage.leftchild := v.successorpage;
      v.successorpage := nextpagepointer;
      newroot := FALSE;
      IF ptr = rootpointer THEN
        newroot := TRUE;
        rootpage.leftchild := rootpointer;
        getnextpage(  nextpointer  );
        rootpointer := nextpointer;
        rootpage.pagedata[  1  ].info := v.info;
        rootpage.pagedata[  1  ].duplicates := duplicates;
        rootpage.pagedata[  1  ].successorpage :=
          nextpagepointer;
        rootpage.numberkeys := 1;
      END(* if then *);
      writepage(  nextpagepointer,  newpage  );
      IF newroot THEN
        writepage(  rootpointer,  rootpage  );
      END(* if then *);
    END(* if then *);
  END(* with *);
END insertion;


BEGIN (* search *)
  IF ptr = 0 THEN
    h := TRUE;
    v.info := inputitem;
    v.duplicates := 1;
    v.successorpage := 0; (* NIL *)
  ELSE
    getcurrentpage( ptr );
```

```
    WITH currentpage DO
      left := 1;
      right := numberkeys;
      (* do a binary search for the input key *)
      LOOP
        IF right = 0 THEN
          EXIT
        END(* if then *);
        k := ( left + right ) DIV 2;
        IF lessthan( inputitem, pagedata[  k  ].info ) OR
           equal( inputitem, pagedata[ k ].info )
        THEN
          right := k - 1;
        END(* if then *);
        IF NOT lessthan( inputitem, pagedata[  k  ].info )
        THEN
          left := k + 1;
        END(* if then *);
        IF right < left THEN
          EXIT;
        END(* if then *);
      END(* loop *);
      IF left - right > 1 THEN
        (* The inputitem is already in the file, increment
           duplicates.                                        *)
        INC(  pagedata[  k  ].duplicates  );
        writepage(  ptr,  currentpage  );
        IF ptr = rootpointer THEN
          rootpage := currentpage;
        END(* if then *);
        h := FALSE;
      ELSE
        (* The inputitem is not currently in the file. *)
        IF right = 0 THEN
          (* Inputitem less than all keys in this page. *)
          q := leftchild;
        ELSE
          (* inputitem greater than pagedata[ right ].info *)
          q := pagedata[  right  ].successorpage
        END(* if then *);
        search(  inputitem,  q,  h,  u  );
        IF split THEN
          getcurrentpage( ptr );
        END(* if then *);
        IF h THEN
          insertion;
        END(* if then *);
      END(* if then *);
    END(* with *);
  END(* if then *);
END search;
```

```
BEGIN (* insert *)
  split := FALSE;
  search(  inputitem,   rootpointer,   h,   u );
END insert;
```

We will examine many of the branch paths in algorithm insert by walking through a case study that causes a double-page split to occur. The B-tree in Figure 9.19 represents our starting point for the insertion of key 17. We leave it as an exercise for the reader to confirm the page numbers labeled in Figure 9.19. The steps in procedure insert required to insert key 17 are given below. We suggest that you consult the appropriate lines in Listing 9.9 as you read this walk-through.

```
insert( 17.0 )
split = false
search( 17.0, 3, h, u )
bring page 3 into active memory
left = 1
right = 4
After binary search loop, left = 5, right = 4
q = 6
  search( 17.0, 6, h, u )
  bring page 6 into active memory
  left = 1
  right = 4
  After binary search loop, left = 5, right = 4
  q = 0
    search( 17.0, 0, h, u )
    h = true
    v.pagekey = 17, v.duplicates = 1, v.successorpage = 0
  ( At this level of recursion, v becomes u.)
  insertion
  bring 6 into active memory
  (page 6 is full, so must split it)
  split = true
  nextpointer = 7 = nextpagepointer
  (insert u in the right page)
  right = 4 - 2 = 2
```

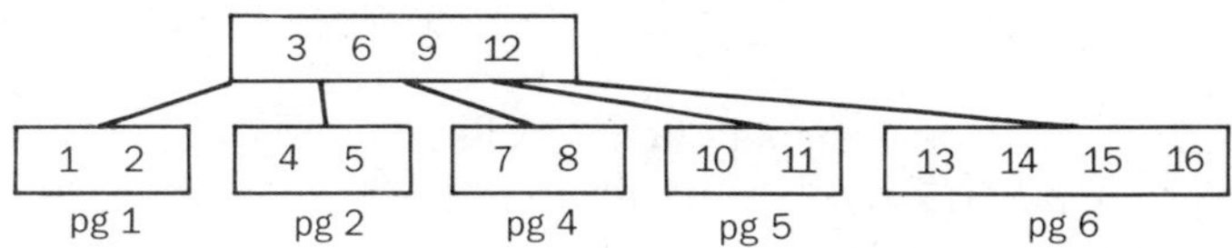

Figure 9.19 Insertion into a B-Tree

```
  v = record associated with third key in page 6, namely
      item 15
  newpage.pagedata[ 1 ] = record associated with fourth key
      in page 6, namely item 16
  newpage.pagedata[ 2 ] = u (record associated with item 17)
  numberofkeys = 2 (for page 6)
  write page 6 to disk
  numberofkeys = 2 (for new page 7)
  newpage.leftchild = 0
  v.successorpage = 7
  write page 7 to disk
Because split is true, read current page, page 3 from disk
      insertion
(page is full so we must split it)
nextpointer = 8 = nextpagepointer
(insert u, item 15, in the right page)
right = 2
v = third item on page 3, namely item 9
(u = 15 from the previous level of recursion)
newpage.pagedata[ 1 ] = item 12
newpage.pagedata[ 2 ] = item 15 ( u )
numberkeys( page 3 ) = 2
write page 3 to the disk
rootpage = currentpage
numberkeys( page 8 ) = 2
newpage.leftchild = 0
v.successorpage = 8
rootpage.leftchild = 3
nextpointer = 9
rootpointer = 9
rootpage.pagedata[ 1 ] = item 9
rootpage.duplicates = 1
rootpage.pagedata[ 1 ].successorpage = 8
rootpage.numberkeys = 1
write root page to the disk
```

The B-tree resulting from the insertion of key 17 is shown in Figure 9.20.

We note that during a page split, we do not actually erase the pagedata[3] and pagedata[4]. Instead, the numberkeys field of the page is set to 2.

9.11 Implementation of Procedures ispresent and display

In Listing 9.10 we present the implementation of procedures ispresent and display.

Noting that procedure display behaves like an inorder traversal of the B-tree, we leave it as an exercise for the reader to walk through procedures ispresent and display.

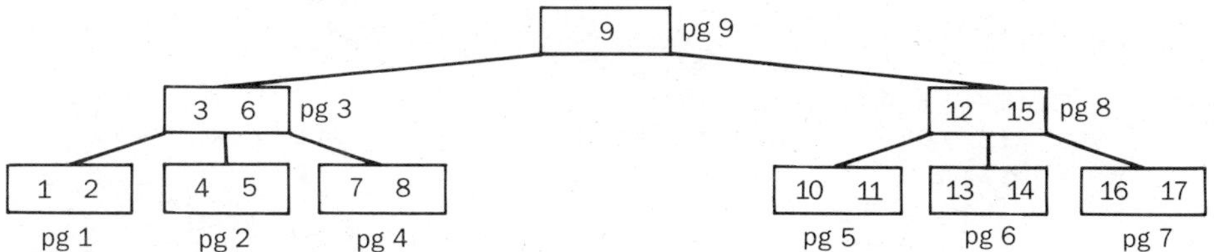

Figure 9.20 B-Tree of Figure 9.19 after Insertion

Listing 9.10 Implementation of B-Tree Procedures ispresent and display

```
PROCEDURE ispresent
          (     inputitem  : elementtype      (* in      *);
                equal      : equaltype        (* in      *);
                lessthan   : lessthantype     (* in      *) ) :
                BOOLEAN;

VAR
     found                : BOOLEAN;


  PROCEDURE search
            (     ptr       : pagepointer     (* in      *) );

    VAR
          k,
          left,
          right                : CARDINAL;
          q                    : pagepointer;

  BEGIN
    IF (  ptr # 0   ) AND (   NOT found   )
    THEN
      getcurrentpage( ptr );
      WITH currentpage DO
        left := 1;
        right := numberkeys;
        (* do a binary search for the input key *)
        LOOP
          IF right = 0
          THEN
            EXIT
          END(* if then *);
          k := ( left + right ) DIV 2;
          IF lessthan( inputitem, pagedata[  k  ].info ) OR
             equal( inputitem, pagedata[ k ].info )
```

```
          THEN
            right := k - 1;
          END(* if then *);
          IF NOT lessthan( inputitem, pagedata[  k  ].info )
          THEN
            left := k + 1;
          END(* if then *);
          IF right < left
          THEN
            EXIT;
          END(* if then *);
        END(* loop *);
        IF left - right > 1
        THEN
          found := TRUE;
        ELSE
          IF right = 0
          THEN
            (* inputitem less than all keys in this page *)
            q := leftchild;
          ELSE
            (* inputitem greater than
               pagedata[ right ].info                        *)
            q := pagedata[  right  ].successorpage;
          END(* if then *);
          search(  q  );
        END(* if then *);
      END(* with *);
    END(* if then *);
  END search;


BEGIN
  found := FALSE;
  getpage(  rootpointer,  rootpage  );
  search(  rootpointer  );
  RETURN found;
END ispresent;


PROCEDURE display
        (     displayproc  : displaytype   (* in     *) );


  PROCEDURE inorder
          (     ptr        : pagepointer   (* in     *) );

    VAR
          key                : CARDINAL;
```

```
  BEGIN
    IF ptr # 0
    THEN
      getpage(  ptr, currentpage  );
      IF currentpage.leftchild > 0
      THEN
        (* There is a key with a value less than
           pagedata[1].info.                                  *)
        inorder(  currentpage.leftchild  );
        getpage( ptr, currentpage );
      END(* if then *);
      FOR key := 1 TO currentpage.numberkeys DO
        WriteString( " page number → " );
        WriteCard( ptr, 1 );
        WriteString( "   " );
        displayproc(  currentpage.pagedata[  key  ].info );
        WriteLn;
        IF currentpage.pagedata [  key  ].successorpage > 0
        THEN
          (* Keys with a value greater than
             pagedata[key].pagekey exist in a successor
             page.                                            *)
          inorder( currentpage.pagedata[ key ].
                   successorpage );
          getpage(  ptr, currentpage  );
        END(* if then *);
      END(* for loop *);
    END(* if then *);
  END inorder;


BEGIN (* display *);
  inorder( rootpointer );
END display;
```

9.12 Implementation of B-Tree Deletion

In Listing 9.11, we present the procedure for B-tree deletion.

Listing 9.11 Implementation of B-Tree Deletion

```
PROCEDURE delete
         (      inputitem     : elementtype     (* in      *);
                equal         : equaltype       (* in      *);
                lessthan      : lessthantype    (* in      *) );
```

```
VAR
    h                   : BOOLEAN;

  PROCEDURE deletion
          (     inputitem   : elementtype  (* in  *);
                a           : pagepointer  (* in  *);
            VAR h           : BOOLEAN      (* out *) );

   VAR
        key               : CARDINAL;
        k                 : CARDINAL;
        left              : CARDINAL;
        right             : CARDINAL;
        apage             : page;
        q                 : pagepointer;


   PROCEDURE underflow
     (     ancestorpagepointer,
           underflowpagepointer : pagepointer    (* in *);
           s                    : CARDINAL       (* in *);
       VAR h                    : BOOLEAN        (* in *) );

   (* If underflow page is undersize, then h = true.     *)

     VAR
           ancestorpage         : page;
           underflowpage        : page;
           adjacentpage         : page;
           adjacentpagepointer  : pagepointer;
           key                  : CARDINAL;
           k                    : CARDINAL;
           itemsancestor        : CARDINAL;
           itemsadjacent        : CARDINAL;

   BEGIN (* underflow *)
     getpage(  ancestorpagepointer,  ancestorpage  );
     getpage(  underflowpagepointer,  underflowpage  );
     itemsancestor := ancestorpage.numberkeys;
     IF s < itemsancestor
     THEN
       INC( s );
       adjacentpagepointer :=
       ancestorpage.pagedata[  s  ].successorpage;
       getpage(  adjacentpagepointer,  adjacentpage  );
       itemsadjacent := adjacentpage.numberkeys;
       (* k is the number of items available on right
          page                                            *)
       k := ( itemsadjacent - minpagesize + 1 ) DIV 2;
       underflowpage.pagedata[  minpagesize  ] :=
```

```
        ancestorpage.pagedata[ s ];
      underflowpage.pagedata[ minpagesize ].successorpage :=
        adjacentpage.leftchild;
      IF k > 0
      THEN
        (* Move k items from adjacentpage to underflow
           page.                                        *)
        FOR key := 1 TO k - 1 DO
          underflowpage.pagedata[  key + minpagesize  ] :=
            adjacentpage.pagedata[  key  ];
        END(* for loop *);
        ancestorpage.pagedata[  s  ] :=
        adjacentpage.pagedata[  k  ];
        ancestorpage.pagedata[  s  ].successorpage :=
        adjacentpagepointer;
        adjacentpage.leftchild :=
          adjacentpage.pagedata[  k  ].successorpage;
        itemsadjacent := itemsadjacent - k;
        FOR key := 1 TO itemsadjacent DO
          adjacentpage.pagedata[  key  ] :=
            adjacentpage.pagedata[  key + k  ];
        END(* for loop *);
        adjacentpage.numberkeys := itemsadjacent;
        underflowpage.numberkeys := minpagesize - 1 + k;
        h := FALSE;
      ELSE
        (* Merge pages underflow and adjacentpage *)
        FOR key := 1 TO minpagesize DO
          underflowpage.pagedata[  key + minpagesize  ] :=
            adjacentpage.pagedata[  key  ];
        END(* for loop *);
        FOR key := s TO itemsancestor - 1 DO
          ancestorpage.pagedata[  key  ] :=
            ancestorpage.pagedata[  key + 1  ];
        END(* for loop *);
        underflowpage.numberkeys := maxpagesize;
        ancestorpage.numberkeys := itemsancestor - 1;
        IF (  ancestorpagepointer = rootpointer  ) AND
           ( ancestorpage.numberkeys = 0 )
        THEN
          rootpointer := underflowpagepointer;
          rootpage := underflowpage;
          dispose( ancestorpagepointer );
        END(* if then *);
        adjacentpage.numberkeys := 0;
        dispose(  adjacentpagepointer  );
        h := ancestorpage.numberkeys < minpagesize;
      END(* if then *);
    ELSE
      (* Use page to the left of underflow page.        *)
```

```
IF s <= 1
THEN
  adjacentpagepointer := ancestorpage.leftchild;
ELSE
  adjacentpagepointer :=
    ancestorpage.pagedata[  s - 1  ]. successorpage;
END(* if then *);
getpage(  adjacentpagepointer,  adjacentpage  );
itemsadjacent := adjacentpage.numberkeys + 1;
IF itemsadjacent >= minpagesize
THEN
  k := ( itemsadjacent - minpagesize ) DIV 2;
ELSE
  k := 0;
END(* if then *);
IF k > 0
THEN
  (* Move k items from adjacent page to underflow
     page.                                              *)
  FOR key := minpagesize - 1 TO 1 BY - 1 DO
    underflowpage.pagedata[  key + k  ] :=
      underflowpage.pagedata[  key  ];
  END(* for loop *);
  underflowpage.pagedata[  k  ] :=
  ancestorpage.pagedata[  s  ];
  underflowpage.pagedata[  k  ].successorpage :=
    underflowpage.leftchild;
  itemsadjacent := itemsadjacent - k;
  FOR key := k - 1 TO 1 BY - 1 DO
    underflowpage.pagedata[  key  ] :=
      adjacentpage.pagedata[  key + itemsadjacent  ];
  END(* for loop *);
  underflowpage.leftchild :=
    adjacentpage.pagedata[ itemsadjacent ].
    successorpage;
  ancestorpage.pagedata[  s  ] :=
    adjacentpage.pagedata[  itemsadjacent ];
  ancestorpage.pagedata[  s ].successorpage :=
  underflowpagepointer;
  adjacentpage.numberkeys := itemsadjacent - 1;
  underflowpage.numberkeys := minpagesize - 1 + k;
  h := FALSE;
ELSE
  (* Merge pages underflow and adjacent.              *)
  IF s >= 1
  THEN
    adjacentpage.pagedata[  itemsadjacent  ] :=
      ancestorpage.pagedata[  s  ];
  ELSE
    adjacentpage.pagedata[  itemsadjacent  ] :=
```

```
            ancestorpage.pagedata[  s + 1  ];
        END(* if then *);
        adjacentpage.pagedata[  itemsadjacent  ].
        successorpage := underflowpage.leftchild;
        FOR key := 1 TO minpagesize - 1 DO
          adjacentpage.pagedata[  key + itemsadjacent  ]:=
            underflowpage.pagedata[  key  ];
        END(* for loop *);
        adjacentpage.numberkeys := maxpagesize;
        IF itemsancestor >= 1
        THEN
          ancestorpage.numberkeys := itemsancestor - 1;
        ELSE
          ancestorpage.numberkeys := 0;
        END(* if then *);
        IF (  ancestorpagepointer = rootpointer  ) AND
           (  ancestorpage.numberkeys = 0  )
        THEN
          rootpointer := adjacentpagepointer;
          rootpage := adjacentpage;
          dispose( ancestorpagepointer );
        END(* if then *);
        underflowpage.numberkeys := 0;
        dispose(  underflowpagepointer  );
        h := ancestorpage.numberkeys < minpagesize;
      END(* if then *);
    END(* if then *);
    writepage(  ancestorpagepointer,  ancestorpage  );
    writepage(  adjacentpagepointer,  adjacentpage  );
    writepage(  underflowpagepointer,  underflowpage  );
  END underflow;


  PROCEDURE del
            (     p   : pagepointer    (* in    *);
              VAR h   : BOOLEAN        (* out   *) );

    VAR
          q                     : pagepointer;
          pg                    : page;

  BEGIN
    getpage( p,  pg );
    IF ( apage.numberkeys > 0 ) AND ( pg.numberkeys > 0 )
    THEN
      q := pg.pagedata[ pg.numberkeys ].successorpage;
      IF q # 0
      THEN
        del(  q,  h  );
        getpage( p,  pg );
```

```
        IF h
        THEN
          underflow( p, q, pg.numberkeys, h );
          getpage( p, pg );
          getpage( a, apage );
        END(* if then *);
      ELSE
        pg.pagedata[ pg.numberkeys ].successorpage :=
          apage.pagedata[ k ].successorpage;
        apage.pagedata[ k ] := pg.
          pagedata[ pg.numberkeys ];
        pg.numberkeys := pg.numberkeys - 1;
        h := pg.numberkeys < minpagesize;
      END(* if then *);
      writepage( a, apage );
      IF a = rootpointer
      THEN
        rootpage := apage;
      END(* if then *);
      writepage( p, pg );
      IF p = rootpointer
      THEN
        rootpage := pg;
      END(* if then *);
    END(* if then *);
  END del;



BEGIN (* deletion *)
  IF a = 0
  THEN
    WriteLn;
    WriteLn;
    h := FALSE;
  ELSE
    getpage( a, apage );
    left := 1;
    right := apage.numberkeys;
    REPEAT
      IF ( left + right ) >= 0
      THEN
        k := ( left + right ) DIV 2;
      ELSE
        k := 0;
      END(* if then *);
      IF k >= 1
      THEN
        IF lessthan( inputitem, apage.pagedata[ k ].info )
           OR equal( inputitem, apage.pagedata[ k ].info )
```

```
        THEN
          right := k - 1;
        END(* if then *);
        IF NOT lesstham( inputitem,
                         apage.pagedata[ k ].info )
        THEN
          left := k + 1;
        END(* if then *);
      END(* if then *);
    UNTIL left > right;
    IF right = 0
    THEN
      q := apage.leftchild;
    ELSE
      q := apage.pagedata[ right ].successorpage;
    END(* if then *);
    IF left - right > 1
    THEN
      IF q = 0
      THEN
        apage.numberkeys := apage.numberkeys - 1;
        h := apage.numberkeys < minpagesize;
        FOR key := k TO apage.numberkeys DO
          apage.pagedata[ key ] := apage.
            pagedata[ key + 1 ];
        END(* for loop *);
      ELSE
        del( q,  h );
        IF h
        THEN
          underflow( a,  q,  right,  h );
          getpage(  a,  apage  );
        END(* if then *);
      END(* if then *);
    ELSE
      deletion(  inputitem,  q,  h );
      getpage(  a,  apage  );
      IF h
      THEN
        underflow( a,  q,  right,  h );
        getpage(  a,  apage  );
      END(* if then *);
    END(* if then *);
  END(* if then *);
  writepage( a,  apage );
  IF a = rootpointer
  THEN
    rootpage := apage;
  END(* if then *);
END deletion;
```

```
BEGIN (* delete *)
  deletion(  inputitem,   rootpointer,   h  );
END delete;
```

We leave it for the reader (see exercise 9.25) to exercise the branch paths of the algorithm given in Listing 9.11 by doing a walk-through of the code.

9.13 Initialization Code in a B-Tree Module

We conclude our presentation of the B-tree implementation with Listing 9.12, the initialization section of the implementation module.

Listing 9.12 Initialization Code for B-Tree Module

```
BEGIN(* initialization code *)
  pagesize := TSIZE(  page  );
  Lookup( btree, "BTREE", FALSE );
  new := btree.res = notdone;
  Lookup(  btree, "BTREE", TRUE );
  Lookup(  rootptr, "ROOT", TRUE );
  Lookup(  next, "NEXT", TRUE );
  IF new
  THEN
    (* A new B-tree must be created. *)
    WriteLn;
    centermessage( "A new B-tree is being created." );
    WriteLn; WriteLn;
    rootpointer := 1;
    nextarray[  0  ] := 2;
    nextarray[  1  ] := 1;
    FOR key := 2 TO maxpages - 1 DO
      nextarray[  key  ] := key + 1;
    END(* for loop *);
    nextarray[  maxpages  ] := 0;
    rootpage.numberkeys := 0;
    rootpage.leftchild := 0;
    FOR key := 1 TO maxpagesize DO
      rootpage.pagedata[  key  ].successorpage := 0;
      rootpage.pagedata[  key  ].info := initialvalue;
      rootpage.pagedata[  key  ].duplicates := 1;
    END(* for loop *);
    writepage( rootpointer, rootpage )
```

```
  ELSE
    SetRead( rootptr );
    ReadNBytes(  rootptr, ADR( rootpointer ),
                 SIZE( rootpointer ), read  );
    SetRead( next );
    ReadNBytes(  next, ADR( nextarray ), SIZE( nextarray ),
                 read  );
    getpage( rootpointer, rootpage );
  END(* if then *);
END Btree.
```

The file commands given in the initialization code are implementation specific. They are presented for completeness. Many of these lines of code would have to be rewritten for a different Modula-2 implementation.

9.14 B-Tree Test Program

In Listing 9.13, we display a simple test program that exercises the procedures given in the B-tree interface.

Listing 9.13 B-Tree Test Program

```
MODULE BTreeTest;

  FROM RealInOut IMPORT
    (* proc *) WriteReal;

  FROM elements IMPORT
    (* proc *) elementtype;

  FROM Btree IMPORT
    (* proc *) insert, delete, display, ispresent, save;

  FROM InOut IMPORT
    (* proc *) WriteLn, WriteString, WriteCard;

  FROM util IMPORT
    (* proc *) spacebar, rand;

  FROM screen IMPORT
    (* proc *) clrscreen;
```

```
PROCEDURE equalid
          (     item1, item2 : elementtype    (* in  *) ) :
                BOOLEAN;


BEGIN
  RETURN item1.idnumber = item2.idnumber;
END equalid;


PROCEDURE lessthanid
          (     item1, item2 : elementtype    (* in  *) ) :
                BOOLEAN;


BEGIN
  RETURN item1.idnumber < item2.idnumber;
END lessthanid;


PROCEDURE displayproc
          ( VAR item : elementtype             (* out    *)


BEGIN
  WriteLn;
  WriteReal(  item.idnumber,  20  );
END displayproc;

VAR
      i                  : CARDINAL;
      r                  : ARRAY[  1..200   ] OF REAL;
      item               : elementtype;

BEGIN
  WriteString( " Generating random number array " );
  WriteLn;
  FOR i := 1 TO 200 DO
    r[  i  ] := rand() * 10.0;
  END(* for loop *);
  WriteLn; WriteLn;
  WriteString( " Performing insertions " );
  WriteLn;
  FOR i := 2 TO 200 BY 2 DO
    item.lastname :=" " ;
    item.firstname :=" " ;
    item.idnumber := r[  i  ];
    insert(  item,  equalid,  lessthanid  );
  END(* for loop *);
  FOR i := 1 TO 199 BY 2 DO
```

```
    item.lastname :=" " ;
    item.firstname :=" " ;
    item.idnumber := r[  i  ];
    insert(  item,  equalid,  lessthanid  );
  END(* for loop *);
  item.lastname :=" " ;
  item.firstname :=" " ;
  item.idnumber := 7.0;
  insert(  item,  equalid,  lessthanid  );
  item.idnumber := 6.2;
  IF ispresent(  item,  equalid,  lessthanid  )
  THEN
    WriteLn;
    WriteString( " 6.2 is present." )
  ELSE
    WriteLn;
    WriteString( " 6.2 is not present." );
  END(* if then *);
  spacebar;
  clrscreen;
  WriteString( " Performing deletions " );
  WriteLn;
  FOR i := 200 TO 51 BY - 1 DO
    item.idnumber := r[  i  ];
    delete(  item,  equalid,  lessthanid  );
  END(* for loop *);
  WriteString( " Performing some more insertions " );
  WriteLn;
  FOR i := 60 TO 51 BY - 1 DO
    item.lastname :=" " ;
    item.firstname :=" " ;
    item.idnumber := r[  i  ];
    insert(  item,  equalid,  lessthanid  );
  END(* for loop *);
  item.idnumber := -11.0;
  insert( item, equalid, lessthanid );
  item.idnumber := -13.0;
  insert( item, equalid, lessthanid );
  item.idnumber := 2.0;
  insert(  item,  equalid,  lessthanid  );
  WriteString( " Performing final deletions " );
  WriteLn;
  FOR i := 1 TO 60 DO
    item.idnumber := r[  i  ];
    delete(  item,  equalid,  lessthanid  );
  END(* for loop *);
  item.lastname := " ";
  item.firstname := " ";
  item.idnumber := 9.0;
  insert( item, equalid, lessthanid );
```

```
  WriteLn;
  WriteLn;
  display(  displayproc  );
  save;
END BTreeTest.
```

The test program creates an array of 200 random real numbers (id numbers), which will be used as keys for insertion into the B-tree. The id numbers in the even-array positions are inserted into the B-tree. Next the id numbers in the odd-array positions are inserted into the B-tree. Next, id number 7.2 is inserted into the B-tree. The presence of id number 6.2 is tested.

The id numbers in array positions 200 to 51 are deleted from the B-tree. Next the id numbers in array positions 60 to 51 are reinserted. Next the id keys −11.0, −13.0, and 2.0 are inserted. Next the id numbers in array positions 1 to 60 are deleted, and finally, the id key 9.0 is inserted into the B-tree.

When the B-tree is displayed, the correct sequence of −13.0, −11.0, 2.0, 7.2, 9.0 appears.

Suppose we wish to use the field lastname as a key in building the B-tree, rather than id. A client program would have to use different lessthan and equal procedures. We present these modified procedures in Listing 9.14.

Listing 9.14 Modified Procedures equal and lessthan

```
PROCEDURE equallastname
          (      item1, item2 : elementtype   (* in *) ) :
                 BOOLEAN;

VAR
      len1,
      len2                    : CARDINAL;
      i                       : CARDINAL;

BEGIN
  len1 := Length(  item1.lastname   );
  len2 := Length(  item2.lastname   );
  IF len1 # len2
  THEN
    RETURN FALSE;
  ELSE
    i := 0;
    WHILE (  i < len1  ) AND
          (  item1.lastname[  i  ] = item2.lastname[  i  ] )
```

```
    DO
      INC(  i  );
    END(* while loop *);
    RETURN item1.lastname[  i  ] = item2.lastname[  i  ];
  END(* if then *);
END equallastname;


PROCEDURE lessthanlastname
          (     item1, item2 : elementtype (* in *) ) :
                BOOLEAN;

VAR
      len1,
      len2                 : CARDINAL;
      minlength            : CARDINAL;
      i                    : CARDINAL;

BEGIN
  len1 := Length(  item1.lastname  );
  len2 := Length(  item2.lastname  );
  IF len1 < len2
  THEN
    minlength := len1;
  ELSE
    minlength := len2;
  END(* if then *);
  i := 0;
  WHILE (  i < minlength  ) AND
        ( item1.lastname[  i  ] = item2.lastname[  i  ] ) DO
    INC(  i  );
  END(* while loop *);
  IF item1.lastname[  i  ] = item2.lastname[  i  ]
  THEN
    RETURN len1 < len2;
  ELSE
    RETURN item1.lastname[  i  ] < item2.lastname[  i  ];
  END(* if then *);
END lessthanlastname;


PROCEDURE displayproc
          ( VAR item    : elementtype     (* out *) );

BEGIN
  WriteLn;
  WriteString(  item.lastname  );
END displayproc;
```

Exercises

9.1 Develop two separate definitions for "near balance" in a search tree.

9.2 Prove that the search tree property is preserved under the operations left and right rotate.

9.3 Create several examples that exercise all the branch paths in the AVL insertion algorithm given in Listing 9.2

9.4 Justify that in Listing 9.2, the code blocks with the comments "left right rotate" and "right left rotate" perform the indicated operations.

9.5 Prove that with AVL deletion, it is possible that every node in the search path to the deleted node may serve as a pivot node for rotational correction.

9.6 Using the tree shown in Figure 9.12*a*, walk through Listing 9.3 and justify each logical branch that you encounter.

9.7 What is the purpose of PROCEDURE del in Listing 9.3? Sketch a tree that exercises PROCEDURE del.

9.8 Why do you think AVL deletions require fewer rotational interventions than AVL insertions?

9.9 Write a Modula-2 program that:

- **(a)** Constructs an AVL tree of 2000 nodes using random integer keys.
- **(b)** Outputs the number of nodes requiring (i) a single rotational correction and (ii) a double rotational correction.
- **(c)** Design an experiment to determine the number of nodes, during deletion, that require one or more rotational corrections. What fraction of deleted nodes require any rotational intervention? What is the total number of rotations required during deletion?

9.10 Sketch an AVL tree built from the following integer keys:

12, 45, 23, 67, 34, 22, 20, 18, 16, 13, 10, 8, 46, 50,
52, 34, 76, 75, 77, 79, 15, 44, 49, 23, 97, 0, 28, 99.

9.11 If the following nodes are deleted from the tree of exercise 9.10, sketch the resulting tree:

23, 67, 22, 20, 16, 13, 10, 46, 50, 52, 34, 75, 15, 23, 0, 99.

9.12 Prove that when a node is added or deleted from an internal-path-balanced (IPB) tree, the only nodes that may go out of balance are those in the search path from the root to the inserted/deleted node.

9.13 Write and test a Modula-2 procedure for deleting a node from a weight-balanced tree.

9.14 Write a Modula-2 program simulation that compares the number of rotations required to build an AVL tree with the number required to build a weight-balanced tree. Each tree should contain 5000 randomly generated real keys (use the same keys for both trees).

9.15 Walk through procedure checkrotations and insert in Listing 9.4 in building a weight-balanced tree with integer keys:

14, 17, 19, 12, 11, 9, 8, 3, 1, 2, 20, 18, 16, 13, 10, 7,
26, 24, 25, 29, 27, 22, 23, 34, 32, 31, 33, 15

9.16 Sketch the AVL tree resulting from the insertion of the sequence of integer keys given in exercise 9.15.

9.17 Explain the rationale for the global rebalancing algorithm given in Listing 9.5.

9.18 Compute the number of keys in a four-level B-tree of order 500 levels if each page is three-quarters filled (i.e., contains 750 keys).

9.19 Sketch a B-tree of order 2 formed by the keys:

21, 34, 56, 78, 32, 10, 17, 18, 5, 4, 2, 1, 11, 12, 19,
16, 23, 22, 24, 25, 27, 26, 28, 31, 34, 41, 44, 43, 42,
47, 49, 50

9.20 Sketch a B-tree of order 3 formed by the set of keys given in exercise 9.19.

9.21 Sketch the B-tree, that results if keys 56, 78, 17, 5, 4, 2, 1, 12, 19, 16, 23, 22, 27, 34, 41, 43, 47, and 50 are deleted from the B-tree of exercise 9.19.

9.22 Repeat exercise 9.21 using the B-tree of exercise 9.20.

9.23 Modify the B-tree code given in this chapter to allow many B-tree files to coexist and to be accessible from each procedure.

9.24 Write a new test program for the B-tree using the modified lessthanid, equalid, and displayproc procedures given in Listing 9.13.

9.25 Walk through the deletion algorithm given in Listing 9.11 by deleting key 9 from the B-tree shown in Figure 9.20.

10

The Search Table Implemented Using Hash Tables

In Chapters 8 and 9 we defined the search table abstraction and implemented it with binary trees. We saw that for a height-balanced tree (e.g., AVL, or weight balanced), the search time increased as O($\log_2 n$), where n represents the number of nodes in the search tree.

In this chapter we examine the implementation of search tables using hash functions. Under proper conditions, with a well-constructed hash function, the search time as a function of the number of nodes or data points in the table is constant. That is, the search time does not increase as the number of data points increases. This feature of a hash table makes it very attractive when run-time efficiency is important.

10.1 Concept of Hashing

A hash function, h(key), maps a data type, key, to a table address, h(key). In this chapter we will assume, unless stated otherwise, that a hash table is implemented as an array. Therefore, the address, h(key), is an index location in such a hash table array.

Ideally, each key would map to a unique hash address, h(key). For exmaple, if we define data type key as a string of 3 characters representing a 3-letter English word with lowercase letters, a hash function that uniquely maps each word to a hash table address would be computed as follows:

Given a 3-letter string, key (i.e., key[0], key[1], key[2]):

1. Convert key[2] to a cardinal from 0 to 26. Blank maps to 0, 'a' maps to 1, 'b' maps to 2, . . ., 'z' maps to 26. Call the value obtained z.
2. Convert key[1] to a cardinal from 0 to 26 in the same way. Call the value y.
3. Convert key[0] to a cardinal from 0 to 26 in the same way. Call the value x.
4. h(key) = $26x^2 + 26y^1 + z$.

It should be evident that each 3-letter word maps to a unique hash address from 0 (for a blank word) to 18278 (for "zzz").

Unfortunately, this one-to-one mapping from the key domain to the target domain of the hash table is rarely possible in practical situations. For example, to create a hash table for any English word of length equal to or less than 20, we would need a hash table with index locations greater than 200,000,000,000,000,000,000 to uniquely map each English word to a hash address. This is of course difficult to implement.

In practice, we allow an equivalence class of keys, K, to map to the same location h(k), where k is in the set K. A collision occurs when two members of this equivalence class map to the same location. We use a collision-resolution algorithm to assign (or fetch) members of K to (from) the hash table.

The two principal problems associated with implementing a hash table are finding a good hash function and developing a good collision-resolution strategy.

In section 10.2 we discuss well-known methods for finding a good hash function. In section 10.3 we discuss important collision-resolution algorithms. In sections 10.4, and 10.5 we introduce some advanced hashing techniques.

10.2 Hash Functions

A good hash function maps a random selection of keys uniformly across the hash table. That is, the frequency distribution of address or index values, h(key), should be uniformly distributed from 0 to maxindex, where maxindex is the largest index address in the hash table array.

A uniform distribution of keys into the hash table minimizes the need for collision resolution. Consider the consequences of using a poor hash function, that is, a hash function that clusters its values in one section of the table (primary clustering). Figure 10.1 depicts a good hash function and a poor one. The shading represents the density of hash indices in the table.

A poor hash function results in frequent collisions, because of primary clustering. In fact, the effective size of a hash table is reduced when a poor hash function is used.

To illustrate and compare various hashing functions, we will assume keys from the domain of English words or strings of characters. In the subsections 10.2.1 and 10.2.2, we present algorithms for hashing referred to as extraction and compression.

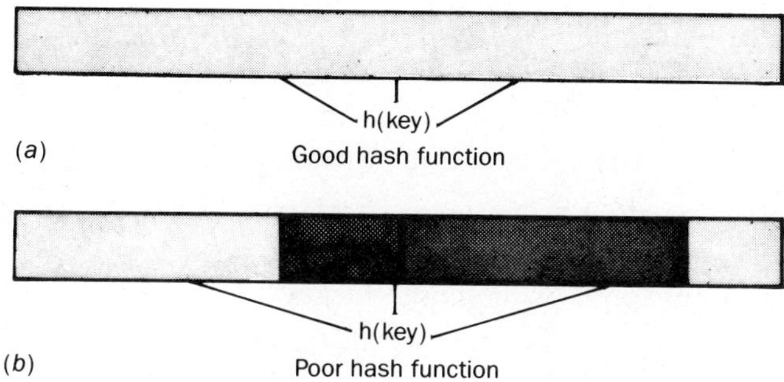

Figure 10.1 Hash Functions

10.2.1 Extraction

Suppose we first convert each character of the key to a 5-bit binary string as follows:

```
blank → 00000
'a'   → 00001
'b'   → 00010
'c'   → 00011
...
'z'   → 11010.
```

The word "by" would then map to:

```
00010|11001
  b     y
```

As an example, a simple extraction scheme takes the fourth bit from the left, the sixth bit from the left, and the next to the last three bits on the right. Using this scheme, "by" would become $11100_2 = 28$.

The word "hello" would map to:

```
00100|00101|01100|01100|01111
  h     e     l     l     o
```

and using extraction would become $00111_2 = 7$.

This particular extraction scheme assumes that the domain of keys is very small, since h(key) is a number between 0 and 31.

Extraction is considered a poor method for computing a hash address. As an exercise, we ask you to demonstrate this. In general, a hash function should utilize every bit of information in the key.

10.2.2 Compression

Using compression, we force the value of h(key) to be within the range 0 ..maxindex. We accomplish this using the MOD function. There are two common methods, division and multiplication.

Suppose we first convert key to a number n by, for example, using extraction. We describe another method below.

Using division, we compute h(key) as follows:

```
h( key ) = n MOD ( maxindex + 1 )
```

Using the division method, it is very desirable for maxindex + 1 to be prime. In exercise 10.7, you are asked why this is true.

Using multiplication, we compute h(key) as follows:

```
h( key ) = TRUNC( maxindex * frac( n*m ) ) + 1
```

In the multiplication method, m is a multiplicative constant between 0 and 1, and frac(r) returns the fractional part of r.

As an example, suppose maxindex = 100, n = 63221, and m = 0.3819660113. Then using division, we have:

```
h( key ) = 63221 MOD 101 = 96
```

Using multiplication, we write:

```
h( key ) = TRUNC( 100 * frac( 63221 * 0.3819660113 ) ) + 1
         = 28
```

A common method for computing n is the following:

1. Break the key into groups of 5-bit binary strings, as before.
2. Form clusters of 15 bits from right to left, and number them sequentially, as shown below.
3. For the second cluster, shift all the bits one space to the left. The most significant bit is transferred to the least significant bit location. For the third cluster, we shift all the bits two spaces to the left. The two most significant bits are transferred to the two least significant bit locations. This process is continued until all clusters are accounted for.
4. Compute the sum of modified clusters from step 3 using the XOR operator on the clusters.

We illustrate this algorithm by computing h(key) when key = "goodbye".

```
00111|01111|01111|00100|00010|11001|00101
  g     o     o     d     b     y     e
```

15-Bit Clusters

Cluster 1:
000101100100101 - bye
Cluster 2:
011110111100100 - ood   shifted 1 bit → 111101111001000
Cluster 3:
000000000000111 - g   shifted 2 bits → 000000000011100

XOR Sum

000101100100101
XOR
111101111001000

111000011101101
XOR
000000000011100

111000011110001
Now, 111000011110001 = 28913_{10}.

Using the method of division, h(key) = 28913 MOD 101 = 27.

The value *m*, in the method of multiplication, should not be chosen arbitrarily. We do not want *m* too close to 0 or 1 because this would force small words to cluster at the ends of the table (see exercise 10.6). Refer to Reingold and Hansen (1983) for additional constraints on *m*.

Before presenting our two advanced methods for hashing in sections 10.4 and 10.5, we turn to examine collision-resolution strategies.

10.3 Collision Resolution

Four common methods for collision resolution are: linear chaining, double hashing, coalesced chaining, and separate chaining. For each algorithm presented in subsection 10.3.1 to 10.3.4, we assume that we are inserting a key into the hash table. The algorithms for determining the presence of a key are almost identical. We assume that the hash table is implemented as an array, with subscript range 0 .. maxindex.

10.3.1 Linear Chaining

In linear chaining, perhaps the simplest of all collision-resolution methods, the hash table is conceptually a circular array. The algorithm for linear chaining is presented below.

```
Algorithm Linear Chaining
(* n represents the number of keys currently in the hash
      table which we assume is less than maxindex.          *)
(* address denotes the index location in the hash table
      array.                                                *)

  address ← h( key )
  found ← false
  while ( table( address ) not empty ) and ( found = false )
      loop
    if table( address ) = key
```

```
    then
      found ← true
    else
      address ← ( address + 1 ) MOD ( maxindex + 1 )
      (* We leave one blank space in the hash table to
         assure termination of the while loop.                *)
    end if
  end loop
  if found = false
  then
    if n = maxindex
    then
      overflow error
    else
      n ← n + 1
      table( address ) ← key
    end if
  end if
end Algorithm
```

In words, linear chaining works as follows: if an element of value different from the key is already present at the first hash address, go to the adjacent index location in the hash table (array). If this index location has an element of different value from the key, try the next adjacent index location, and so forth. Continue linearly scanning the array until either a matchup or a blank index location occurs. Insert the key into this index location.

Linear chaining may lead to the formation of clusters of keys within the table, as illustrated in Figure 10.2. The principle that the big get bigger applies to these clusters. For example, if there are 100 index locations in a hash table and a cluster of 20 keys already exists, then if we assume that the next hash value (index location) is uniformly distributed from 0 to 99, the probability that the 20-element cluster will grow in size by 1 is 20 percent. If the new hash value "hits" any of the existing keys in the cluster, linear chaining will deposit this new key into the 21st space, just to the right of the existing cluster. Because there are already 20 potential "hit" locations out of 100 possible index locations, the probability of a hit is 20 percent.

Load factor, *LF*, is an important parameter that determines the collision-resolution performance using any method of collision resolution. We define the load factor as the ratio of the number of keys present in the table to the total number of index locations in the table. That is:

$$LF = \frac{n}{\text{maxindex} + 1}$$

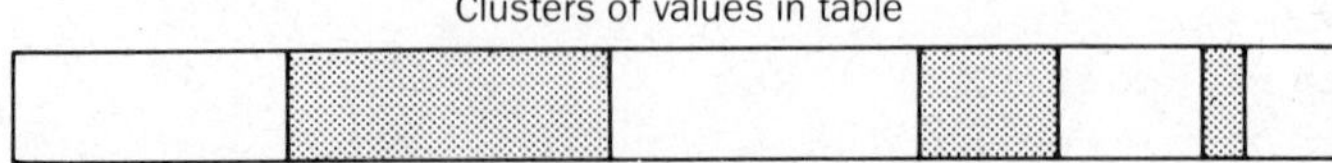

Figure 10.2 Primary Clustering

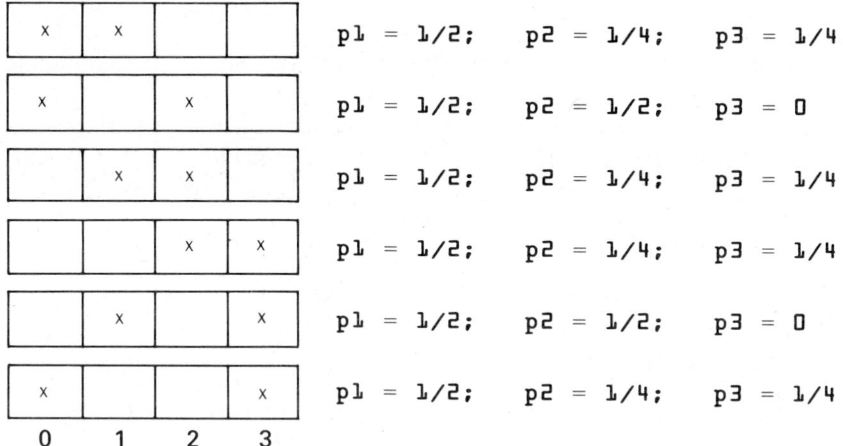

Figure 10.3 Probing a Hash Table

An important measure of performance for a hash table is the average number of probes for a successful search and for an unsuccessful search. We will denote these values S and U, respectively. It is of course desirable that both values be kept as low as possible because each is a measure of computational effort and thus computation time in searching the table.

It is important to compute or estimate S and U as funcitons of the load factor LF for a given collision-resolution strategy. We would expect S and U to increase with LF.

It may be instructive to compute U for a small table using linear chaining to gain insight into the mechanism that determines U. Suppose we have a hash table with four index locations and two keys already present. The load factor is 1/2. In Figure 10.3 we show the six possible configurations of keys in the table and list probabilities p1, p2, and p3 of one, two, and three probes for an unsuccessful search. We assume a perfect hash function; that is, one that uniformly distributes the keys across the hash table.

For the third configuration given in Figure 10.3, the probability of one probe for an unsuccessful search is 1/2 because locations 0 and 3 are empty. If we hit either of these locations with our hash function, we count this hit as one probe because we must determine that the location is empty.

The probability of two probes for an unsuccessful search is 1/4 because if we hit location 2, we must chain to location 3 before concluding that the key is not present.

The probability of three probes for an unsuccessful search is 1/4 because if we hit location 1, we must chain to location 2 and then location 3 before concluding that the key is not present.

If all six configurations have equal probability of occurring, the total probabilities of one, two, or three probes are computed as the average of the six probabilities given.

Thus p1 = 1/2 p2 = 1/3, and p3 = 1/6. The average number of probes for an unsuccessful search is thus computed as follows:

$$U = 1(1/2) + 2(1/3) + 3(1/6) = 5/3$$

As an exercise, we ask the reader to compute S for the configuration shown in Figure 10.3.

As the load factor increases, the performance of linear probing decreases. In the limit, when the load factor is 1, the number of probes for an unsuccessful search equals the number of index locations in the array. Under these conditions, the hash table performs like a linked list.

In subsection 10.3.5 we simulate the performance of linear chaining and estimate the average number of probes versus LF.

10.3.2 Double Hashing

The double hashing algorithm for collision resolution is a variation of linear chaining that attempts to eliminate clustering. The algorithm is given as follows:

```
Algorithm Double Hashing

  address1 ← h( key )
  address2 ← q( key )
  oldaddress ← address1
  overflow ← false
  found ← false
  while ( table( address1 ) is not empty ) and ( found =
          false ) and ( not overflow ) loop
    if table( address1 ) = key
    then
      found ← true
    else
      address1 ← ( address1 + address2 ) MOD ( maxindex + 1 )
      if oldaddress = address1 then overflow ← true end if
    end if
  end loop
  if not found
  then
    if n = maxindex
    then
      overflow error
    else
      n ← n + 1
      table( address1 ) ← key
    end if
  end if
end Algorithm
```

With double hashing, an index location address2 units away is sought, whereas with linear chaining an index location equal to address1 + 1 is sought. If the second hash function q() uniformly distributes the hash addresses across the hash table, clustering should be avoided.

The price that must be paid to achieve less clustering is the evaluation of an additional hash function. In some instances, this price may be too high. We estimate and compare the performance of double hashing with linear chaining below (subsection 10.3.5).

10.3.3 Coalesced Chaining

The algorithm for coalesced chaining is given as follows:

```
Algorithm Coalesced Chaining
  free ← maxindex + 1
  address ← h( key )
  found ← false
  if table( address ) is not empty
  then
    i ← address
    repeat
      if table( i ) = key
      then
        found ← true
      else
        previous ← i
        i ← link( i )
      end if
    until ( found = true ) or ( i = -1 )
    (*-1 corresponds to nil *)
  end if
  if found = false
  then
    if table( address ) is empty
    then
      table( address ) ← key
    else
      repeat
        free ← free -1
      until table( free ) is empty
      if free = -1
      then
        overflow error
      else
        link( previous ) ← free
        table( free ) ← key
        link( free ) ← -1
      end if
    end if
  end if
end Algorithm
```

We initially set the variable free to equal maxindex and link(index) = −1 for index = 0 … maxindex.

Using coalesced chaining, we form a linked list (chain) each time a collision occurs. The variable free, decremented until an empty location is found, is used to locate the index of the next element in the linked list. The long cluster chains, typical of linear chaining, are avoided because it would be unusual for free to be adjacent to the last element in the linked list.

Subsection 10.3.5 estimates and compares the performance of coalesced chaining with double hashing and linear chaining

10.3.4 Separate Chaining

The structure of the hash table is different for separate chaining. Instead of using a fixed size array, we instead use a fixed size array of pointers, each pointer acting as the header to a linked list of elements. After h(key) has been computed, the appropriate linked list is found and the element key inserted at the end of the list. For a structure such as this, it is possible for the load factor to exceed 1 because there may be more elements in the hash structure than header nodes in the fixed size array.

We leave it as an exercise for the reader to construct such a hash table and estimate and compare its performance to the other collision-resolution strategies.

10.3.5 Simulation to Compare the Performance of Collision-Resolution Strategies

A random number generator is used to simulate a hash function. We assume that each key is distinct and thus do not test for key matchup.

A hash table with 1000 locations ranging from 0 to 999 is used. The simulation program controls the load factor by the number of keys inserted into the table.

The average number of probes for a successful search is computed as each search table is built. The cumulative number of probes required to insert the keys into each table divided by the total number of keys equals the average number of probes for a successful search. Obviously, the keys inserted earlier require fewer probes than the keys inserted later.

We leave it as an exercise for the reader to simulate the average number of probes for an unsuccessful search.

In Listing 10.1 we present the code for a simulation experiment that compares linear chaining, double hashing, and coalesced chaining under the assumption of a random hash function.

Listing 10.1 Simulation to Compare Collision-Resolution Strategies

```
MODULE collisionresolution;

  FROM Utilities IMPORT
    (* proc *) Rand2;
    (* A random cardinal from 0 to 32767 *)
```

```
   FROM InOut IMPORT
     (* proc *) WriteLn, WriteString;

   FROM RealInOut IMPORT
     (* proc *) WriteReal;


   PROCEDURE random () : CARDINAL;

   BEGIN
     RETURN TRUNC( FLOAT( Rand2() ) / 32767.0 * 999.0 );
   END random;


TYPE hashtable = ARRAY[ 0 .. 999 ] OF BOOLEAN;

VAR
   table1      : hashtable; (*Used for linear chaining.    *)
   table2      : hashtable; (*Used for double hashing.     *)
   table3      : hashtable; (*Used for coalesced chaining. *)
   numprobes1  : REAL;      (*Used for linear chaining.    *)
   numprobes2  : REAL;      (*Used for double hashing.     *)
   numprobes3  : REAL;      (*Used for coalesced chaining. *)
   free        : CARDINAL;
   link        : ARRAY[ 0 .. 999] OF INTEGER;


PROCEDURE linearchaining
          ( VAR address : CARDINAL (* in/out *) );

BEGIN
  numprobes1 := numprobes1 + 1.0;
  WHILE ( table1[ address ] )DO
   address := ( address + 1 ) MOD 1000;
   numprobes1 := numprobes1 + 1.0;
  END(* while loop *);
END linearchaining;


PROCEDURE doublehashing
          ( VAR address : CARDINAL (* in/out *) );

BEGIN
  numprobes2 := numprobes2 + 1.0;
  WHILE ( table2[ address ] ) DO
    address := ( address + random() ) MOD 1000;
    numprobes2 := numprobes2 + 1.0;
  END(* while loop *);
END doublehashing;
```

```
PROCEDURE coalesced
          ( VAR address : CARDINAL (* in/out *) );

VAR
    previous : INTEGER;
    i        : INTEGER;
    intable  : BOOLEAN;

BEGIN
  numprobes3 := numprobes3 + 1.0;
  intable := table3[ address ];
  IF intable
  THEN
    i := address;
    REPEAT
      previous := i;
      numprobes3 := numprobes3 + 1.0;
      i := link[ i ];
    UNTIL i = -1;
  END(* if then *);
  IF NOT intable
  THEN
    RETURN; (* with address unchanged *)
  ELSE
    REPEAT
      DEC( free );
    UNTIL NOT table3[ free ];
    link[ previous ] := free;
    link[ free ] := -1;
    address := free;
  END(* if then *);
END coalesced;


PROCEDURE simulate( upper : CARDINAL );    (* in *) );


VAR
   index     : CARDINAL;
   address   : CARDINAL;
   temp      : CARDINAL;

BEGIN
  free := 1000;
  FOR index := 0 TO 999 DO
    link[ index ] := -1;
  END(* for loop *);
  FOR index := 0 TO upper DO
    temp := random();
    address := temp;
```

```
        linearchaining( address );
        table1[ address ] := TRUE;
        address := temp;
        doublehashing( address );
        table2[ address ] := TRUE;
        address := temp;
        coalesced( address );
        table3[ address ] := TRUE;
    END(* for loop *);
    WriteLn;
    WriteString(" LC average number of probes for a ");
    WriteString("successful search = ");
    WriteReal( numprobes1 / ( FLOAT( upper ) + 1.0 ) , 1 );
    WriteLn;
    WriteString(" DH average number of probes for a ");
    WriteString("successful search = ");
    WriteReal( numprobes2 / ( FLOAT( upper ) + 1.0 ) , 1 );
    WriteLn;
    WriteString(" CC average number of probes for a ");
    WriteString("successful search = ");
    WriteReal( numprobes3 / ( FLOAT( upper ) + 1.0 ) , 1 );
END simulate;

PROCEDURE initializetable;

VAR index : CARDINAL;

BEGIN
    FOR index := 0 TO 999 DO
        table1[ index ] := FALSE;
        table2[ index ] := FALSE;
        table3[ index ] := FALSE;
    END(* for loop *);
END initializetable;


BEGIN
    initializetable;
    WriteLn; WriteString("          Set load factor to 25%. ");
    WriteLn;
    numprobes1 := 0.0;  numprobes2 := 0.0;  numprobes3 := 0.0;
    simulate( 249 );
    initializetable;
    WriteLn;
    WriteLn; WriteString("          Set load factor to 50%. ");
    WriteLn;
    numprobes1 := 0.0;  numprobes2 := 0.0;  numprobes3 := 0.0;
    simulate( 499 );
    WriteLn;
    WriteLn;
```

```
  WriteString("                        Set load factor to 75%.");
  WriteLn;
  initializetable;
  numprobes1 := 0.0;  numprobes2 := 0.0;  numprobes3 := 0.0;
  simulate( 749 );
  WriteLn;
  WriteLn;
  WriteString("                        Set load factor to 85%.");
  WriteLn;
  initializetable;
  numprobes1 := 0.0;  numprobes2 := 0.0;  numprobes3 := 0.0;
  simulate( 849 );
  WriteLn;
  WriteLn;
  WriteString("                        Set load factor to 90%. ");
  WriteLn;
  initializetable;
  numprobes1 := 0.0;  numprobes2 := 0.0;  numprobes3 := 0.0;
  simulate( 899 );
  WriteLn;
  WriteLn;
  WriteString("                        Set load factor to 95%.");
  WriteLn;
  initializetable;
  numprobes1 := 0.0;  numprobes2 := 0.0;  numprobes3 := 0.0;
  simulate( 949 );
  WriteLn;
END collisionresolution.
```

In Table 10.1 we present the results of the simulation experiment.

It is clear from Table 10.1 that coalesced hashing is the most efficient, next double hashing, and finally linear chaining. It would appear from the simulation results that for a load factor of 95 percent, the ratios of performance are:

Coalesced chaining	1.000
Double hashing	1.748
Linear chaining	5.997

A CPU timing test was performed for the insertion of 949 keys into each table. The results of this test show the following ratios of performance:

Coalesced chaining	1.000
Double hashing	2.108
Linear chaining	2.791

Double hashing appears to perform worse in the actual timing analysis than in the average number of probes simulation. The reason should be clear.

TABLE 10.1 Results of Simulation Experiment

Load Factor	Collision-Resolution Strategy	Average Number of Probes
0.25	Linear chaining	1.124
0.25	Double hashing	1.144
0.25	Coalesced chaining	1.120
0.50	Linear chaining	1.462
0.50	Double hashing	1.330
0.50	Coalesced chaining	1.300
0.75	Linear chaining	2.601
0.75	Double hashing	1.909
0.75	Coalesced chaining	1.481
0.85	Linear chaining	3.442
0.85	Double hashing	2.112
0.85	Coalesced chaining	1.662
0.90	Linear chaining	4.009
0.90	Double hashing	2.558
0.90	Coalesced chaining	1.651
0.95	Linear chaining	10.71
0.95	Double hashing	3.122
0.95	Coalesced chaining	1.786

The double hash algorithm requires the computation of an additional hash function, which shows up in the timing run but not in the simulation.

Coalesced chaining compared with linear chaining looks worse in the actual timing analysis than in the average number of probes simulation because the overhead associated with traversing the linked lists, in algorithm coalesced chaining, does not appear in the number of probes. Thus coalesced chaining performs worse with respect to linear chaining in the actual timing runs. It is still, by far, the best of the three methods.

It should be clear from Table 10.1 that the performance, measured in average number of probes, does not vary significantly with the number of keys in the table (load factor) as long as the load factor is below 50 percent. This relatively constant performance with load continues much further with the coalesced hashing method. This is in sharp contrast to tree implementations of a search table.

We emphasize that Table 10.1 was obtained from a simulation experiment that used a random number generator to simulate a hash function. In practice, one would expect the average number of probes to be slightly higher because of the imperfect nature of real hash functions.

What about deletion from a hash table? (Thus far, we have discussed the operations insertion and ispresent.) Deletion, however, requires a careful repositioning of the keys in a collision chain and is difficult; it is not discussed in this book.

In constructing a hash table, the most frequently accessed keys should be inserted before the keys less frequently accessed. As indicated earlier, the probability of a collision during insertion increases as the number of keys in the table increases. See exercise 10.14.

10.4 Probabilistic Hashing

The hash methods discussed in section 10.2 are all based on the assumption that the key being hashed is stored in the hash table. This arrangement may be practical for relatively small hash tables, but it is impractical for very large tables. For example, suppose one wishes to use a hash table as a dictionary for a spelling checker. Assume a hash table of size 60,000. To store such a table in an array, if each word occupies 23 characters, would require a machine with a random access memory of 1,380,000 bytes. Few machines can dedicate this much RAM space to a hash table.

Probabilistic hashing permits a tradeoff between speed and memory, allowing a significant reduction in the storage required for the hash table at the expense of some search speed.

Using probabilistic hashing, n distinct hash functions are used to map a key to n values, hopefully distinct values. Instead of storing the key in the table, each of the n values is stored in a set consisting of cardinal index values. Each key thus adds n cardinal values to the set. To determine whether a key is present in the table, the presence of all n hash values is determined. If one or more values are missing, the key is deemed not to be in the set. If all n values are present, the key is deemed to be in the set.

Using this scheme it is possible to detect as being in the table a key that is not in fact there. In the case of a spelling checker, a misspelled word would be incorrectly identified as correctly spelled. This type of error does not exist when the key is stored in the table. We note that there is no possibility for a key that is in the table to be incorrectly identified as not being present (e.g., a correctly spelled word cannot be identified as incorrectly spelled).

How can we estimate the error of a key outside the table colliding with a key in the table?

If we assume that each hash function is perfect (i.e., yields a uniform distribution of index locations across the table), the probability of a key outside the table producing n hash values that are all contained in the index set is the load factor raised to the nth power, where the load factor is the ratio of the number of indices in the set to the total number that can be accommodated by the set. Because we are not storing the full word in the table, we can use a much larger table for a given computer memory and therefore reduce the load factor. Each key occupies exactly n bits in the table, whereas a 23-character word would occupy 23 bytes or 184 bits. The memory compression is therefore $184/n$.

If we choose $n = 10$, and $LF = 1/4$, we can limit the error of a key outside the table being incorrectly identified as in the table to 1/4 raised to the 10th power, which is 0.00000954. The name "probabilistic hashing" derives from the fact that we are able to limit this risk of error to an acceptable level. We see a direct tradeoff between the risk of an error and the degree of memory compression.

Probabilistic hashing may be attractive on small computers because of the tremendous memory compression that is possible.

10.5 Virtual Hashing

The beginning reader may wish to skip this section on first reading because it uses advanced features of Modula-2.

The algorithm presented in this section was developed by Wiener (1985).

Virtual hashing, like probabilistic hashing, does not deposit a key in the hash table. In the case of virtual hashing, a major key (cardinal) determines the index location in an array and a minor key (cardinal) is placed in the table (virtual address). That is, a cardinal is stored as a surrogate for the key. For an erroneous collision to occur for a key outside the table, the outside key must have exactly the same major and minor key as a legitimate key in the table.

If we construct the table with, say, 8091 major keys and 65,536 minor keys, the chances of an accidental hit are close to zero.

Since an array of cardinals is required for a virtual hash table, considerably less storage is needed than would be the case if the keys were in the table. On many machines, a cardinal requires 2 bytes of storage, whereas a 23-character word requires 23 bytes of storage. Thus, for these values, a memory compression exceeding 10 : 1 is possible using virtual hashing. Even more remarkable, we are able to achieve tremendous improvements in run-time efficiency because of the use of low-level bit manipulations in computing the major and minor addresses.

Before presenting the algorithm for virtual hashing, we briefly review some pertinent facts concerning bit manipulation in Modula-2. The reader is referred to Ford and Wiener (1985) for more details.

10.5.1 Brief Review of Bit Manipulation in Modula-2

Two important facilities of Modula-2 are used in the construction of the virtual hash algorithm: type transfer (type coercion) and bitsets.

Type transfer, which has been achieved in Pascal using (or misusing) variant records, is a mechanism for interpreting a structure of given size in two or more ways. For example, on a machine in which a character requires 1 byte of storage and an integer 2 bytes, we may construct the following type transfer:

```
TYPE string2 = ARRAY [ 1 .. 2 ] OF CHAR;

VAR
     i : INTEGER;
     a : string2;
```

The following operations are legal:

```
i := INTEGER( a );

a := string2( i );
```

These operations are legal because the object and the target occupy exactly the same amount of memory. This is the crucial requirement that supports type transfers. Actually no processing of information occurs, the function name notwithstanding. Rather, the type transfer accomplishes a reinterpretation of a bit pattern.

A BITSET, in Modula-2, is a set of cardinals that are in one-to-one correspondence with the binary digits of a machine word (a bit vector). The presence of a cardinal in a bitset implies the presence of a 1 bit in the corresponding position in the machine word bit vector. We have the following correspondence between bitsets and bit vectors:

{} 0000000000000000
{0, 1, 13, 15 } → 1100000000000101

We will assume for this application that a cardinal requires exactly one machine word. Thus there exists a two-way mapping from bitset to cardinal and from cardinal to bitset.

We will also assume the presence of a 32-bit integer (two-word integer) called type LONGINT. Many implementations of Modula-2 support such long integers.

Using type transfers and bitsets, the following code plays a major role in implementing the virtual hash algorithm:

```
(* We convert a long integer to an array of two words using
type transfer. We then extract the middle 16 bits of the
resulting 32-bit word to form a new bitset, which we then
convert to a cardinal.      *)

TYPE widemask = ARRAY [ 1..2 ] OF WORD;

VAR
    m            : widemask;
    wideobject   : LONGINT; (* 32 bit integer *)

    m := widemask( wideobject ); (* an array of two words *)
    bitset := {};  (* null set *)
    FOR pos := 8 TO 15 DO
      IF pos IN bitset( m[ 2 ] )
      THEN
        INCL ( bitset, pos - 8 );
      END(* if then *);
    END(* for loop *);
    FOR pos := 0 TO 7 DO
      IF pos IN BITSET( m[ 1 ] )
```

```
      THEN
        INCL( bitset, pos + 8 );
      END(* if then *);
    END(* for loop *);
```

The resulting bitset may be converted to a cardinal by applying a type transfer function:

```
key := CARDINAL( bitset );
```

10.5.2 Algorithm for Virtual Hashing

Before presenting pseudo-code for the virtual hash algorithm, we state the algorithm. We assume that the key is an English word.

For English words of 4 characters or more, we combine and map the first two characters of the word into a 32-bit long integer, wide1. We combine and map the next two characters of the word into another long integer, wide2. We multiply the two long integers and retain only 32 bits of the product, getting a third long integer, wide3.

Using type transfer, we interpret wide3 as an array of two words. Using bitsets, we retrieve the middle 16 bits of wide3 and combine the integer value of this bitset with 0 to form a new long integer, wide1. If appropriate (based on the length of the English word), we continue to chain multiply wide1 with a new long integer formed by the next two characters in the word. An odd number of characters in the word is treated as a special case. When the chain multiplication is finished, the middle 16 bits of the resultant long integer determine the minor key, and 13 bits taken from each side of the long integer form the major key (a number from 0 to 8091).

These low-level operations may be performed quickly. The number of chain multiplication iterations is approximately equal to half the number of characters in the word minus 4. The extraction of middle and end bits from the resultant product assures a fairly even distribution of major and minor hash addresses (virtual addresses).

We now present the virtual hash algorithm in pseudo-code.

```
Algorithm compute
  ( w : wordtype         (* in  *)
    minorkey : integer (* out *)
    majorkey : integer (* out *)

  length ← Length( w )
  numberiterations ← ( length DIV 2 ) - 2
  wide1 ← convert( ORD( w[ 0 ], ORD( w[ 1 ] ) )
  wide2 ← convert( ORD( w[ 2 ], ORD( w[ 3 ] ) )
  (* Function convert maps two 16-bit cardinals into a
     32-bit long integer.                                    *)
  wide3 ← multiply( wide1, wide2 )
  m[ 1 ] ← first machine word (16 bits) of wide3
```

```
m[ 2 ] ← second machine word (16 bits) of wide3
BITSET b ← empty
for pos ← 8 to 15 loop
  if pos in m[ 2 ]
  then
    add( pos - 8 ) to BITSET b
  end if
end loop
for pos ← 0 to 7 loop
  if pos in m[ 1 ]
    then
      add ( pos + 8  ) to BITSET b
  end if
end loop
for iteration ← 1 to numberiterations loop
  wide1 ← convert( 0, CARDINAL( BITSET b ) )
  wide2 ← convert( ORD( w[ 2 * iteration + 2 ] ),
                   ORD( w[ 2 * iteration + 3 ] ) )
  wide3 ← multiply( wide1, wide2 )
  m[ 1 ] ← first 16 bits of wide3
  m[ 2 ] ← second 16 bits of wide3
  BITSET b ← empty
  for pos ← 8 to 15 loop
    if pos in m[ 2 ]
    then
      add( pos - 8 ) to BITSET b
    end if
  end loop
  for pos ← 0 to 7 loop
    if pos in m[ 1 ]
    then
      add ( pos + 8 ) to BITSET b
    end if
  end loop
  if length is odd
  then
  wide1 ← convert( ORD( w[ 1 ] ), CARDINAL( BITSET b ) )
  wide2 ← convert( ORD( w[ 0 ] ), ORD( w[ length - 1 ] ) )
    m[ 1 ] is first 16 bits of wide3
    m[ 2 ] is second 16 bits of wide3
  end if
  majorkeybitset = {}
  for pos ← 8 to 15 loop
    if pos in m[ 2 ]
    then
      add ( pos - 8 ) to majorkeybitset
    end if
  end loop
  if pos ← 0 to 4 loop
    if pos in m[ 1 ]
```

```
      then
        add ( pos + 8 ) to majorkeybitset
      end if
    end loop
    minorkeybitset = {}
    for pos ← 0 to 7 loop
      if pos in m[ 2 ]
      then
        add( pos ) to minorkeybitset
      end if
    end loop
    for pos ← 8 to 15 loop
      if pos in m[ 1 ]
      then
        add( pos ) to minorkeybitset
      end if
    end loop
    majorkey ← CARDINAL( majorkeybitset )
    minorkey ← CARDINAL( minorkeybitset )
  end Algorithm
```

In Listing 10.2, we present a definition module that contains the interface to the virtual hash table. Listing 10.3 implements procedures compute and ispresent. We omit the code for procedure insert because it is similar to the code for procedure ispresent.

In procedure ispresent, English words of length 3 or less are checked separately using a one-to-one mapping as described at the beginning of the chapter.

We assume that procedure makewide which converts two ordinary integers to a long integer) and Mul (which multiplies two long integers) are available elsewhere.

Listing 10.2 Interface to Virtual Hash Table

```
DEFINITION MODULE HashTable;

  EXPORT QUALIFIED
    (* type *) wordtype,
    (* proc *) ispresent,
    (* proc *) insert;

  CONST upperword = 22;

  TYPE wordtype = ARRAY[ 0 .. upperword ] OF CHAR;

  PROCEDURE ispresent
            ( inputkey : wordtype     (* in *) ) : BOOLEAN;
```

```
  PROCEDURE insert( inputkey : wordtype );

END HashTable.
```

Listing 10.3 Some Implementation Details of Virtual Hashing

```
PROCEDURE compute
          ( w            : wordtype (* in  *);
            VAR mkey     : CARDINAL (* out *);
            VAR minkey   : CARDINAL (* out *) );

VAR
    length      : CARDINAL;
    pos         : CARDINAL;
    b           : BITSET;
    majorkey    : BITSET;
    minorkey    : BITSET;
    m           : widemask;
    w1, w2, w3  : LONGINT;
    numberit    : CARDINAL;
    iteration   : CARDINAL;
    even        : BOOLEAN;

BEGIN (* compute *)
  length := Length(w);
  numberit := (length DIV 2) - 2;
  even := (length MOD 2 = 0);
  w1 := MakeWide( ORD(w[0]), ORD(w[1]) );
  w2 := MakeWide( ORD(w[2]), ORD(w[3]) );
  w3 := Mul(w1,w2);
  m  := widemask(w3);
  b := {};
  FOR pos := 8 TO 15 DO
    IF pos IN BITSET( m[2] )
    THEN
      INCL( b,pos - 8 );
    END(* if then *);
  END(* for loop *);
  FOR pos := 0 TO 7 DO
    IF pos IN BITSET( m[1] )
    THEN
      INCL( b,pos + 8 );
    END(* if then *);
  END(* for loop *);
```

```
  FOR iteration := 1 TO numberit DO
    w1 := MakeWide( 0, CARDINAL(b) );
    w2 := MakeWide( ORD(w[2*iteration + 2]),
                    ORD(w[2*iteration + 3]) );
    w3 := Mul( w1, w2 );
    m  := widemask( w3 );
    b := {};
    FOR pos := 8 TO 15 DO
      IF pos IN BITSET( m[2] )
      THEN
        INCL( b,pos - 8 );
      END(* if then *);
    END(* for loop *);
    FOR pos := 0 TO 7 DO
      IF pos IN BITSET( m[1] )
      THEN
        INCL( b,pos + 8 );
      END(* if then *);
    END(* for loop *);
  END(* for loop *);
  IF NOT even
  THEN
    w1 := MakeWide( ORD(w[1]), CARDINAL(b) );
    w2 := MakeWide( ORD(w[0]), ORD(w[length-1]) );
    w3 := Mul( w1, w2 );
    m  := widemask( w3 );
  END(* if then *);
  (* Determine the major key. *)
  majorkey := {};
  FOR pos := 8 TO 15 DO
    IF pos IN BITSET( m[2] )
    THEN
      INCL( majorkey, pos - 8 );
    END(* if then *);
  END(* for loop *);
  FOR pos := 0 TO 4 DO
    IF pos IN BITSET( m[1] )
    THEN
      INCL( majorkey,pos + 8 );
    END(* if then *);
  END(* for loop *);
  minorkey := {};
  FOR pos := 0 TO 7 DO
    IF pos IN BITSET( m[2] )
    THEN
      INCL( minorkey,pos );
    END(* if then *);
  END(* for loop *);
  FOR pos := 8 TO 15 DO
    IF pos IN BITSET( m[1] )
```

```
    THEN
      INCL( minorkey,pos );
    END(* if then *);
  END(* for loop *);
  mkey   := CARDINAL( majorkey );
  minkey := CARDINAL( minorkey );
END compute;


PROCEDURE ispresent
        ( inputkey : wordtype       (* in *) ) : BOOLEAN;


VAR
   minorkey    : CARDINAL;
   majorkey    : CARDINAL;
   tablevalue  : CARDINAL;


  PROCEDURE insmall
          ( w : wordtype            (* in *) ) : BOOLEAN;

  VAR length : CARDINAL;

  BEGIN
    length := Length( w );
    IF length = 1
    THEN
      IF w[0] IN setofchar{'a'..'z'}
      THEN
        RETURN smalltable[ ORD(w[0]) - 96 ] = TRUE;
      ELSE
        RETURN FALSE;
      END(* if then *);
    ELSIF length = 2
    THEN
      IF ( w[0] IN setofchar{'a'..'z'} ) AND
         ( w[1] IN setofchar{'a'..'z'} )
      THEN
        RETURN smalltable[ ORD(w[0]) - 96 +
                           c2*(ORD(w[1]) - 96) ] =
               TRUE;
      ELSE
        RETURN FALSE;
      END(* if then else *);
    ELSE
       IF ( w[0] IN setofchar{'a'..'z'} ) AND
          ( w[1] IN setofchar{'a'..'z'} ) AND
          ( w[2] IN setofchar{'a'..'z'} )
       THEN
```

```
            RETURN smalltable[ ORD(w[0]) - 96 +
                               c2*(ORD(w[1]) - 96) +
                              c3*(ORD(w[2]) - 96) ] = TRUE;
          ELSE
            RETURN FALSE;
          END(* if then *);
      END(* if then *);
    END insmall;


BEGIN (* ispresent *)
  IF Length( inputkey ) < 4
  THEN
    RETURN insmall( inputkey );
  END(* if then *);
  compute( inputkey, majorkey, minorkey );
  firstletter := CAP ( inputkey[ 0 ] );
  IF setnumber( firstletter ) # setnumber( lastletter )
  THEN
    lastletter := firstletter;
    readrecord( firstletter );
  END(* if then *);
  tablevalue := hashtable[ majorkey ];
  WHILE ( tablevalue # 0 ) AND ( tablevalue # minorkey ) DO
   majorkey := (majorkey + 1) MOD 8191;
   IF majorkey = 0
   THEN
     INC( majorkey );
   END(* if then *);
   tablevalue := hashtable[ majorkey ];
  END(* while loop *);
  RETURN tablevalue = minorkey;
END ispresent;
```

10.5.3 Test Results Using Virtual Hashing

To test the likelihood of collisions between incorrectly spelled words and the approximately 35,000 words that were loaded into 14 hash tables, it is necessary to generate many misspelled words quickly. The technique used is to produce 100,000 permutations of the word ''shavingbt'' (any large word with distinct characters may be used) and test each of these permutations against the hash dictionaries. Each unique word identified as correctly spelled is inserted into a search table and displayed at the end of the experiment. We present the procedure permute, in Listing 10.4, for generating 100,000 misspelled words.

The test results yield 11 misspelled words identified as correctly spelled from the 100,000 misspelled words. For the reader interested in trivia, the words incorrectly identified as correctly spelled were: asihngvbt, avngisbht,

Listing 10.4 Procedure for Generating 100,000 Misspelled Words

```
PROCEDURE permute
         ( n         : INTEGER  (* in  *);
           VAR word : wordtype (* out *) );
(* This procedure generates n! permutations of word.          *)

VAR
    i, j : INTEGER;
    temp : CHAR;

BEGIN
  IF n > 0
  THEN
    permute( n-1, word );
    FOR i := n - 1 TO 0 BY -1 DO
      temp := word[ n ];
      word[ n ] := word[ i ];
      word[ i ] := temp;
      permute( n-1, word );
      temp := word[ n ];
      word[ n ] := word[ i ];
      word[ i ] := temp;
    END(* for loop *);
  ELSE
    IF ispresent( word )
    THEN
      searchtable.insert( tab, word );
    END(* if then *);
    numbertested := numbertested + 1.0;
    IF numbertested = numbertests
    THEN
      WriteLn; WriteLn;
      WriteString("The number tested = ");
      WriteReal(  numbertested, 1 );
      WriteLn; WriteLn;
      Spacebar;
      WriteLn; WriteLn;
      searchtable.Display( tab );
      WriteLn; WriteLn;
      Spacebar;
      HALT;
    END(* if then *);
  END(* if then else *);
END permute;
```

banshtvig, gasvhibnt, inshgvabt, isvgnahtb, nsbahvitg, sanihvtbg, sanihvtbg, sighnbvat, stibvahng, tsvnahigb (not suitable for naming children!).

The error rate of 0.00011 applies to incorrectly spelled words as input, not correctly spelled words. It would take an extremely large test of words written by a poor speller to force an error in the virtual hash spelling checker.

For speed comparisons, the average processing rate during the test of 100,000 words was 30.77 words per second, which compares very favorably with 8.5 words per second tested using a B-tree algorithm and 4 words per second using an indexed search into a large file.

Exercises

10.1 Show with an example that the method of extraction is a poor method of hashing (perhaps a good method in dentistry).

10.2 Using the hashing function given in section 10.2, the method of compression with multiplication, compute the hash functions for the following words (assume that maxindex = 1003 and $m = 0.3819660113$): the, word, computer, university, to, give, some, sum, more, node, done.

10.3 Write and test a Modula-2 procedure:

```
hash( key : keytype ) : CARDINAL;
```

that uses the method of compression, given in subsection 10.2.2, with multiplication. Assume the same values for maxindex and m as in exercise 10.2

10.4 Write and test another Modula-2 procedure, hash, using the method of compression with division. Assume that maxindex = 1003.

10.5 **(a)** Write and test your own algorithm for computing n as a variation of the method given in subsection 10.2.2.

(b) Using your algorithm, recompute the hash values for the list of words given in exercise 10.2.

10.6 Show that if m is 0.9999 or 0.00001, small-length words map, using the method of compression with multiplication, to the ends of the hash table.

10.7 Why is it desirable for maxindex + 1 to be prime using the method of division?

10.8 Discuss the reasons for additional constraints on m in the method of compression using multiplication.

10.9 Compute the average number of probes for a successful search, S, for the configuration shown in Figure 10.3.

10.10 Why do we always leave one blank space in a hash table?

10.11 Using coalesced chaining, suppose we only allow h(key) to take on values from 0 to max < maxindex. We initially set free to maxindex. For values of max equal to 1/2 maxindex, 3/4 maxindex, and 4/5 maxindex, estimate and compare the performance of this variation of coalesced chaining with the algorithm given in subsection 10.3.3. What advantage, if any, might there be to restricting h(key) to the range 0, . . ., max?

10.12 Using the methods of subsection 10.3.5, construct a hash table using separate chaining and estimate and compare its performance to lincar chaining, double hashing, and coalesced chaining.

10.13 Add some additional procedures to the simulation given in Listing 10.1, to compare the average number of probes for an unsuccessful search.

10.14 Build a hash table of 1000 keys using linear chaining. Assume that the first 500 insertions have a probability of access that is 10 times the next 500 insertions. Use a weighting function on the number of probes to compute the new average number of probes per successful search.

10.15 Repeat exercise 10.14, only this time assume that the first 500 insertions have a probability of access that is 10 times the next 500 insertions. Compute the new average number of probes per successful search.

10.16 Implement probabilistic hashing for words of various lengths.

10.17 Write a complete spelling checker program. Implement a virtual hash table for table lookup in the dictionary. Test your program by generating 1,000,000 incorrectly spelled words and computing the error rate.

11

Applications of Data Structures to Sorting

Sorting a list of items into a specified order is a common and useful operation that appears in many applications. A sorted list of items makes it easier to search a list for a specified item. For example, if the telephone directory was not sorted by name, it would be a useless list.

Sorting routines are very widely used in a variety of software systems. Indeed the efficiency of an entire software system may depend on the efficiency of the underlying sorting algorithm. Because of this, we must be able to measure the efficiency of sorting algorithms so that we can determine which methods are best. Efficiency of a sorting algorithm is usually based on the number of comparisons required to put the list in sorted order. We will find that the number of comparisons for some sorting algorithms is proportional to the square of the number of items in the list, and for other algorithms it is proportional to the number of items times the logarithm of the number of items. We will also discover that the efficiency of some sorting algorithms varies substantially depending on whether the initial list of items is random, almost sorted, or sorted in reverse order.

The list of items to be sorted may be large, so we must also consider the storage requirements for each sorting algorithm. In some cases, it may not be possible to sort large lists of items directly in computer memory. Algorithms that sort lists stored on an external device such as a tape or disk are called external sorting algorithms, whereas algorithms that sort lists stored in memory are called internal sorting algorithms. Our principal concern in this chapter is algorithms of the latter type.

No sorting algorithm is best for every situation. The selection of a sorting algorithm depends on the number of items to be sorted, the computer memory available, the size of disks and tapes, the extent to which the items are already sorted, and other problem-dependent considerations.

The problem of sorting a list of integers is easy to understand. We know the ordering of the integers, so we need only specify whether they should be sorted in ascending order or descending order. The same remarks are applicable to a list of reals. If we have a list of names consisting of both a first name and a last name, we usually sort the list based on the last name, which is considered to be the key field or the field on which the sorting is based. A common problem that arises in many applications involves sorting a list of records when each record may contain a number of fields. One field of the record is usually chosen as the key field on which to sort the list of records. The sorted keys can then be used as an index to the records. The sorting problem is completely defined when we specify an ordering relation on the key field.

Historically, sorting procedures have often been rewritten to reflect each new data type to be sorted. In this chapter, we present a user interface to sorting that is applicable for all our sorting algorithms and can be used for any user-defined data type for which an ordering relation can be specified. Thus, we will not need to change a single line in any sorting algorithm presented here, irrespective of the types of item to be sorted.

We began with Listing 11.1, the user interface for all the sorting algorithms to be developed in this chapter.

The definition module for sorting imports the type of items to be sorted from the user-defined module elements. This type is referred to as elementtype. The sorting procedure sort accepts as a parameter a list of items to be sorted. The list is an array of elementtype. The ARRAY OF elementtype is referred to as an open-array type in Modula-2 and permits us to sort the list independent of the subscript range or subscript type used to reference items in the list. In the

Listing 11.1 Sorting Interface

```
DEFINITION MODULE sorting;

  FROM elements IMPORT
    (* type *) elementtype;

  EXPORT QUALIFIED
    (* proc *) sort;

  TYPE lessthantype = PROCEDURE( elementtype, elementtype ) :
                                 BOOLEAN;

  PROCEDURE sort
          ( VAR items    : ARRAY OF elementtype (* in/out *);
                lessthan : lessthantype         (* in *) );

END sorting.
```

implementation of the sort procedure, we can reference items with subscripts 0 to HIGH(items). The number of items, n, to be sorted is n = HIGH(items) + 1. The sorting problem is completely specified if we define an ordering relation for the list of items. The procedure type, lessthantype, is a user-defined procedure that specifies the order relation for the items.

Let us consider several examples. If we wish to sort an array of integers with subscript range −50 to 100, elementtype is defined by:

```
DEFINITION MODULE elements;

  EXPORT QUALIFIED
    (* type *) elementtype;

  TYPE
        elementtype = INTEGER;

END elements.
```

and the ordering relation is defined by :

```
PROCEDURE lessthan ( p, q : elementtype ) : BOOLEAN;
BEGIN
  RETURN p < q
END;
```

Our main program would contain the declaration:

```
VAR integeritems : ARRAY [ -50 .. 100 ] OF elementtype;
```

After we have assigned values to the array integeritems, we can sort them by calling the sorting algorithm:

```
sort( integeritems, lessthan );
```

If we wish to sort the list integeritems in descending order rather than ascending order, we need only change the ordering relation as follows:

```
PROCEDURE lessthan ( p, q : elementtype ) : BOOLEAN;
BEGIN
  RETURN p > q
END;
```

To enhance program readability, we might also wish to change the name of the procedure to greaterthan.

If we wish to sort an array of reals, we need only change INTEGER to REAL in the preceding elementtype definition. Note that the subscripts used in the list of items are not relevant to the sorting problem; they are important only to the applications program that is calling the sort procedure. For example, the following declarations:

```
TYPE months = ( Jan, Feb, Mar, Apr, May, Jun, Jul, Aug,
                Sep, Oct, Nov, Dec );
VAR items : ARRAY [ months ] OF elementtype;
```

lead to a list of items that are indexed by the months of the year, but can be sorted by the simple call:

```
sort( items, lessthan );
```

Now let us consider a more interesting example, sorting a list of records. We make the following elementtype definition:

```
DEFINITION MODULE elements;

  EXPORT QUALIFIED
    (* type *) elementtype;

  TYPE string = ARRAY [ 0 .. 79 ] OF CHAR;
       elementtype = RECORD
                       lastname   : string;
                       firstname  : string;
                       salary     : REAL;
                       age        : CARDINAL
                     END (* record *);

END elements.
```

and we assume that the following declarations occur in the program that calls the sort procedure:

```
CONST numberemployees = 100;

VAR employeerecords = ARRAY [ 1 .. numberemployees ] OF
                      elementtype;
```

Once we have created our list of employee records, we can sort the list based on any field in the record by an appropriately defined procedure of type lessthantype. This field is called the key field. For example, to sort the list of employees based on age, we define the order relation:

```
PROCEDURE ageorder( p, q : elementtype ) : BOOLEAN;
BEGIN
  RETURN p.age < q.age
END ageorder;
```

and call:

```
sort( employeerecords, ageorder );
```

To sort the list of employees based on salary from highest salary to lowest salary, we define the order relation:

```
PROCEDURE salaryorder( p, q : elementtype ) : BOOLEAN;
BEGIN
  RETURN p.salary > q.salary
END salaryorder;
```

and call:

```
sort( employeerecords, salaryorder );
```

Finally, to sort the employee records based on the alphabetical order of the last name of each employee, we can use the procedure lessthan defined in Listing 5.1 without any changes and call:

```
sort( employeerecords, lessthan );
```

For some purposes, we might wish to see a listing of employee records sorted by age with the last names alphabetically ordered within each age group. This can be achieved by sorting the employee records twice, as follows:

```
sort( employeerecords, lessthan );
sort( employeerecords, ageorder );
```

The first call to sort puts the employee records into alphabetical order by last name. The output from the first sort is input to the second call to sort which puts the employee records into age order. This gives us the desired output if the sorting algorithm preserves the original order of items with identical key values.

11.1 Elementary Sorting Techniques

11.1.1 Selection Sort/Exchange Sort

We first consider the sorting algorithm called the selection sort or exchange sort. This is most likely the algorithm you would use if someone handed you a sheet of paper containing items to be sorted. You would find the item that should go first and write it at the top of a second sheet of paper. Then you would cross out the item on the original list. From the remaining items on the first sheet, you would find the item that now should be first, transfer it over as the next item on the second sheet, and cross out the item on the first sheet. This process would be continued until all the items on the first sheet had been crossed out and written to the second sheet, which then would contain the items in sorted order.

Let us consider the implementation of this simple sorting algorithm. The preceding description implies that storage space must be available for two copies of the items, since we transfer items from the original to a second copy, which eventually becomes the sorted items. This is an unacceptable requirement, especially if the list of items to be sorted is large. However, a simple modification to the algorithm eliminates the need for a second copy of the items. Suppose we do not have the second sheet of paper referred to above. Then when we find the item that belongs first we swap it with the item that is currently at the top of the list. After an item has been placed in its ordered position, we need only examine the items after that position to determine which item comes next.

The preceding algorithm—called selection sort, since the next item is selected from the remaining items that have not yet been sorted—can be formally described by the following, where number = HIGH(items) and the number of items to be sorted is number + 1:

```
for index = 0 to number - 1 do
  set position to index
  for j = index + 1 to number do
    if lessthan( items[ j ], items[ position ] )
    then
      position = j
    end if
  end for
  swap( items[ position ], items[ index ] )
end for
```

The swap procedure is defined by:

```
PROCEDURE swap( VAR p, q : elementtype );
  VAR temp : elementtype;
BEGIN
  temp := p;
  p := q;
  q := temp
END swap;
```

This swap procedure is used in many of the sorting algorithms developed in this chapter.

To illustrate this algorithm we sort the following list of integers:

25 7 74 1 60 13 54 14 43 21

Figure 11.1 shows the items after each iteration of the outer for loop.

Listing 11.2 presents the implementation of the selection sort algorithm.

Note that in this algorithm the subscript range on the items to be sorted is from 0 to number. This is a consequence of the use of the ARRAY OF elementtype parameter passing in Modula-2. This algorithm requires very little addi-

1	7	74	25	60	13	54	14	43	21
1	7	74	25	60	13	54	14	43	21
1	7	13	25	60	74	54	14	43	21
1	7	13	14	60	74	54	25	43	21
1	7	13	14	21	74	54	25	43	60
1	7	13	14	21	25	54	74	43	60
1	7	13	14	21	25	43	74	54	60
1	7	13	14	21	25	43	54	74	60
1	7	13	14	21	25	43	54	60	74

Figure 11.1 Illustration of Selection Sort

Listing 11.2 Selection Sort

```
PROCEDURE selectionsort
        ( VAR items    : ARRAY OF elementtype (* in/out *);
              lessthan : lessthantype         (* in *) );

  VAR index, number, position, j : CARDINAL;

BEGIN
  number := HIGH( items );
  FOR index := 0 TO number - 1 DO
    position := index;
    FOR j := index + 1 TO number DO
      IF lessthan( items[ j ], items[ position ] )
      THEN
        position := j
      END (* if then *)
    END (* for loop *);
    swap( items[ position ], items[ index ] )
  END (* for loop *)
END selectionsort;
```

tional storage. Except for a few variables for indexing, the only other storage required is space for one item for use in the swap procedure.

Analysis of Selection Sort

The outer for loop is executed $n - 1$ times, where n is the number of items in the list. Each execution of the outer loop performs a swap, so this algorithm requires $n - 1$ swaps. The inner for loop is executed $n - 1, n - 2, n - 3, \ldots, 1$ times as index is incremented in the outer loop. The number of comparisons is thus:

$$\begin{aligned}\text{number comparisons} &= (n - 1) + (n - 2) + (n - 3) + \cdots + (1)\\ &= \frac{n(n - 1)}{2}\end{aligned}$$

This algorithm requires $n(n - 1)/2$ comparisons and $n - 1$ swaps.

11.1.2 Insertion Sort

Our next sorting algorithm is called the insertion sort because it inserts an item in its proper position in an already sorted list. Suppose we wish to insert a new item in its ordered position into a list of sorted items. We can compare the new item with each item in the sorted list either starting with the first item in the list and proceeding to the last item or vice versa. When we find the ordered position for the item, we insert it into the sorted list, thereby creating a sorted list with one additional item.

From an implementation point of view, inserting an item into a list requires us to move existing items to make space for the new item. In addition, we need to be able to use this approach to sort a list of items that are not already sorted. Both these implementation concerns can be addressed as follows. We begin by considering the first item in the list as our sorted list containing a single item. We then consider the next item in the unsorted list and determine where to insert it into the sorted list. Since the insert will require us to make space for the new item, we begin our comparison with the last item in the sorted list and proceed toward the beginning. As we compare the new item with each item in the sorted list, we also move each item down one position, making space for the new item. When the ordered position is found, we insert the new item into the space. This process is repeated for each item in the list.

The implementation of the insertion sort algorithm is given in Listing 11.3.

Listing 11.3 Insertion Sort

```
PROCEDURE insertionsort
        ( VAR items : ARRAY OF elementtype      (* in/out *);
              lessthan : lessthantype           (* in *) );

  VAR item                        : elementtype;
      index, number, position     : CARDINAL;
      found                       : BOOLEAN;

BEGIN
  number := HIGH( items );
  FOR index := 1 TO number DO
    found := FALSE;
    item := items[ index ];
    position := index;
    WHILE ( position > 0 ) AND NOT found DO
      IF lessthan( item, items[ position-1 ] )
      THEN
        items[ position ] := items[ position-1 ];
        DEC( position )
      ELSE
        found := TRUE
      END (* if then *)
    END (* while loop *);
    items[ position ] := item
  END (* for loop *)
END insertionsort;
```

7	25	74	1	60	13	54	14	43	21
7	25	74	1	60	13	54	14	43	21
1	7	25	74	60	13	54	14	43	21
1	7	25	60	74	13	54	14	43	21
1	7	13	25	60	74	54	14	43	21
1	7	13	25	54	60	74	14	43	21
1	7	13	14	25	54	60	74	43	21
1	7	13	14	25	43	54	60	74	21
1	7	13	14	21	25	43	54	60	74

Figure 11.2 Illustration of Insertion Sort

The inner while loop is designed to handle insertion into the sorted portion of the list, as well as the case of an item that is inserted at the beginning of the list.

Using again the example above, we present in Figure 11.2 the configuration of the list after each execution of the outer for loop.

Analysis of Insertion Sort

The outer for loop is executed $n - 1$ times. In the worst case the inner while loop is executed $1, 2, 3, \ldots, n - 2, n - 1$ times as index is incremented in the outer for loop. In the worst case, we have:

$$\text{number comparisons} = (1) + (2) + \cdots + (n - 2) + (n - 1)$$
$$= \frac{n(n - 1)}{2}$$

If the items are already sorted, the while loop will be executed only once each time the outer for loop is executed. In this case, the number of comparisons will be $n - 1$. It can be shown that the average case still requires a number of comparisons proportional to n^2. Notice that this algorithm does not perform swaps explicitly. Instead it moves the items to make room for a new item to be inserted. Each move requires about one-third the work of one swap, since a move involves only one assignment statement, whereas a swap requires three assignment statements.

This algorithm might be improved by replacing the while loop, which finds the position in the sorted items for inserting the new item, with a binary search algorithm. The while loop search is equivalent to a linear search. This is left to the exercises.

11.1.3 Bubble Sort

The bubble sort is a selection sort that uses a different method for finding the largest or smallest item. The approach is so named because it "bubbles" either the largest or the smallest item to the top of the list of items, depending on the definition of the lessthan procedure.

Each iteration moves the appropriate item from the unsorted portion of the list to its correct position, but it may also change the positions of the other items in the unsorted portion of the list. The first iteration moves the appropriate item to the first position. We start with the last item and compare successive pairs of items. These two items are swapped whenever the order relation is not satisfied. In this way, the appropriate item "bubbles" up to the top or front of the list. The next iteration places the appropriate item from the unsorted portion of the list into the second position in the list using the same method. This process is continued until the last two items have been examined, at which time the list is in sorted order.

The bubble sort algorithm can be formally described by:

```
for index = 0 to number - 1 do
  for position = number to index + 1 by -1 do
    if lessthan( items[ position ], items[ position-1 ] )
    then
      swap( items[ position ], items[ position-1 ] )
    end if
  end for
end for
```

Using the same example again, we illustrate in Figure 11.3 the configuration of the items in the list after each execution of the outer for loop.

Notice that each iteration of the outer for loop causes some intermediate changes in the order of the list of items. It is possible that the list of items will become completely sorted before the outer for loop is executed its full number of times. For example, consider the following list of items:

7 1 14 21 13 43 25 60 74 54

The items are completely sorted after one iteration of the outer loop, but the procedure continues to execute. All further iterations perform a number of unnecessary comparisons, since no swaps will be made once the list has been sorted. Can we modify the preceding algorithm to terminate when the list has become sorted? Yes, we can, by noting whether the inner loop performed a swap. If no swap was performed, the list is in sorted order. We modify the preceding algorithm by adding a boolean flag that indicates whether a swap

1	25	7	74	13	60	14	54	21	43
1	7	25	13	74	14	60	21	54	43
1	7	13	25	14	74	21	60	43	54
1	7	13	14	25	21	74	43	60	54
1	7	13	14	21	25	43	74	54	60
1	7	13	14	21	25	43	54	74	60
1	7	13	14	21	25	43	54	60	74
1	7	13	14	21	25	43	54	60	74

Figure 11.3 Illustration of Bubble Sort

Listing 11.4 Bubble Sort

```
PROCEDURE bubblesort
        ( VAR items    : ARRAY OF elementtype (* in/out *);
              lessthan : lessthantype         (* in *) );

  VAR number, index, position : CARDINAL;
      swapped                 : BOOLEAN;

BEGIN
  number := HIGH( items );
  index := 0;
  swapped := TRUE;
  WHILE ( index < number ) AND swapped DO
    position := number;
    swapped := FALSE;
    WHILE position > index DO
      IF lessthan( items[ position ], items[ position-1 ] )
      THEN
        swap( items[ position ], items[ position-1 ] );
        swapped := TRUE
      END (* if then *);
      DEC( position )
    END (* while loop *);
    INC( index )
  END (* while loop *)
END bubblesort;
```

occurred in the inner loop. The implementation of the modified algorithm is given in Listing 11.4.

Analysis of Bubble Sort

The outer for loop of the original bubble sort algorithm is executed $n - 1$ times. The inner for loop is executed $n - 1, n - 2, \ldots, 2, 1$ times as the index of the outer loop is incremented. The inner loop in the bubble sort algorithm makes $n(n - 1)/2$ comparisons, and the worst case each comparison results in a swap.

In the modified algorithm, we set a boolean flag to indicate when a swap occurs in the inner loop. If the inner loop is executed and no swap is performed, the item are in their final sorted order and we can terminate the process. Suppose that for index $= k$, this occurs. Then the number of comparisons is:

$$\begin{aligned}\text{number comparisons} &= (n - 1) + (n - 2) + \cdots + (n - k)\\ &= \frac{n(n - 1)}{2} - \frac{(n - k)(n - k - 1)}{2}\\ &= \frac{2kn - k^2 - k}{2}\end{aligned}$$

Potentially, a swap may occur for every comparison, so the number of swaps could be as many as the number of comparisons. In the worst case, for $k = n$ and the items in reverse order we make $n(n - 1)/2$ comparisons and swaps.

11.2 The Computational Complexity of Sorting

Our concern with efficiency is important when many items are to be sorted. If we have a small number of items to sort, say 16, the efficiency of the sorting algorithm is relatively unimportant, since the number of comparisons and swaps will be small. However, as the size of the problem increases, the number of comparisons and swaps grows even faster.

The computational complexity of an algorithm is often expressed in terms of the size of the problem using a mathematical notation called order of magnitude or "big-oh" (O) notation. For example, if the complexity or some measure of work of an algorithm is:

$$2n^3 + \frac{n^2}{3} - n$$

we say that the algorithm is of order 3 or "big oh" of 3. This is usually written as follows:

$$O(n^3)$$

since the highest order term will dominate as n gets large. This notation ignores the lower order terms and the coefficient of the highest order term. The notation expresses the proportionality of the work or the complexity of the algorithm to the cube of the size of the problem.

If an algorithm is $O(1)$, work or complexity is not proportional to the size of the problem but requires a constant computing time irrespective of problem

TABLE 11.1 Relationship of Problem Size and Complexity

n	$\log_2 n$	$n \log_2 n$	n^2	n^3
1	0	0	1	1
2	1	2	4	8
4	2	8	16	64
8	3	24	64	512
16	4	64	256	4,096
32	5	160	1,024	32,768
64	6	384	4,096	262,144
128	7	896	16,384	2,097,152
256	8	2,048	65,536	16,777,216
512	9	4,608	262,144	134,217,728
1024	10	10,240	1,048,576	1,073,741,824

size. An algorithm that is $O(n)$ is more efficient than an algorithm that is $O(n^2)$, and an algorithm that is $O(n^3)$ is less efficient than an $O(n^2)$ algorithm. Often in analyzing algorithms we find the work proportional to log n or n log n. In these cases, we have algorithms of $O(\log n)$ and $O(n \log n)$, respectively.

In Table 11.1, we show the relationship between the size of the problem, n, and the computing time or work depending on the complexity of the problem.

Notice that $n \log_2 n$ grows more slowly than n^2 as the size of the problem, n, increases.

We now relate the preceding sorting algorithms to this notation. Based on our previous analysis of these algorithms, we can generate Table 11.2.

In Table 11.2, "worst case" refers to the maximum number of comparisons and swaps, whereas "best case" refers to the items already in sorted order. All three of these sorting algorithms have complexity $O(n^2)$, since the complexity of a sorting algorithm is based on the number of comparisons.

Our first bubble sort algorithm is definitely $O(n^2)$. To determine the complexity of the second bubble sort algorithm with the boolean flag, we need to determine the order of magnitude of $(2kn - k^2 - k)/2$. The term that is increasing most rapidly relative to n is $2kn$. We know that k is less than or equal to n, so k is $O(n)$. Therefore, the magnitude of the term $2kn$ is n^2, and so the second bubble sort is also $O(n^2)$. In the best case (when the items are sorted) and we are using the second bubble sort algorithm, only $n - 1$ comparisons are required, and so the bubble sort is $O(n)$.

Analysis of the insertion sort is similar to that for the bubble sort. In the best case (when the items are already sorted), only one comparison is made for each outer iteration, so the sort is $O(n)$. However, in the worst case (when the items are in reverse order), the number of comparisons is identical to the bubble sort. The selection sort is always $O(n^2)$ regardless of whether the items are in sorted order.

Which of the three sorting algorithms presented so far is the best? Since the insertion sort does not actually swap items but moves them only when

TABLE 11.2 Complexity of Simple Sorting Algorithms

	Worst Case		Best Case	
Method	Comparisons	Swaps	Comparisons	Swaps
Selection sort	$\frac{n(n-1)}{2}$	$n - 1$	$\frac{n(n-1)}{2}$	$n - 1$
Insertion sort	$\frac{n(n-1)}{2}$	$\frac{n(n+1)}{6}$	$n - 1$	0
Bubble sort	$\frac{n(n-1)}{2}$	$\frac{n(n-1)}{2}$	$n - 1$	0

TABLE 11.3 Performance of Simple Sorting Algorithms

Method	Random	Ordered	Inverse Order
Selection sort	248.35	248.17	254.08
Insertion sort	183.58	0.95	367.27
Bubble sort	377.77	0.57	483.37

necessary, one could conclude that the insertion sort algorithm is most likely the best of these three. Also the insertion sort takes into account whether the items are in sorted order. The selection sort should most likely outperform the bubble sort, since the selection sort performs far fewer swaps. However, if the items are already sorted, the bubble sort should outperform the selection sort.

Table 11.3 presents timing results for three sorting algorithms. The items sorted consisted of 1000 randomly generated integers between 0 and 10,000. It is the relative difference between the sorting algorithms that is important, so the numbers in the table can be viewed as arbitrary units of time. The results in Table 11.3 confirm our analysis of these algorithms.

Can we develop sorting algorithms that are better than $O(n^2)$ in complexity? The answer is yes. The next section gives three sorting algorithms with complexity $O(n \log n)$.

11.3 Advanced Sorting Techniques

11.3.1 Quick Sort

The quick sort algorithm is based on the fact that it is easier and faster to sort two small lists than one large list. We select an item from the list of items and place the selected item in its proper position in the list, thereby dividing the list into two parts: one part containing all items less than the selected item and the other part containing all items greater than the selected item. This process is continued on each part until the resulting part contains a single item. When all parts have been processed to a single item, the list is sorted.

The preceding strategy suggests a recursive algorithm, since each attempt to sort a list of items divides the list and then uses the same strategy to sort each of the smaller lists. The basic algorithm is:

```
quick( first, last )
  if first is less than last
  then
    split( first, last, splitpoint )
    quick( first, splitpoint - 1 )
    quick( splitpoint + 1, last )
  end if
end quick
```

where first and last are the first index and last index to the part of the list of items to be sorted. Splitpoint is the index where the selected item is placed in the list of items. The recursive algorithm halts when first is greater than or equal to last. This situation arises when there is at most one item in the list to be sorted.

To sort the original list of items, the initial call to quick is:

```
quick( 0, number )
```

where number = HIGH(items).

The difficult part of this algorithm is defining the split operation. We will select item = items[first] as the splitting value. After the call to split, all items that satisfy the order relation with item will be to the left of the splitpoint index and all items that do not will be to the right. Note that we do not know the value of splitpoint until the splitting process is finished. We then swap item with the value at the splitpoint.

The call qsort(left, splitpoint − 1) sorts the portion of the list to the left of the splitpoint and the call qsort(splitpoint + 1, right) sorts the portion of the list to the right. The item at the splitpoint is in its correct position.

The splitting algorithm must get all the items that satisfy the order relation with item to the left of the splitpoint and all other items to the right of the splitpoint. The interface to the split procedure is:

```
split( left, right, splitpoint )
```

We use a pair of indices, leftindex and rightindex, to accomplish this. The leftindex is initialized to left + 1, since the selected item is items[left]. We increment the leftindex until we find an item that does not satisfy the order relation. Then we decrement the rightindex until we find an item that satisfies the order relation. We swap these two items, increment the leftindex, decrement the rightindex, and continue this process until the leftindex is greater than the rightindex. Finally, we swap the selected item with the item at the rightindex. The splitting point is the rightindex. The implementation of the splitting algorithm is given in Listing 11.5.

Listing 11.5 Splitting Algorithm for Quick Sort

```
PROCEDURE split
        (      left, right  : INTEGER             (* in *);
           VAR splitpoint   : INTEGER             (* out *) );

  VAR item         : elementtype;
      leftindex    : INTEGER;
      rightindex   : INTEGER;

BEGIN
  item := items[ left ];
  leftindex := left + 1;
```

```
  rightindex := right;
  REPEAT
    WHILE ( leftindex <= rightindex ) AND
            lessthan( items[ leftindex ], item ) DO
      INC( leftindex )
    END (* while loop *);
    WHILE ( leftindex <= rightindex ) AND
            lessthan( item, items[ rightindex ] ) DO
      DEC( rightindex )
    END (* while loop *);
    IF leftindex <= rightindex
    THEN
      swap( items[ leftindex ], items[ rightindex ] );
      INC( leftindex );
      DEC( rightindex )
    END (* if then *);
  UNTIL leftindex > rightindex;
  swap( items[ left ], items[ rightindex ] );
  splitpoint := rightindex
END split;
```

Figure 11.4 illustrates the first call to the splitting algorithm for the list of integers used in previous examples.

The splitting algorithm we defined results in lopsided splits of the list if the original list is in sorted order, almost in sorted order, reverse order, or almost reverse order. For example, if the list is sorted, the split results in no items on one side of the split point and all the remaining items except for the splitting item on the other side. In this case, our quick sort algorithm would not be very quick!

Can we modify the splitting algorithm to prevent this situation? The previous splitting algorithm appears to work best with the items in random order; however, it is not unusual to have to sort a list of items that are almost sorted. In such cases, selecting the item in the middle of the list would seem to be a better choice. That is, select:

```
items[ (first + last) DIV 2 ]
```

as the splitting item. Computational experiments indicate that this is a better choice for the splitting algorithm if the data is sorted or almost sorted or in reverse order or almost reverse order. We leave it as an exercise to modify and implement the quick sort algorithm for this choice of splitting item. An alternative approach is to use a random number generator to select the splitting item.

Listing 11.6 presents the complete implementation of the quick sort algorithm.

```
 25     7    74     1    60    13    54    14    43    21
 ↑      ↑                                               ↑
item  left                                            right
      index                                           index

 25     7    74     1    60    13    54    14    43    21
             ↑                                          ↑
            left                                      right
            index                                     index

 25     7    21     1    60    13    54    14    43    74
                    ↑                             ↑
                   left                         right
                   index                        index

 25     7    21     1    60    13    54    14    43    74
                         ↑                 ↑
                        left             right
                        index            index

 25     7    21     1    14    13    54    60    43    74
                               ↑     ↑
                              left  right
                              index index

 25     7    21     1    14    13    54    60    43    74
                               ↑     ↑
                             right  left
                             index  index

 13     7    21     1    14    25    54    60    43    74
                               ↑
                           splitpoint
```

Figure 11.4 Illustration of Splitting Algorithm

Listing 11.6 Quick Sort

```
PROCEDURE quicksort
        ( VAR items : ARRAY OF elementtype    (* in/out *);
              lessthan : lessthantype         (* in *) );

  VAR number : CARDINAL;

  (* Insert procedure split here. *)

  PROCEDURE quick( first, last : INTEGER );
    VAR splitpoint : INTEGER;
```

```
  BEGIN
    IF first < last
    THEN
      split( first, last, splitpoint );
      quick( first, splitpoint - 1 );
      quick( splitpoint + 1, last )
    END (* if then *);
  END quick;

BEGIN
  number := HIGH( items );
  quick( 0, number )
END quicksort;
```

Analysis of Quick Sort

On the first call to split, every item in the list is compared with the selected item using the order relation. Hence, $O(n)$ comparisons are performed. The list of items is then split into two parts, which are examined next. We refer to this configuration as level 1. The total number of comparisons over the two parts in $O(n)$. These two parts are next split into four parts, giving the level 2 configuration. Again the total number of comparisons over the four parts is $O(n)$. If the splits at each level divide each sublist at the level into approximately equal sublists, it takes $O(\log_2 n)$ levels to arrive at sublists of length 1. Since each level requires $O(n)$ comparisons, the quick sort algorithm requires $O(n \log_2 n)$ comparisons. This algorithm should be much quicker than the $O(n^2)$ sorting algorithms presented in section 11.1

However, if the list is in sorted order or reverse order, the splits are lopsided. In these cases it takes $O(n)$ levels to arrive at sublists of length 1, so the quick sort algorithm becomes an $O(n^2)$ algorithm. This is not the case, however, if we modify the splitting algorithm to select the middle item of each sublist as the splitting item rather than the first item.

11.3.2 Merge Sort

The merge sort algorithm is based on merging two ordered sequences of items into a single, ordered sequence. Merging is considered to be a much simpler operation than sorting. Before developing the merge sort algorithm, we need to know how to merge two sorted lists of items thereby creating a third sorted list.

Suppose we have two lists of sorted items that are both contained in the array x. One list is x[low] through x[middle] and the second list is x[middle+1] through x[high]. These two lists are to be merged to form a sorted list z[low] through z[high] in the array z. The basic idea is to examine pairs of items, with respect to the order relation, one from each of the sublists

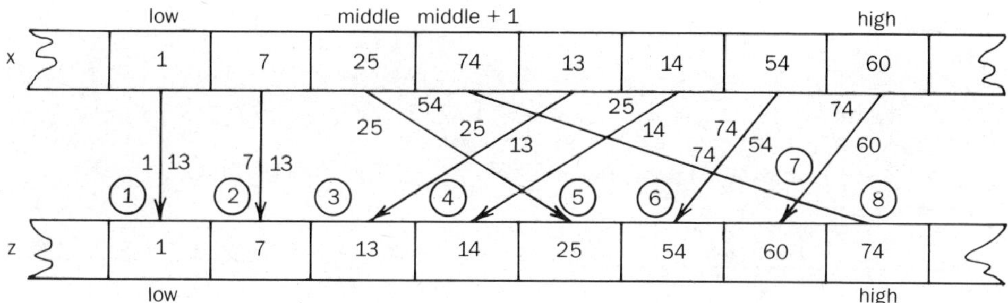

Figure 11.5 Illustration of Merge

of x, and move an item from the appropriate x sublist to the z sublist. When an item is moved from an x sublist, the next item to be considered is the next item in that sublist. This process is continued until one of the x sublists is exhausted, at which point we can simple copy the items in the remaining x sublist to z to obtain the final ordered list. Figure 11.5 illustrates the merge process and Listing 11.7 presents the implementation of the merge algorithm.

Listing 11.7 The Merge Algorithm

```
PROCEDURE merge
        ( VAR x, z : ARRAY OF elementtype      (* in/out *);
              low, middle, high : INTEGER      (* in *) );
  VAR i, k, j, p : INTEGER;
BEGIN
  i := low;
  k := low;
  j := middle + 1;
  WHILE ( i <= middle ) AND ( j <= high ) DO
    IF lessthan( x[ i ], x[ j ] )
    THEN
      z[ k ] := x[ i ];
      INC( i )
    ELSE
      z[ k ] := x[ j ];
      INC( j )
    END (* if then *);
    INC( k )
  END (* while loop *);
  IF i > middle
  THEN
    FOR p := j TO high DO
      z[ k ] := x[ p ];
      INC( k )
    END (* for loop *);
```

```
  ELSE
    FOR p := i TO middle DO
      z[ k ] := x[ p ];
      INC( k )
    END (* for loop *);
  END (* if then *);
END merge;
```

We now show how to use the merge algorithm to develop a two-way merge sort, which we simply refer to as merge sort. This sort begins by interpreting the initial list to be sorted as n sorted lists, each of length 1, where n is the number of items in the initial list. Successive pairs of sublists are then merged to form sorted sublists of length 2. If n is odd, one sublist is of length 1. Successive pairs of these $n/2$ sublists are then merged to form $n/4$ sorted sublists of length 4. This process is continued until we are left with only one list of length n, so that no more merges can occur. The name "two-way merge" refers to the combining of successive pairs of sublists. Figure 11.6 illustrates the process.

We next develop an algorithm to perform one merge pass. This algorithm merges adjacent pairs of sublists of length size from list x to list z. When we get near the end of sublist x, if the length of the remaining list is less than 2*size but larger than size, we merge the list of length size with the shorter list at the end of list x. Otherwise, we copy the short list (length less than size) at the end of list x to the list z. This algorithm is presented in Listing 11.8.

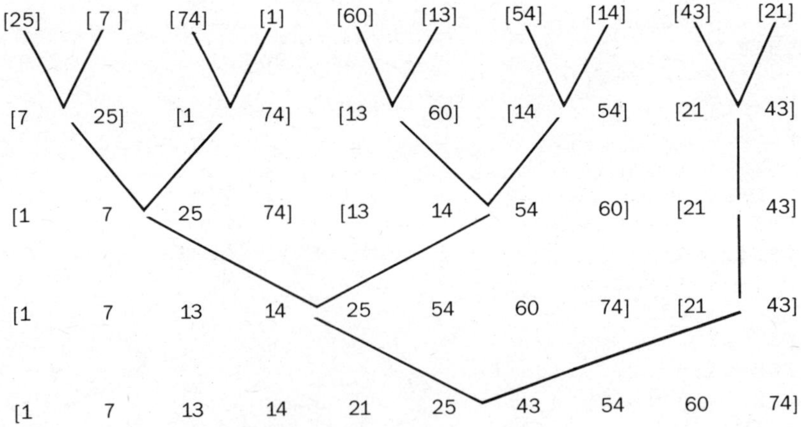

Figure 11.6 Illustration of Merge Sort Process

Listing 11.8 Merge Sort

```
PROCEDURE mergesort
        ( VAR items    : ARRAY OF elementtype (* in/out *);
              lessthan : lessthantype         (* in *) );

  (* Procedure merge goes here. *)

  PROCEDURE mpass( VAR x, z    : ARRAY OF elementtype;
                       n, size : INTEGER );
    VAR i, k : INTEGER;
  BEGIN
    i := 0;
    WHILE  i  <= n - 2 * size DO
      merge( x, z, i, i+size-1, i+2*size-1 );
      INC( i, 2*size )
    END (* while loop *);
    IF i + size - 1 < n
    THEN
      merge( x, z, i, i+size-1, n )
    ELSE
      FOR k := i TO n DO
        z[ k ] := x[ k ]
      END (* for loop *);
    END (* if then *)
  END mpass;


  PROCEDURE msort
          ( VAR items : ARRAY OF elementtype (* in/out *);
                copy  : ARRAY OF elementtype (* in *) );
    VAR size, n  : INTEGER;
  BEGIN
    n := HIGH( items );
    size := 1;
    WHILE size < n + 1 DO
      mpass( items, copy, n, size );
      INC( size, size );
      mpass( copy, items, n, size );
      INC( size, size )
    END (* while loop *)
  END msort;

BEGIN
  msort( items, items )
END mergesort;
```

The complete merge sort algorithm requires us to call the merge pass algorithm a number of times. The merge operation requires an additional copy of the list of items to be sorted. To keep a consistent user interface to the sorting algorithms developed in this chapter, we create the procedure msort, which makes a copy of the items to be sorted. In msort, we perform alternate merges from items to copy and then from copy to items. The while loop of procedure msort exits with the sorted items in the original list. Listing 11.8 presents the complete merge sort algorithm.

Analysis of Merge Sort

An analysis of the merge procedure indicates that each iteration of the while loop increments k by 1 and that the total increment in k is at most high − low + 1. Procedure mpass merges all sublists of x to y by calling merge. This results in the while loop in merge being executed a total of n times for each call to mpass.

The merge sort process implemented in procedure msort requires several passes (calls to mpass) over the list of items to be sorted. In the first pass, sublists of length 1 are merged. In the second pass, the size of the sublists is 2. On the ith pass the sublists being merged are of size $2i$. Hence, at most $log_2 n$ passes are required. Since each merge pass (call to mpass) requires $O(n)$ comparisons, the merge sort algorithm is $O(n \log_2 n)$.

A serious shortcoming of the merge sort algorithm, as presented, is the requirement for additional storage space equivalent in size to that necessary to store the entire initial list of items to be sorted. One of the exercises addresses this storage space concern for merge sort.

11.3.3 Heap Sort

The heap sort algorithm is based on the heap data structure for representing a collection of items. The items in a heap may be of any ordered type. Figure 11.7 shows a heap of 10 integers:

The binary tree in Figure 11.7 is a heap because it satisfies two properties that characterize the heap data structure: order and shape. These properties can be defined as follows:

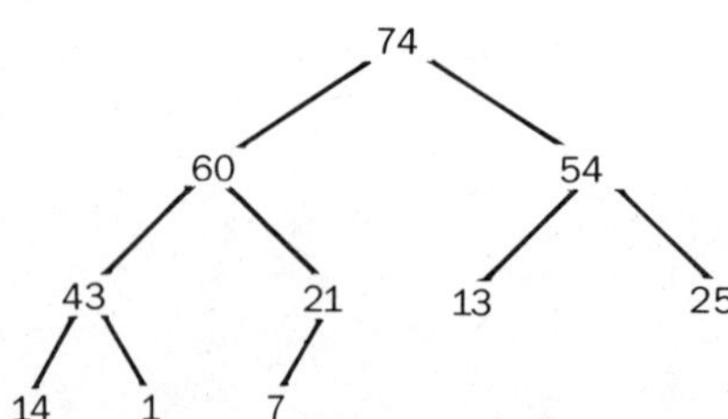

Figure 11.7 Heap of 11 Integers

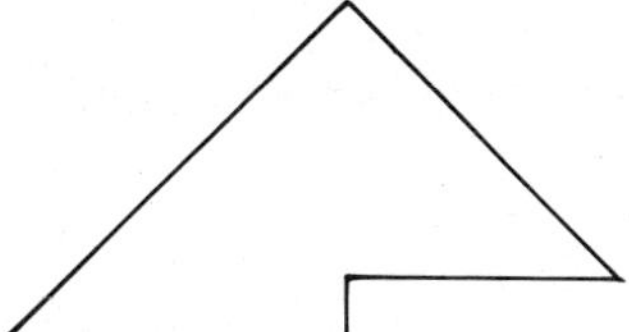

Figure 11.8 The Shape Property

Order. The item at any node must satisfy an order relation with the items of the node's children, e.g., parent larger than its children.

Shape. The binary tree has its terminal nodes on at most two levels, with those on the bottom level as far left as possible.

The order property implies that either the maximum or minimum item is at the root of the tree, depending on the order relation, but it does not imply anything about the relative order of left and right children. The shape property implies that there are no "holes" in the tree. That is, there is a nonnegative integer k such that every terminal node in the tree is at level k or at level $k + 1$, and if a node in the tree has a right child at level $k + 1$, all its left children that are terminal nodes are also at level $k + 1$. Figure 11.8 captures the concept of the shape property. If the tree contains n nodes, no node is more than $\log_2 n$ levels from the root node. By constrast, the binary tree in Figure 11.9 is not a heap because it does not satisfy the shape property. Node 74 has a right child at level 3 (nodes 7 and 10) but a left child at level 2 (node 21).

Let us now turn to the implementation of heaps. There are many representations for heaps, including pointers. Our goal is to sort a list of items stored as an array of a user-defined element type. The array of items can have arbitrary subscripts, but the subscript range in the implementation is from 0 to number where number = HIGH(items). A 12-item tree with shape is implemented as a 12-item array as shown in Figure 11.10.

In this representation of a binary tree, the root node is items[0], its children are items[1] and items[2], and so forth. If item = items[i], the left child of item is items[2 i + 1], the right child of item is items[2 (i + 1)], and the parent of item is items[(i − 1) DIV 2]. The shape property is guaranteed with this representation.

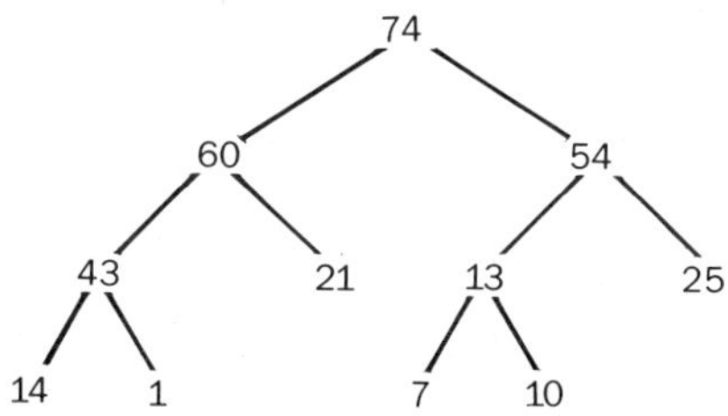

Figure 11.9 Binary Tree That Does Not Satisfy the Shape Property

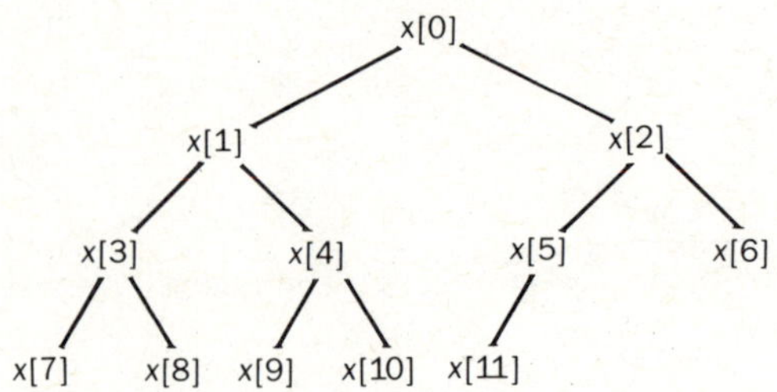

Figure 11.10 Twelve-Item Tree with Shape

Using this representation, the heap property can be restated as follows:

```
for all 1 ≤ i ≤ n,
  lessthan( items[ i ], items[ (i-1) DIV 2 ] )
is true.
```

where lessthan defines the order relation on the list of items. We define the notation heap(p, q) to mean that the order lessthan(items[i], items[(i−1) DIV 2]) is true for $2p + 1 \leq i \leq q$.

We now develop two procedures, siftup and siftdown, for fixing a heap whose heap property has been broken at one end of the heap or the other.

If we start with heap(0, $n-1$), placing an item in items[n] will most likely not yield heap(0, n). The siftup procedure reestablishes the heap in this case. The siftup procedure sifts the new item up the tree as far as it should go, swapping it with its parent along the way. The siftup process is illustrated in Figure 11.11, where the new item 67 is sifted up the heap until it is in its proper position. Listing 11.9 gives the implementation of siftup.

The while loop terminates when item[n] finds its proper position or if $i =$ 0, which means that i has no parent and the heap property holds everywhere. If i has a parent, its index is p and if lessthan(items[i], items[p]) is true, the heap property holds everywhere and we can terminate the loop. If items[i] is out of

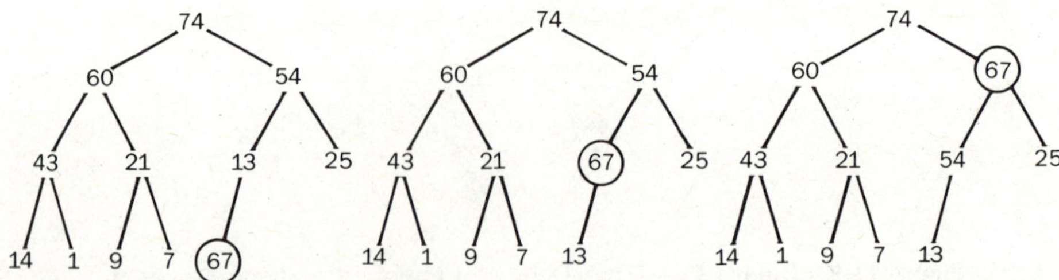

Figure 11.11 Illustration of Siftup

Listing 11.9 Implementation of Siftup

```
PROCEDURE siftup
        ( n : INTEGER                                   (* in *) );
  VAR i, p : INTEGER;
      done : BOOLEAN;
BEGIN
  i := n;
  done := FALSE;
  WHILE ( i > 0 ) AND NOT done DO
    p := (i - 1) DIV 2;
    IF lessthan( items[ i ], items[ p ] )
    THEN
      done := TRUE
    ELSE
      swap( items[ i ], items[ p ] );
      i := p
    END (* end if *)
  END (* end while *)
END siftup;
```

order with its parent, we swap items[i] and items[p]. The siftup procedure has complexity $O(\log_2 n)$ because the heap has that many levels.

If we have heap(1, n), assigning a new item to items[0] is not likely to yield heap(0, n). The siftdown procedure makes heap(0, n) true. The siftdown procedure does this by sifting items[0] down the tree either until it has no children or until it is less than or equal to the children it has. Figure 11.12 shows 18 being sifted down the heap until it satisfies the order relation with respect to its single child. Sifting down requires that an out-of-order item be swapped with its proper child. Listing 11.10 gives the implementation of the siftdown procedure.

The loop in the siftdown procedure is similar to the loop in the siftup procedure. If $c \geq n$ then items[i] has no children, so we terminate the loop. If items[i] has one child, the item with index c is the left child. If there are two children, we set c to the index of the one that does not satisfy the order relation.

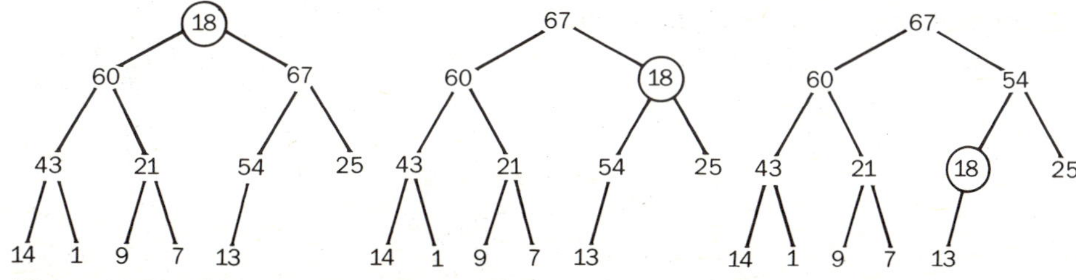

Figure 11.12 Illustration of Siftdown

Listing 11.10 Implementation of Siftdown

```
PROCEDURE siftdown
        ( n : INTEGER                                  (* in *) );
  VAR i, c : INTEGER;
      done : BOOLEAN;
BEGIN
  i := 0;
  c := 0;
  done := FALSE;
  WHILE ( c < n ) AND NOT done DO
    c := 2 * i + 1;
    IF c <= n
    THEN
      IF ( c < n ) AND lessthan( items[ c ], items[ c+1 ] )
      THEN
        INC( c )
      END (* if then *);
      IF lessthan( items[ c ], items[ i ] )
      THEN
        done := TRUE
      ELSE
        swap( items[ c ], items[ i ] );
        i := c
      END (* if then *);
    END (* if then *);
  END (* while *);
END siftdown;
```

If lessthan(items[c], items[i]) is true, we terminate the loop; otherwise we progress toward the bottom of the heap by swapping items[c] and items[i] and assigning i to c.

Like siftup, this procedure has complexity $O(\log_2 n)$, since it does a fixed amount of work at each level of the heap.

We next show how to use the siftup and siftdown procedures to develop the heap sort algorithm, a two-stage process. The first n steps build the array of items into a heap and the second n steps extract the items in order and build the final sorted sequence from right to left.

The first stage is to build the heap. If items[0] to items[$i-1$] form a heap, siftup(i) makes heap(0, i). The starting heap can be created with the following code:

```
number := HIGH( items );
FOR i := 1 TO number DO
  siftup( i )
END (* for loop *);
```

The second stage uses the heap to build the sorted sequence. If items[0] to items[*i*] form a heap and items[i+1] through items[n] are sorted, swapping items[0] and items[i] extends the sorted sequence by one item. That swap probably destroys the heap property for items[0] to items[$i-1$], but we can reestablish the heap property by sifting down the new top element. The second-stage code is:

```
FOR i := number TO 1 BY -1 DO
  swap( items[ 0 ], items[ i ] );
  siftdown( i - 1 )
END (* for loop *)
```

The heap sort algorithm uses $n - 1$ siftups and $n - 1$ siftdowns. Since each of these is $O(\log_2 n)$, the entire heap sort algorithm is $O(n \log_2 n)$.

11.3.4 Complexity of Advanced Sorting Algorithms

The quick sort algorithm has worst-case performance of $O(n^2)$ when the items to be sorted are almost sorted initially. The merge sort algorithm has a complexity of $O(n \log_2 n)$ in the worst case and as its average behavior; however, it requires additional storage proportional to the number of items being sorted. The heap sort algorithm requires essentially no extra storage and is $O(n \log_2 n)$ in all cases.

Which of these advanced sorting algorithms is best? All three algorithms are $O(n \log_2 n)$. The heap sort has a storage advantage over merge sort and a worst-case performance advantage over quick sort. To examine the actual performance of these three sorting algorithms, we repeated our earlier computational experiment of sorting 1000 randomly generated integers between 0 and 10,000. The results, presented in Table 11.4, are in the same units of time as the results in Table 11.3. Note the significant improvement in performance when we use an $O(n \log_2 n)$ algorithm compared to an $O(n^2)$ algorithm.

How important is our choice of sorting algorithm if the list of items to be sorted is small? All the sorting algorithms have some overhead in addition to the number of comparisons. This overhead contributes to the constant of proportionality for the algorithm, which we have ignored in our "big-oh" notation. We have also ignored the lower order terms, which become more significant if n is small. The $O(n \log_2 n)$ sorting algorithms tend to be more complex, with more

TABLE 11.4 Performance of Advanced Sorting Algorithms

Method	Random	Ordered	Inverse Order
Quick sort	7.18	250.13	234.83
Merge sort	8.18	6.30	6.20
Heap sort	16.18	22.40	14.68

TABLE 11.5 Performance of Sorting Algorithms on Small Lists

	Random		Ordered		Inverse Order	
Method	100	16	100	16	100	16
Selection sort	2.53	0.08	2.52	0.08	2.58	0.08
Insertion sort	1.82	0.08	0.12	0.03	3.68	0.10
Bubble sort	3.65	0.12	0.07	0.02	4.80	0.13
Quick sort	0.50	0.05	2.65	0.10	2.63	0.10
Merge sort	0.59	0.07	0.51	0.07	0.48	0.07
Heap sort	1.05	0.10	1.35	0.12	0.92	0.10

overhead and most likely a larger constant of proportionality. These considerations may cause anomalies in the relative performance of the sorting algorithms when n is small. In this case, n^2 is not much larger than $n \log_2 n$, so that an $O(n^2)$ sort may actually run faster than an $O(n \log_2 n)$ sort because of a smaller constant of proportionality. In Table 11.5, we present timing results for all the algorithms in this chapter for lists of 100 and 16 items. Clearly for 16 items, it makes relatively little difference which sorting algorithm is used.

Many of the algorithms presented in this chapter call the swap procedure to interchange two items. It may be desirable for the sake of efficiency to streamline the code by placing the swap procedure in-line. Procedure calls require extra overhead, which we may want to avoid in sorting algorithms.

11.4 More About Sorting and External Sorting

All the sorting algorithms just presented require us to swap items. If the items swapped are large records, the swap operation can be rather costly in computer time. This time can be reduced by defining an array of pointers to the records and then sorting the pointers rather than the actual records. This approach is illustrated in Figure 11.13.

Note that after sorting the items, the records are still in the same physical locations. Only the pointers have been swapped.

This scheme can also be used to sort an array of records with the sort based on several different keys or fields of the record. For example, consider the following declarations:

```
TYPE elementtype = RECORD
                     lastname  : string;
                     firstname : string;
                     salary    : REAL;
                     age       : CARDINAL
                   END (* record *);
```

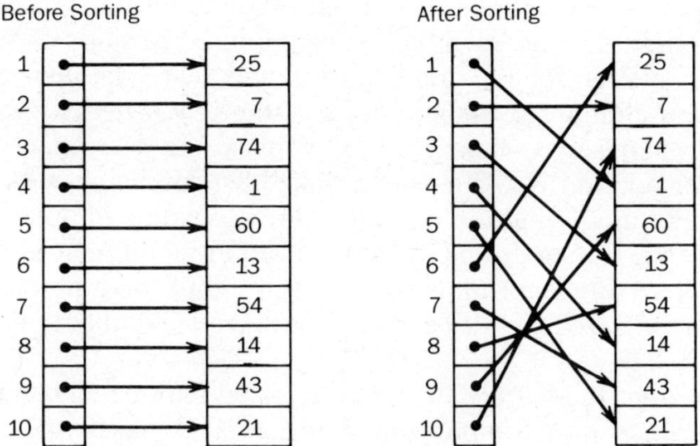

Figure 11.13 Sorting an Array of Records with Pointers

```
VAR employeerecords = ARRAY [ 1 .. numberemployees ] OF
                      elementtype;
```

In Figure 11.14, we show the data physically stored according to the lastname field, the primary key. The arrays salaryorder and ageorder contain pointers to the employee records. This permits us to keep the employee records ordered with respect to salary and age, which are referred to as secondary keys. The salary order is from highest to lowest salary. The age order is from youngest to oldest.

1	Adam John 32000 29
2	Jones Robert 49000 37
3	Madsen Mary 35500 33
4	Olson Richard 45000 52
5	Smith Janet 21000 43

	salaryorder
1	2
2	4
3	3
4	1
5	5

	ageorder
1	1
2	3
3	2
4	5
5	4

Figure 11.14 Sorting Records with Secondary Arrays of Pointers

In Chapter 4, we defined the "place" operation for a linked list, which inserts a new item in the list in its proper ordered position based on a user-defined order relation for the items in the linked list. The construction of the place operation eliminated the need to sort the list of items. But suppose we wish to sort an unsorted linked list of items or to rearrange it based on a different order relation. The items in a linked list can be placed in any desired order by simply modifying the pointer field associated with each node in the linked list. Hence, to sort a linked list we need to modify our implementations of the various sorting algorithms so that we modify the pointer fields of each node in the list to achieve the specified order. We leave these implementations as exercises.

On occasion, the list of items, to be sorted may be so large that the sort cannot be performed in computer memory. In such cases, we must resort to external sorting methods rather than the internal methods presented so far. We assume that the list of items is either stored as a disk file or maintained as a file stored on some other external device such as a magnetic tape. We describe only one external sorting algorithm, the natural merge sort, which is very similar to the merge sort algorithm described earlier.

Suppose we are given a file of records, say C, to sort based on a specified order relation, say lessthan. We define A and B as two auxiliary files to be used in the sort process. The natural merge sort algorithm is based on identifying

```
Identify runs
C     [25]  [7   74]  [1  60] [13   54] [14   43] [21]

Distribute
A     [25]        [ 1    60]  [14    43]
B     [7    74] [13    54]   [21]

Merse
C      [7    25   74]  [1   13   54   60] [14   21    43]

Distribute
A      [7    25   74]          [14 21      43]
B      [1    13   54    60]

Merse
C      [1     7   13    25   54   60    74] [14   21    43]

Distribute
A     [ 1     7   13    25   54   60    74]
B     [14    21   43]

Merse
C      [1     7   13    14   21   25    43    54    60   74]
```

Figure 11.15 Illustration of Natural Merge Sort with Files

subsequences that satisfy the order relation. These subsequences are called runs. Merging is the process of combining two or more runs into a single run.

Each pass of the merge sort algorithm consists of a distribution phase and a merge phase. The distribution phase distributes runs from C onto A and B alternately. The merge phase merges runs from A and B back again to C. This process is illustrated in Figure 11.15. Runs are enclosed in brackets.

The natural merge sort algorithm is $O(n \log_2 n)$, but disk seek time and disk read or write time can have a significant impact on the overall efficiency of the algorithm. The implementation of this algorithm is left as an exercise.

11.5 Searching

Previously defined structures that can be used to hold data include linked lists, search trees, and hash tables. Often the objective is to be able to access the data efficiently. In this section, we describe two methods for searching for a specified item in a sorted list of items. We consider only internal searching, where the sorted list is stored completely in memory.

The interface to our search procedures should be compatible with the interface already defined for our sort procedures. The sort procedures required an order relation on the items to be sorted. The search procedures not only need the same order relation for the items in the list but also need an equality relation that specifies the meaning of equality for two items.

What information should be returned by a search procedure? The search should return the position of the specified item in the list if the search is successful; otherwise, it should return an error indicator or an illegal value for position. However, if we use the open-array type to pass the list of items to the search procedure, the search procedure has no knowledge of the subscript range or subscript type used to reference the items in the list. This means that the search procedure can return only the relative position or offset that the desired item is from the beginning of the list. Thus position is a value between 0 and HIGH(items). If the specified item is not in the list, the search procedure returns the illegal position value of -1.

The interface to our search procedures is presented in Listing 11.11.

Listing 11.11 Searching Interface

```
DEFINITION MODULE searching;

  FROM elements IMPORT
    (* type *) elementtype;

  EXPORT QUALIFIED
    (* proc *) search;
```

```
  TYPE equaltype =    PROCEDURE( elementtype, elementtype ):
                                 BOOLEAN;

       lessthantype = PROCEDURE( elementtype, elementtype ):
                                 BOOLEAN;

  PROCEDURE search
         ( VAR items    : ARRAY OF elementtype (* in *);
               item     : elementtype          (* in *);
           VAR position : INTEGER              (* out *);
               equal    : equaltype            (* in *);
               lessthan : lessthantype         (* in *) );

END searching.
```

11.5.1 Linear Search/Sequential Search

The simplest search algorithm is the linear or sequential search. We begin with the first item in the list and examine each subsequent item until the desired item is found or the list is exhausted. This search algorithm can be used on sorted as well as unsorted lists. However, if the list is sorted, we can improve the efficiency of the algorithm by terminating the search before the list is exhausted if the specified item is not in its ordered position in the list.

The implementation of this search procedure is given in Listing 11.12.

Listing 11.12 Linear Search

```
PROCEDURE linearsearch
       ( VAR items    : ARRAY OF elementtype (* in *);
             item     : elementtype          (* in *);
         VAR position : INTEGER              (* out *);
             equal    : equaltype            (* in *);
             lessthan : lessthantype         (* in *) );
  VAR index : CARDINAL;
      found : BOOLEAN;
BEGIN
  index := 1;
  position := -1;
  found := FALSE;
  IF equal( item, items[ 0 ] )
  THEN
    position := 0
  ELSE
```

```
    WHILE ( index <= HIGH( items ) ) AND
            NOT lessthan( item, items[ index-1 ] ) AND
            NOT found DO
      IF equal( item, items[ index ] )
      THEN
        found := TRUE;
        position := index
      ELSE
        INC( index )
      END (* if then *)
    END (* while loop *)
  END (* if then *)
END linearsearch;
```

The while loop uses the user-defined lessthan procedure to compare item with items[index−1]. This may seem a bit strange at first, but since the user-defined order relation can be in the terms of <, <=, >, or >=, we must permit the loop to increment index, possibly one time too many, so that the equality check can be performed on all items in the list that can be equal to the specified item, regardless of how the order relation is defined. The structure of the while loop necessitates the special check for equality of the item with items[0].

Analysis of Linear Search

In the worst case, the while loop is executed $n - 1$ times with a total of n checks for equality, where n is the number of items in the list. On the average we would expect $n/2$ checks for equality regardless of whether the specified item is in the list. Hence, linear search is $O(n)$.

11.5.2 Binary Search

A version of the binary search procedure was presented in Chapter 6 as a recursive algorithm. The basic idea of binary search is to examine the middle item in the list. If the middle item is the specified item, we stop searching. If the order relation between the specified item and the middle item is satisfied, we binary search the first half of the list; otherwise we binary search the second half.

The implementation of the binary search algorithm is given in Listing 11.13.

Listing 11.13 Binary Search

```
PROCEDURE binarysearch
        ( VAR items    : ARRAY OF elementtype     (* in *);
              item     : elementtype              (* in *);
```

```
        VAR position : INTEGER                          (* out *);
            equal    : equaltype                        (* in *);
            lesthan  : lessthantype                     (* in *) );


PROCEDURE search
        (      low, high : INTEGER                    (* in *);
           VAR position  : INTEGER                    (* out *) );
  VAR middle : INTEGER;
BEGIN
  IF low <= high
  THEN
    middle := ( low + high ) DIV 2;
    IF equal( item, items[ middle ] )
    THEN
      position := middle
    ELSIF lessthan( item, items[ middle ] )
    THEN
      search( low, middle - 1, position )
    ELSE
      search( middle + 1, high, position )
    END (* if then *);
  ELSE
    position := -1
  END (* if then *);
END search;

BEGIN
  search( 0, HIGH( items ), position )
END binarysearch;
```

Analysis of Binary Search

Each recursive call to search halves the size of the list left to be searched. Hence, the maximum number of comparisons is $\log_2 n$ and so binary seach $O(\log_2 n)$. For small lists, binary search may not be more efficient than linear search because of the extra overhead associated with the former.

Exercises

11.1 Sort 1000 randomly generated real numbers and develop a table similar to Tables 11.3 and 11.4.

11.2 Generate 1000 records containing the following record structure:

```
RECORD
   lastname   : string;
   firstname  : string:
```

```
      salary      : REAL;
      age         : CARDINAL
   END;
```

Sort these records on the salary field and compare the execution time with that obtained in exercise 11.1.

11.3 Place all the sorting algorithms developed in this chapter together into one sorting module by defining an appropriate definition module and a corresponding implementation module.

11.4 A sorting algorithm is called stable if for all records i and j such that the key field of items[i] is equal to the key field of items[j], if items[i] precedes items[j] in the original list, then items[i] precedes items[j] in the sorted list. Which of the sorting algorithms described in this chapter are stable? Does the user-defined order relation that is specified in the lessthantype procedure affect the stability of a sorting algorithm?

11.5 Modify the insertion sort algorithm so that it is defined for a linked list. Instead of physically moving a record, modify the link fields to reflect the change in position of that record in the linked list.

11.6 Modify the quick sort algorithm so that the splitting item is selected as the middle item in that part of the list under consideration. Perform some computational experiments to determine the performance of the modified algorithm on random data, sorted data, and data in reverse order. Rework this problem, selecting the splitting item randomly using a random number generator.

11.7 Implement quick sort as a nonrecursive algorithm using the stack ADT. The stack contains the left and right indices of the items yet to be sorted. These indices can be determined using the split procedure.

11.8 The radix sort for sorting an array integers uses 10 queues, one for each of the digits 0 through 9. The algorithm examines the integers to be sorted one digit at a time, starting with the rightmost (least significant) digit. The steps are:

(a) Examine the least significant digits and move each integer to the appropriate queue.

(b) Reconstruct the array of integers by concatenating the elements in the queues in order from 0 through 9.

(c) Repeat steps a and b on the second digit, third digit, and so on, until all digits have been examined, at which time the array of integers is in order.

Implement the radix sort using the queue ADT.

11.9 Modify the siftdown procedure so that given heap(p+1, q), the siftdown procedure forms heap(p, q). What is the complexity of this procedure? Show how it can be used to build an n-item heap in $O(n)$.

Use this siftdown procedure to construct a heap sort algorithm. Is your heap sort algorithm faster than the one presented in the text?

11.10 Modify the merge sort algorithm by making one pass over the initial list to be sorted to determine sequences of items that satisfy the order relation and then use these as the initially sorted sublists. This modified algorithm, called natural merge sort, takes into account the existing order in the initial list of items. What is the complexity of this algorithm on an initially ordered list?

11.11 Modify algorithm merge so that it merges two sublists of array x without the additional array y. Try to develop a merge algorithm that uses as little extra storage space as possible but still has complexity $O(n)$. As an alternative, use some ideas presented in connection with the insertion sort. In the alternative case, is the complexity still $O(n)$? Use this modified merge algorithm to develop a recursive merge sort algorithm as follows:

```
PROCEDURE msort( low, high : CARDINAL );
  VAR middle : CARDINAL;
BEGIN
  IF low <> high
  THEN
    middle := ( low + high ) DIV 2;
    msort( low, middle );
    msort( middle + 1, high );
    merge( low, middle, high )
  END (* if then *)
END msort;
```

We assume that x is a global variable that is visible to msort.

11.12 Develop and implement the merge sort algorithm for linked lists.

11.13 Implement the natural merge sort algorithm for files that is described in section 11.4. Perform timing comparisons between this external sorting algorithm and the internal merge sort algorithm presented in Listing 11.8.

11.14 Perform computational experiments using linear search and binary search to find specified items at various positions in the ordered list. Generate a table that gives timing comparisons for lists of various sizes.

12

Memory Management

12.1 The Issues in Memory Management

Throughout, we have tended to implement abstract data types as opaque types. An opaque type can be any type, but compilers usually impose implementation restrictions. Typically, in Modula-2 opaque types are implemented as an address of storage so that the compiler can allocate memory storage. However, since most of the interesting ADTs presented in this book require more than one word of memory for the underlying data structure, we were forced to use pointer variables and dynamic storage allocation. We did not worry about the scheme used to allocate computer memory—we simply used the scheme provided with the Modula-2 implementation we were using.

In some cases, we did do our own storage management for our abstract data type. For example, we implemented a stack, a queue, and a list in an array of records. We did our own storage management in these implementations. This was rather simple, since each new node was the same size and the address of the nodes was just an index into the array.

In this chapter, we examine how the computer system allocates and deallocates dynamic storage. In a multiuser system, the operating system must allocate blocks of memory for user programs and data. These typically large blocks are allocated and deallocated rather infrequently as new jobs enter and finished jobs leave the system. Since the blocks are large, the hardware configuration usually influences the allocation scheme. In addition, each user program may also allocate and deallocate blocks of memory while executing. Typically these are small blocks that are frequently allocated and deallocated, such as for nodes of a stack, list, or tree.

The performance of a memory management system is influenced by factors such as the statistical distribution of the size of the memory requests, the lengths of time the blocks of memory are required, and the frequency of requests and releases of memory. A memory management scheme can be optimized for large blocks and infrequent allocation or for small blocks and frequent allocation, but it is virtually impossible to devise a memory management scheme that is optimal for allocation and deallocation requests of all kinds.

For these reasons a number of memory management systems have been devised for different applications. Some of the most common are known by the names first-fit, best-fit, and the buddy system. The interested reader is referred to Knuth (1968) and Tremblay and Sorenson (1976) for more detailed discussions on memory management.

The memory management process is simple to describe. The system must maintain a list of all the blocks of memory. Some of these blocks will be free and some will be currently allocated to a user. When an allocation request is made, the system must locate a free block of memory of sufficient size and allocate all or part of it. When a deallocation request is made, the system must recover the deallocated block of memory. In addition, the system should be able to find adjacent free blocks and combine them into a single larger block, to maximize the probability of being able to satisfy a large allocation request.

The interesting feature of the memory management process is the allocation and deallocation of variable size blocks of memory. The memory can become fragmented if a large number of blocks of memory are allocated and later deallocated but adjacent free blocks are not combined. This causes the average free block size to become small and large blocks to become scarce. When an allocation request is made, it may fail because there is no single block of memory large enough, even though the total amount of available memory is much larger than the requested amount. On the other hand, we might attempt to inhibit small blocks by allocating blocks that are larger than the requested size if splitting a block would result in a small block on the free list. In this case, we waste space by allocating more than is requested and as a consequence may not be able to satisfy a later allocation request even though the amount of wasted space is more than adequate to satisfy the request.

We begin our implementation of a memory management system by defining in Listing 12.1 the definition module for the system. The definition module

Listing 12.1 The Storage Management Definition Module

```
DEFINITION MODULE STORAGE;

  FROM  SYSTEM IMPORT
    (* type *) ADDRESS;

  EXPORT QUALIFIED
    (* proc *) ALLOCATE, DEALLOCATE;
```

```
  PROCEDURE ALLOCATE
          ( VAR  blockaddress : ADDRESS       (* out *);
                 blocksize    : CARDINAL      (* in  *) );

  PROCEDURE DEALLOCATE
          ( VAR  blockaddress : ADDRESS       (* in/out *);
                 blocksize    : CARDINAL      (* in *) );

END STORAGE.
```

exports two operations, ALLOCATE and DEALLOCATE, through which the user can access the storage management system. Each operation has two parameters: the address and the size of the block to be allocated or deallocated. Since the ADDRESS data type is compatible with all pointer types, it is possible to allocate and deallocate storage for variables identified by any pointer type. Notice that this definition module is essentially identical to the module Storage, which is part of a Modula-2 system. Our intent here is to illustrate a possible implementation for this Modula-2 module.

12.2 A First-Fit Storage Management System

The first-fit storage management scheme is very simple. The free blocks of memory are linked together in a list that is not ordered with respect to memory locations or the size of the free blocks. When an allocation request is received, the list is searched for the first block large enough to satisfy the request, as suggested by the name "first-fit." That block is removed from the list. If it is larger than the requested size, it is broken into two blocks: one is given to the requesting program and the other is placed back on the free list.

The implementation for the first-fit storage management scheme, given in Listing 12.2, is reprinted by permission from Ford and Wiener (1985).

Listing 12.2 First-Fit Storage Implementation

```
IMPLEMENTATION MODULE STORAGE;

(* This module maintains a linked list of free blocks.  It
   uses a first-fit allocation algorithm to allocate storage
   from a statically allocated first block.                *)

  FROM InOut IMPORT
    (* proc *) WriteLn, WriteCard, WriteString;
```

```
FROM SYSTEM IMPORT
  (* type *) ADDRESS, WORD,
  (* proc *) TSIZE, ADR;
CONST
  maxblocksize = 1000; (* size of first block *)
TYPE
  storageunit = WORD;     (* Memory unit for storage
                             allocation.                    *)
  freeblockptr = POINTER TO freeblock;
  freeblock    = RECORD
                   blocksize : CARDINAL;
                   next      : freeblockptr
                 END (* record *);

VAR
  minblocksize : CARDINAL;
  freelist     : freeblockptr;
  firstblock   : ARRAY [ 1..maxblocksize ] OF storageunit;


PROCEDURE failure;
(* Allocation failure procedure.  This procedure should be
   modified to print an appropriate message, abort
   execution, etc. depending on the application.           *)
BEGIN
  WriteLn;
  WriteString( 'Allocation failure.' );
  WriteLn
END failure;


PROCEDURE insertblock
        ( block : freeblockptr              (* in *) );
  (* Inserts block at the front of the freelist.            *)
BEGIN
  block^.next := freelist;
  freelist := block
END insertblock;


PROCEDURE removeblockafter
        ( block : freeblockptr              (* in *) );
  (* Removes block from the freelist.                       *)
BEGIN
  IF block <> NIL
  THEN  (* Block is not first in the free list *)
    block^.next := block^.next^.next
  ELSE  (* Block is first in the free list *)
    freelist := freelist^.next
  END (* if then *)
END removeblockafter;
```

```
PROCEDURE ALLOCATE
        ( VAR  blockaddress : ADDRESS        (* out *);
               blocksize    : CARDINAL       (* in  *) );
  VAR
    actualsize   : CARDINAL;
    newblock     : freeblockptr;
    testblock    : freeblockptr;
    prevblock    : freeblockptr;
    blockfound   : BOOLEAN;


BEGIN
  actualsize := blocksize + TSIZE( CARDINAL );
  IF actualsize < minblocksize
  THEN
    actualsize := minblocksize
  ELSIF ODD( actualsize )
  THEN
    INC( actualsize )
  END (* if then *);
  testblock := freelist;
  prevblock := NIL;
  blockfound := FALSE;
  WHILE NOT blockfound AND ( testblock <> NIL ) DO
    IF testblock^.blocksize >= actualsize
    THEN  (* Block of sufficient size found. *)
      blockfound := TRUE;
      IF testblock^.blocksize - actualsize < minblocksize
      THEN  (* Allocate the entire block. *)
        removeblockafter( prevblock );
        newblock := testblock
      ELSE  (* Allocate only a piece of the block. *)
        testblock^.blocksize := testblock^.blocksize -
                                actualsize;
        newblock := freeblockptr( CARDINAL( testblock ) +
                                  testblock^.blocksize );
        newblock^.blocksize := actualsize
      END (* if then *)
    ELSE  (* Advance to next block. *)
      prevblock := testblock;
      testblock := testblock^.next
    END (* if then *)
  END (* while loop *);
  IF blockfound
  THEN
    blockaddress := freeblockptr( CARDINAL( newblock ) +
                                  TSIZE( CARDINAL ) )
  ELSE
    failure
  END (* if then *)
```

```
END ALLOCATE;
PROCEDURE DEALLOCATE
        ( VAR blockaddress : ADDRESS      (* in/out *);
              blocksize    : CARDINAL     (* in *) );
  VAR
    releasedblock     : freeblockptr;
    testblock         : freeblockptr;
    prevblock         : freeblockptr;
    combinedbefore    : BOOLEAN;
    combinedafter     : BOOLEAN;

 BEGIN
  releasedblock := freeblockptr(CARDINAL( blockaddress ) -
                                   TSIZE( CARDINAL ) );
  testblock := freelist;
  prevblock := NIL;
  combinedbefore := FALSE;
  combinedafter  := FALSE;
  WHILE NOT ( combinedbefore AND combinedafter ) AND
            ( testblock <> NIL ) DO
    IF freeblockptr( CARDINAL( testblock ) +
               testblock^.blocksize ) = releasedblock
    THEN  (* Testblock is immediately before released
             block. *)
      removeblockafter( prevblock );
      testblock^.blocksize := testblock^.blocksize +
                               releasedblock^.blocksize;
      releasedblock := testblock;
      combinedbefore := TRUE
    ELSIF freeblockptr( CARDINAL( releasedblock ) +
                releasedblock^.blocksize ) = testblock
    THEN  (* Testblock is immediately after released
             block. *)
      removeblockafter( prevblock );
      INC(releasedblock^.blocksize,
        testblock^.blocksize);
      combinedafter := TRUE
    ELSE  (* No combining possible; advance to next
             block. *)
      prevblock := testblock
    END (* if then *);
    testblock := testblock^.next
  END (* while *);
  (* Put the released block at the front of the free block
     list. *)
  insertblock( releasedblock )
 END DEALLOCATE;

BEGIN
 minblocksize := TSIZE( CARDINAL )  +  TSIZE( ADDRESS );
```

```
  (* Put the static first block in the free list. *)
  freelist := ADR( firstblock );
  freelist^.blocksize := maxblocksize;
  freelist^.next := NIL
END STORAGE.
```

Let us begin by examining how we should maintain our linked list of free blocks. We must have space for pointers, but since a free block contains storage that is not currently in use, we put these pointers in the free block. We also put the size of the free block into each block. To access these two values, we define the freeblock data type and use a type transfer function to superimpose a record of this type on each free block.

For each used block we will also store the size of the block. This eliminates the need for the user program to save the size of each dynamically allocated data structure. This also enables us to modify our interface to the DEALLOCATION operation so that only the address of the block need be specified.

We now describe the allocation procedure. First, the actual size of the block required to satisfy the request is determined. The requested size is increased by enough space to accommodate the block size field and if the resulting size is odd, we increment the request to make the actual size of the block even. This is done because on many computer systems, storage blocks can be used more easily if they begin at addresses that are a multiple of 2 or 4; we assume 2 here. The actual size is also required to be greater than or equal to a specified minimum block size.

The allocation procedure then performs a linear search of the free block list looking for a block that is large enough to satisfy the request. It removes the first such block from the list and tries to break it into two blocks. One block, the bottom portion of the split block, goes to the user to satisfy the request, and the other is put back on the free list. If the leftover block is smaller than a specified minimum block size, the user is given the entire block rather than just a piece. If no block of sufficient size is found, the system fails. The address sent to the user is the address of the free storage immediately following the block size field.

The deallocation procedure first determines the actual address of the block to be released by decreasing the specified address to the address of the block size field. The list of free blocks is then searched to find adjacent blocks that can be combined. Two blocks are found to be adjacent if the address plus the size of one block equals the address of the other block. If an adjacent block is found, it is removed from the free block list and combined with the deallocated block. The resulting larger block is placed back in the free block list. If the procedure recognizes that two blocks have been combined, it stops searching the free list, since there can be at most one block before and one block after the deallocated block.

The implementation uses the two private procedures: insertblock and removeblockafter. These two procedures manipulate the free block list for the allocate and deallocation procedures.

This implementation does not allocate storage from the heap, since we declare one large static block of storage. When this block of storage is used up, the system will fail. A failure procedure is provided to report failure, but it should be modified by the user to attempt recovery or to abort the program, depending on the application.

The module initialization code specifies the minimum size of a free block to be the size of a CARDINAL plus the size of an ADDRESS. Then the one large block of storage is placed in the free block list.

To illustrate this storage allocation system, we make the following storage allocations: 100, 200, 300, 50, 150, and 75 words. Then we deallocate 300, 150, and 50, followed by an allocation of 350. Figure 12.1 illustrates the memory configuration initially, after the first six allocations, and then after each deallocation and the final allocation.

The preceding first-fit storage allocation scheme can be used with any of the ADT implementations presented in this book. We simply need to change the calls to NEW and DISPOSE to ALLOCATE and DEALLOCATE, respectively. We can use the TSIZE or SIZE operations available in module SYSTEM to determine the size parameter in ALLOCATE.

Since our implementation of the first-fit storage allocation scheme uses a statically allocated block of storage, we could save this block of storage on some peripheral storage unit such as a disk for later use. However, since we use actual computer addresses in this implementation, we may encounter several problems. For example, if we modify the program by declaring new variables, these may be assigned to the same memory locations previously used by the storage allocation scheme. In a multiple-user system, it is very unlikely that our program and code space will occupy the same computer memory locations as on a prior run. These circumstances suggest that we modify our implementation so that the address within the block of storage is relative to the actual address of the starting location of the block of storage. We can then save the block of storage for later use and be assured that there will be no address problems. We leave these modifications to the exercises.

The first-fit implementation is relatively slow in execution speed primarily because both allocation and deallocation require searching potentially long lists of free blocks. It is also subject to failure because it begins with a single large statically allocated block of fixed size. Nevertheless, it is simple to implement, and it illustrates all the concepts associated with dynamic storage allocation.

The objective in considering other storage allocation and deallocation algorithms is to achieve better performance and reliability for a given application. We now briefly describe some of these. The reader is referred to Tremblay and Sorenson (1976) or Knuth (1968) for additional information.

The best-fit approach searches the entire free list for the smallest block of storage that will satisfy the request. This approach tends to save large blocks until they are needed to satisfy a large request. However, the best-fit approach tends to produce large numbers of very small free blocks that are inadequate to

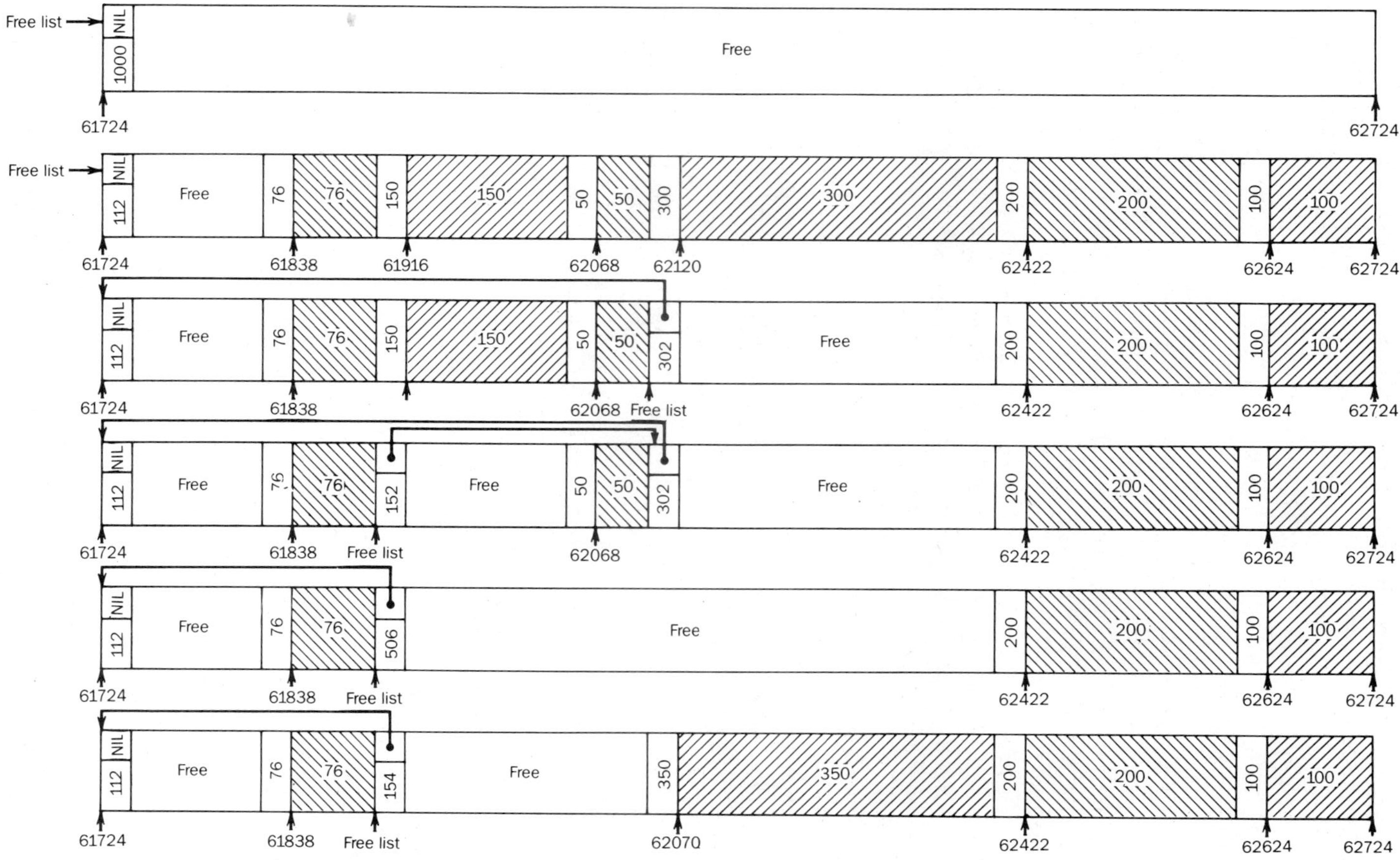

Figure 12.1 Illustration of the First-Fit Storage Allocation System

satisfy most requests. This approach is less efficient than first-fit because it requires that the entire free list be searched for each request.

In both the first-fit and best-fit methods, we made no assumptions on the order of the free list. If the free list is ordered by size, the search time for the best-fit strategy could be reduced. If the order is ascending, first-fit becomes best-fit. If the order is descending, first-fit would take the first block on the free list, since it is largest. Always using the largest block to satisfy storage requests generates many small blocks and is sometimes referred to as worst-fit.

We might also consider ordering the free list by address. This would not affect the search time for blocks to satisfy the allocation request, but it could improve the efficiency of the deallocation scheme. Blocks sorted by address can easily be checked to determine whether they are contiguous, hence should be merged into a single block.

A modification to the first-fit strategy that has been observed to decrease search time is to start a search for a suitable block at the position that the previous search ended. This approach tends to distribute smaller blocks uniformly over the entire list rather than having most of them concentrated near the front.

Another approach to improving the efficiency of the deallocation scheme is referred to as the boundary tag method in which blocks are marked, to permit us to determine, without traversing the free list, whether the predecessor and successor blocks of any block are part of the free list. To do this we examine the two words of storage immediately preceding and following the block to be deallocated. One of these locations contains a flag to indicate whether that block is allocated; the other location contains the size of the block. If we know the size of the preceding block, it is easy to calculate its starting address. This method eliminates searching during the deallocation process but requires us to maintain the free list as a doubly linked list. It also requires more storage, since we need a flag field and a size field at each end of an allocated block of storage. For an unallocated block we need the same fields plus two additional fields to maintain the free list as a doubly linked list. For additional details see Knuth.

Another approach to storage management is to restrict the size of blocks to some fixed set of sizes. To eliminate searches during allocation, we keep separate free lists for each possible block size. When we receive a storage request for a block of a specified size, we access the appropriate list and remove the first block. A request that is not one of the fixed set of sizes is satisfied by allocating a larger block than was requested. This results in some unused storage, but it is a reasonable price to pay for faster allocation. If the fixed size list required to satisfy the request is empty, a block of larger size is split into subblocks, called buddies. The size of these subblocks must be in the prespecified fixed set of sizes. This process is continued until a block of the required size is available.

To eliminate searches during deallocation, we need a method for locating any free block that is adjacent to the block being deallocated. This can be easily achieved by allowing a block to be combined only with its buddy. The address of its buddy can be determined because the sizes of the blocks are fixed relative to one another. The problem with this approach is that two blocks may be contiguous but cannot be merged, since they are not buddies.

The usual approach to implementing such a storage scheme is to define the fixed sizes according to some pattern such as a recurrence relation. The Fibonacci buddy system is based on the Fibonacci number sequence: 1, 1, 2, 3, 5, 8, 13, 21, 34, 55, ... Each term in this sequence, except the first two, can be determined as the sum of the previous two terms. This number sequence defines the fixed set of block sizes allowed. When a block is split into smaller blocks during the allocation process, it is split into blocks, buddies, whose sizes are the previous two terms in the sequence. For additional discussions on this approach to memory management see Tremblay and Sorenson (1976) or Ford and Wiener (1985). Ford and Wiener implement the Fibonacci buddy system in Modula-2.

12.3 Using the Heap

We have just described several methods for allocating and freeing storage. It is easy to determine when to dynamically allocate storage—this is done when the programmer requests it. However, freeing such storage is a more complicated matter. We defined a deallocation procedure for the programmer to use, thereby placing this responsibility in the hands of the programmer. However, it is easy for the programmer to forget to deallocate storage that is assigned to temporary variables. In such cases, this storage is not part of the free list, hence is not available for future use by the program. A more serious problem is the dangling reference or pointer problem. We briefly discuss the subtleties of freeing dynamic storage and the dangling pointer problem in this section. The reader is referred to Tremblay and Sorenson (1976) for additional discussion on these topics.

The definition modules for most of the abstract data types we defined contained several operations related directly to dynamic storage allocation. The define operation initializes objects of the ADT by assigning a NIL pointer or by dynamically allocating and initializing a header node. The makeempty operation deallocates all dynamically allocated storage associated with objects of the ADT. Failure to use the define procedure typically results in an execution error. Failure to use the makeempty operation does not give rise to any execution errors but causes us to lose access to storage in the heap, since dynamically allocated storage is not returned to the free list. If the user is using the DEALLOCATE procedure directly, catastrophic errors may arise because this procedure does not necessarily set a released pointer to NIL.

Also associated with dynamic allocation is the dangling pointer problem, mentioned above. A dangling pointer is a pointer variable that still exists in the program but points to a block of storage that has been released. If this pointer variable is used after the same block of storage has been reallocated for a totally different purpose, catastrophic errors can result. The following program segment illustrates this problem:

```
TYPE realptr = POINTER TO REAL;
     intptr  = POINTER TO INTEGER;

VAR  r          : realptr;
     i,j        : intptr;

BEGIN
  NEW( i );
  i^ := 5;
  j  := i;
  DISPOSE( i );
  (* j is now a dangling pointer *)
  NEW( r );
  r^ := 2.0;
  WriteLn;
  WriteString( ' j = ' );
  WriteInt( j^, 4 );
  . . .
```

After we have deallocated storage associated with the variable *i*, the variable *j* still points to the storage block originally allocated to *i*, even though this storage block is back on the free list. If the allocation request for *r* allocates the same block of storage for *r* and assigns the real value 2 to that memory location, the dereferenced value for *j* in the WriteInt statement will not have a value of 5.

The problem of freeing dynamically allocated storage and detecting dangling pointers can be interpreted as an operating system problem if it can be resolved at that level. Can the operating system or run-time environment detect whether dynamically allocated blocks of storage are currently in use? The answer to this question is yes! When the operating system detects that such storage is not in use, it should return it to the free list. Methods for doing this are called garbage collection algorithms, and blocks of storage that were once needed but are now unused are called garbage.

Modula-2 provides a deallocation procedure for releasing dynamically allocated blocks of storage. The underlying operating system or run-time environment may also have a garbage collection routine. Some languages may not define a deallocation procedure but place the entire issue of garbage collection into the particular implementation and underlying operating system.

There are several approaches to automatic garbage collection. One is to free no storage at all until almost none is left. Another is to free each block as soon as it becomes unused. The first approach requires the interruption of normal program execution to permit the system to invoke a special garbage collection routine. Such a routine traces all access paths from all program and system variables to allocated blocks of storage. These blocks of storage are marked so that a subsequent scan of the entire memory can return unmarked blocks to the free list and reset the marks on the marked blocks in preparation for the next call to the garbage collection routine. The second approach requires more run-time checking, since it is usually implemented using counters that record how many pointers in the program reference each dynamically allocated block of storage. When the reference count has a value of zero, the block is inaccessible and is returned to the free list. In either case, the dangling pointer problem is resolved because a block of storage is returned to the free list only if there are not variables that reference it.

The final question we address is: Can we develop a more powerful abstraction in Modula-2 for opaque types so that the preceding problems are eliminated independent of the underlying run-time environment? To accomplish this, we would need to keep a use count for every object of the ADT. The use count would be an indicator of how many pointers currently reference the object. When the use count has a value of zero, the dynamic block of storage associated with the object can be deallocated. Whenever an opaque value parameter is passed to a procedure, that object's use count is incremented. An opaque VAR parameter does not change the use count of the object. The effect of assignment of an expression's value to a variable and value returning procedures on use count is more complicated and must be handled carefully. Such a scheme would complicate the implementation of abstract data types but would result in more robust implementations with no impact on the user interface. Additional details on this approach are presented by Bilbe (1985).

Exercises

12.1 The STORAGE module of a Modula-2 system contains the operation Available with the following interface:

```
PROCEDURE Available ( size : CARDINAL ) : BOOLEAN;
```

This procedure returns TRUE if a block of storage of the specified size can be allocated. Add this interface to the definition module STORAGE given in Listing 12.1 and implement and test the procedure.

12.2 Use the STORAGE module with a previously implemented ADT. Verify that it works correctly. Note that you will have to change NEW and DISPOSE calls to ALLOCATE and DEALLOCATE calls, respectively.

12.3 Define the interface and implement two additional procedures in STORAGE. Your new procedures should allow you to store the dynamic memory management space as a file on disk and to restore the dynamic memory management space to memory from a disk file. Note that you must modify the current implementation so that all addresses are relative to the starting address of the dynamic memory management space. This must be done, since if the dynamic memory management space is loaded back to memory, it may end up residing in different locations.

12.4 Implement the DISPOSE operation by translating it to a call to the DEALLOCATE operation. The interface to the DISPOSE operation is:

```
PROCEDURE DISPOSE( VAR p : ADDRESS );
```

We can easily do this, since the size of the storage block at the address p was saved with the block when the block was allocated using the ALLOCATE procedure. What problems, if any, are encountered in trying to implement the NEW operation by translating it to a call to the ALLOCATE operation? The interface to NEW is:

```
PROCEDURE NEW( VAR p : ADDRESS );
```

12.5 Implement the best-fit storage management scheme. Perform some simulation experiments to analyze the performance of the best-fit scheme in comparison to the first-fit scheme. See Knuth (1968) for the results of this author's simulation experiments.

12.6 Modify the first-fit storage management scheme so that the search of the free list for a block to satisfy the allocation request begins at the position where the previous search ended.

References

Bilbe, Charles R "Using the Heap for Modula-2 Opaque Types." *Journal of Ada, Pascal, and Modula-2,* Vol. 4, No. 6, 1985.

Chang, Hsi, and S. Iyengar. "Efficient Algorithms to Globally Balance a Binary Search Tree." *Communications of the ACM,* Vol. 27, No. 7, 1984.

Ford, Gary A., and Richard S. Wiener. *Modula-2: A Software Development Approach.* Wiley: New York, 1985.

Gonnet, Gaston. "Balancing Binary Trees by Internal Path Reduction." *Communications of the ACM,* Vol. 26, No. 12, 1983.

Horowitz, Ellis, and Sartaj Sahni. *Fundamentals of Data Structures.* Computer Science Press: 1976.

Knuth, Donald E. *The Art of Computer Programming, Vol. 1, Fundamental Algorithms.* Addison-Wesley: Reading, MA, 1968.

Logitech Inc. *Modula-2 User's Manual,* Release 1.10, 1984. Logitech, 805 Veterans Blvd., Redwood City, CA 94063.

Reingold, Edward, and Wilfred Hansen. *Data Structures.* Little, Brown: Boston, 1983.

Tremblay, J. P., and P. G. Sorenson. *An Introduction to Data Structures with Applications.* McGraw-Hill: New York, 1976.

Tennenbaum, Aaron. *Data Structures Using Pascal.* Prentice-Hall: Englewood Cliffs, NJ: 1981

Wiener, Richard. "An Efficient Virtual Hash Algorithm for a Spelling Checker." *Journal of Pascal, Ada, and Modula-2,* Vol. 5, No. 1, 1986.

Wiener, Richard, and Richard Sincovec. *Software Engineering with Modula-2 and Ada.* Wiley: New York, 1984.

Wirth, Niklaus. *Alogrithms + Data Structures = Programs.* Prentice-Hall: Englewood Cliffs, NJ: 1976.

Wirth, Niklaus. *Programming in Modula-2,* 2nd, corrected ed. Springer-Verlag: New York, 1982, 1983.

APPENDIX A

Dynamic String Implementation

A block of allocation for a string is initially established. The allocation is expanded by another block if more space is required. The price that must be paid is the copying of values from the old block to the new block, assuming that some or most of the data in the block remains the same after reallocation.

A dynamic string is implemented as a pointer to a block. A block contains an array of characters (of a size sufficient to contain a particular string) plus two cardinal fields. A length field keeps track of the current length of the string, and an allocation field keeps track of how large the allocated block is (in bytes). To save computation time, storage is not reallocated after a deletion; we keep the same block and leave some of it unused.

```
IMPLEMENTATION MODULE dynamicstring;

  (*  This module implements a dynamic string abstract data
type. *)


  FROM SYSTEM IMPORT
    (* proc *)  TSIZE;

  FROM InOut IMPORT
    (* type *) EOL,
    (* proc  *) Read, Write;

  FROM Storage IMPORT
    (* proc *)  ALLOCATE, DEALLOCATE;

  CONST
    stringmax = 65535;

  TYPE
    block     = RECORD
                  len       : CARDINAL;
                  alloclen  : CARDINAL;
                  ch        : ARRAY [ 0..stringmax ] OF CHAR
                END(* record *);

    string    = POINTER TO block;


   PROCEDURE mincard
             ( card1, card2 : CARDINAL        (* in *) ) :
   CARDINAL;

   BEGIN
     IF card1 <= card2
     THEN
       RETURN card1
     ELSE
       RETURN card2;
     END(* if then else *);
   END mincard;


   PROCEDURE allocatestring
             ( VAR str          : string        (* out    *);
                   length       : CARDINAL      (* in     *) );
   (* Note that str does not have to be defined.          *)
```

```
BEGIN
  ALLOCATE ( str, 2 * TSIZE ( CARDINAL ) + length );
  (* We assume that an array of characters has a size
     length bytes.                                          *)
  str^.alloclen := length;
  (* alloclen is in bytes.                                  *)
  str^.len := 0
END allocatestring;


PROCEDURE define
          ( VAR str    : string           (* out    *) );

BEGIN
  str := NIL
END define;


PROCEDURE createnull
          ( VAR str    : string           (* in/out *) );

BEGIN
  destroy( str );
  allocatestring ( str, 0 )
END createnull;


PROCEDURE copy
          (      str1  : string           (* in     *);
             VAR str2  : string           (* in/out *) );

  VAR pos : CARDINAL;

BEGIN
  destroy ( str2 );
  allocatestring ( str2, str1^.len );
  FOR pos := 0 TO str1^.len - 1 DO
    str2^.ch[ pos ] := str1^.ch[ pos ]
  END(* for loop *);
  str2^.len := str1^.len
END copy;


PROCEDURE concatenate
          (      str1   : string          (* in     *);
                 str2   : string          (* in     *);
             VAR result : string          (* in/out *) );

  VAR oldpos   : CARDINAL;
      newpos   : CARDINAL;
      tempstr  : string;
```

```
BEGIN
  allocatestring ( tempstr, str1^.len + str2^.len );
  newpos := 0;
  IF str1^.len > 0
  THEN
    FOR oldpos := 0 TO str1^.len - 1 DO
      tempstr^.ch[ newpos ] := str1^.ch[ oldpos ];
      INC ( newpos )
    END(* for loop *);
  END(* if then *);
  IF str2^.len > 0
  THEN
    FOR oldpos := 0 TO str2^.len - 1 DO
      tempstr^.ch[ newpos ] := str2^.ch[ oldpos ];
      INC ( newpos )
    END(* for loop *);
  END(* if then *);
  tempstr^.len := str1^.len + str2^.len;
  destroy ( result );
  result := tempstr;
END concatenate;


PROCEDURE search
          (     str      : string      (* in      *);
                pattern  : string      (* in      *);
                start    : CARDINAL    (* in      *);
            VAR location : CARDINAL    (* out     *) );

  VAR found : BOOLEAN;
      pos   : CARDINAL;

BEGIN
  IF start < 1
  THEN
    location := 0;
    RETURN;
  END(* if then *);
  found := FALSE;
  IF str^.len >= pattern^.len
  THEN
    location := start - 1;
    WHILE ( location <= str^.len - pattern^.len ) AND
            NOT found DO
      INC ( location );
      pos := 0;
      found := TRUE;
      WHILE found AND ( pos < pattern^.len ) DO
        found := str^.ch[ location - 1 + pos ] =
                 pattern^.ch[ pos ];
```

```
        INC ( pos );
      END(* while loop *);
    END(* while loop *);
  END(* if then *);
  IF NOT found THEN location := 0 END;
END search;


PROCEDURE delete
          ( VAR str       : string       (* in/out *);
                start     : CARDINAL     (* in     *);
                count     : CARDINAL     (* in     *) );

  VAR pos : CARDINAL;

BEGIN
  IF ( start >= 1 ) AND ( start + count - 1 <= str^.len )
     AND ( start <= str^.len )
  THEN
    IF str^.len - count - 1 >= 0
    THEN
      FOR pos := start - 1 TO str^.len - count - 1 DO
        str^.ch[ pos ] := str^.ch[ pos + count ]
      END(* for loop *);
    END(* if then *);
    str^.len := str^.len - count
  END(* if then *);
END delete;

PROCEDURE insert
          ( VAR str       : string       (* in/out *);
                substr    : string       (* in     *);
                start     : CARDINAL     (* in     *) );

  VAR tempstr : string;
      pos     : CARDINAL;

BEGIN
  IF ( start >= 1 ) AND ( start <= str^.len + 1 )
  THEN
    IF str^.alloclen  >= str^.len + substr^.len
    THEN (* Insertion will fit in existing allocation. *)
      FOR pos := str^.len - 1 TO
                 start - 1 BY -1 DO
        str^.ch[ pos + substr^.len ] := str^.ch[ pos ]
      END(* for loop *);
      INC( str^.len, substr^.len );
    ELSE (* new allocation is necessary. *)
      allocatestring ( tempstr, str^.len + substr^.len );
      tempstr^.len := str^.len + substr^.len;
      IF start >= 2
```

```
      THEN
        FOR pos := 0 TO start - 2 DO
          tempstr^.ch[ pos ] := str^.ch[ pos ]
        END(* for loop *);
      END(* if then *);
      FOR pos := start - 1 TO str^.len - 1 DO
        tempstr^.ch[ pos + substr^.len ] :=
          str^.ch[ pos ];
      END(* for loop *);
      destroy ( str );
      str := tempstr;
    END(* if then *);
    (* now insert the substring *)
    FOR pos := 0 TO substr^.len - 1 DO
      str^.ch[ start - 1 + pos ] := substr^.ch[ pos ]
    END(* for loop *);
  END(* if then *);
END insert;


PROCEDURE extract
          (     str      : string       (* in     *);
                start    : CARDINAL     (* in     *);
                count    : CARDINAL     (* in     *);
            VAR substr   : string       (* in/out *) );

  VAR pos : CARDINAL;

BEGIN
  destroy ( substr );
  IF ( start >= 1 ) AND ( start + count - 1 <= str^.len )
  THEN
    allocatestring ( substr, count );
    FOR pos := 0 TO count - 1 DO
      substr^.ch[ pos ] := str^.ch[ start - 1 + pos ]
    END(* for loop *);
    substr^.len := count
  ELSE
    allocatestring ( substr, 0 )
  END(* if then *);
END extract;


PROCEDURE length
          (     str      : string       (* in     *) ) :
CARDINAL;

BEGIN
  RETURN str^.len
END length;
```

```
PROCEDURE equal
          (      str1      : string       (* in     *);
                 str2      : string       (* in     *) ) :
BOOLEAN;

  VAR pos : CARDINAL;

BEGIN
  IF str1^.len = str2^.len
  THEN
   pos := 0;
   WHILE ( str1^.ch[ pos ] = str2^.ch[ pos ] ) AND
         ( pos < str1^.len - 1 ) DO
     INC ( pos )
   END(* while loop *);
   RETURN str1^.ch[ pos ] = str2^.ch[ pos ]
  ELSE
   RETURN FALSE
  END(* if then *);
END equal;


PROCEDURE lessthan
          (    str1        : string       (* in     *);
               str2        : string       (* in     *) ) :
BOOLEAN;

  VAR pos   : CARDINAL;
      limit : CARDINAL;

BEGIN
  limit := mincard ( str1^.len, str2^.len ) - 1;
  pos := 0;
  WHILE ( str1^.ch[ pos ] = str2^.ch[ pos ] ) AND
       ( pos < limit ) DO
    INC ( pos )
  END;
  IF str1^.ch[ pos ] = str2^.ch[ pos ]
  THEN
    RETURN str1^.len < str2^.len
  ELSE
    RETURN str1^.ch[ pos ] < str2^.ch[ pos ]
  END(* if then else *);
END lessthan;


PROCEDURE readstring
          ( VAR str      : string       (* in/out *) );

  CONST tempsize   = 100;
```

```
  VAR   tempstr    : string;
        char       : CHAR;
        tempstr2   : string;

BEGIN
  allocatestring ( tempstr, tempsize );
  destroy ( str );
  createnull ( tempstr2 );
  Read( char );
  WHILE ( char # EOL ) DO
    tempstr^.len := 0;
    LOOP
      IF char = EOL
      THEN
        EXIT
      END;
      INC ( tempstr^.len );
      tempstr^.ch[ tempstr^.len - 1 ] := char;
      IF tempstr^.len = tempsize THEN EXIT END;
      Read ( char );
    END(* loop *);
    concatenate ( tempstr2, tempstr, str );
    copy( str, tempstr2 );
  END(* while loop *);
  destroy ( tempstr );
  destroy( tempstr2 );
END readstring;


PROCEDURE writestring
          ( str          : string       (* in      *) );

  VAR pos : CARDINAL;

BEGIN
  IF str^.len > 0
  THEN
    FOR pos := 0 TO str^.len - 1 DO
      write ( str^.ch[ pos ] )
    END(* for loop *);
  END(* if then *);
END writestring;


PROCEDURE convertarray
          (     chars    : ARRAY OF CHAR   (* in      *);
                count    : CARDINAL        (* in      *);
            VAR str      : string          (* in/out *) );
```

```
    VAR pos : CARDINAL;

  BEGIN
    destroy ( str );
    allocatestring ( str, count );
    FOR pos := 0 TO count - 1 DO
      str^.ch[ pos ] := chars[ pos ]
    END;
    str^.len := count
  END convertarray;


  PROCEDURE convertliteral
            (     chars    : ARRAY OF CHAR    (* in      *);
              VAR str      : string           (* in/out *) );

  BEGIN
    convertarray ( chars, HIGH ( chars ) + 1, str )
  END convertliteral;


END dynamic string.
```

APPENDIX B

Syntax of Modula-2

This appendix, taken with permission from Ford and Wiener (1985), presents the collected syntax charts for Modula-2.

compilation unit

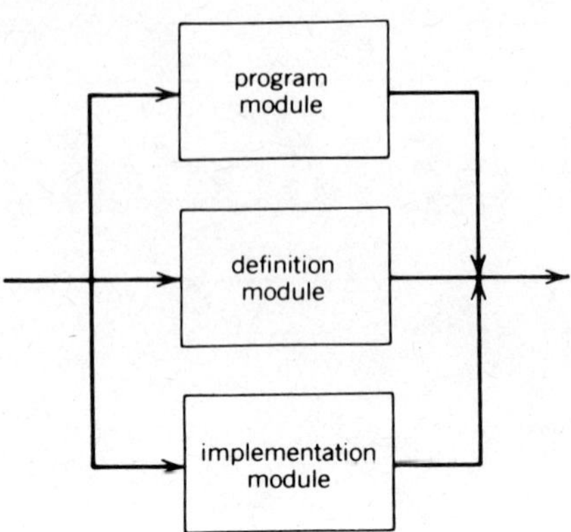

program module

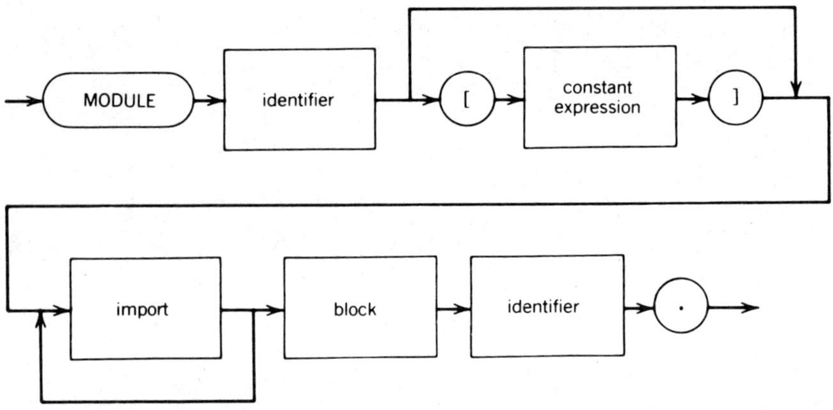

definition module

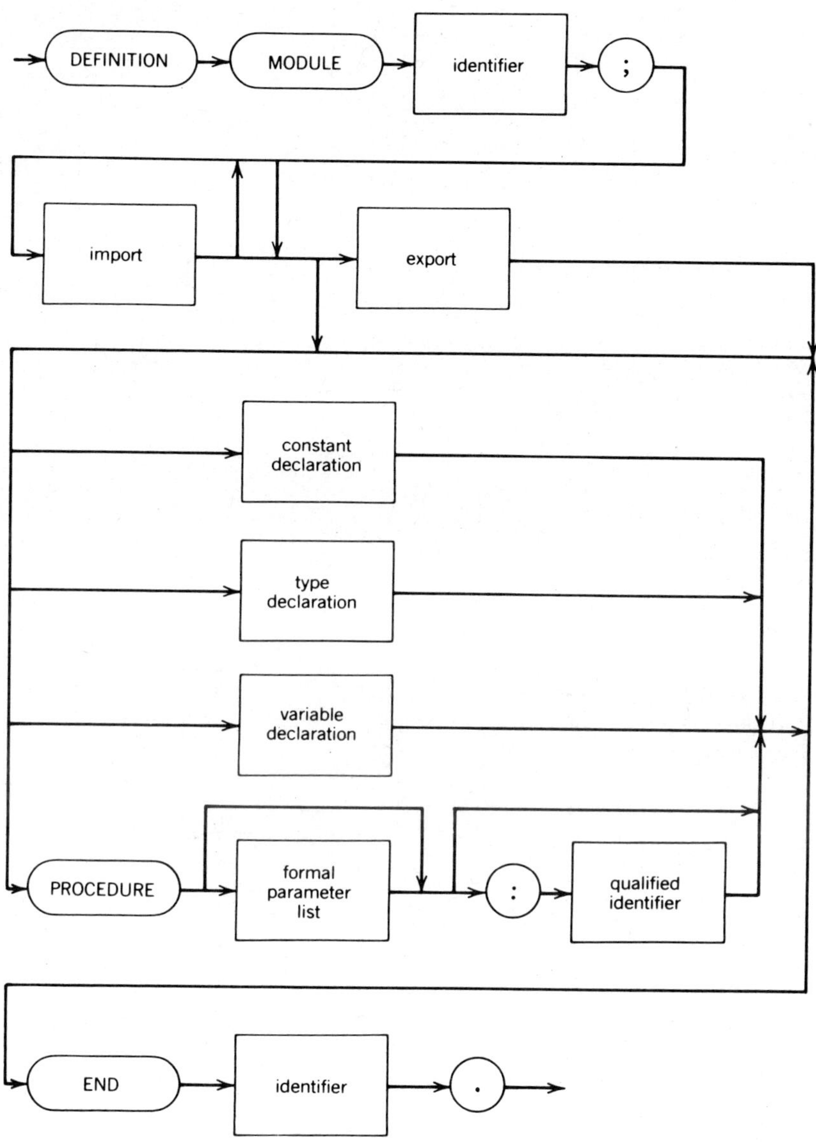

implementation module

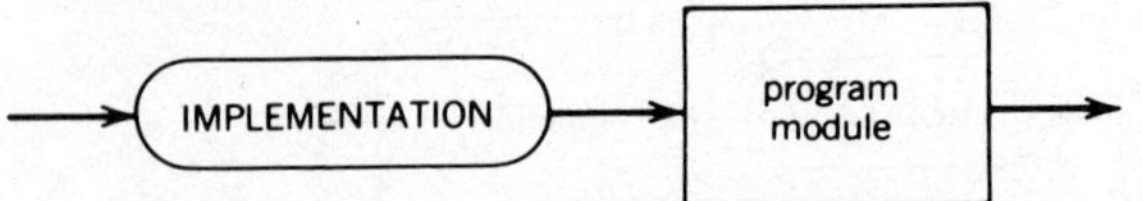

import

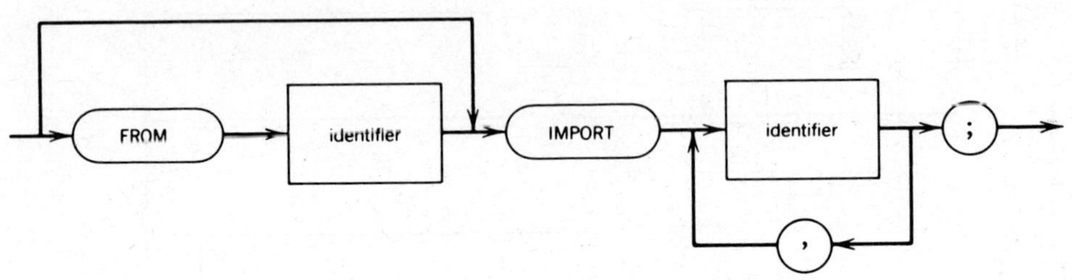

export

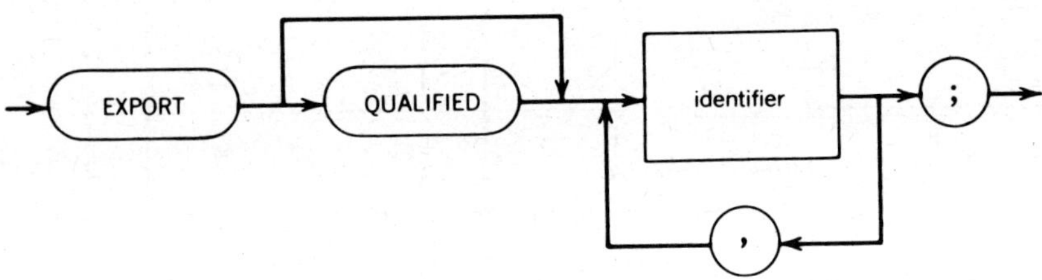

block

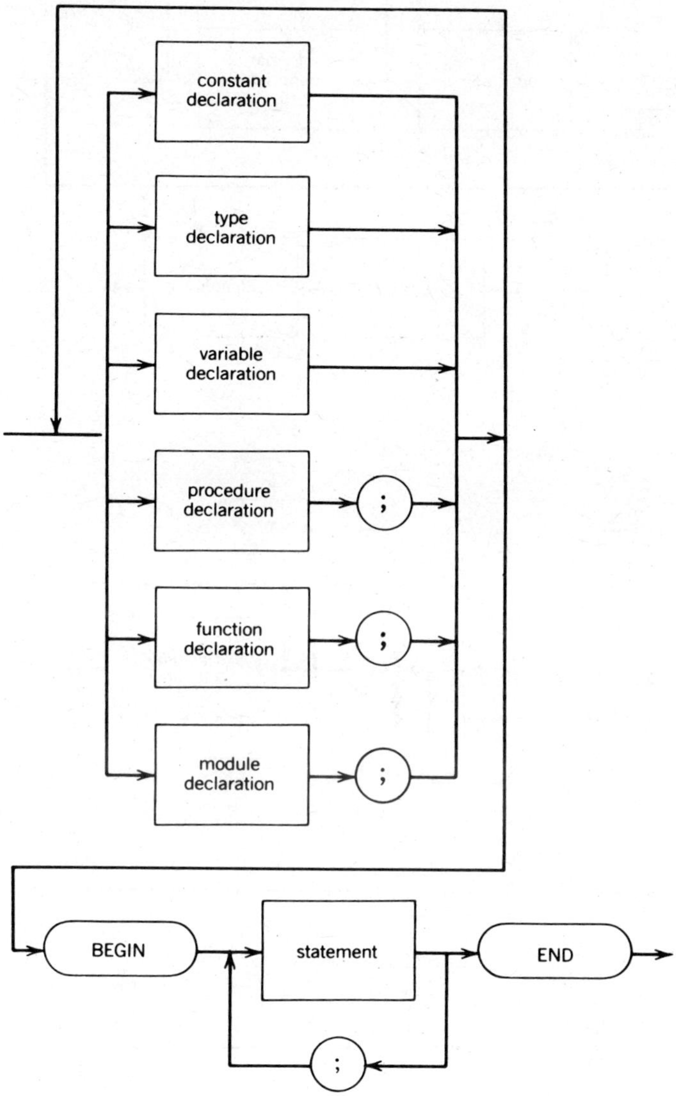

constant declaration

type declaration

variable declaration

procedure declaration

;

function declaration

;

module declaration

;

BEGIN

statement

;

END

procedure declaration

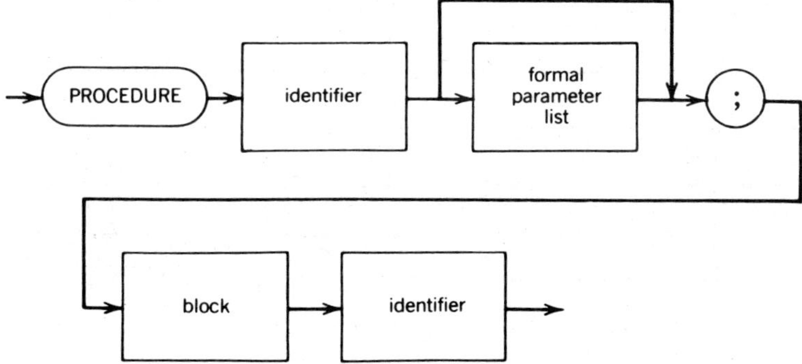

function declaration

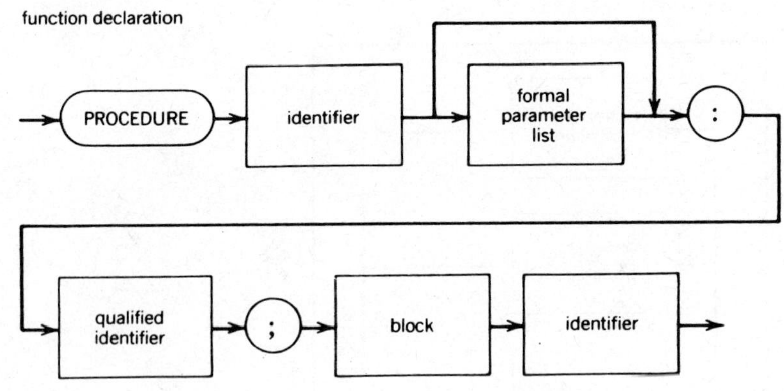

formal parameter list

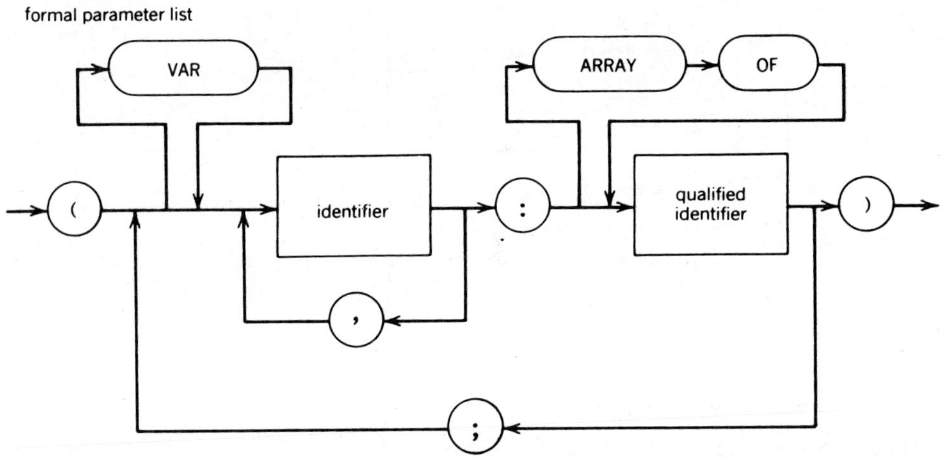

module declaration

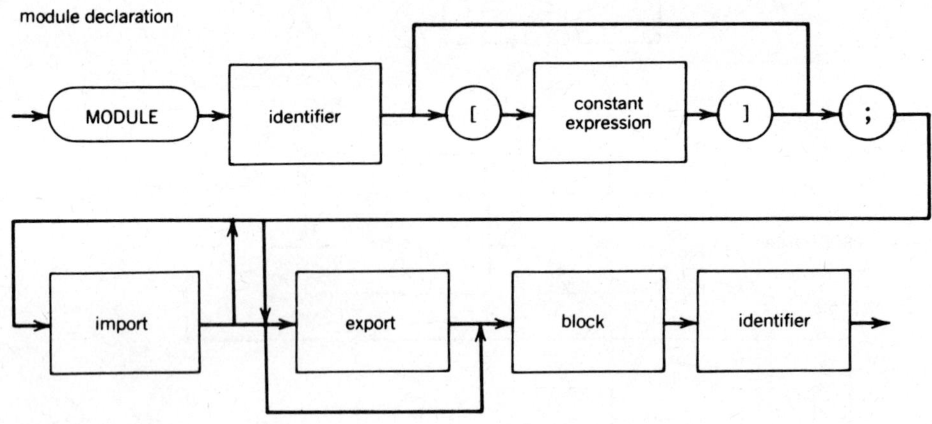

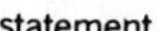
statement

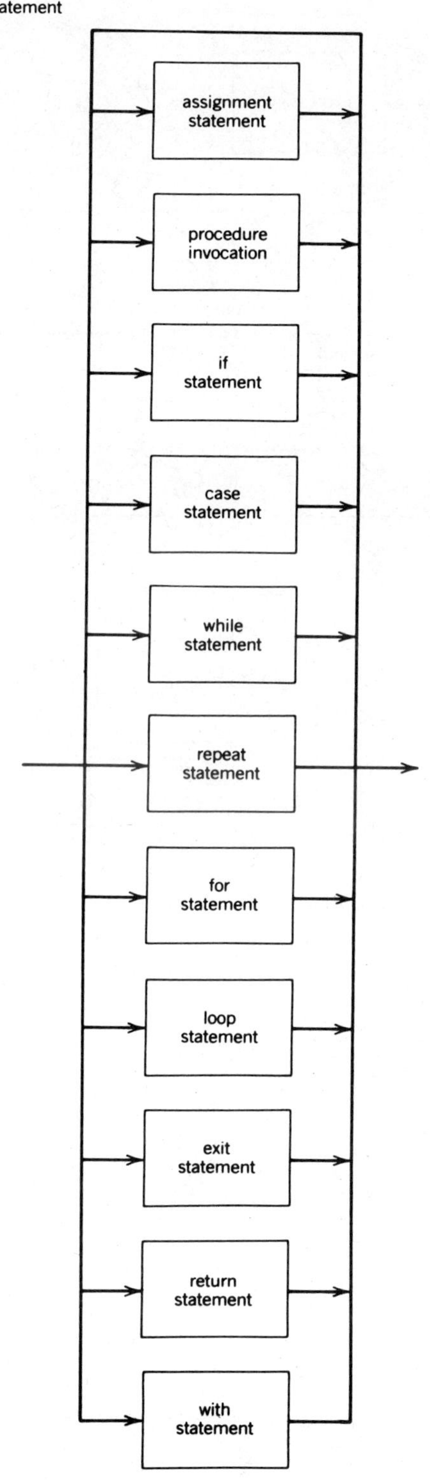
assignment statement
procedure invocation
if statement
case statement
while statement
repeat statement
for statement
loop statement
exit statement
return statement
with statement

assignment statement

designator
: =
expression

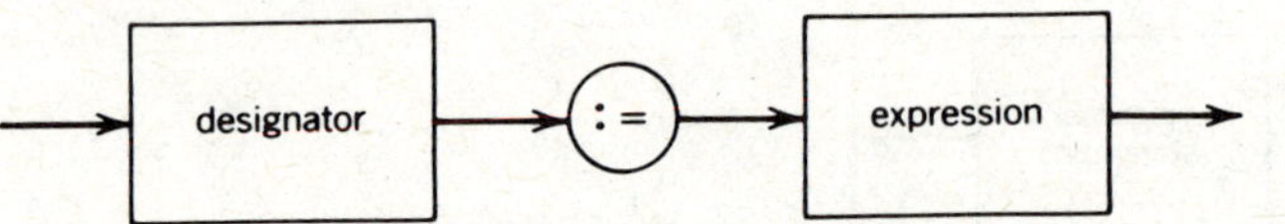

if statement

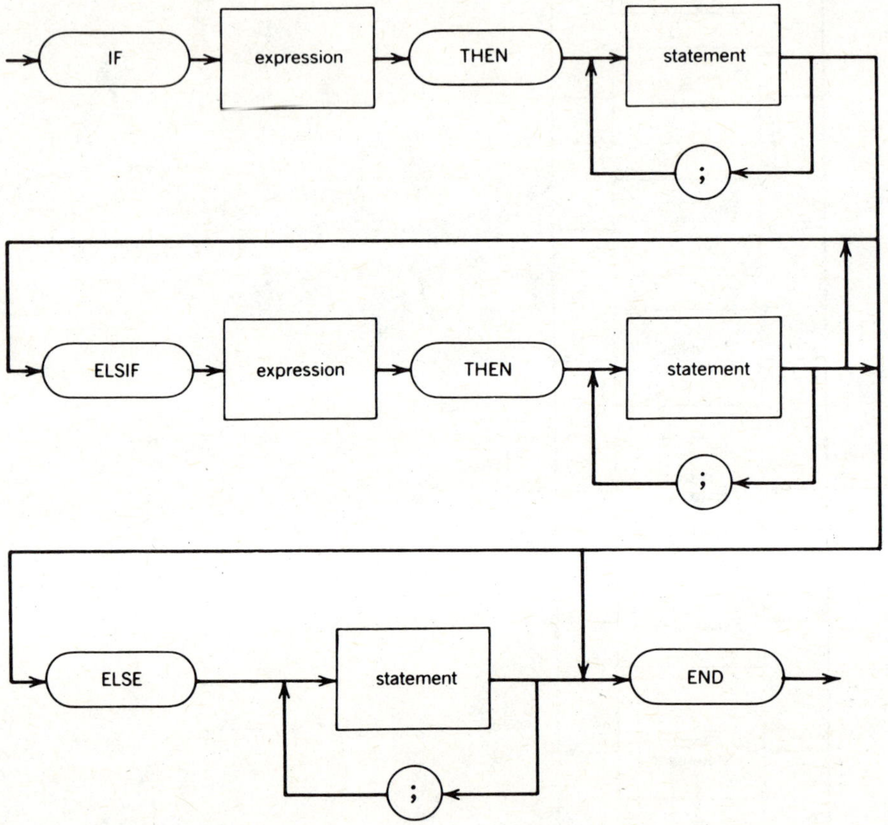

IF
expression
THEN
statement
;
ELSIF
expression
THEN
statement
;
ELSE
statement
;
END

case statement

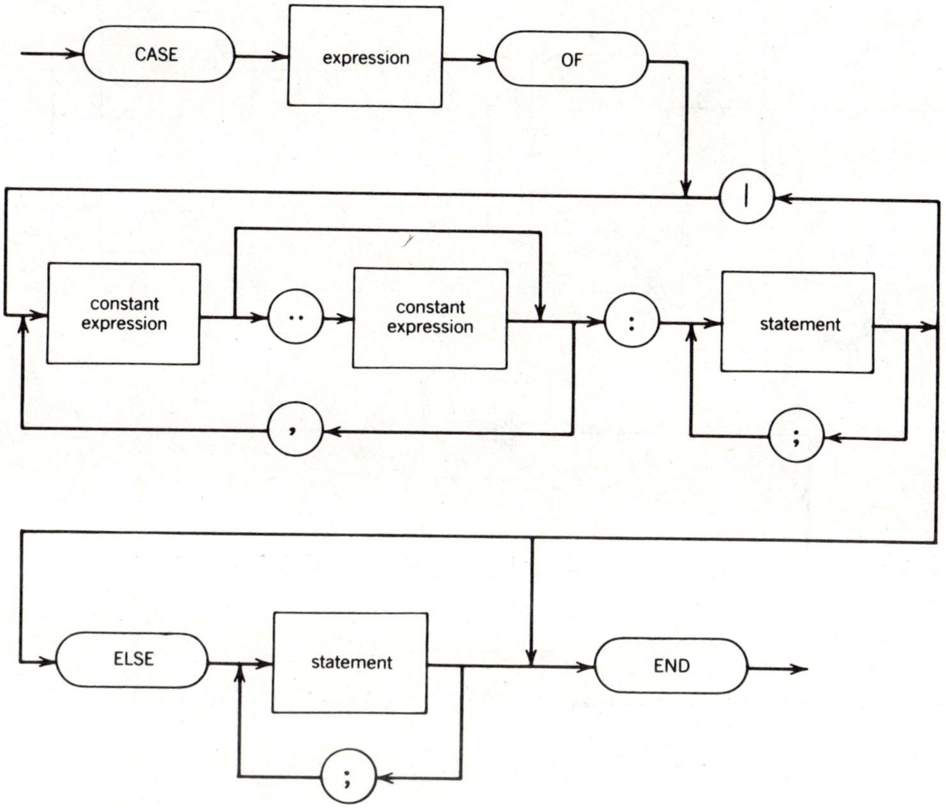

CASE
expression
OF
|
constant expression
..
constant expression
,
:
statement
;
ELSE
statement
;
END

variable declaration

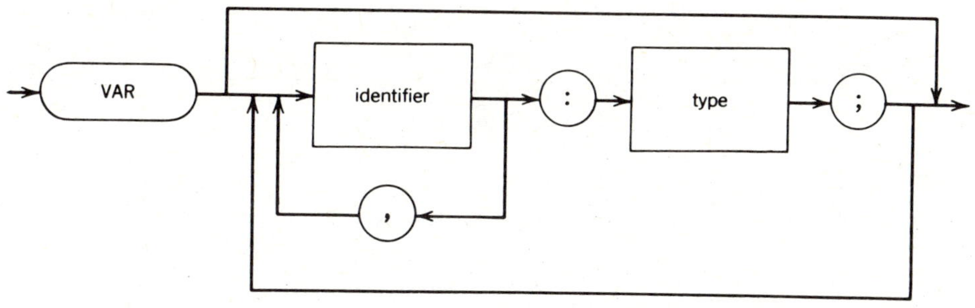

expression

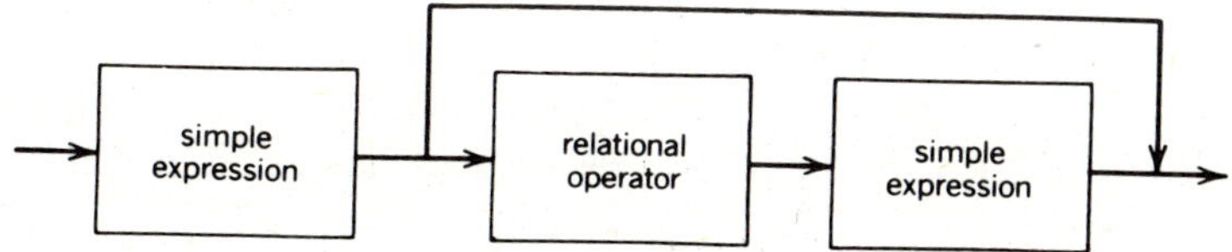

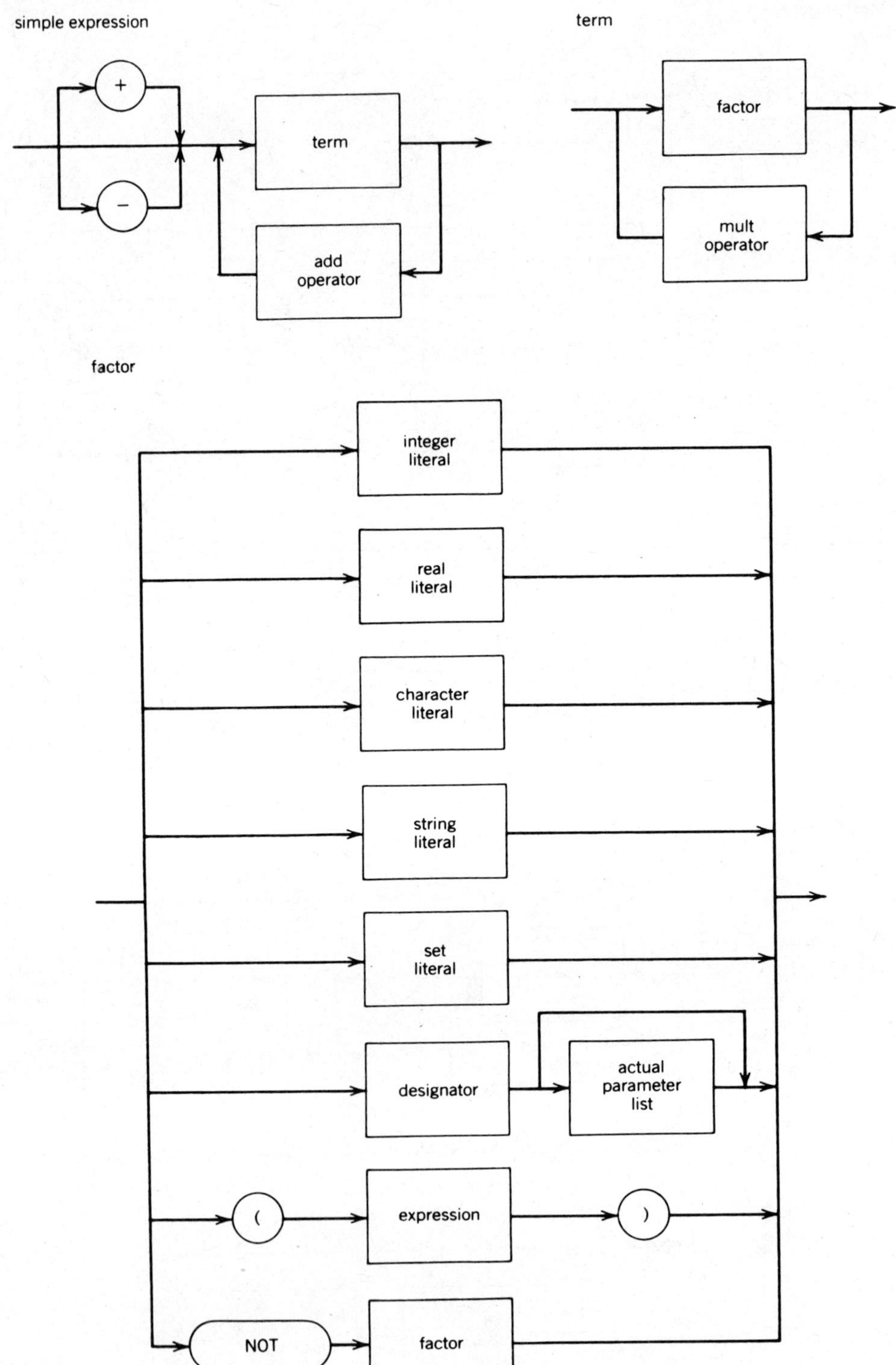
simple expression
+
−
term
add operator
term
factor
mult operator
factor
integer literal
real literal
character literal
string literal
set literal
designator
actual parameter list
(
expression
)
NOT
factor

designator

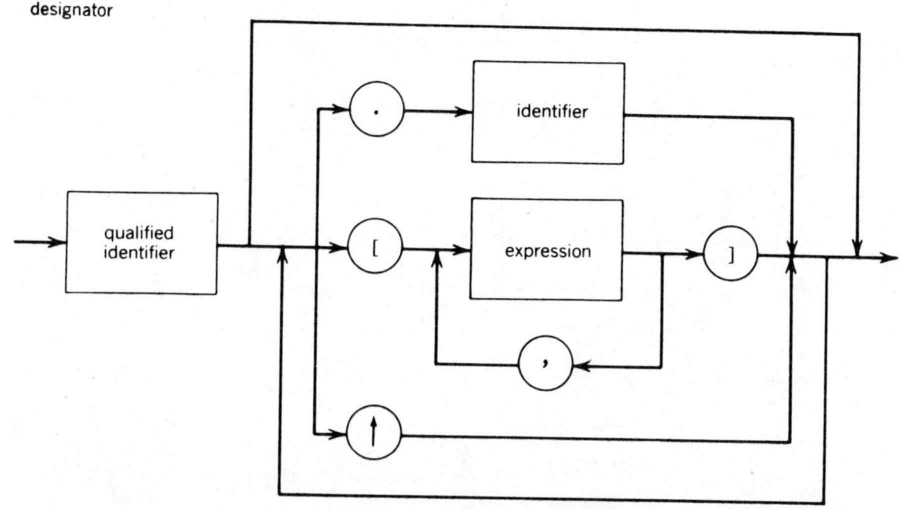

constant expression

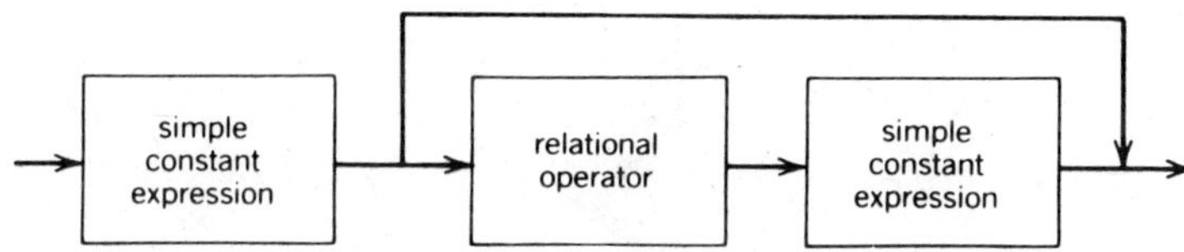

simple constant expression

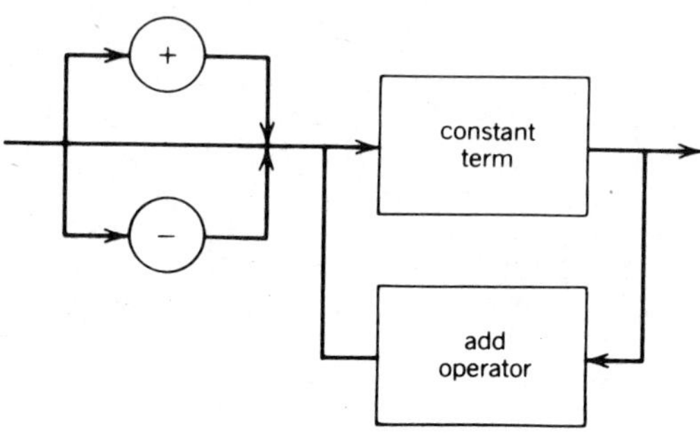

constant term

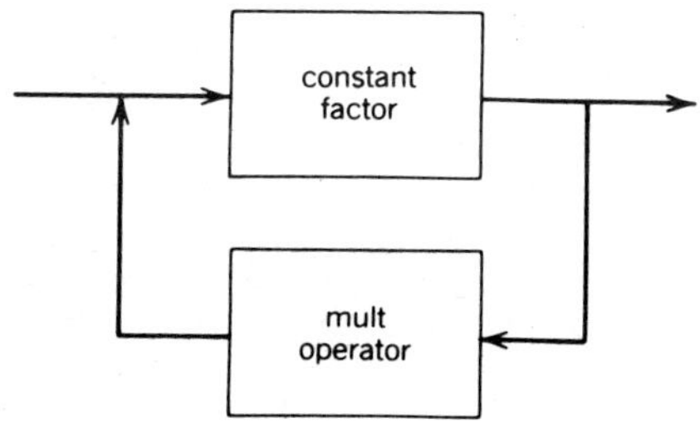

constant factor

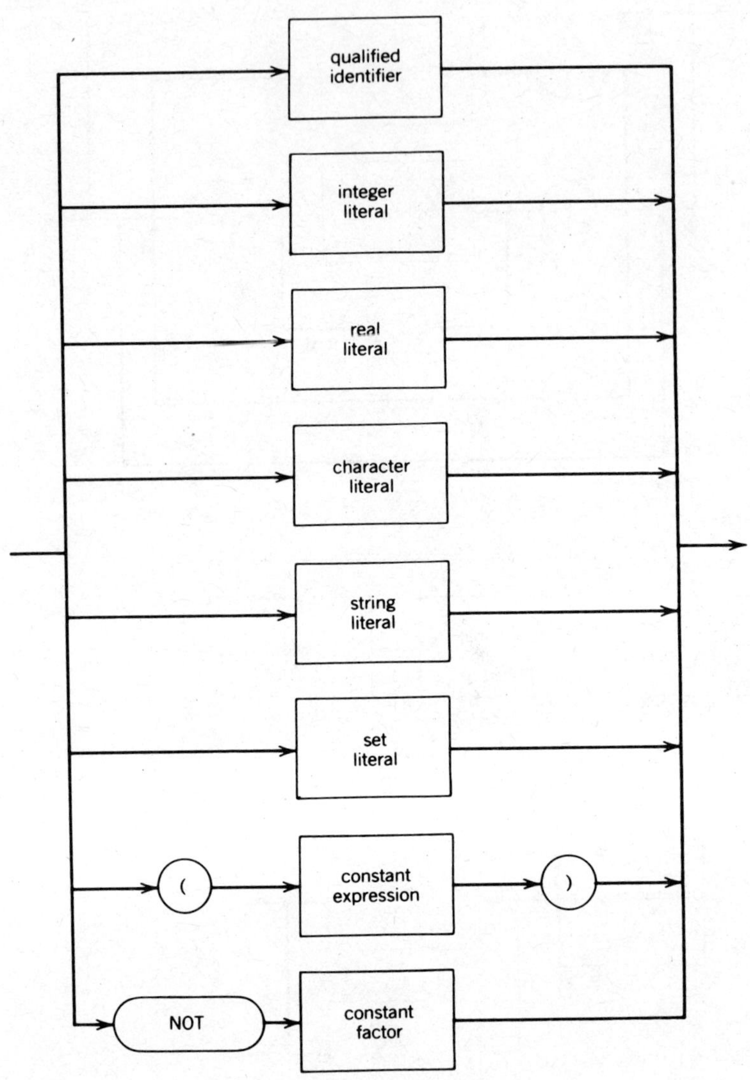

relational operator

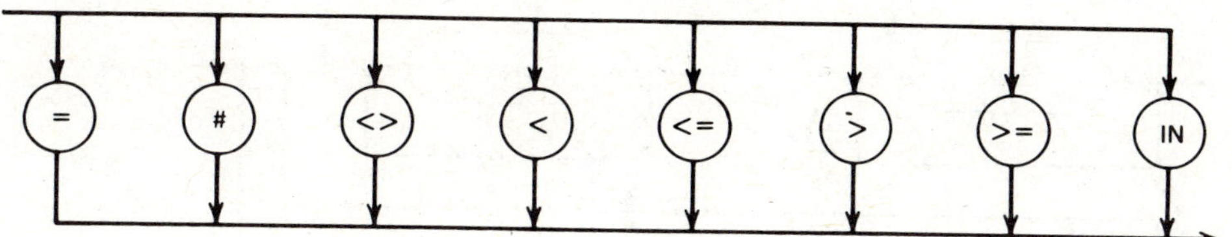

add operator

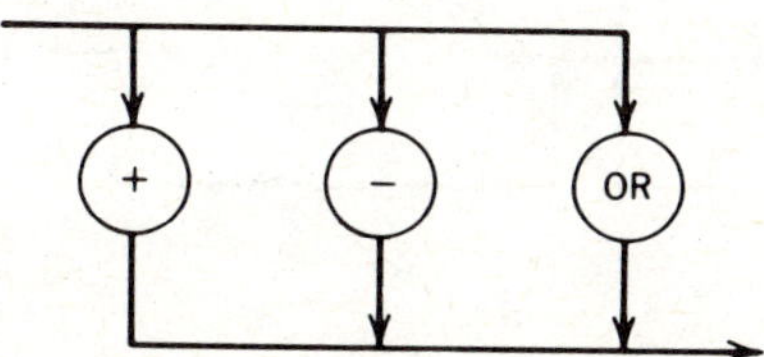

mult operator

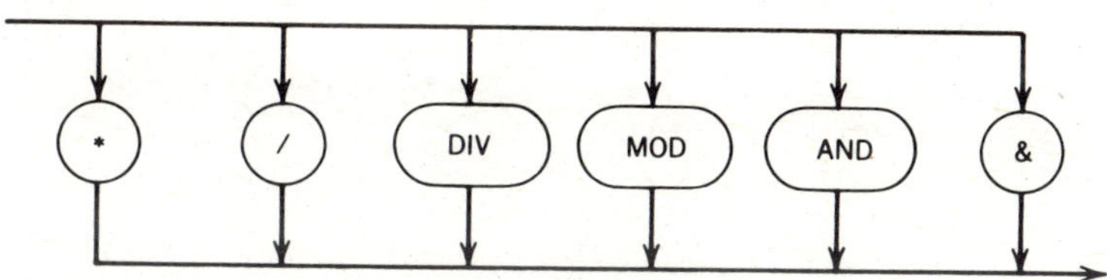

integer literal

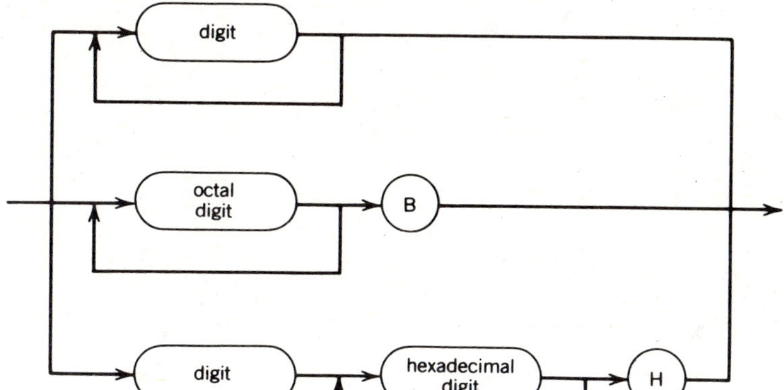

real literal

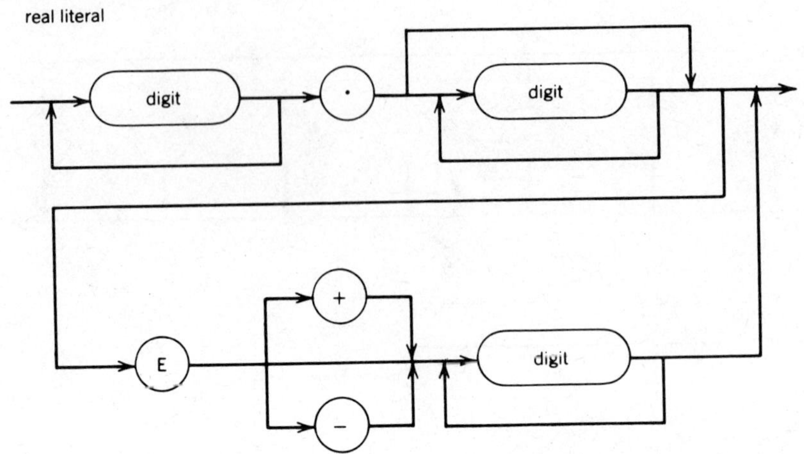

character literal

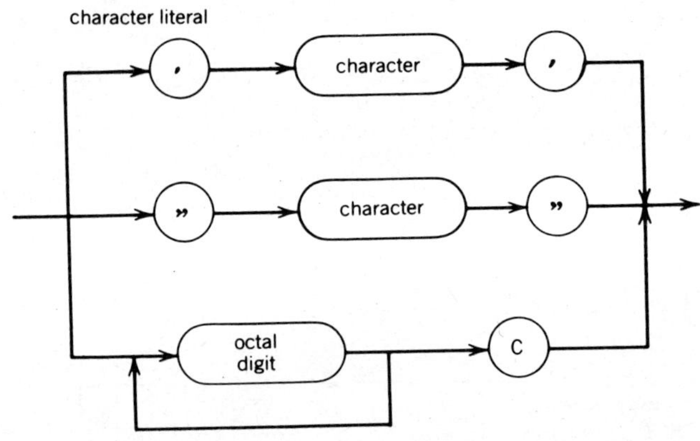

string literal

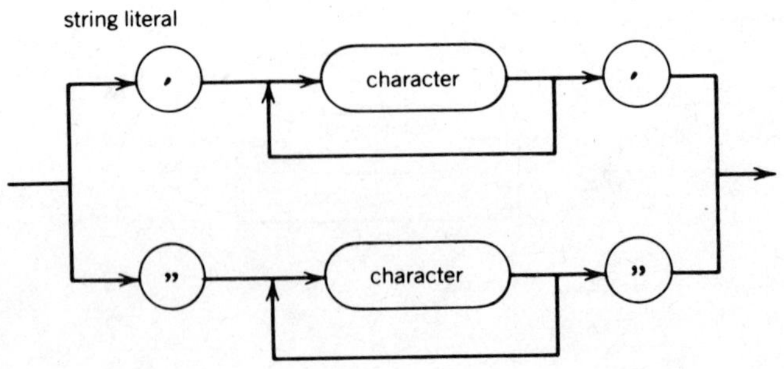

set literal

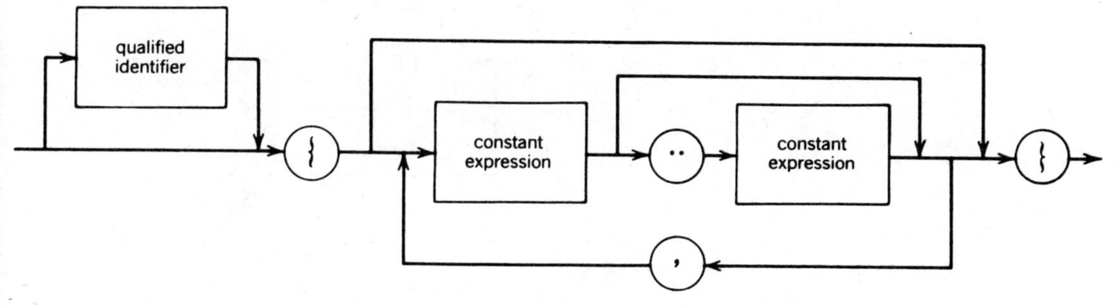

identifier

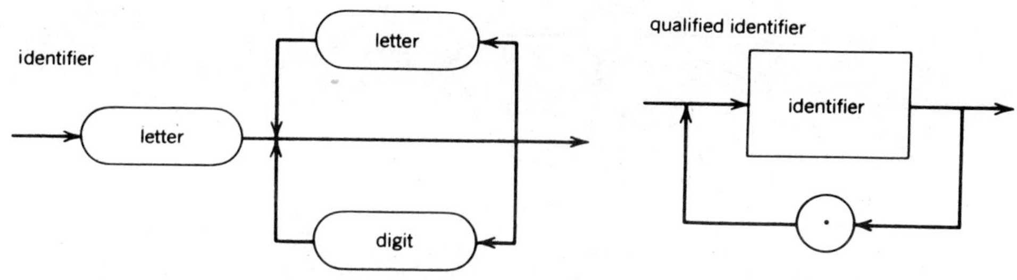

absolute address

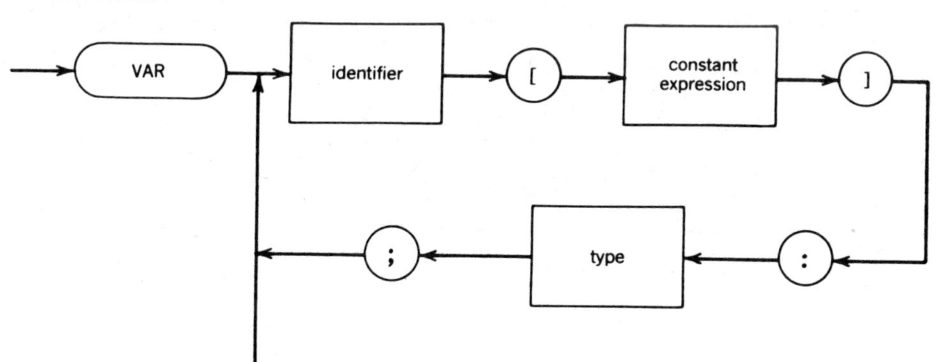

monitor

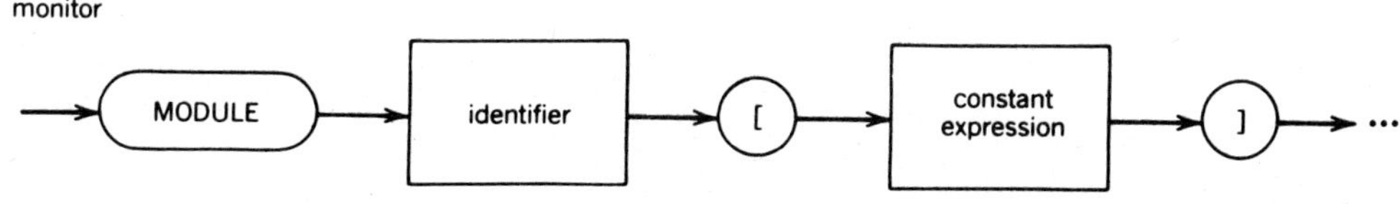

while statement

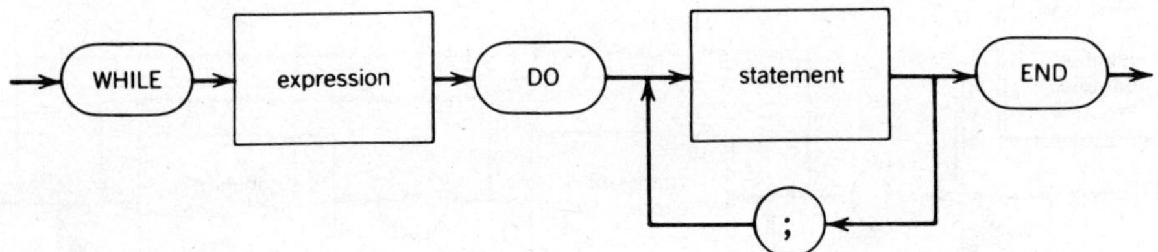

repeat statement

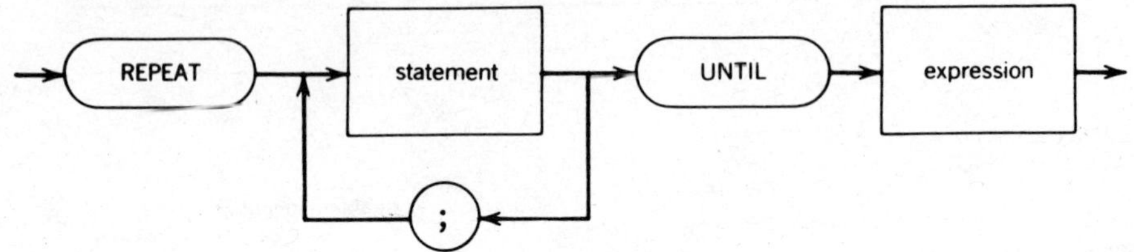

for statement

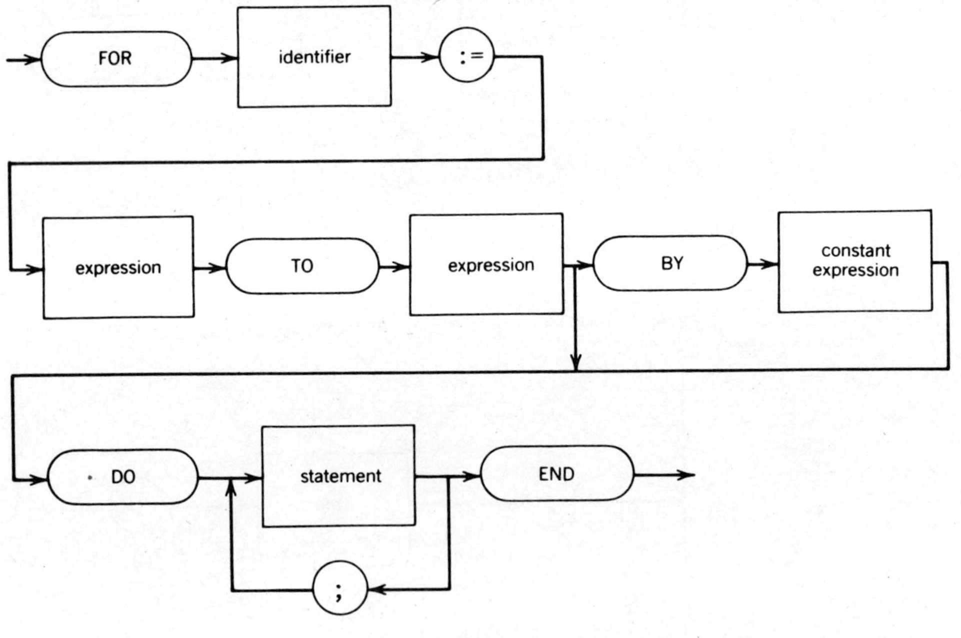

loop statement

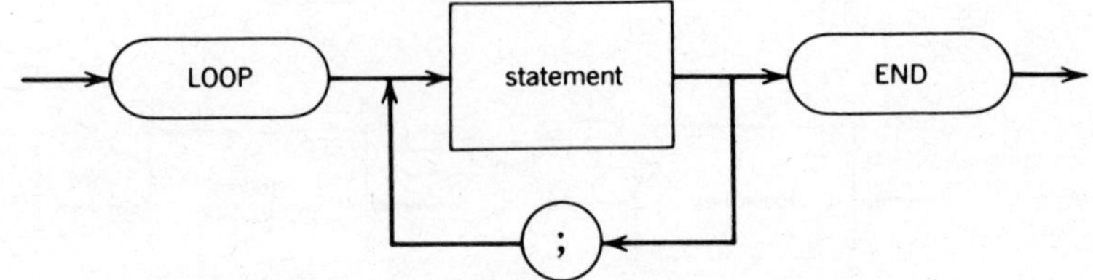

exit statement

with statement

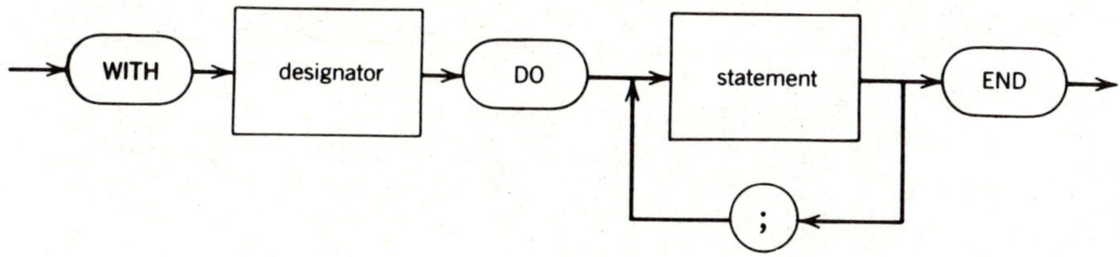

procedure invocation

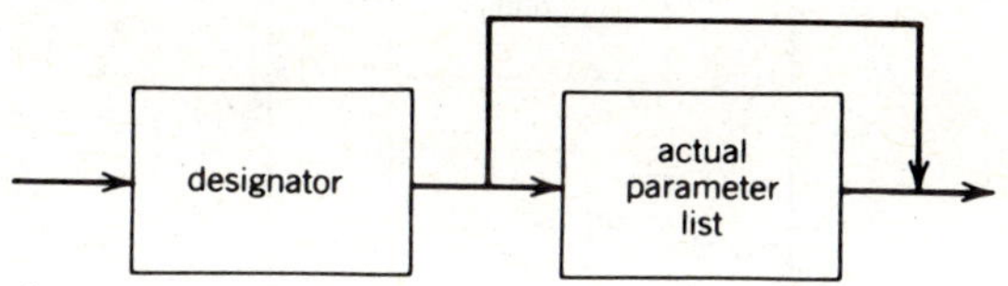

actual parameter list

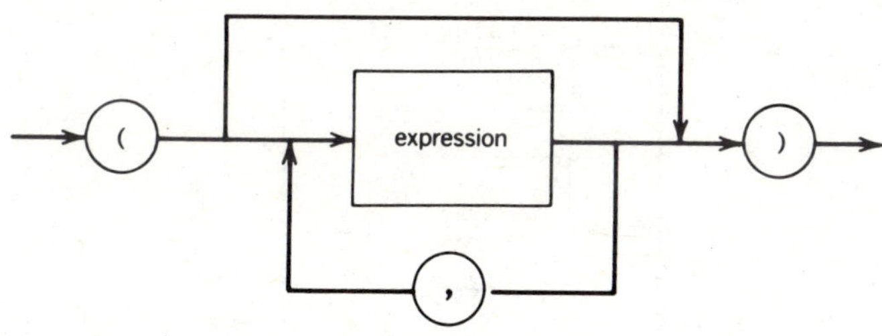

return statement

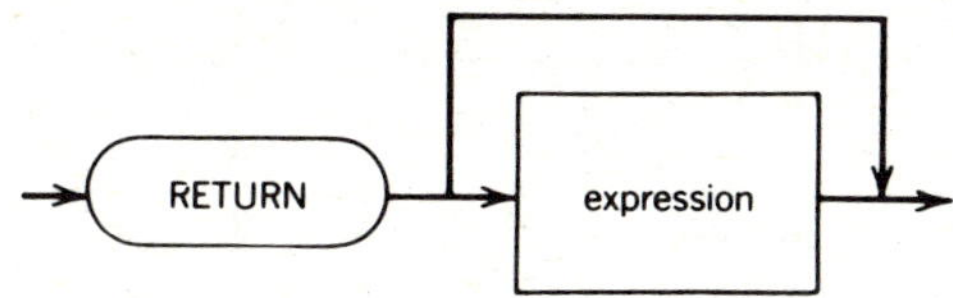

constant declaration

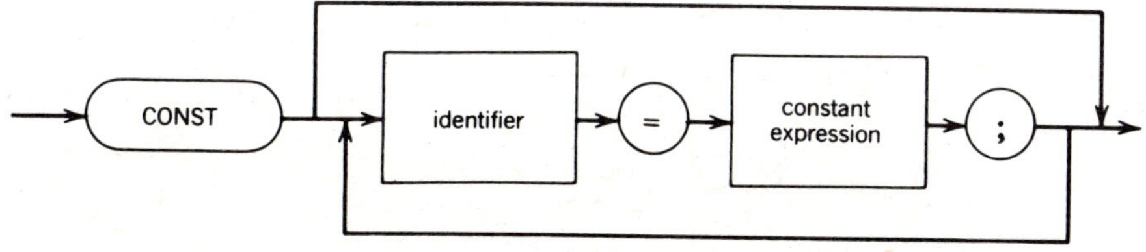

type declaration

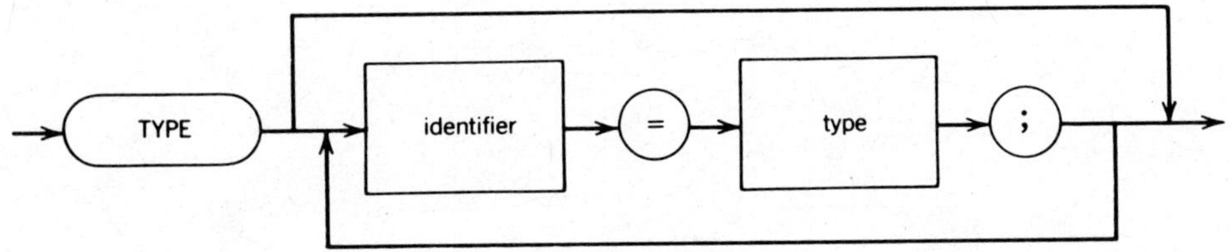

type

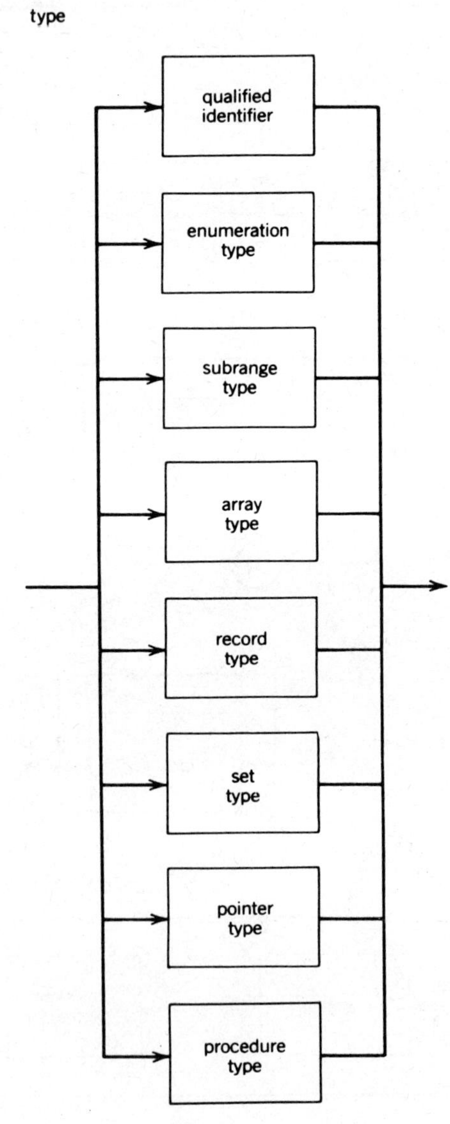

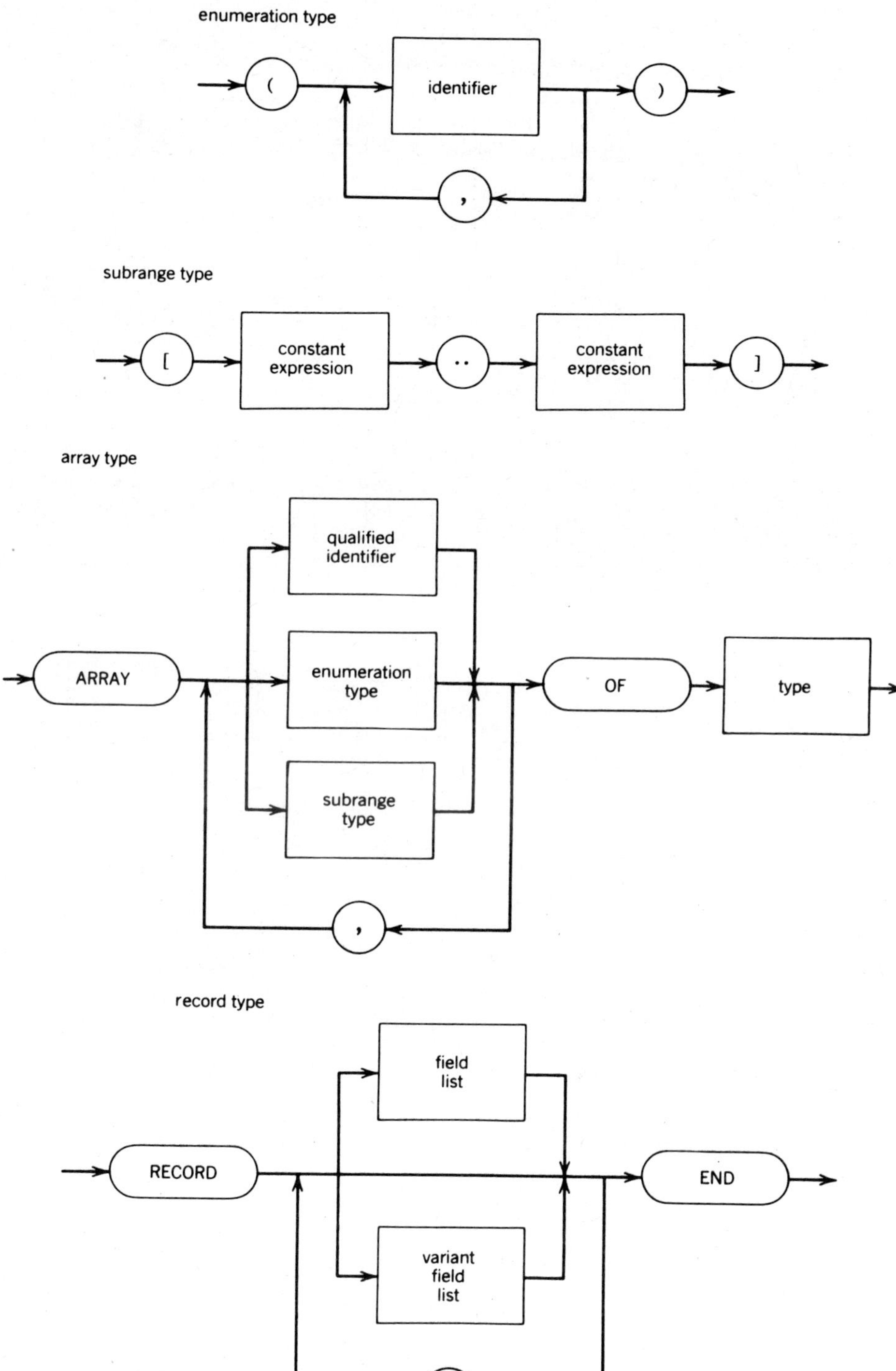
enumeration type
(
identifier
)
,
subrange type
[
constant expression
..
constant expression
]
array type
ARRAY
qualified identifier
enumeration type
subrange type
,
OF
type
record type
RECORD
field list
variant field list
;
END

field list

identifier
:
type
,

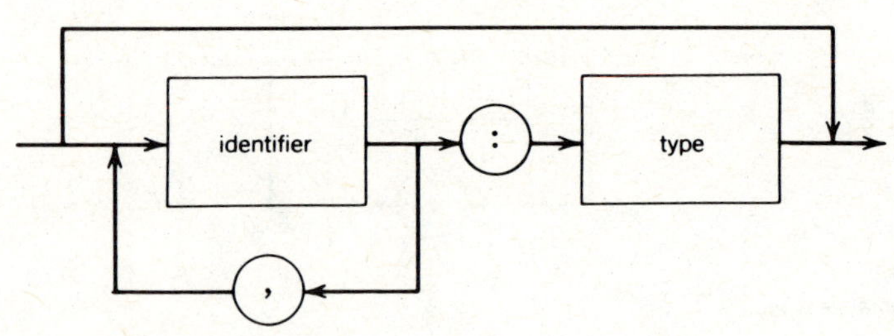

variant field list

CASE
identifier
:
qualified identifier
OF
constant expression
..
constant expression
,
:
field list
variant field list
;
|
ELSE
field list
variant field list
;
END

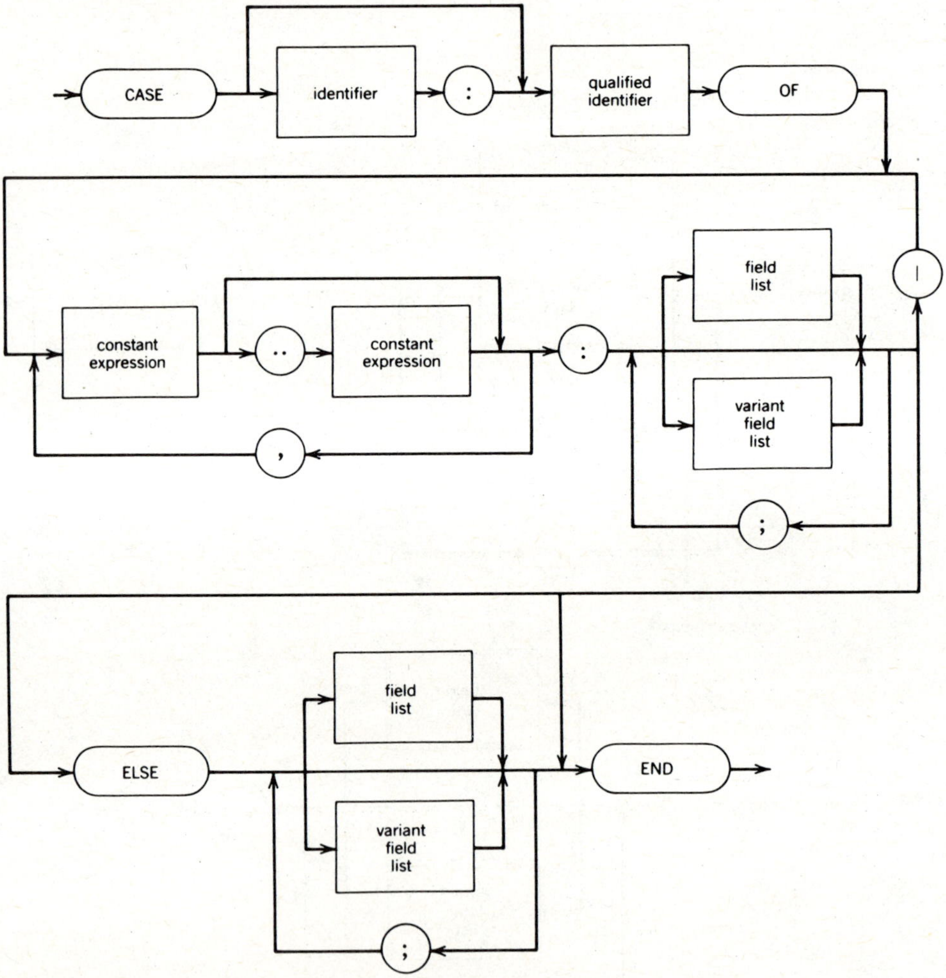

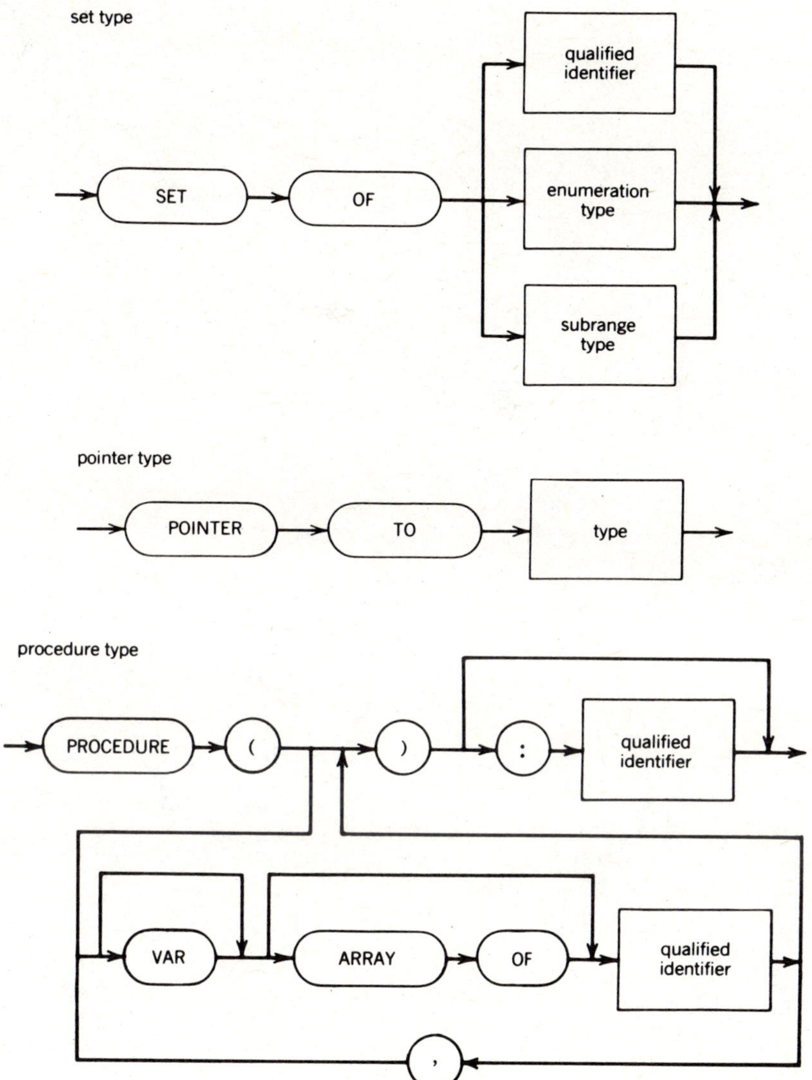
set type
SET
OF
qualified identifier
enumeration type
subrange type
pointer type
POINTER
TO
type
procedure type
PROCEDURE
(
)
:
qualified identifier
VAR
ARRAY
OF
qualified identifier
,

Index